ANDY GOTTS
THE PHOTOGRAPH

ACC ART BOOKS

Table of Contents

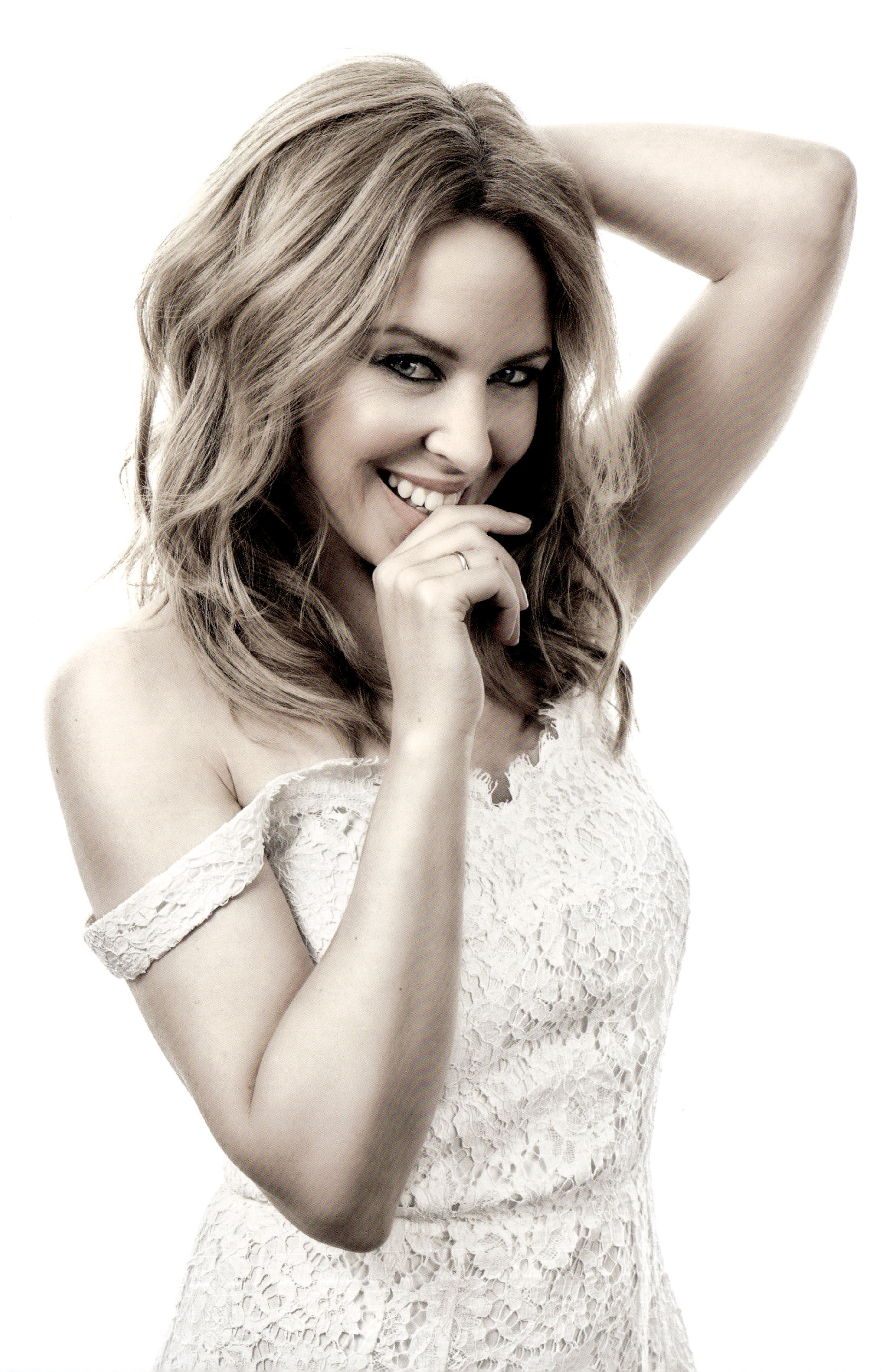

Kylie Minogue

My love for the contact sheet runs deep.

We all know that a photograph captures a moment, but with a contact sheet we're able to see 'the making of' that moment – what happened in the seconds or minutes before, and then what transpired afterwards.

In the pages that follow, we are welcomed into the many moments Andy has captured. We see beyond the 'hero shots' and discover how they came to be.

There is incredible honesty in seeing these images in running order. We know whether it was the start of the roll or the end. We can track the mood, the energy, the 'dance' that happens between photographer and subject... They're warming up, it's not quite right, they've tried a different approach, they're settled and they've found the light, the mood, the magic. CLICK! All those emotions are captured for us, for always.

Perhaps it is an obvious a statement, but in the digital age, it doesn't hurt to mention it: film isn't to be wasted. It also can't be viewed until it is processed and developed, so it requires skill and trust. And patience!

Traditionally, a few Polaroids were taken at the start of photo sessions, which allowed the photographer to assess the light and the composition, and gave the team a sense of what was working. Taking only minutes to develop, they provided vital information as to what the final images would be like. I always had a flutter of excitement when the first Polaroid was developed (I still do!). The team would gather around to view them, to assess and make adjustments. Then any and all Polaroids were pinned to a foam studio board or laid out next to the equipment and it was then time to shoot the first roll of film! At the end of the day, these little paper miracles were swooped upon as references and, in my case, as souvenirs.

As someone in front of the camera, I react differently when being photographed on film. Digital doesn't involve the same calculation of cost or time and therefore can often feel more random, more throwaway. I've lost count of the number of times I've heard the phrases 'There'll be one in there' and 'We'll fix it in post'. There are, of course, beauty and benefits with digital, but I will always have a love affair with film – an admiration for its purity and the precision required. The shutter is opened the split second the photographer senses the shot is right and I, as a subject, feel it.

Andy's contact sheets give us what feels like a VIP pass to spend time with his subjects. We see their beauty, flaws, charisma, humanity and even get a glimpse into their thoughts and process. We see 'the person' inside the portrait.

I'm certain all of the artists in this book were happy to know Andy has the nickname 'One-Shot Gotts'. This was given to him by none other than, swoon, Paul Newman! In the celebrity world, time can be scarce, so the ability to work fast is a valuable one. I can attest to this as when 'One-Shot Gotts' first photographed me in London, in January 2015, it was not only fun, but seemingly over in a flash. We were trying to achieve the perfect hair flick without a wind machine or Photoshop. As one of the only celebrity photographers who doesn't edit or post-produce his portraits, we would either get the shot, or we wouldn't! We DID, and there were many giggles along the way.

This book reminds me of the rush of excitement of seeing, for the first time, the images captured during a photo shoot. The negative film has been processed and cut to size; the images have been projected onto light-sensitive paper and bathed in chemicals. After this journey through the darkroom, where science and magic meet, the contact sheet is revealed – a timeless representation of a single moment.

There is a growing interest in film amongst the younger generation. Perhaps they, too, have been seduced by the thrill, the challenges and romance of this art form. For those of us who, long ago, only knew film, the nostalgia never fades. Its power endures.

Having started out in the entertainment industry many moons ago, I have done countless photo shoots on film. I have also spent a lot of time with contact sheets; a loupe held in one hand and face pressed over the prints, shifting from frame to frame to decide which is 'the one'. Well, this book has many photos Andy can call 'the one' and plenty more captivating shots besides.

Congratulations, Andy, on a tremendous volume of work and thank you to all of his subjects for sharing themselves with us.

Viva film!

Kylie x

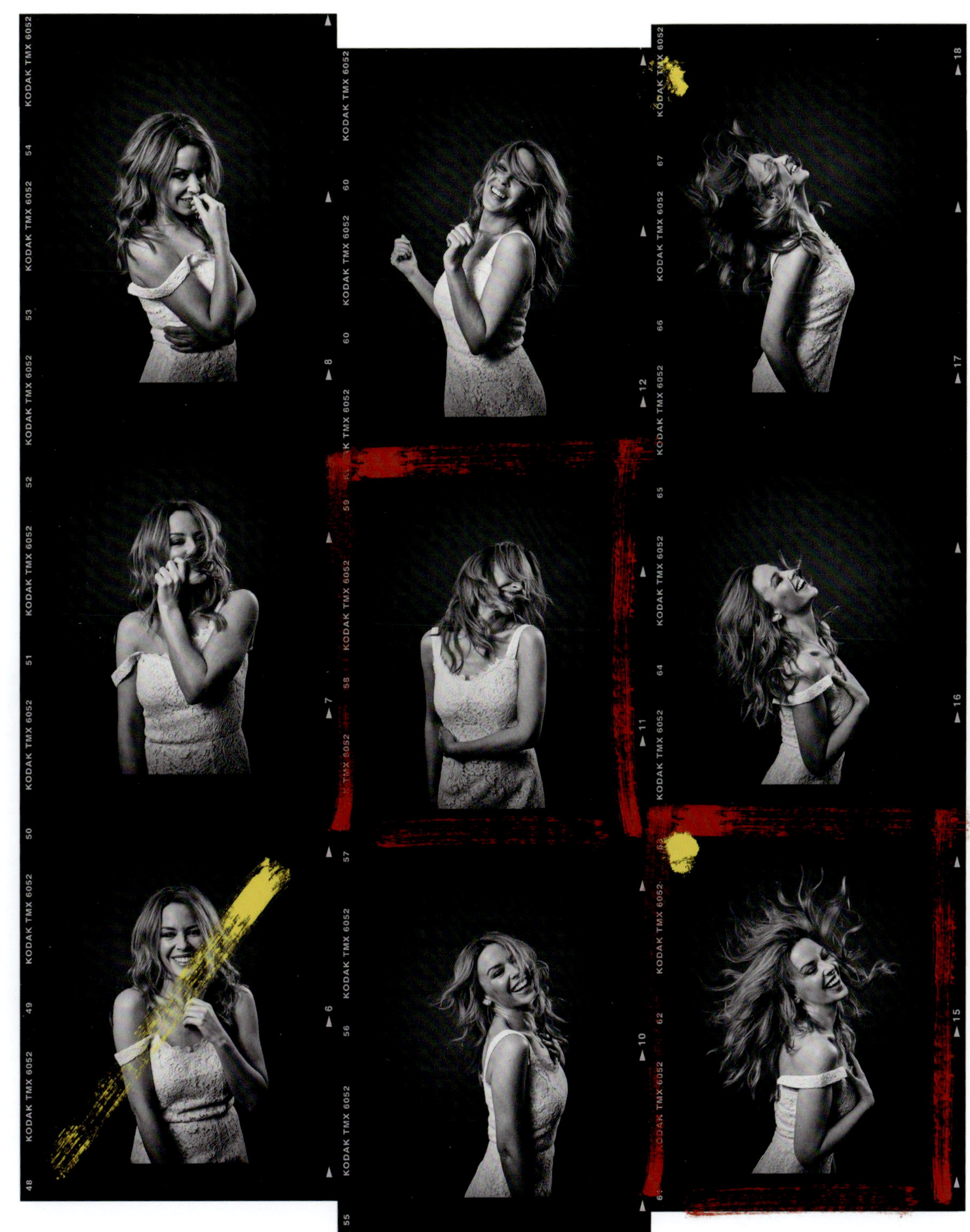

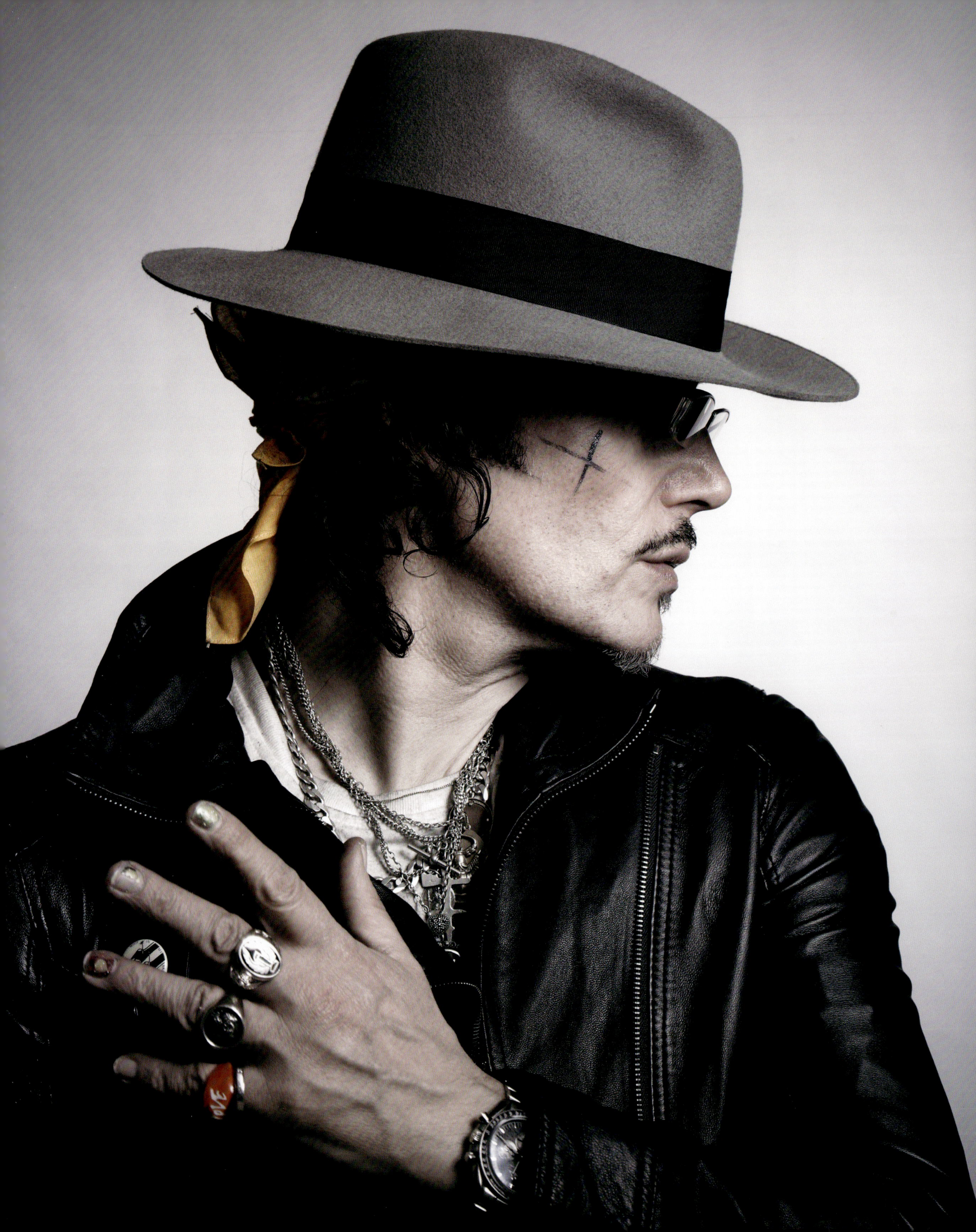

Adam Ant

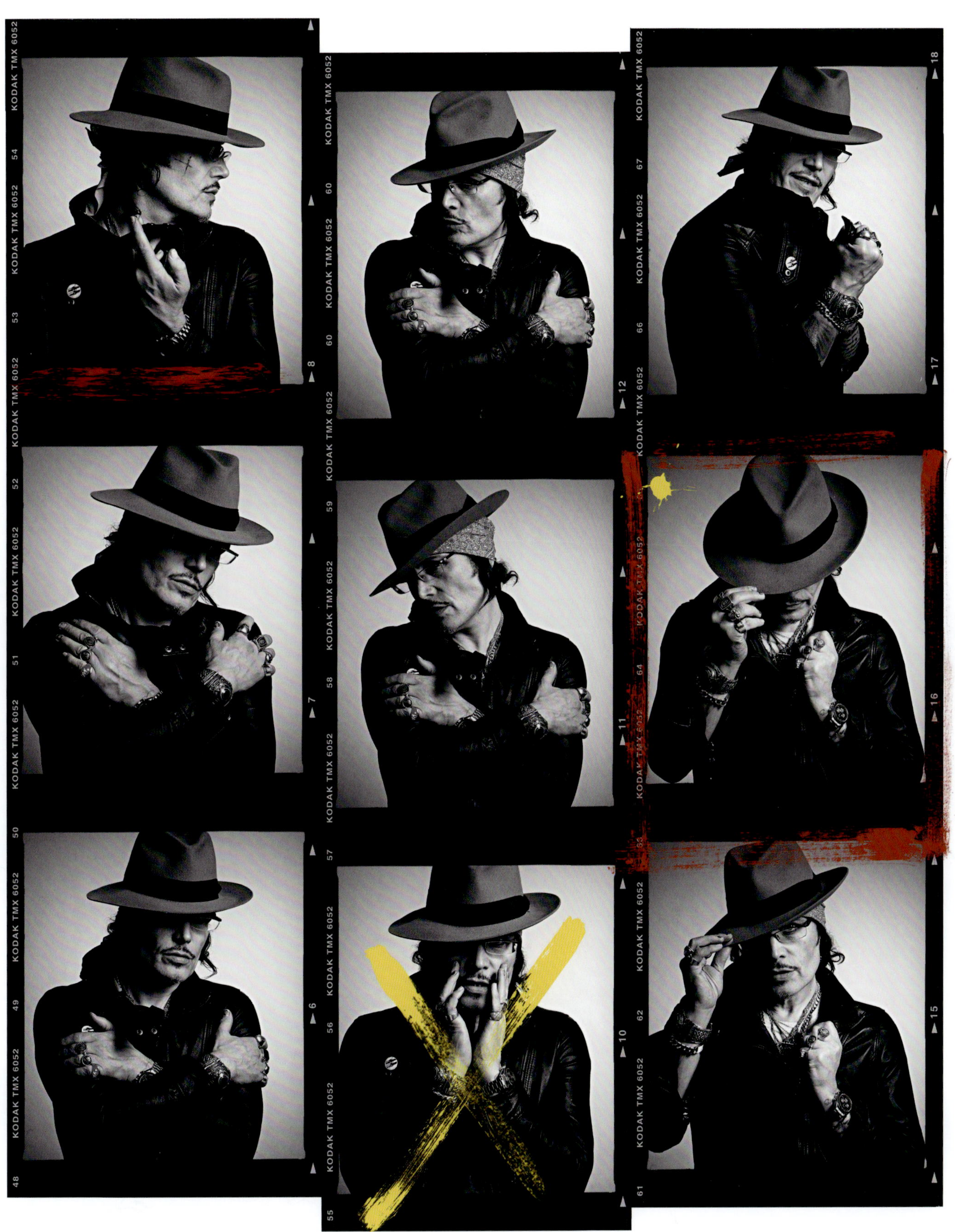

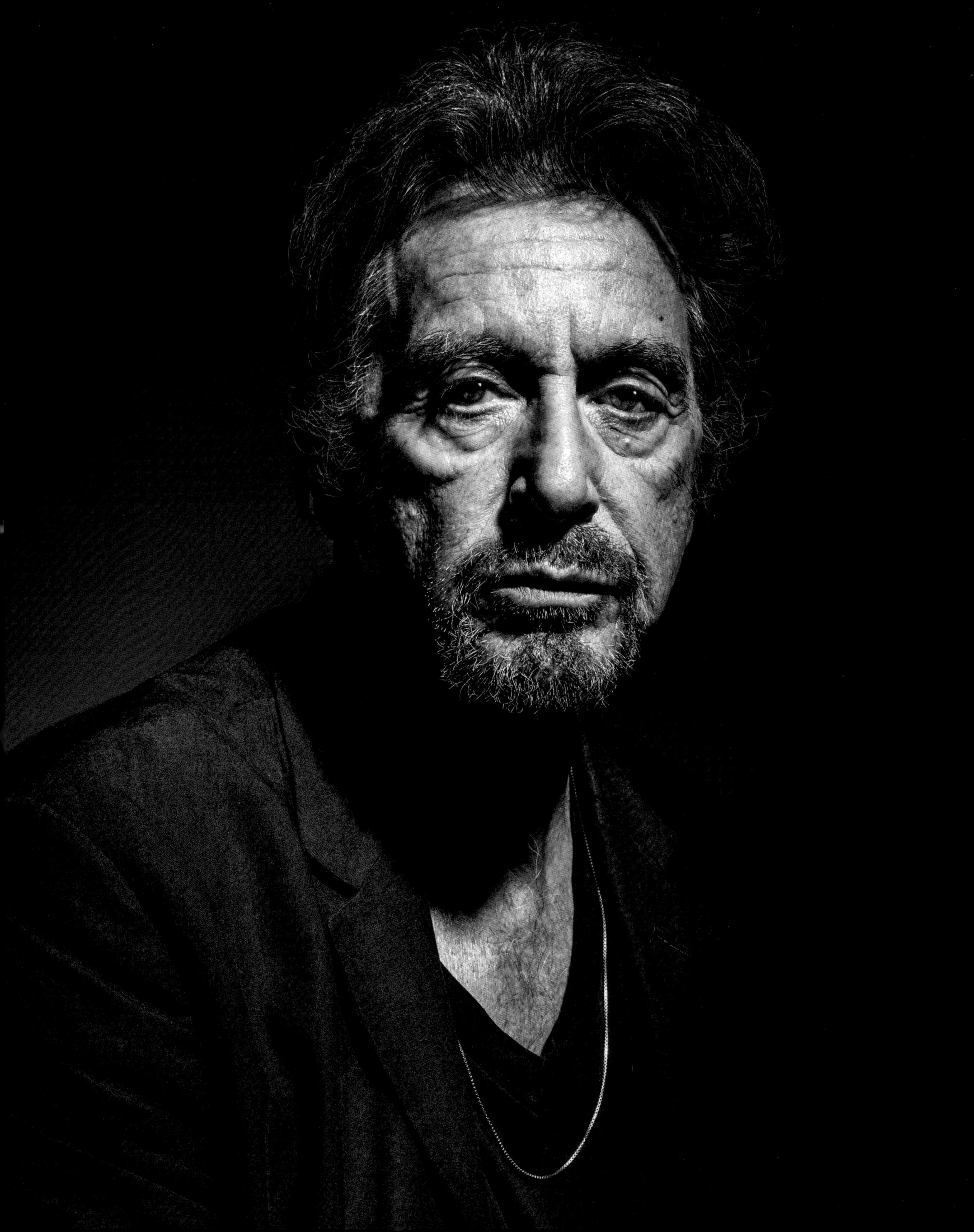

Al Pacino

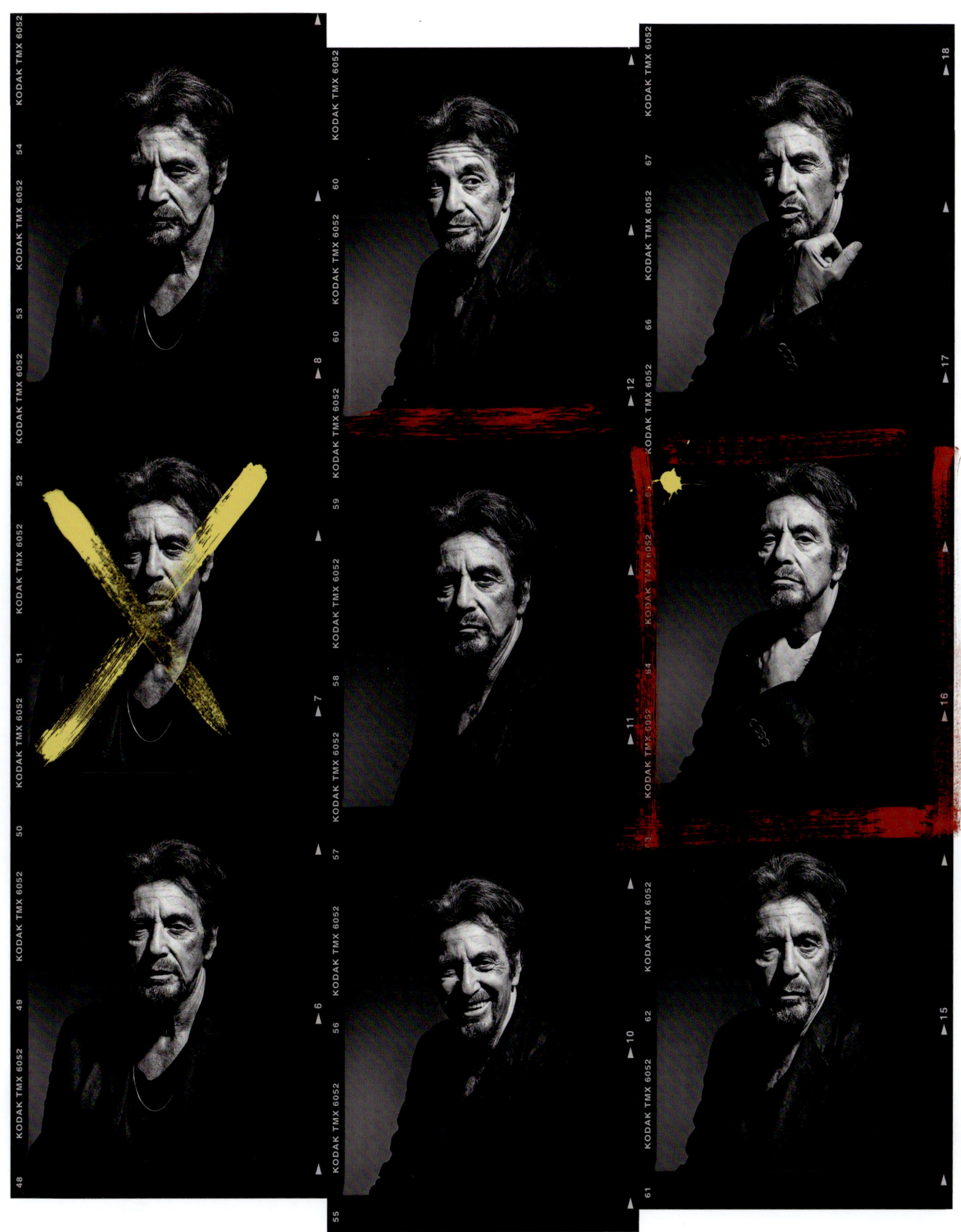

Alan Cumming

Once, twenty-six years ago, Greta Scaachi told me I should let Andy Gotts photograph me. I had just made the film *Emma* with Greta and I would probably have done anything she told me to do because she is clever and enchanting and utterly decent. What I didn't realise at the time was that after our shoot Andy would ask me to suggest someone I thought should be photographed by him – as he was working on his book called *Degrees* – so I asked Saffron Burrows, my girlfriend at the time. So it went on, each of us performing a photographic version of paying it forward, offering a friend the gift of entering Andy's orbit.

It should come as no surprise, then, that Andy has photographed more celebrities than any other photographer. Yes! More than Annie Leibovitz, more than David Bailey, more than Lord Snowdon, COMBINED! And many of those celebrities are here in this book.

These are people for whom being photographed is an occupational hazard. Yet in these pictures, you see not merely professional, dutiful sitters, but happy and relaxed people willing to goof around and bask in that state most vaunted but so rarely achieved by the legions of celebrity snappers: authenticity. Ringo Starr got it. He called Andy 'the Ansel Adams of faces'.

Photo shoots used to be more palpable affairs. There would be the Polaroids at the beginning – test shots for the lighting or an outfit, and souvenirs to take home and show a loved one. In the early days of our relationship, I gave such a Polaroid to my now husband to tell him I was in for the long haul. 'You're the one' I wrote on it and left it on his desk. What would I do nowadays? Text him an image of me on a computer screen, I suppose. Not nearly so romantic.

So, it is both nostalgic and exciting to see contact sheets again, and those illuminating lines through the rejects and squares round the selects, the progression of moments that lead up to 'the one'. Great photographers know when they've got it, and it's fascinating to see the mind of one via these grease pencil lines.

Above all Andy Gotts allows his subjects to shine through, untouched. His artistry does not come afterwards, in Photoshop and all the supposedly flattering trickery technology has taught us to expect. His skill is there in each frame, each moment, in the relationship he has built with his sitter, no matter how short a time they have shared, and the trust he has engendered in them because he is, quite simply, a good man. Anyone who encounters him can sense immediately his openness and kindness and I think this book is most of all a testament to those qualities.

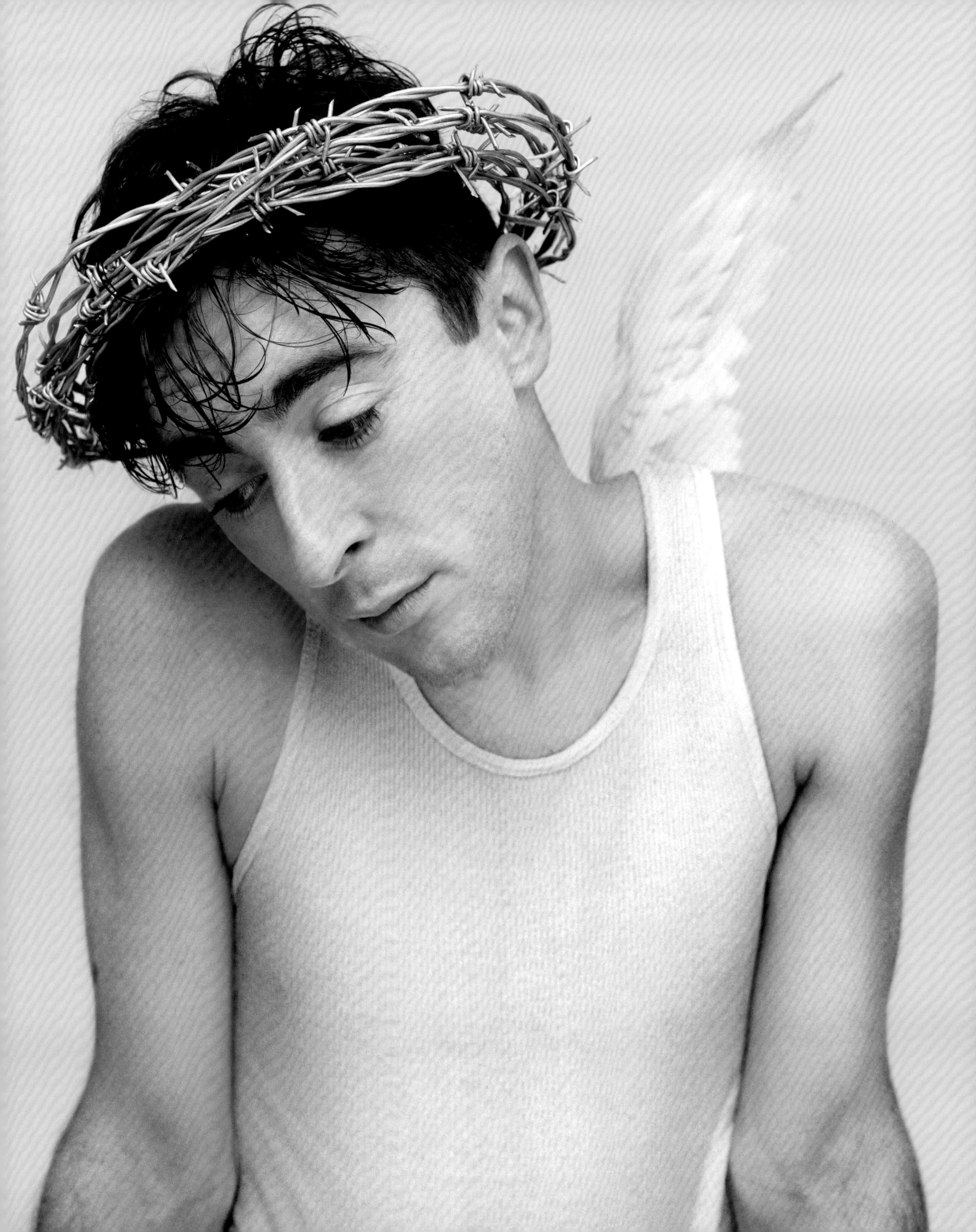

"GREAT PHOTOGRAPHERS KNOW
WHEN THEY'VE GOT IT, AND IT'S FASCINATING."

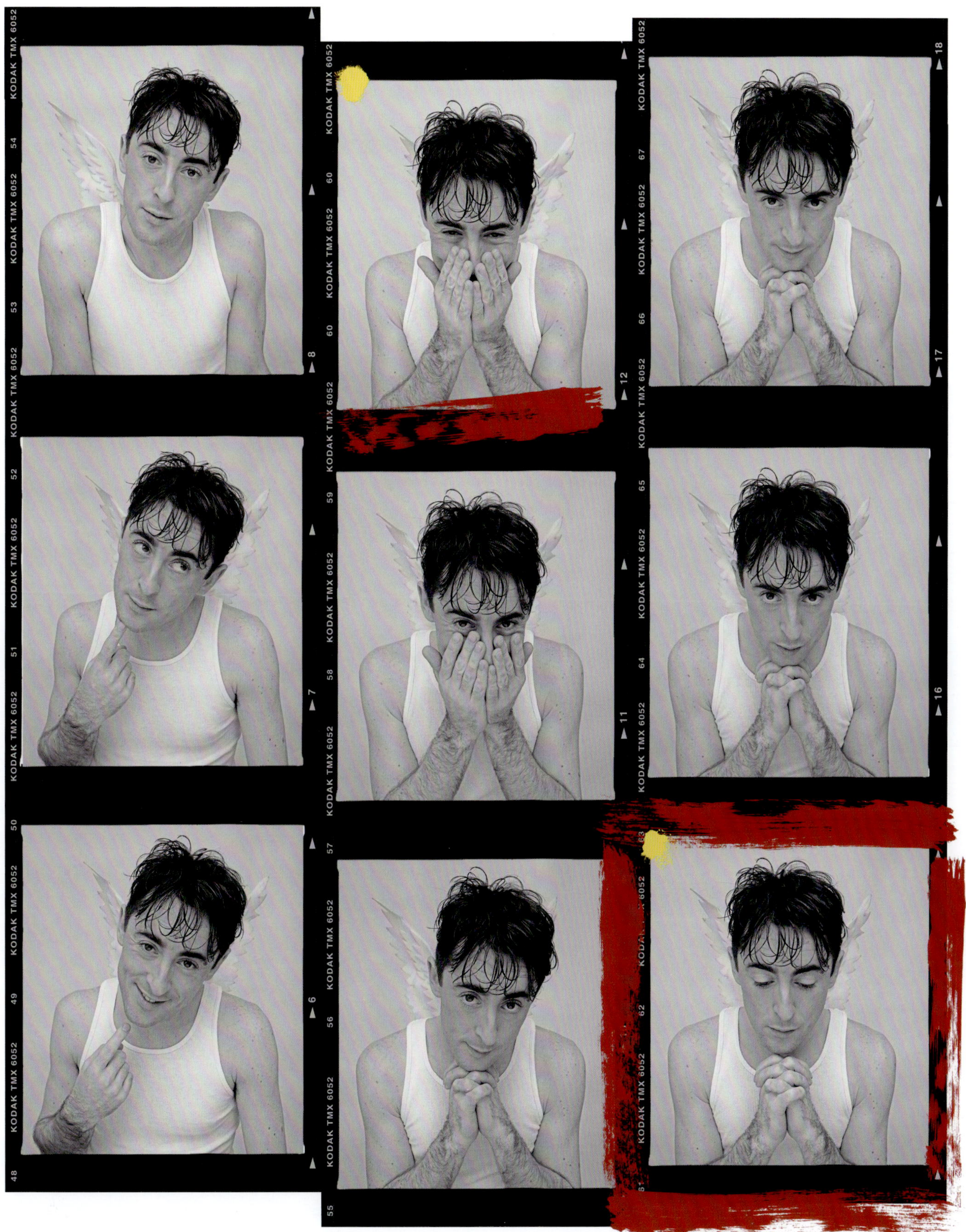

Alan Rickman

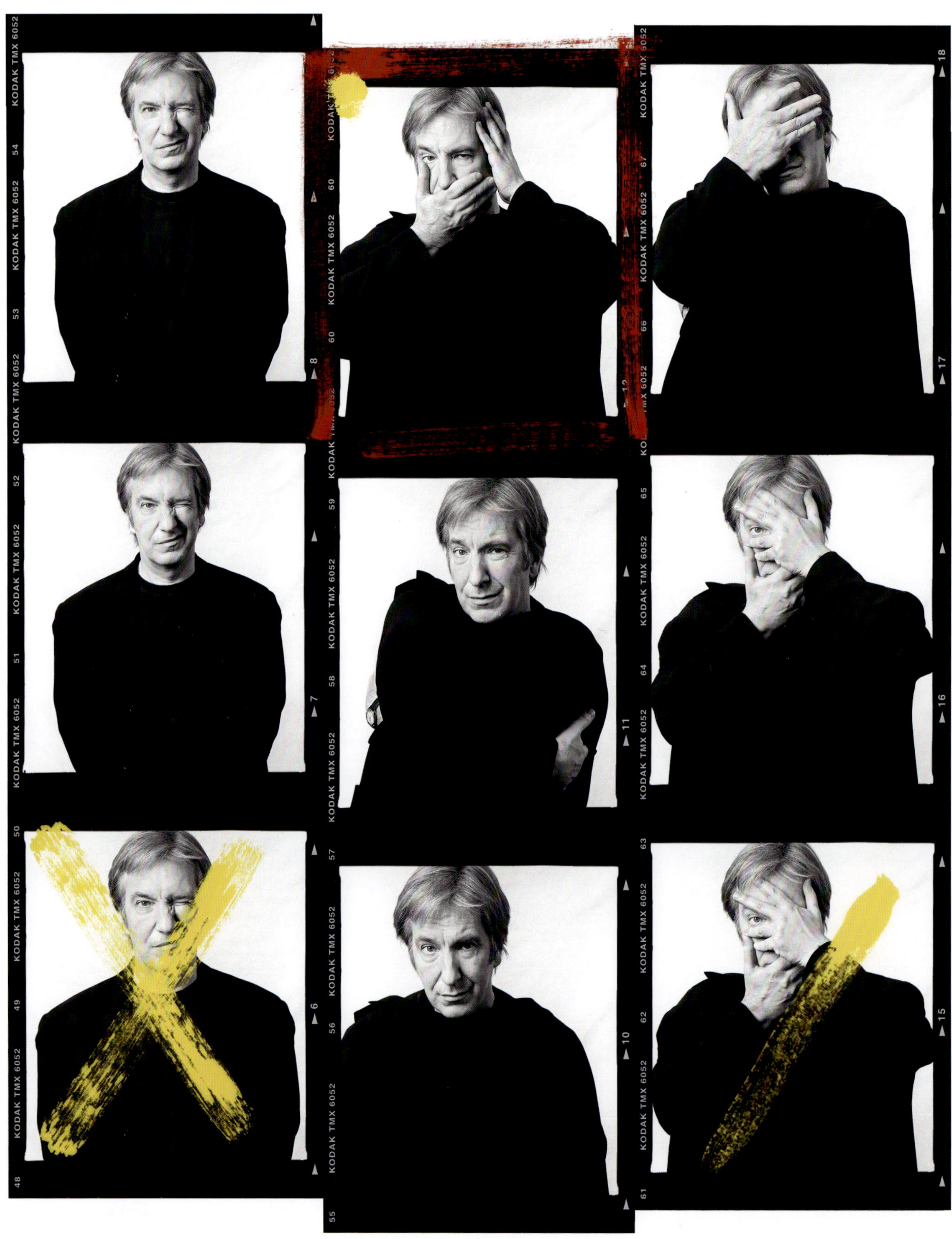

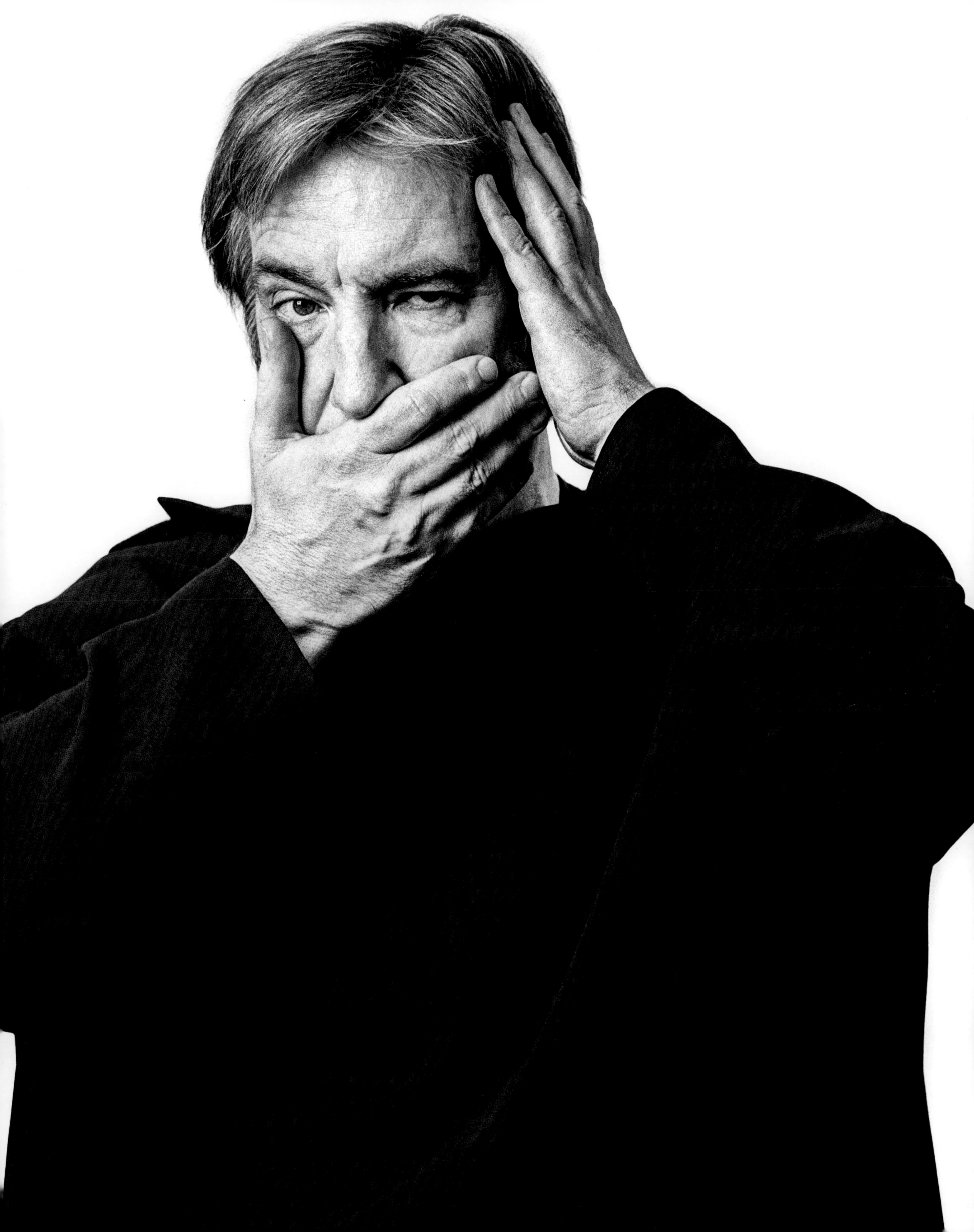

Alice Cooper

I shot Alice (or Vincent) in Flemings Mayfair. What bowled me over was how articulate and knowledgeable he was. He was great friends with Salvador Dalí, and Dalí made several sculptures featuring Alice. But the story that blew me away was how Alice was good friends with Groucho Marx. Groucho was an insomniac and would phone Alice and ask him to pop over to his house at 2-3am. They would sit in bed together and watch old movies. Now THAT would have been a Kodak moment.

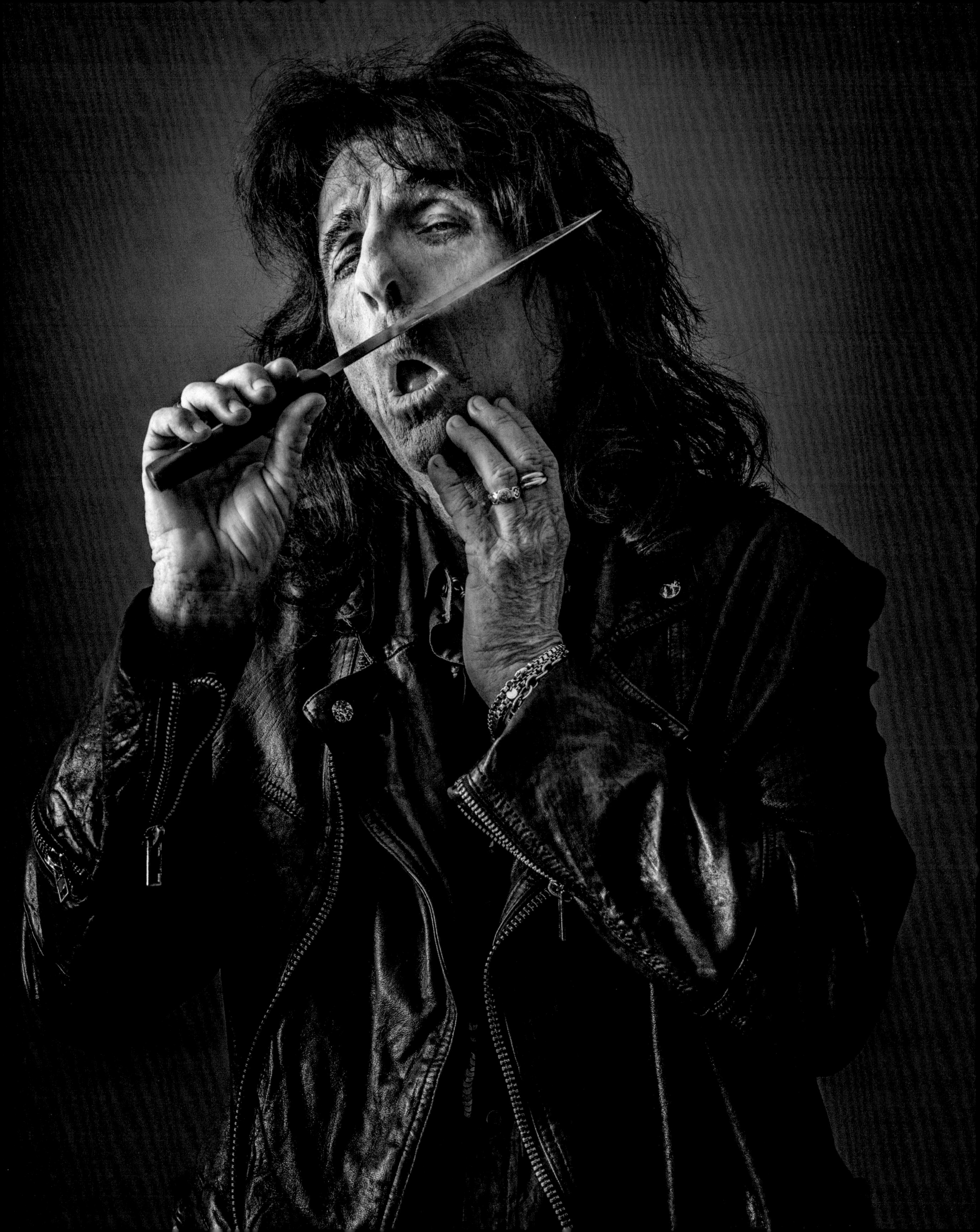

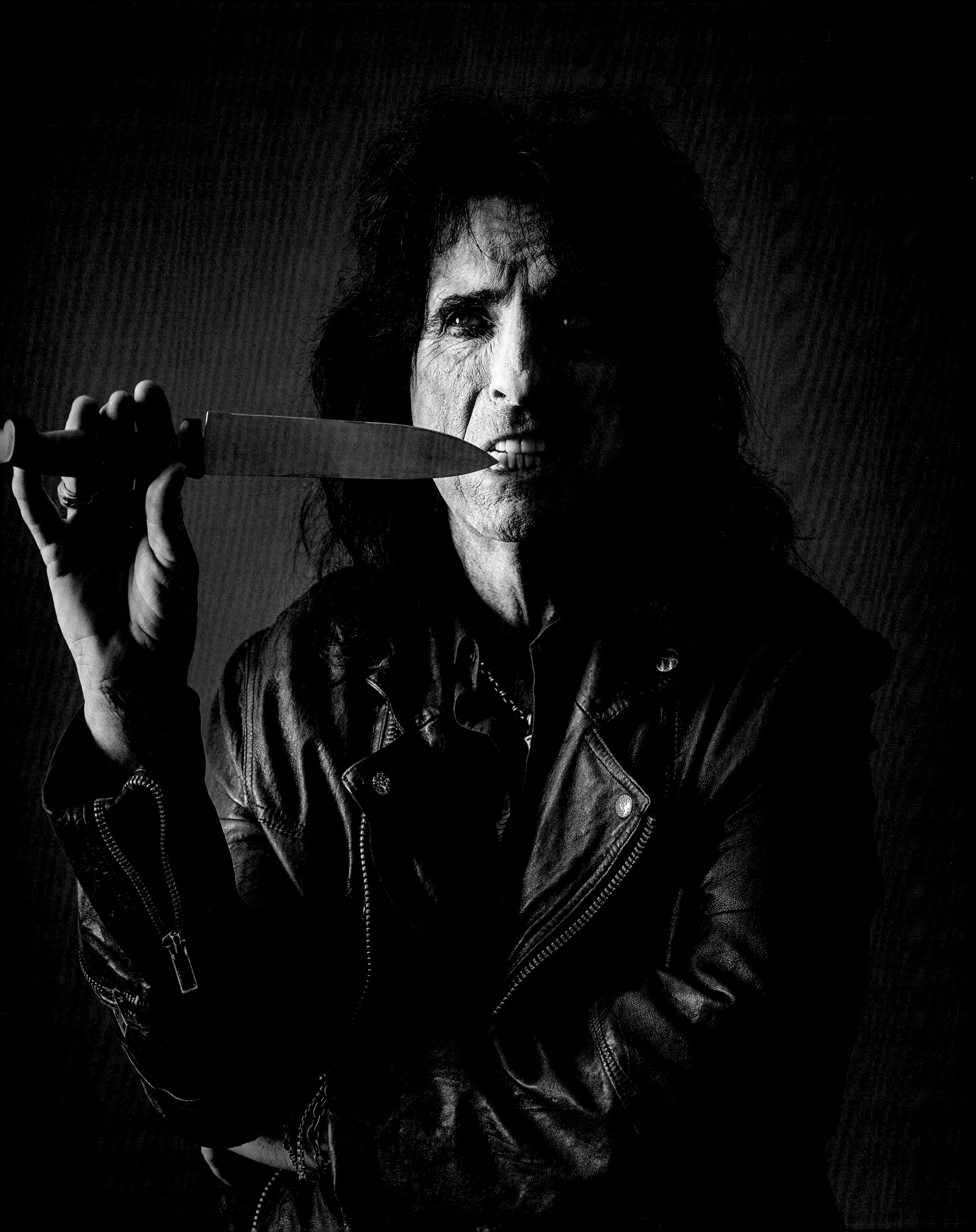

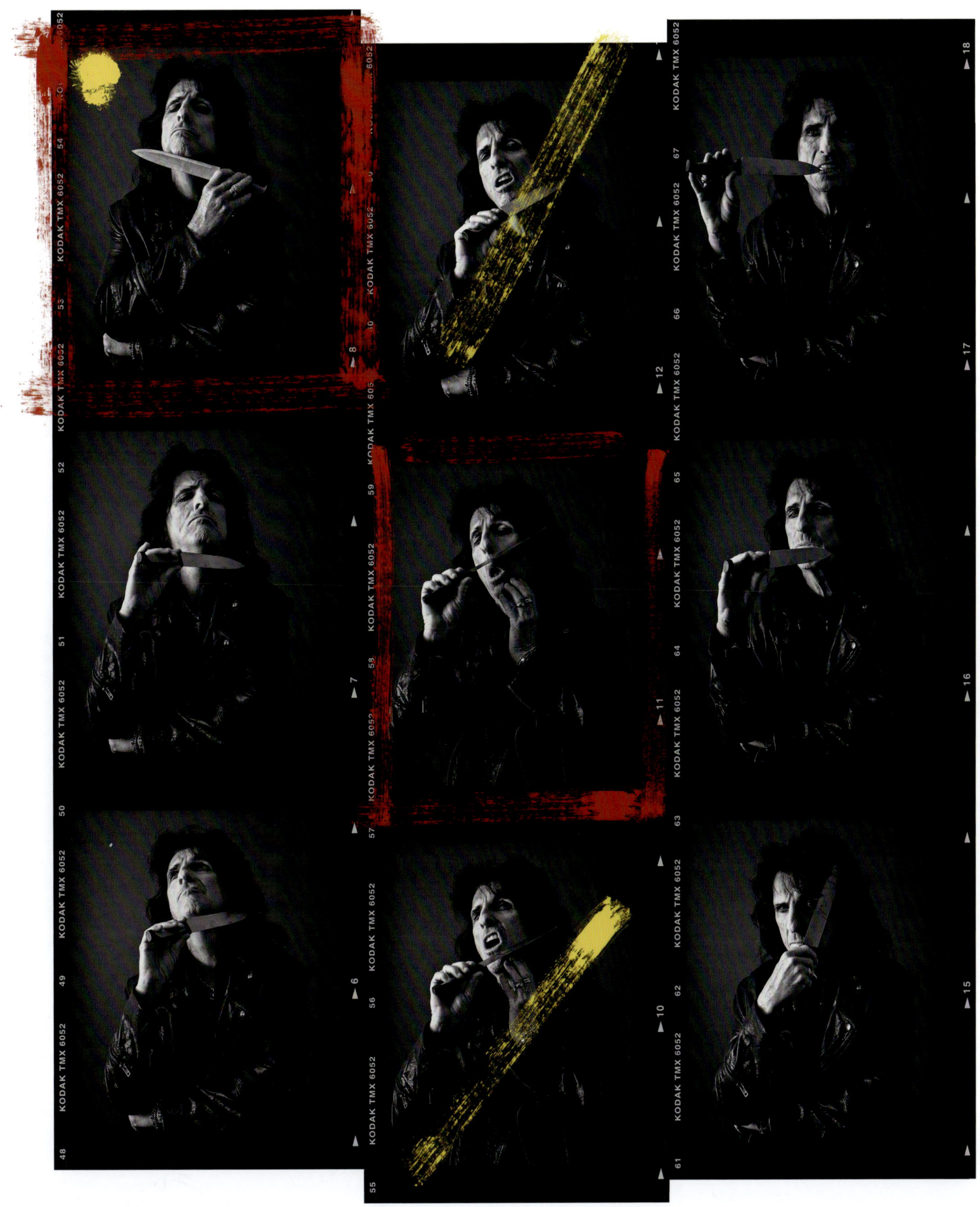

Annie Lennox

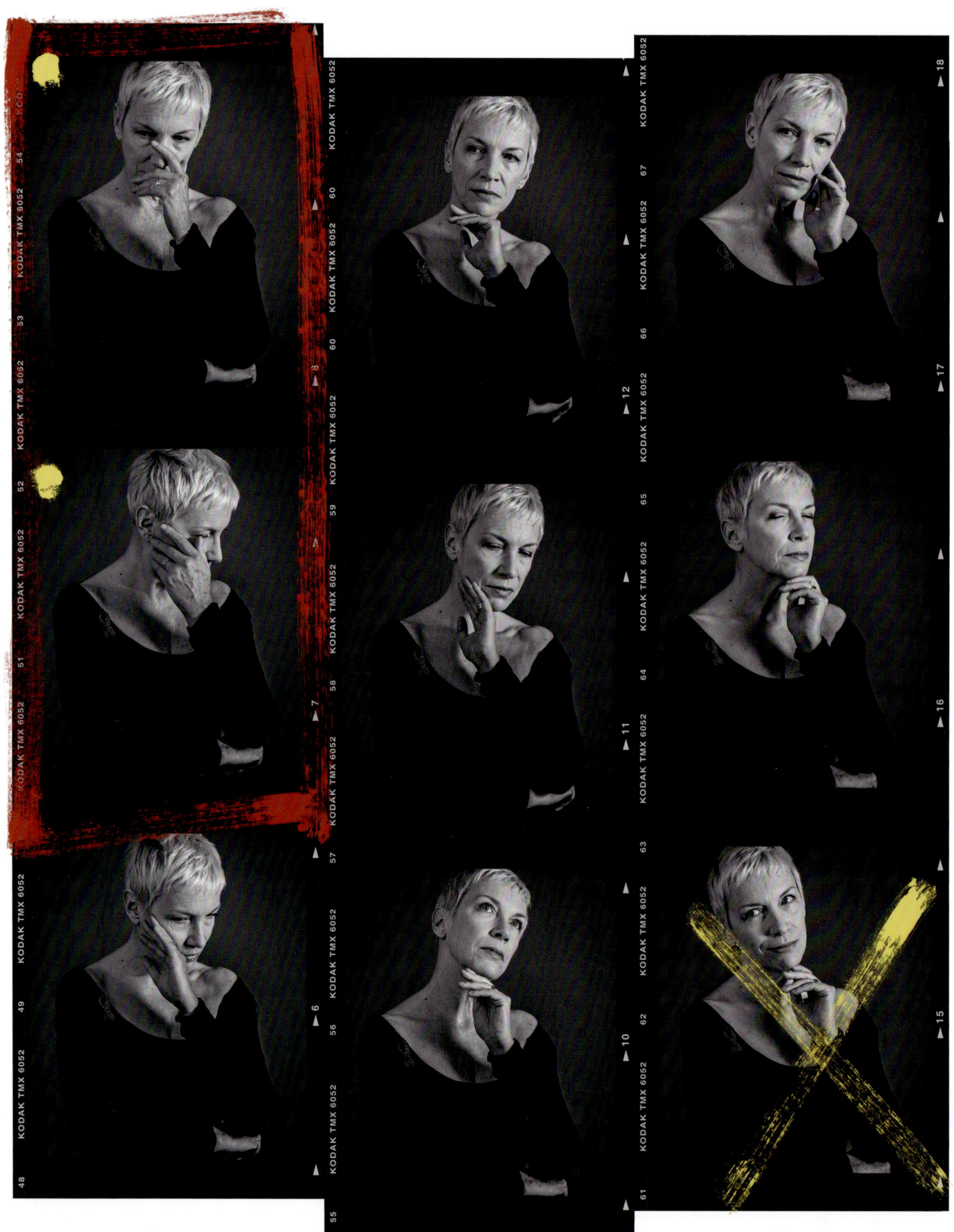

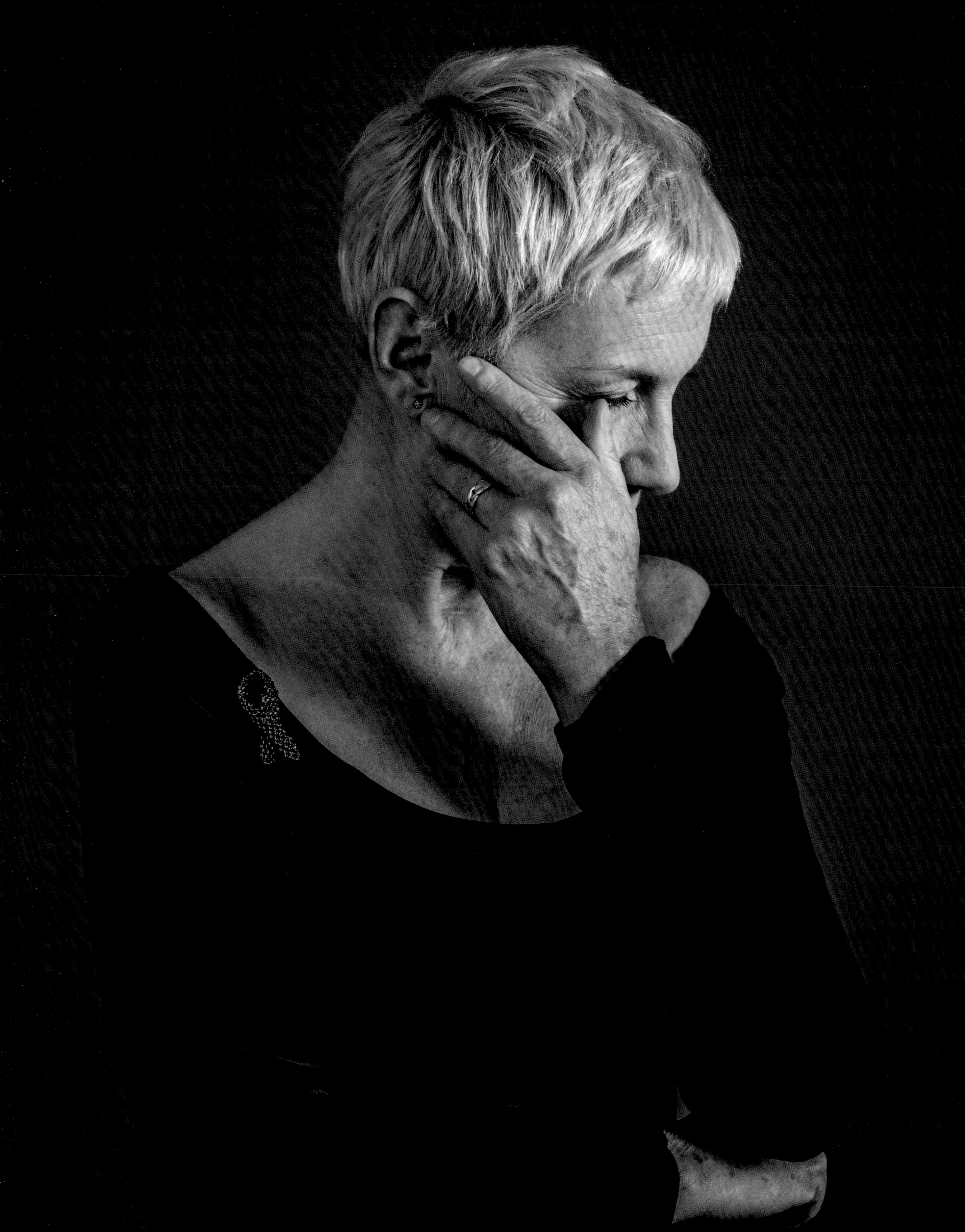

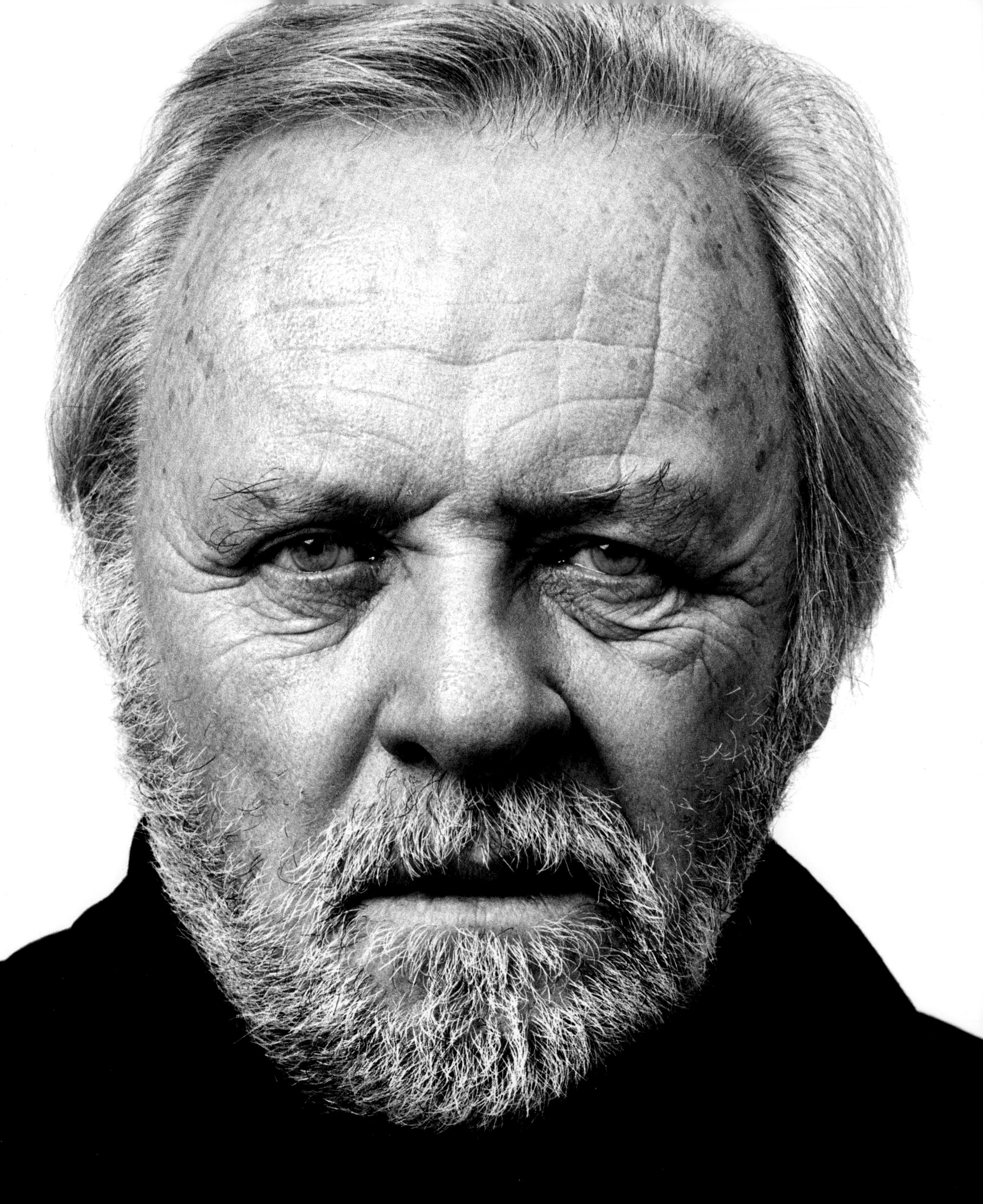

Anthony Hopkins

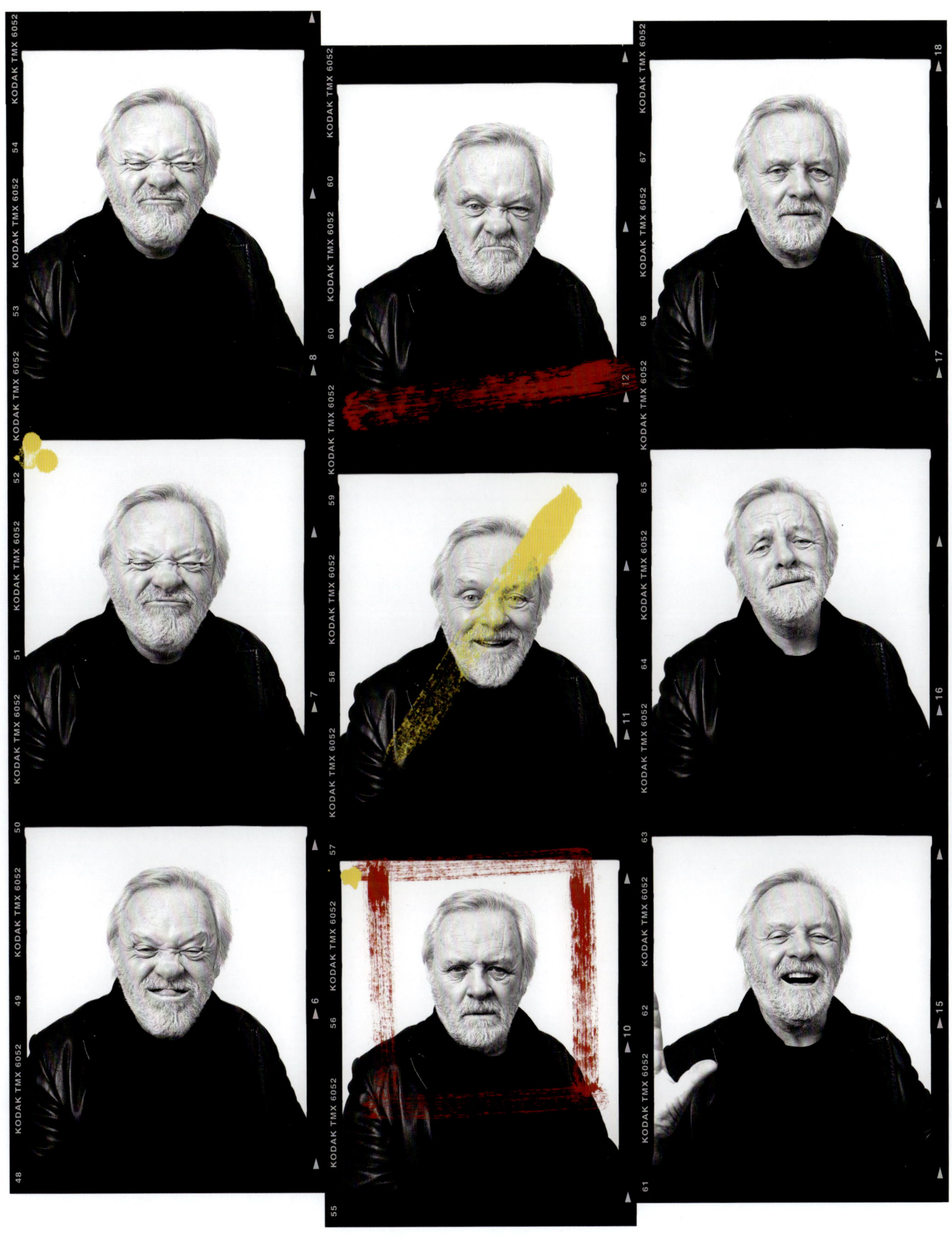

Benedict Cumberbatch

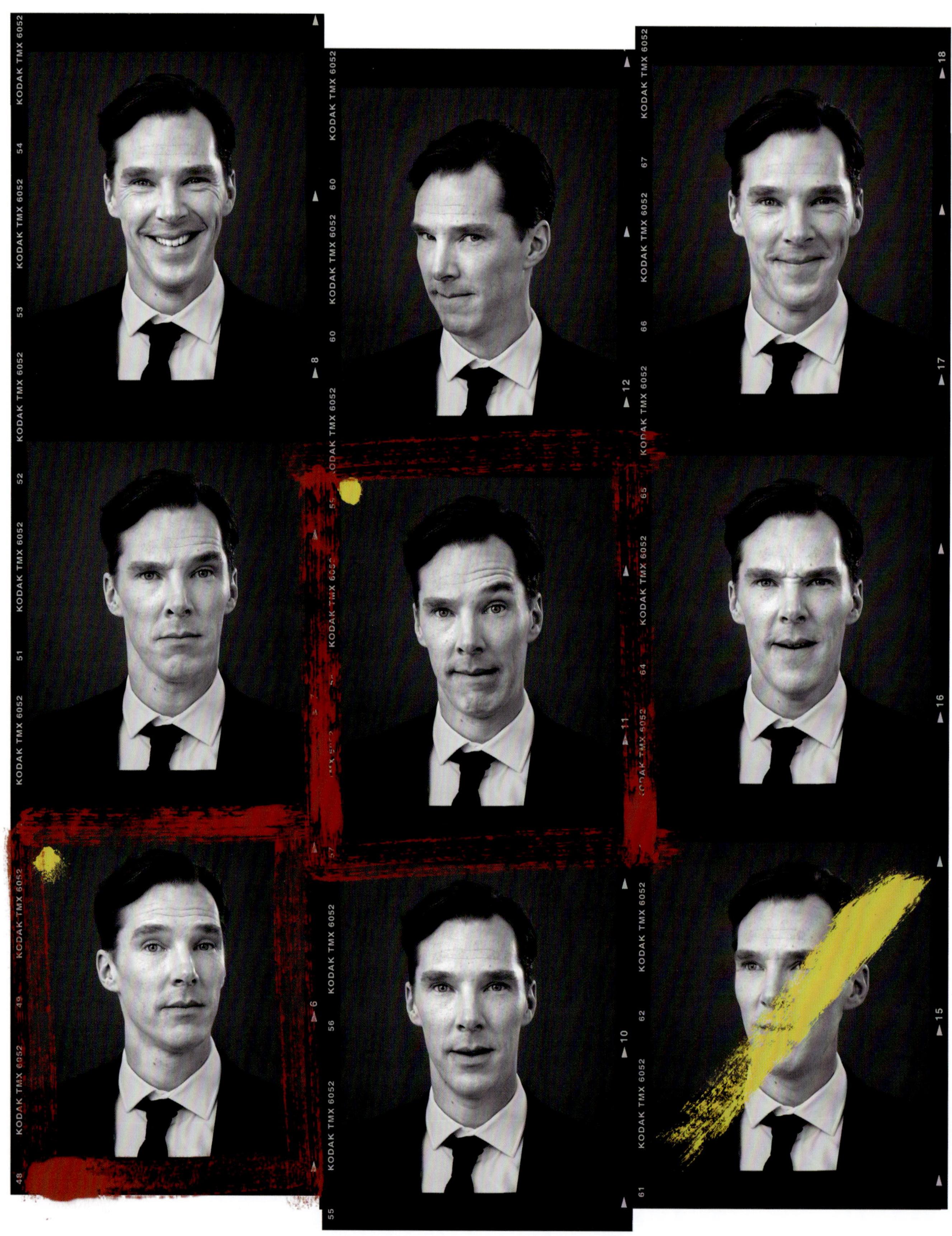

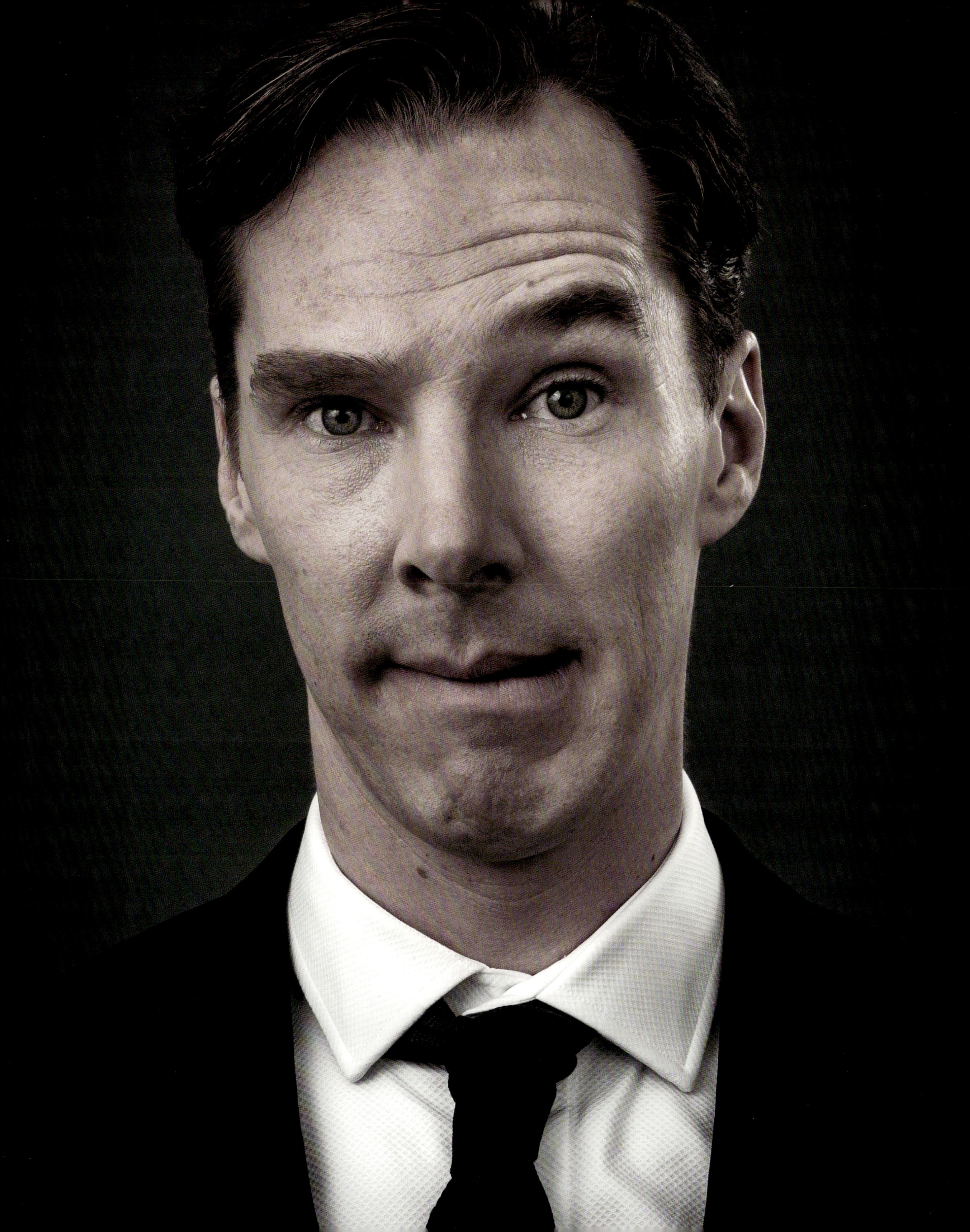

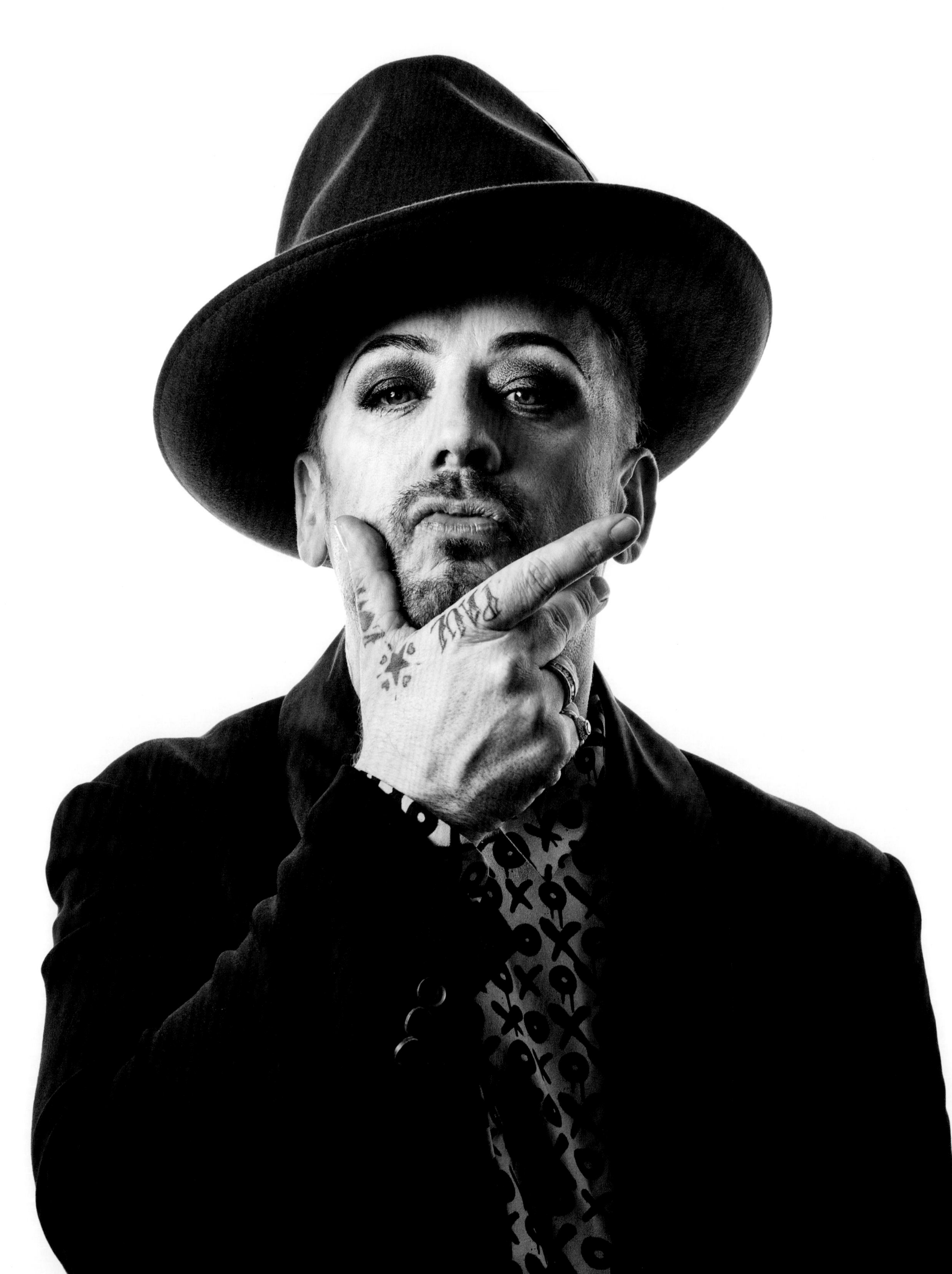

Boy George

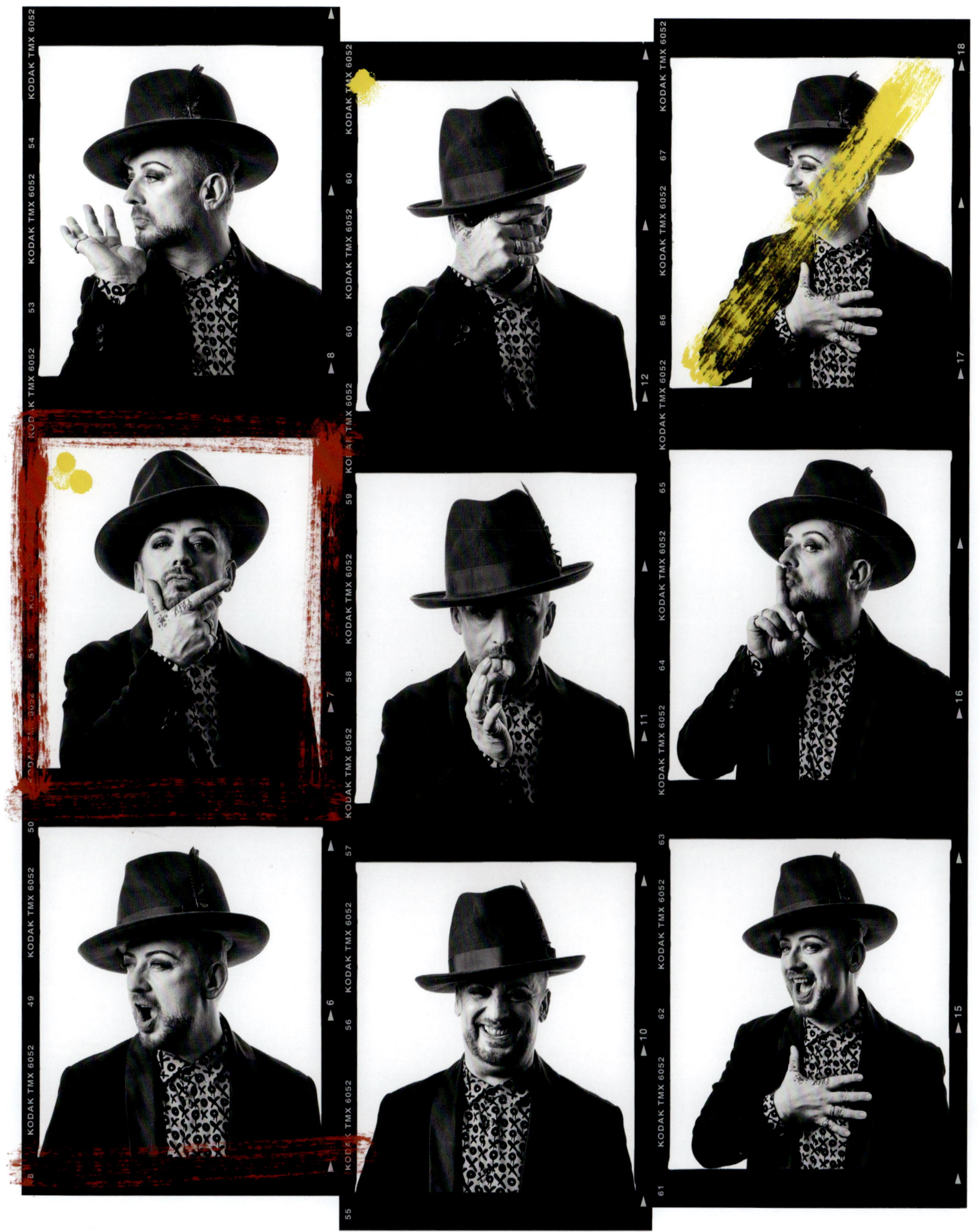

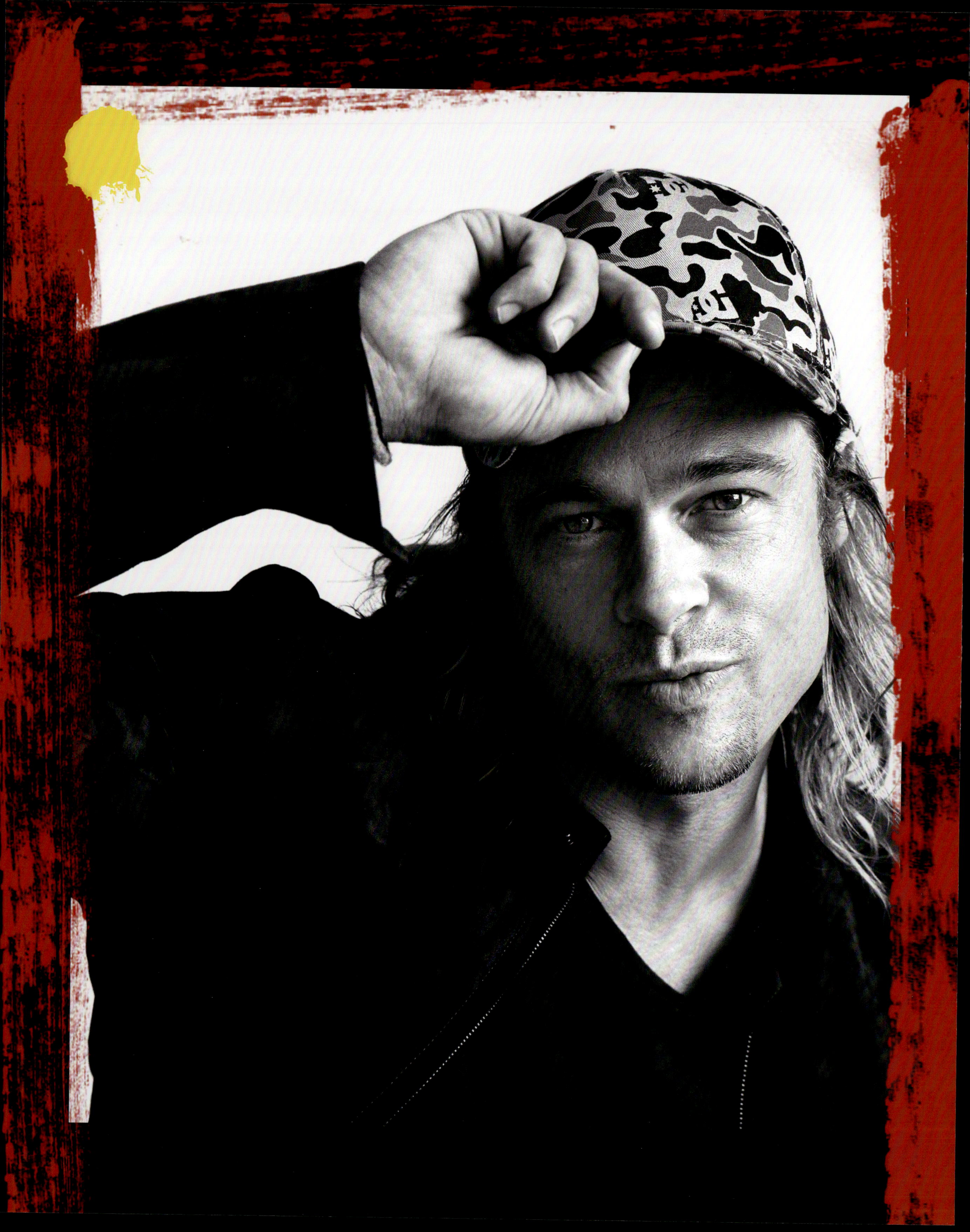

Brad Pitt

This shoot was part of my Degrees project and came through Dustin Hoffman. It took place at Pinewood Studios whilst Brad was filming *Troy* in 2003. I was under strict instructions that I would only have eleven minutes with Brad at 2pm. At around 1pm, there was a knock on the door and in came a guy in a cap and sunglasses with a rucksack... The man lifted his sunglasses to introduce himself as Brad Pitt, like I would not have recognised him otherwise. We spent a lot of the shoot chatting, mostly Brad asking me questions about my life. It created a very relaxed environment and I believe this came across in the images. Brad mentioned that he had been photographed the day before for *Vanity Fair*, by Annie Leibovitz and her cast of thousands. Brad mentioned that he much preferred my less formal way of shooting, just myself and my camera. He felt the experience was more relaxed.

After the shoot Brad asked if the was anything he could do to help my project... to which my juvenile retort was "Do you have any famous friends?". With that he walked into the corner of the studio with his mobile phone and made a quick call. I could hear laughing and merriment occurring ... then Brad came over to me and handed me the phone. "Hey Andy, its George Clooney. I am at Lake Como, do you want to pop over for a shoot?"

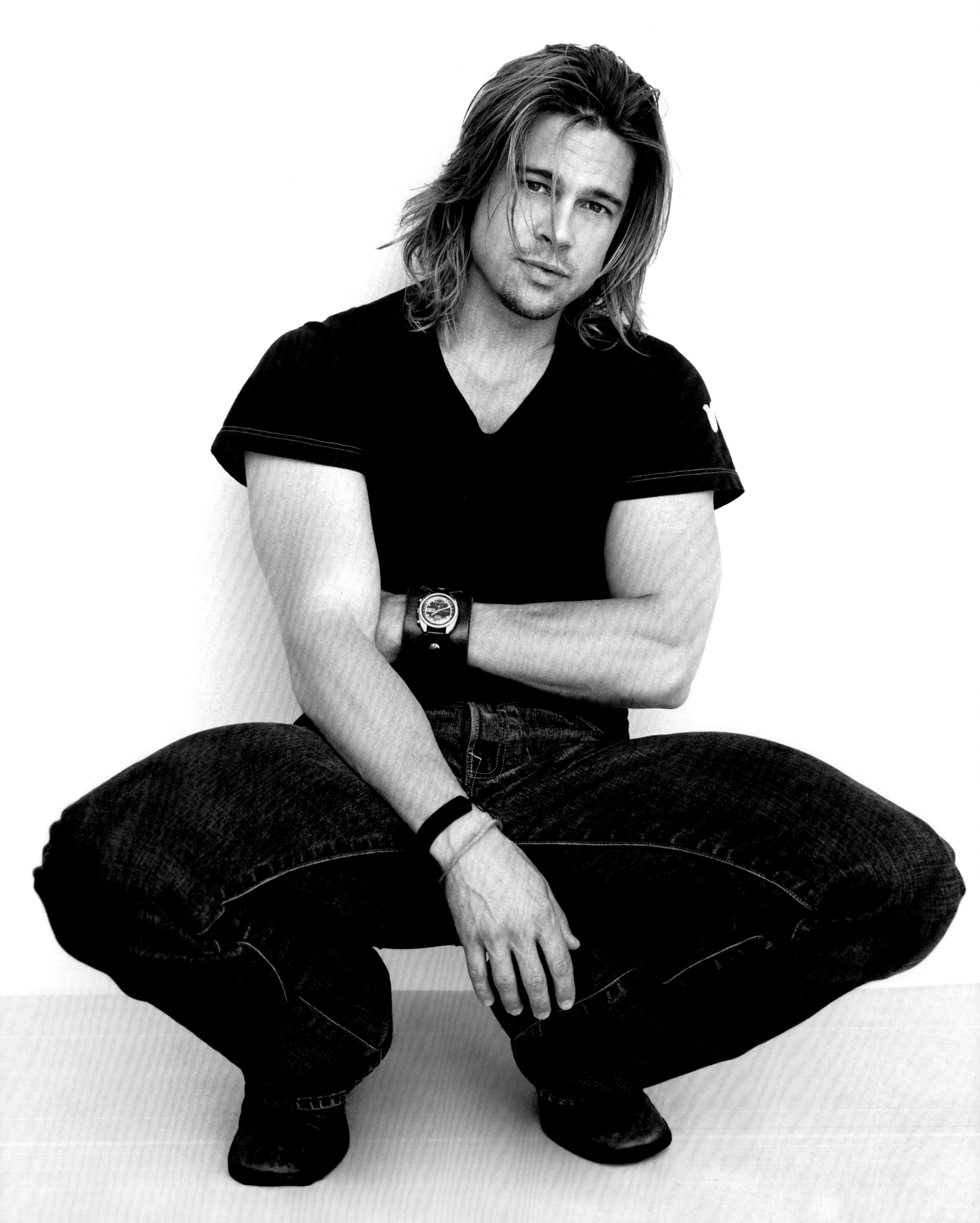

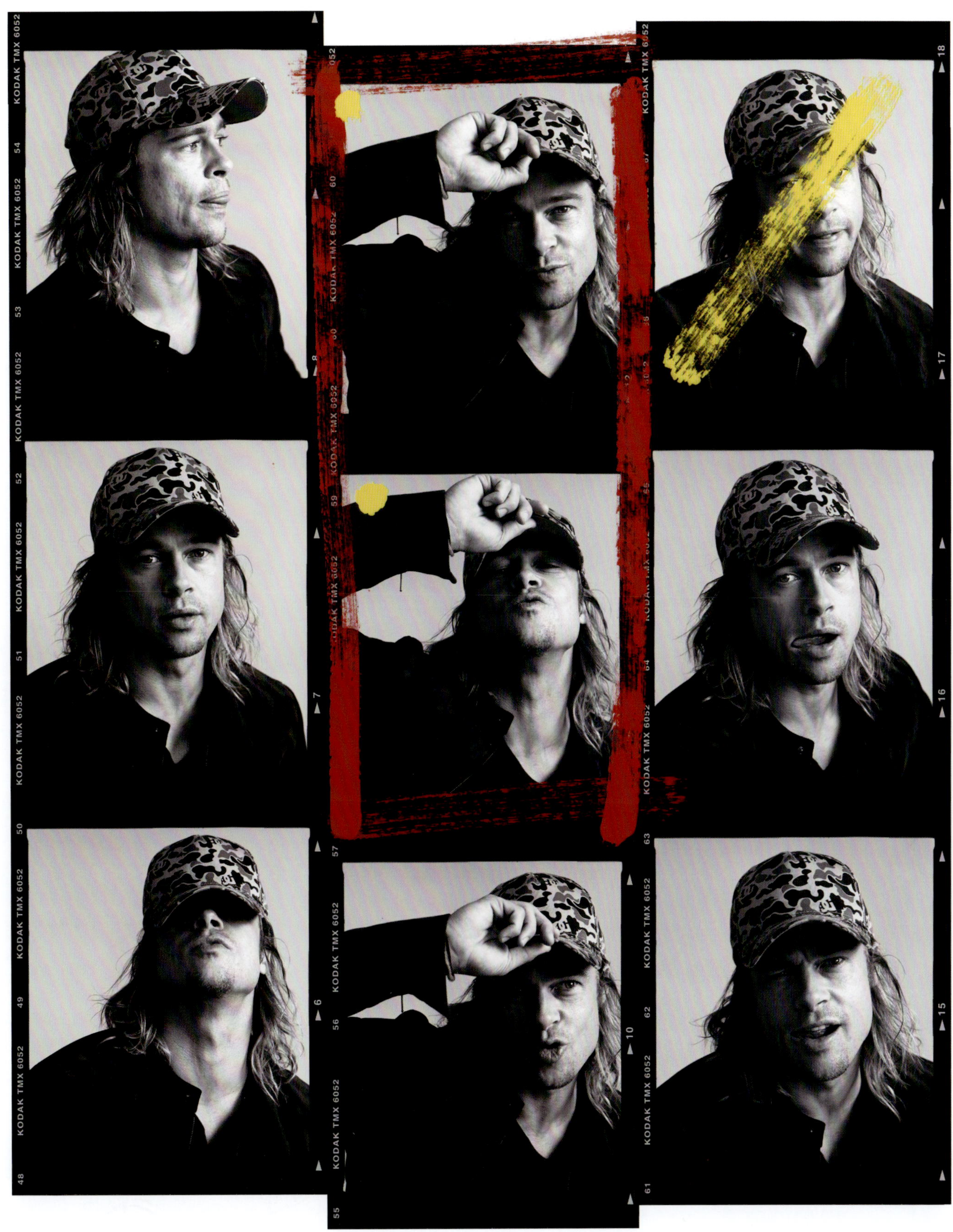
KODAK TMX 6052

Bryan Ferry

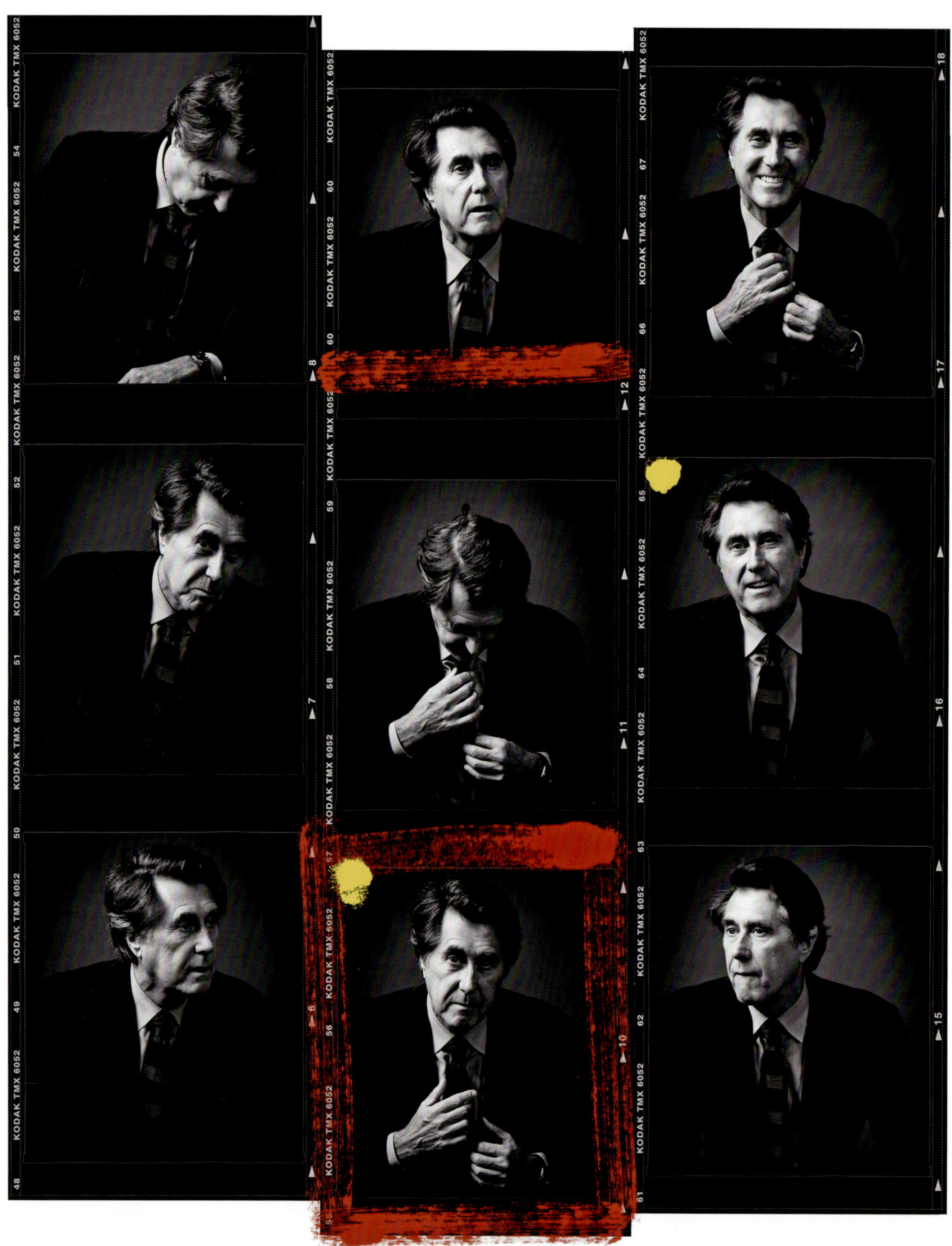

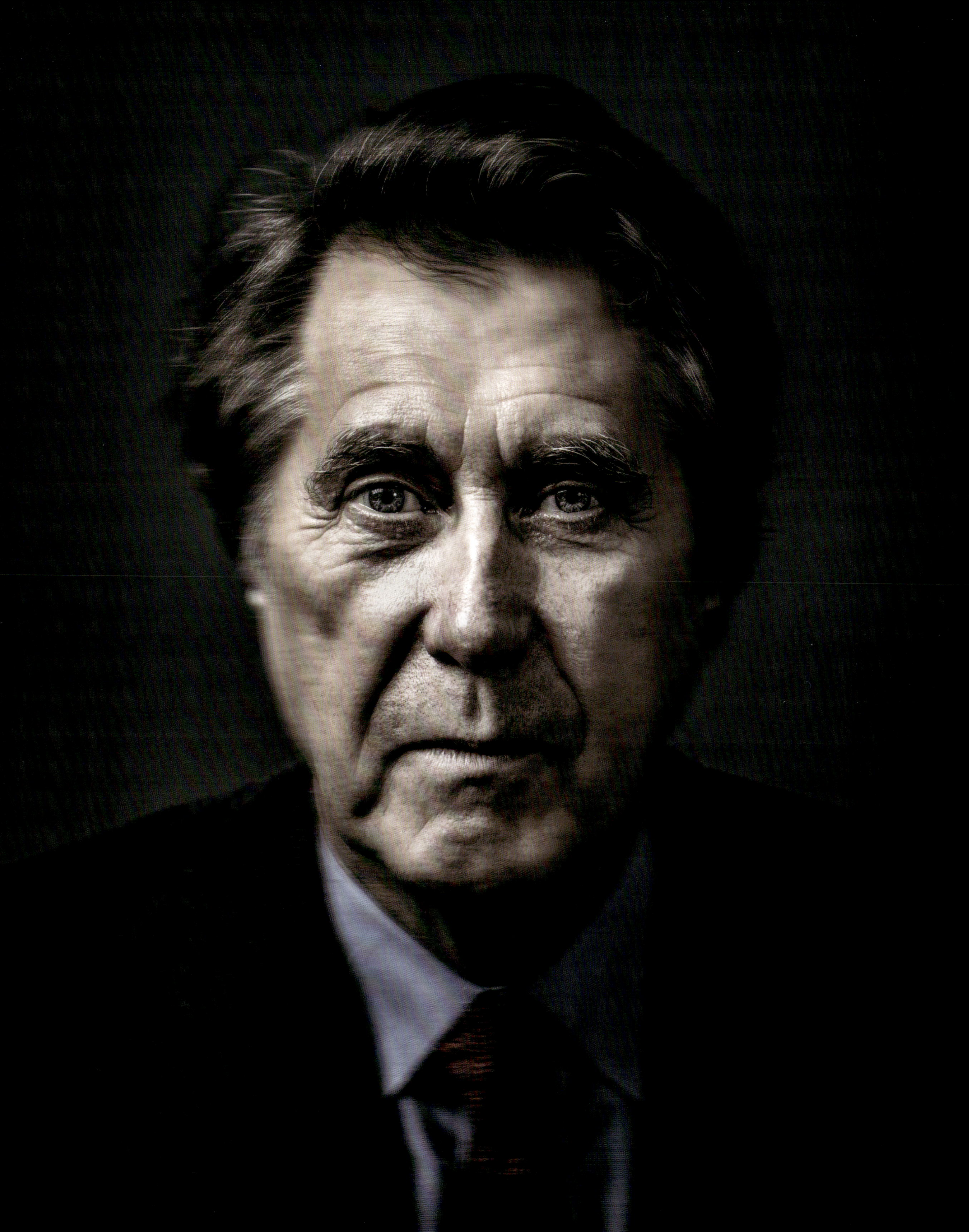

Charlize Theron

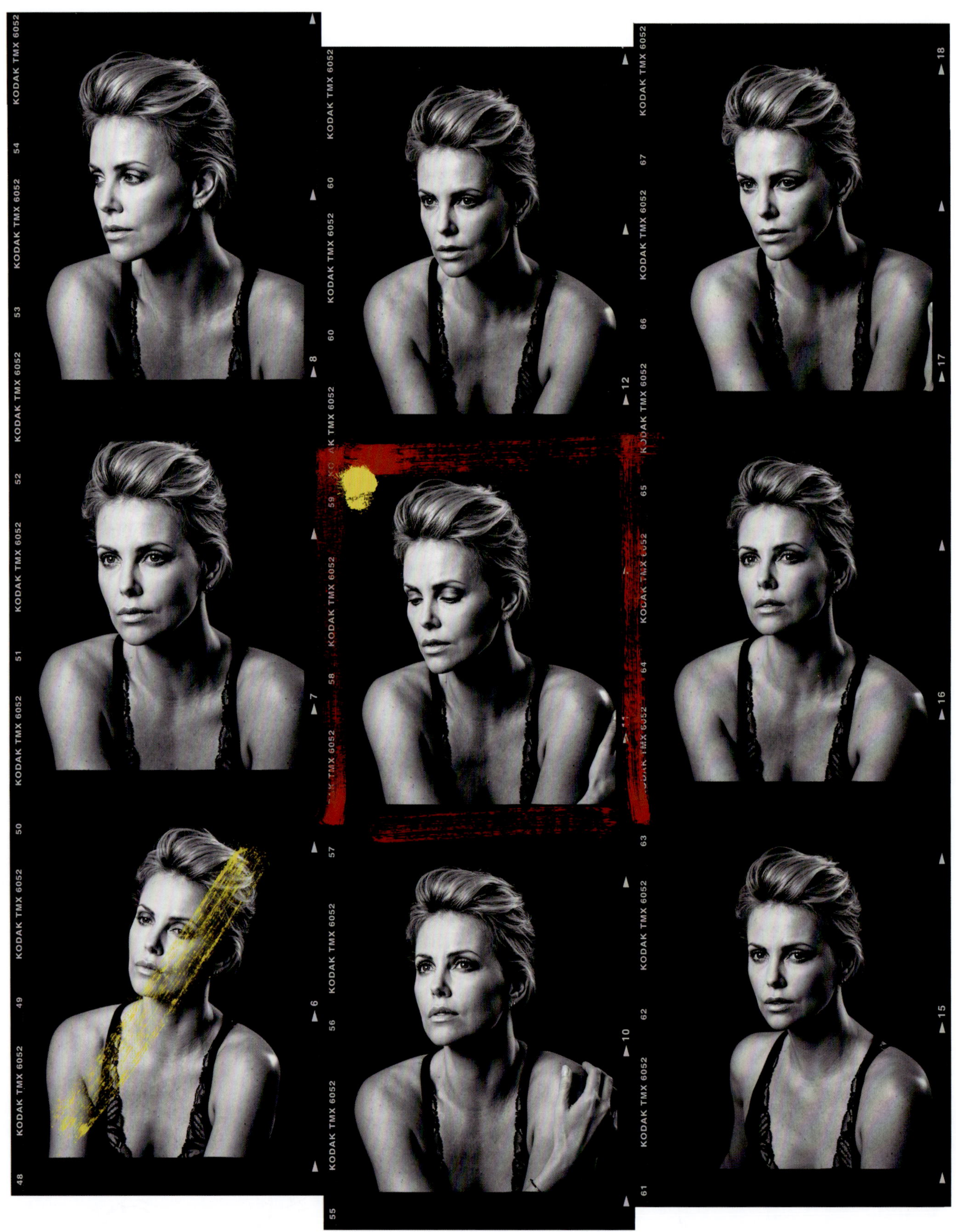

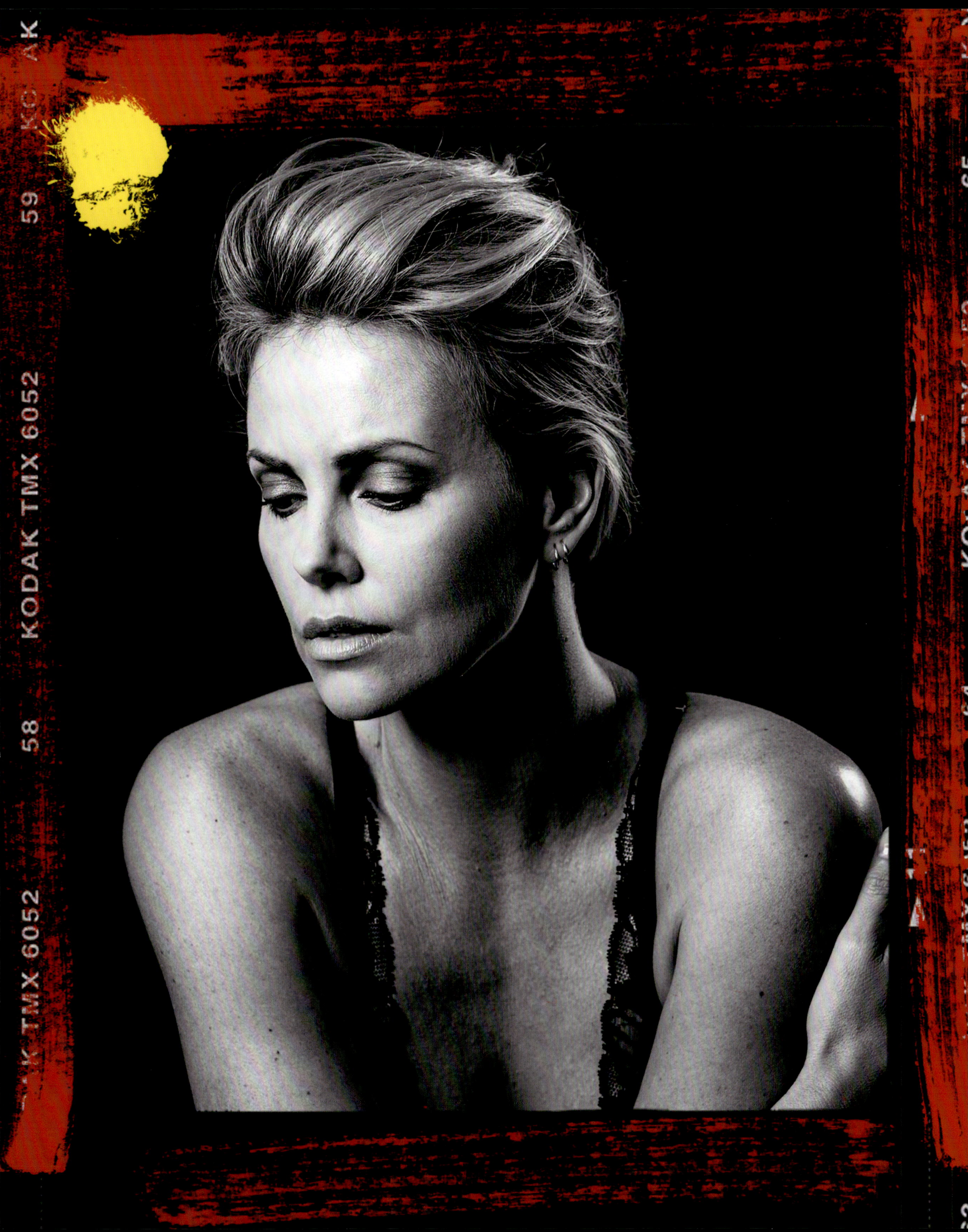
K TMX 6052
58
KODAK TMX 6052
59

Chris Martin

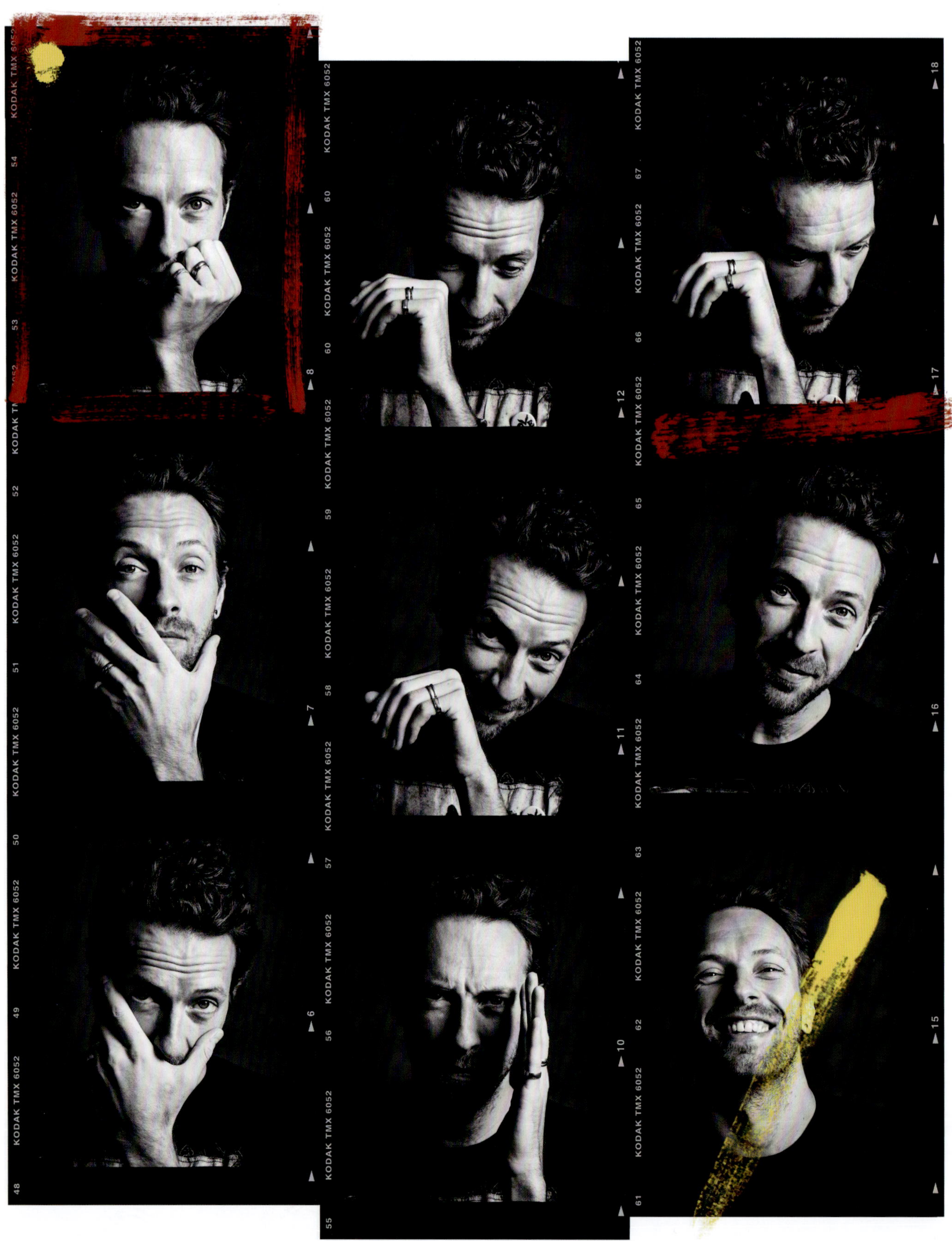

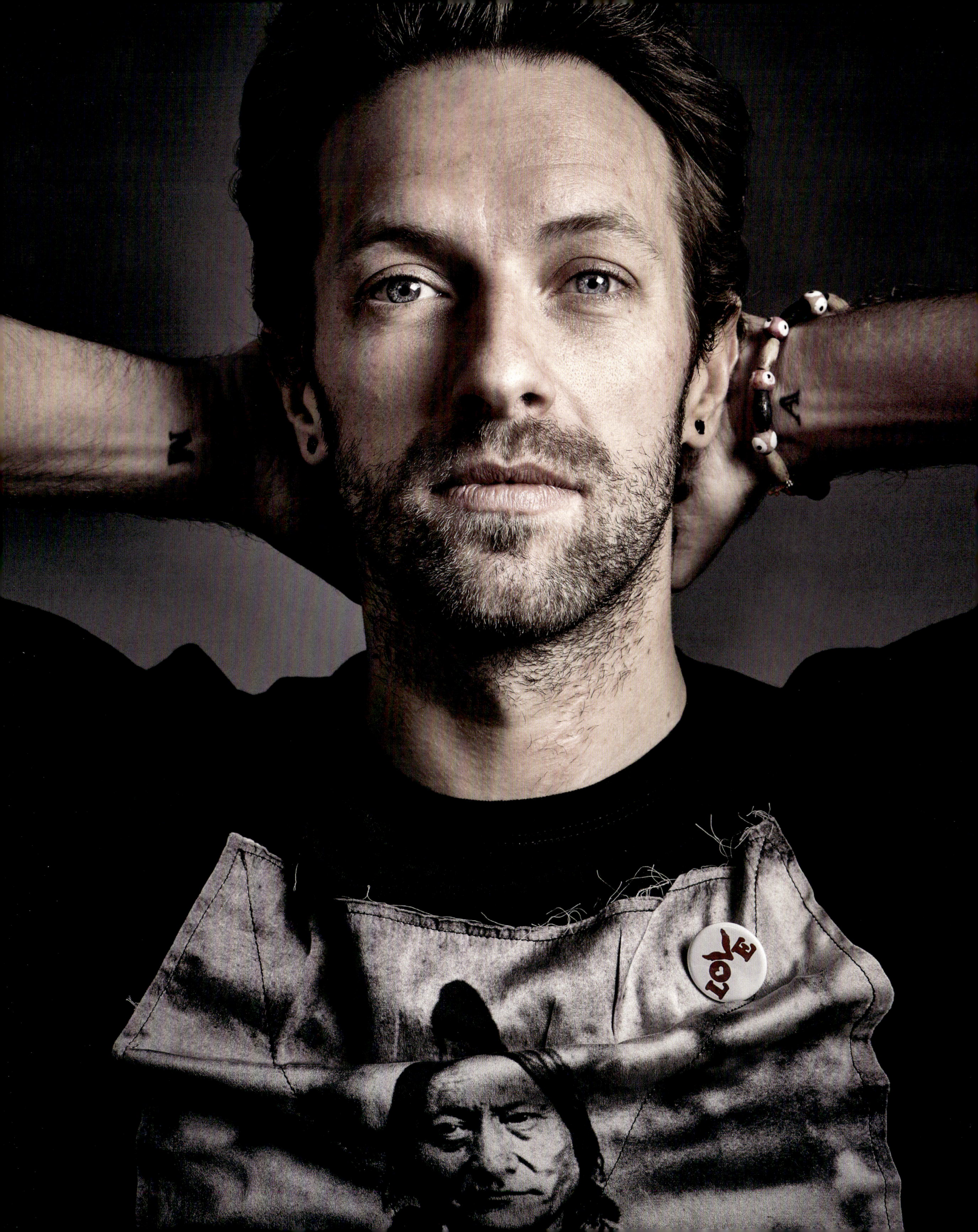
LOVE

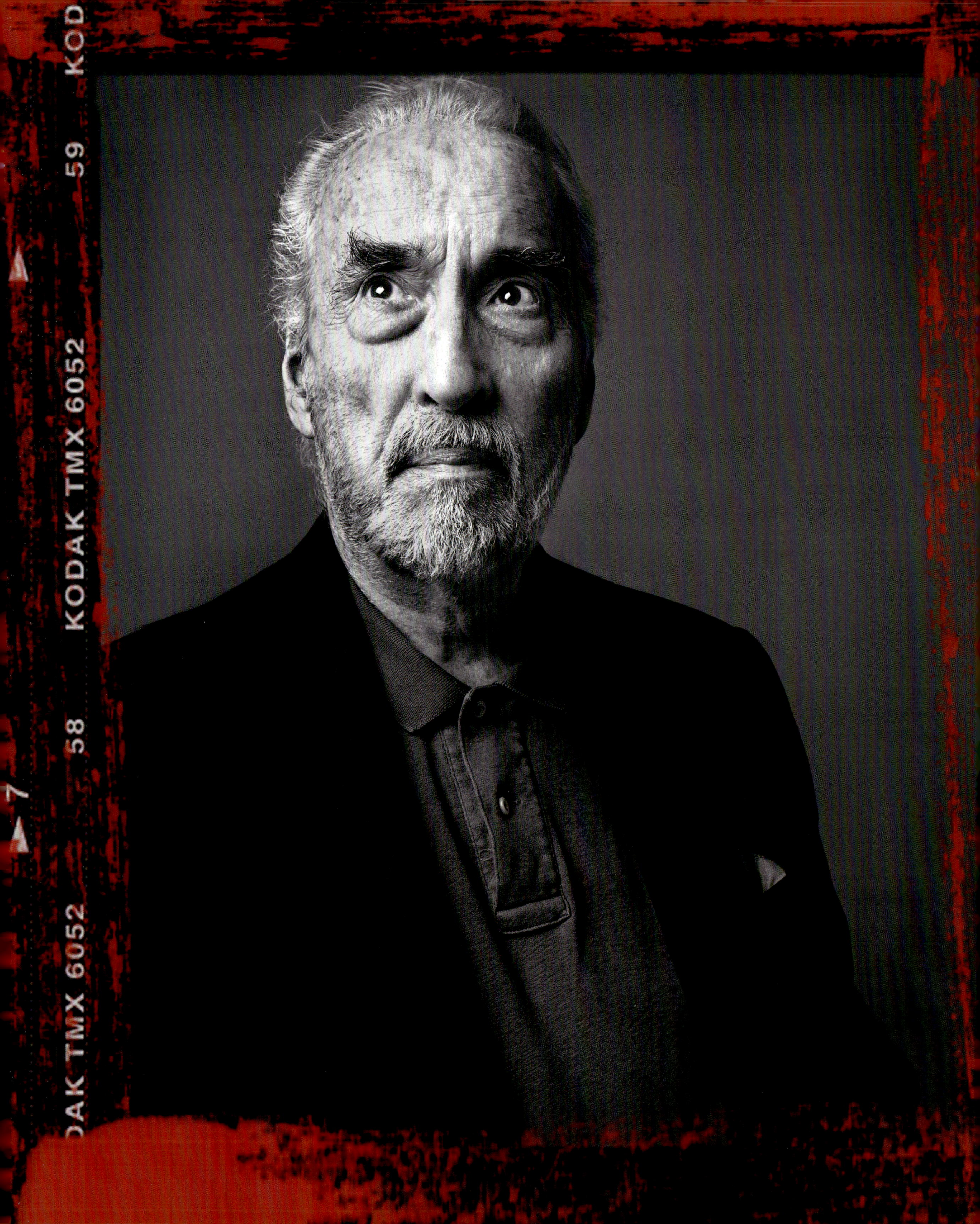
KOD
59
KODAK TMX 6052
58
7
DAK TMX 6052

Christopher Lee

I shot the photos of Christopher in 2005, ten years before he died. Not many people know he was awarded a Guinness World Record in 2007 for the most screen credits for a living actor. As we walked through the Savoy Hotel, Christopher noticed the sheet music on the walls from Gilbert and Sullivan. Christopher said "Did you know I sing every day? I was a classically trained Baritone." He then broke into song with 'Three Little Maids' from *The Mikado*. He belted it out in the hallway of the Savoy and it was an impressive sight. As we got into the room he insisted on tea and a cigar, and as he smoked it, I started shooting. When I originally showed him the images, he particularly loathed the ones of him smoking and asked if I would only show them as a last resort!

A few years passed and Sir Christopher was getting very frail. *The Times Magazine* called me to ask if I had any shots of Christopher that were unpublished. The ones that instantly sprang to mind were the cigar images. I found one that I especially loved and also one that I thought Christopher looked particularly strong in, and sent it over to *The Times*. On the day the magazine was published my phone rang early in the morning. It was Christopher's wife, Lady Lee. Almost guffawing down the phone, she told me Christopher LOVED the shot in *The Times* and asked if I could send him some copies! Obviously over time he had grown to love it, as I always did.

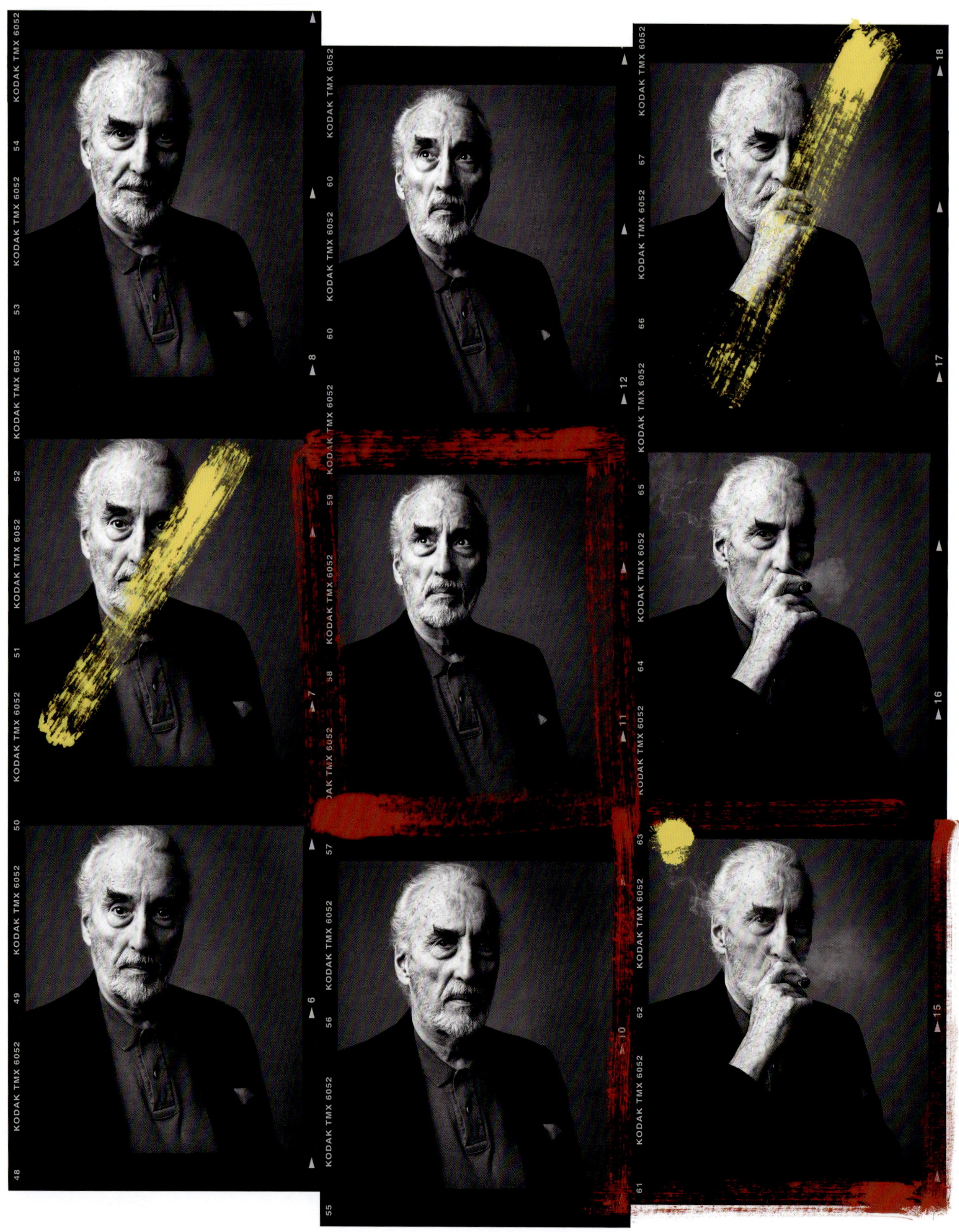
KODAK TMX 6052

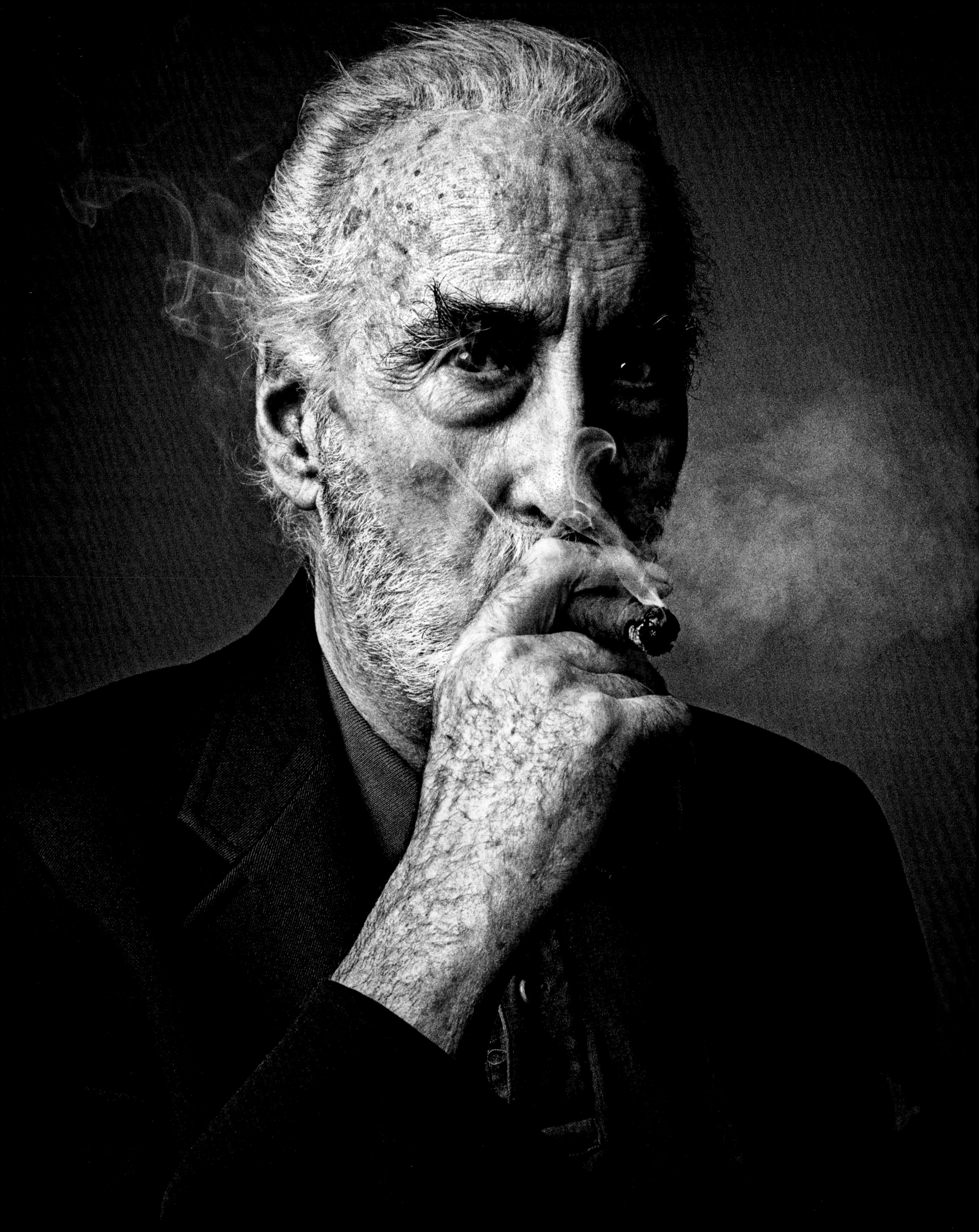

Claudia Schiffer

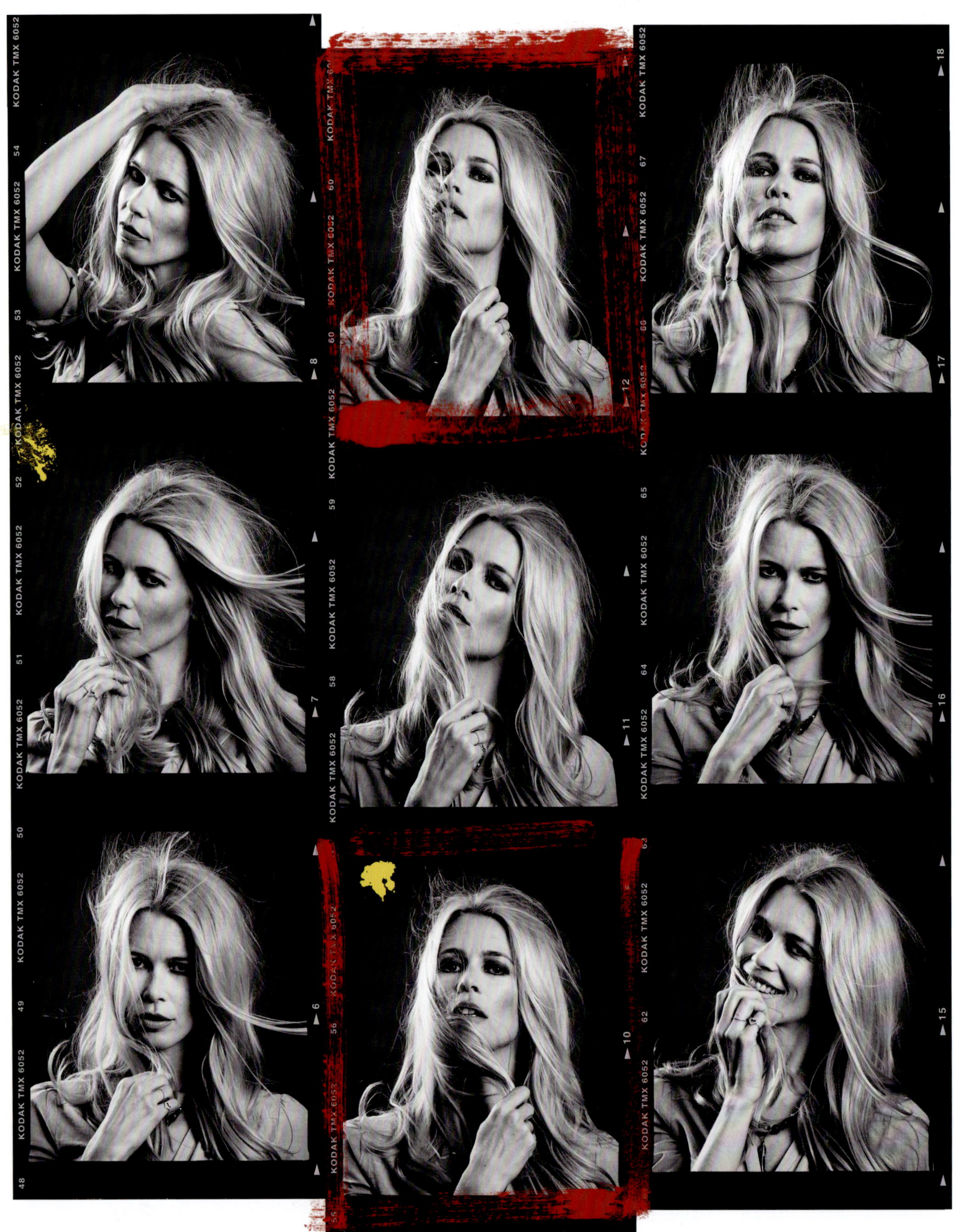

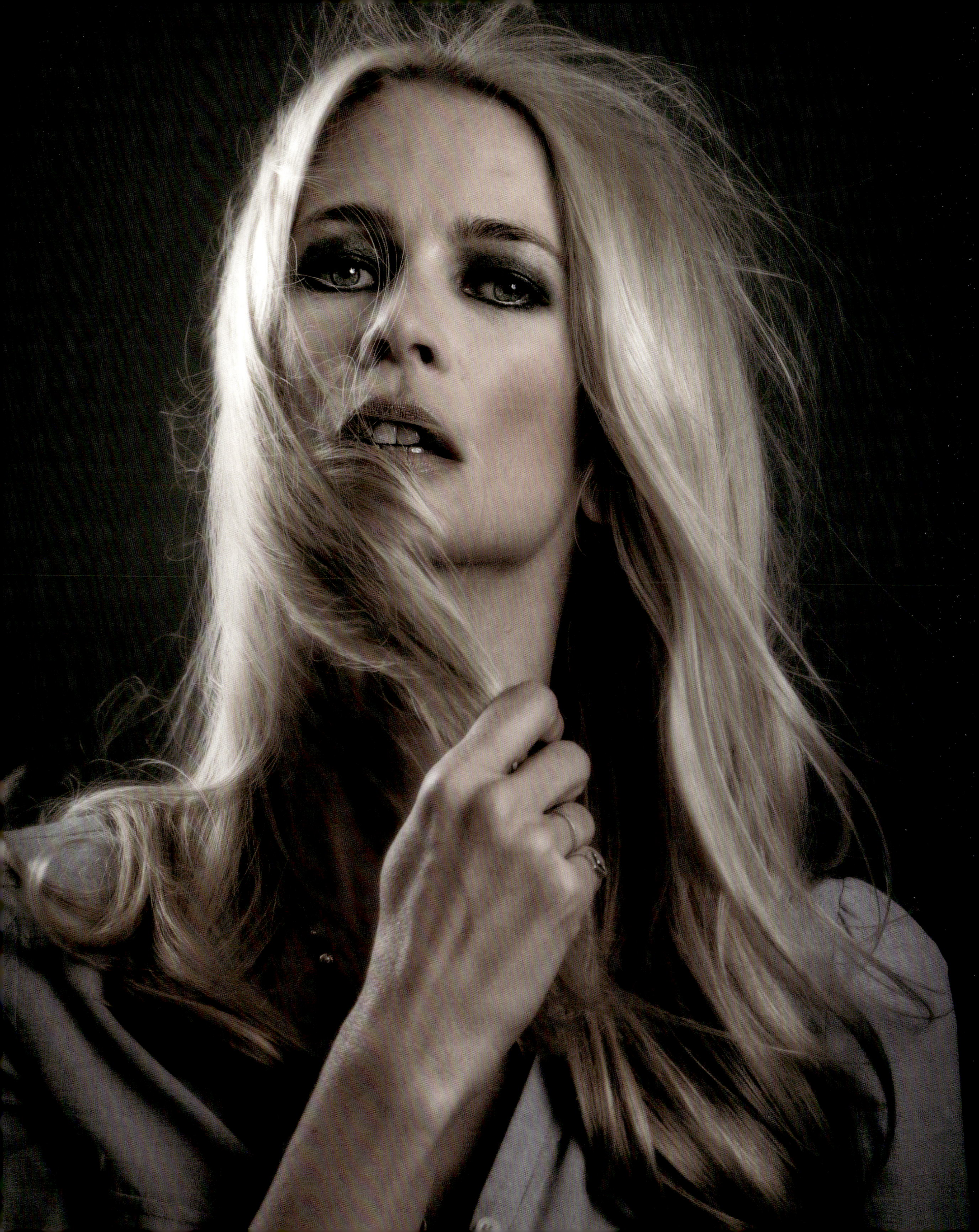

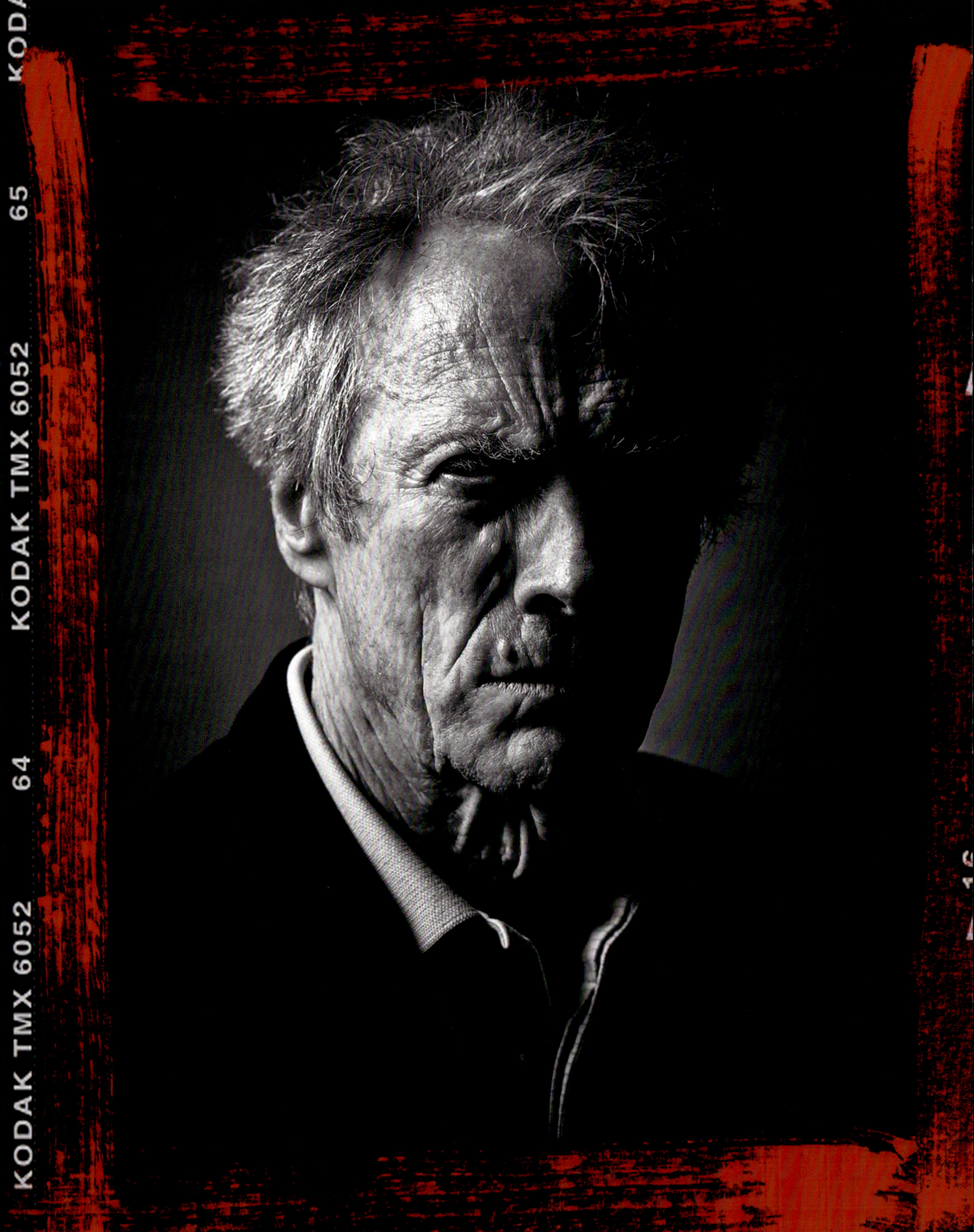
KODAK TMX 6052
64
KODAK TMX 6052
65
KODA

Clint Eastwood

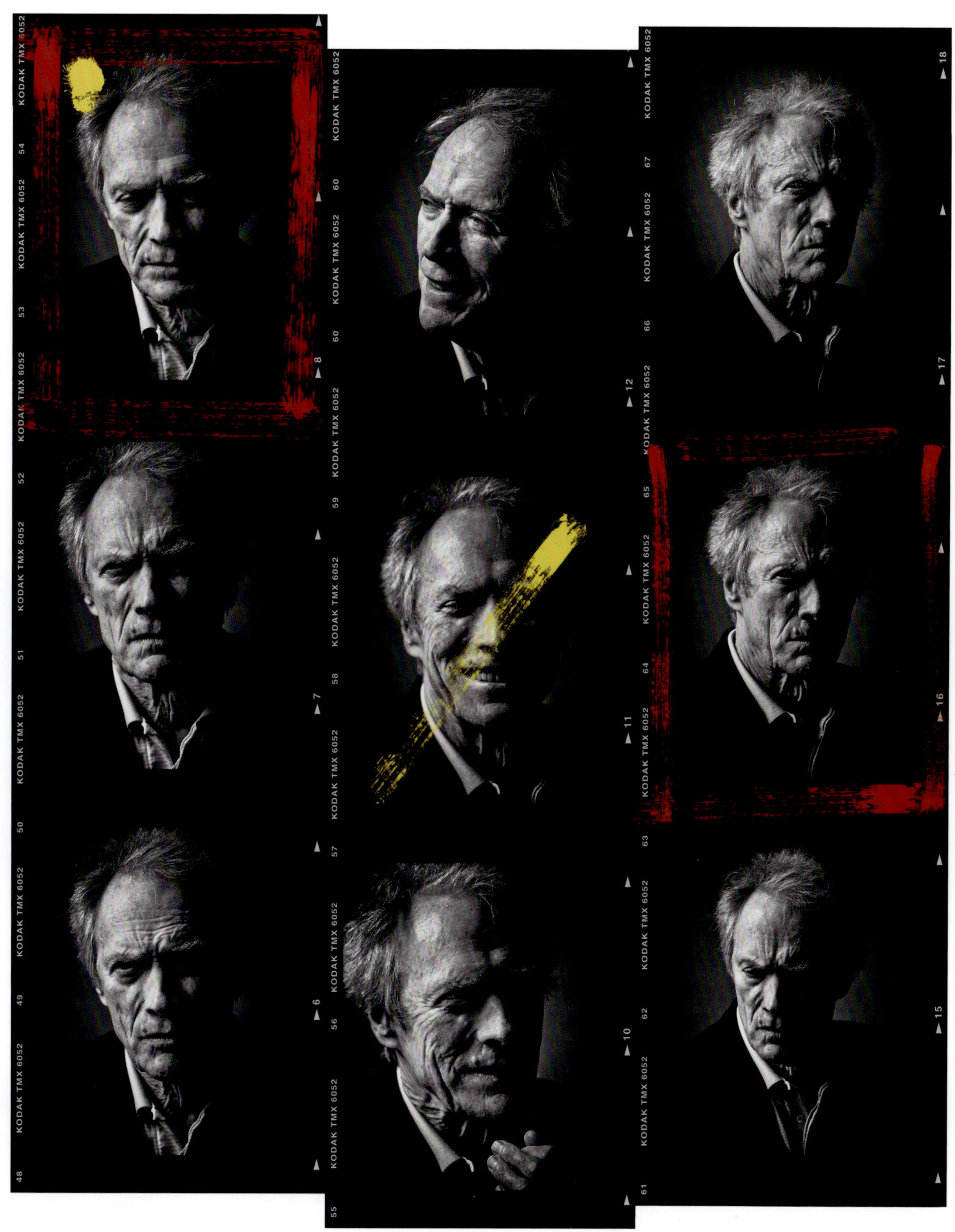

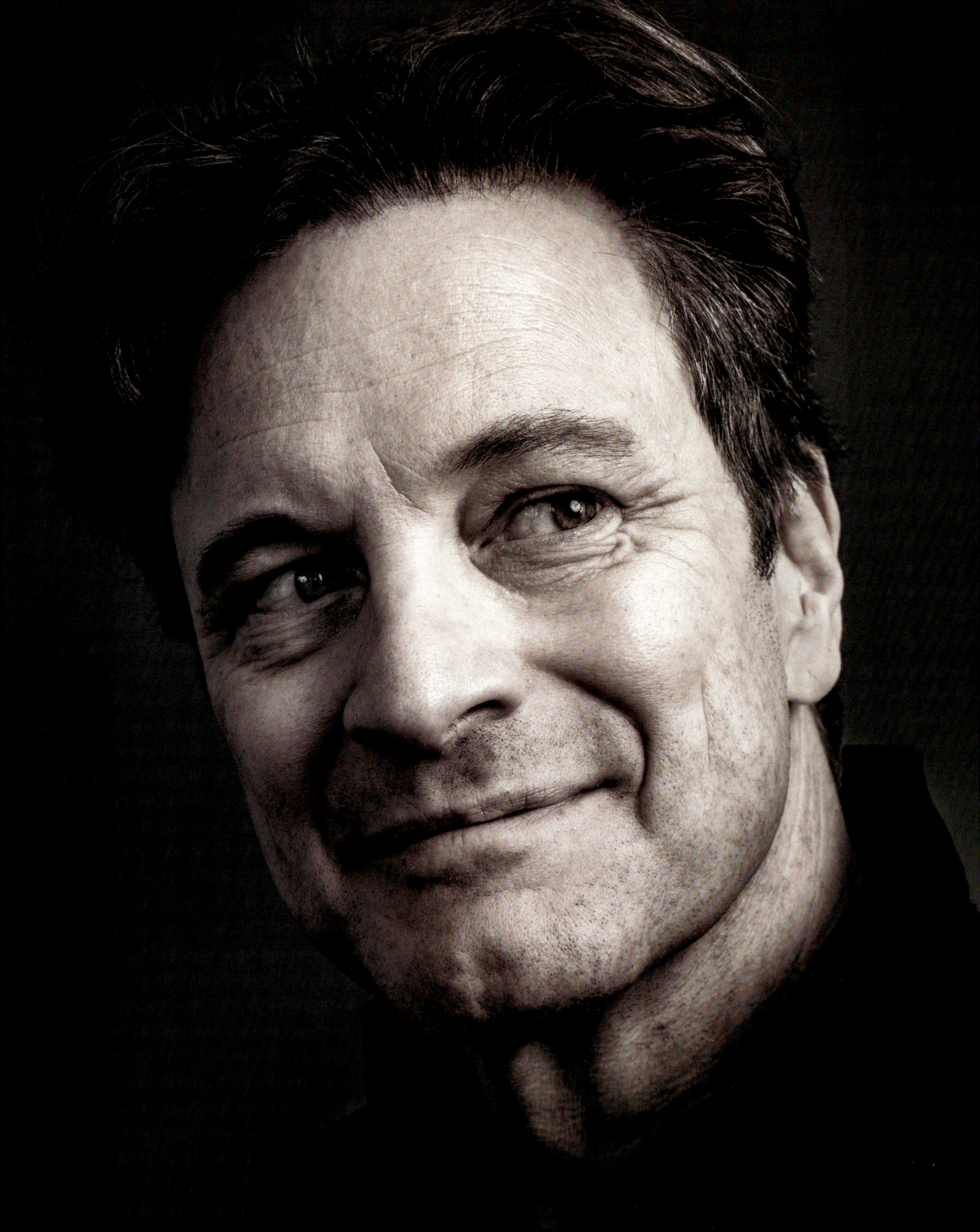

Colin Firth

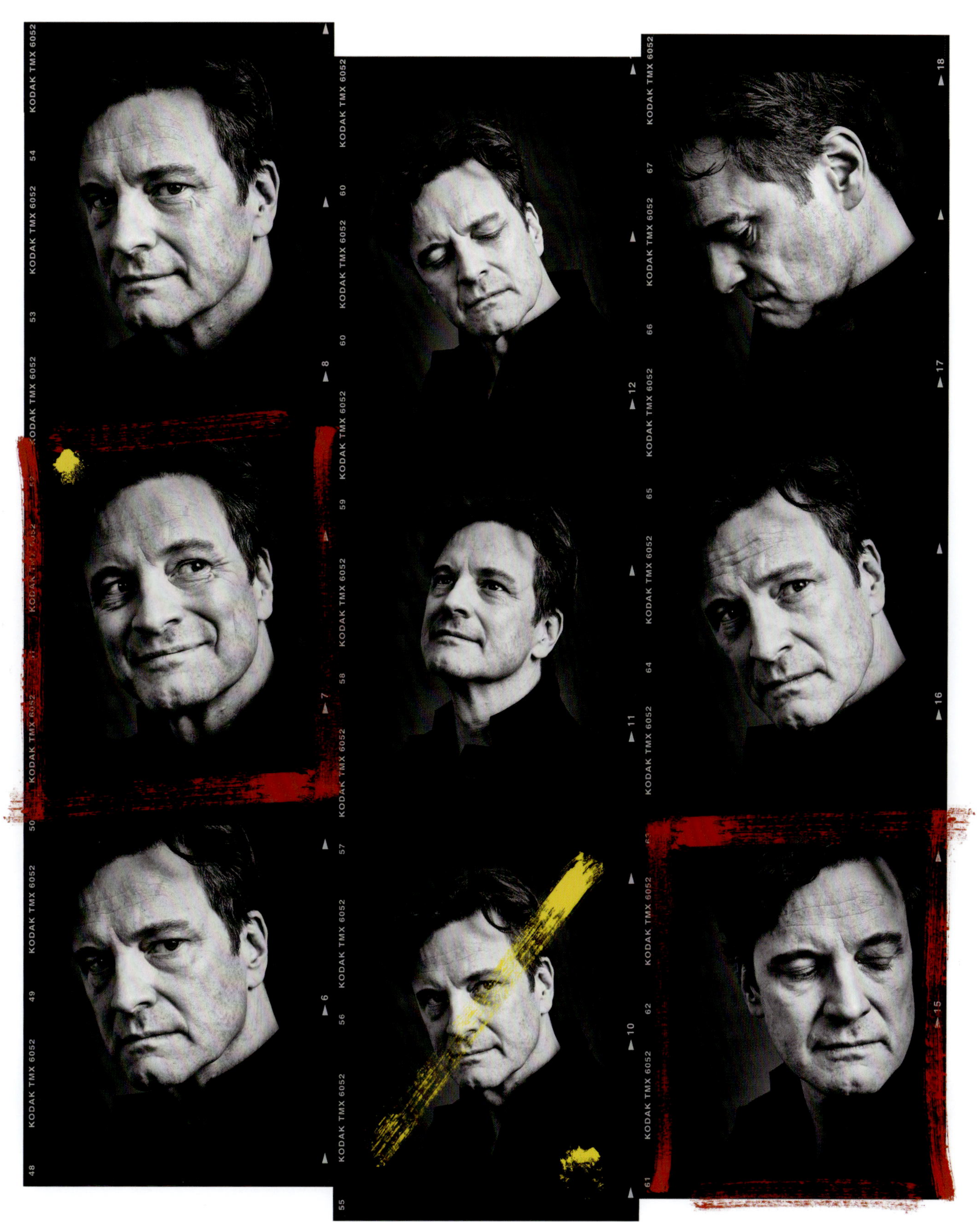

Daniel Craig

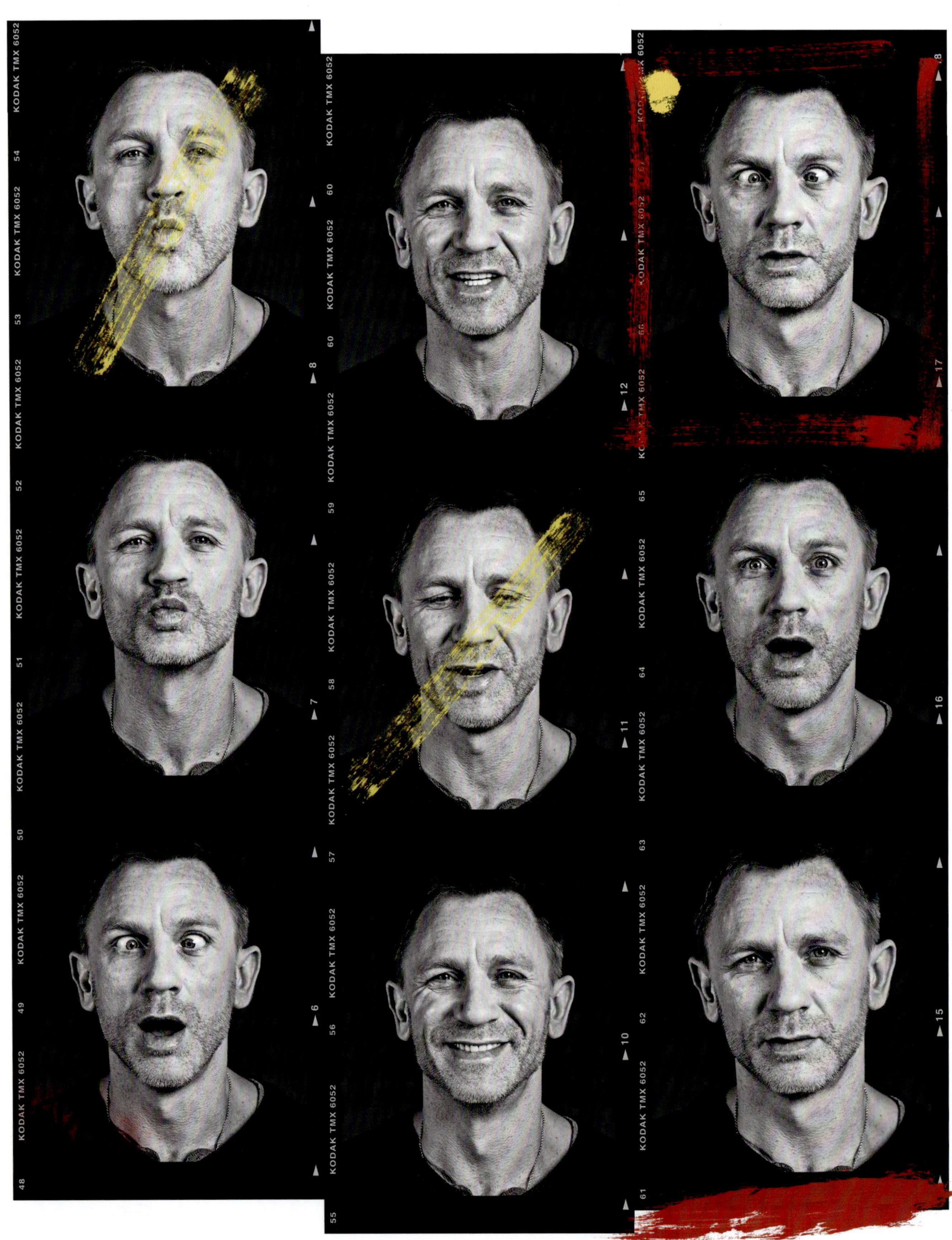

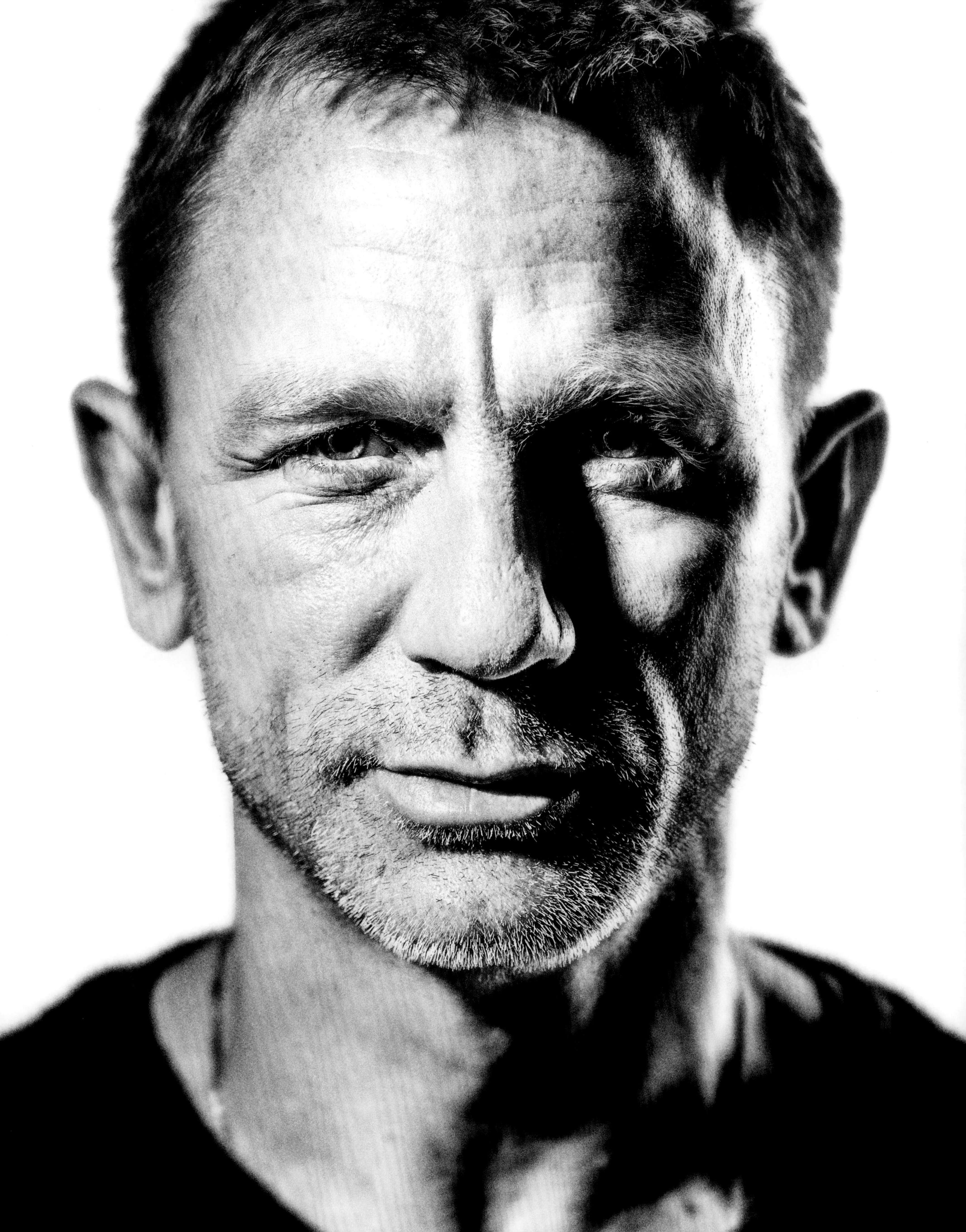

Danny DeVito

I shot Danny at the Savoy Theatre, whilst he was appearing in *Sunshine Boys*. I set up the shoot to happen between his matinee and evening performance. It was a very atmospheric shoot as I set it up on the stage. Danny is generally a very relaxed character, yet got a little too relaxed on this shoot... he fell asleep halfway through. I thought he was doing a series of silly faces, winky eyes – until the snoring started! As I kicked his chair to bring him out of his slumber he apologised profusely. He explained that having been around film sets for so many years, he is a professional at having power naps between takes. Danny is not only a professional napper; he is a professional in every sense of the word. He can turn it on when required of him and he has a library of knowledge when it comes to film. It's an education to be in his presence. With regard to the shoot, I felt he knew what I wanted. He's a bit like Woody Allen that way.

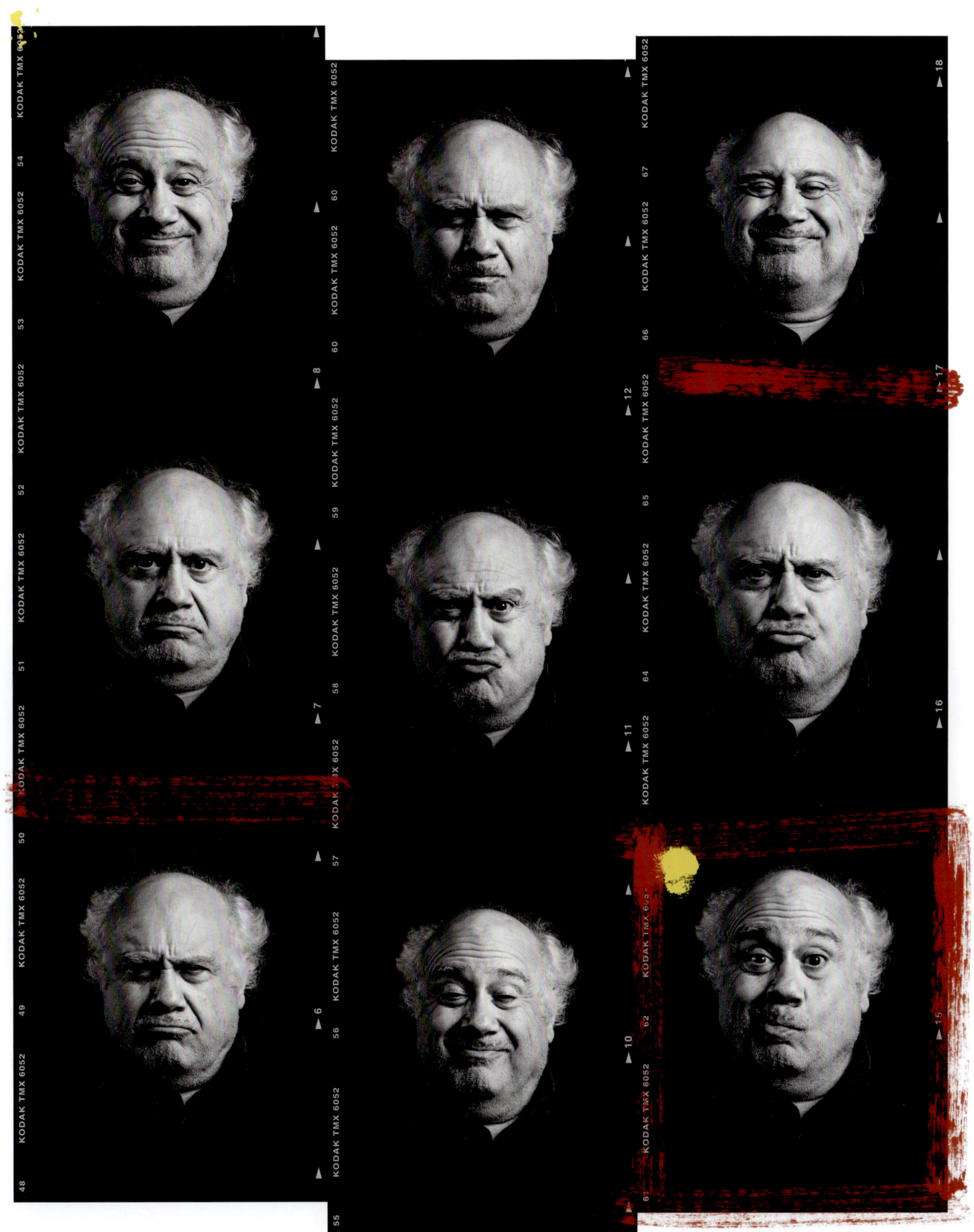

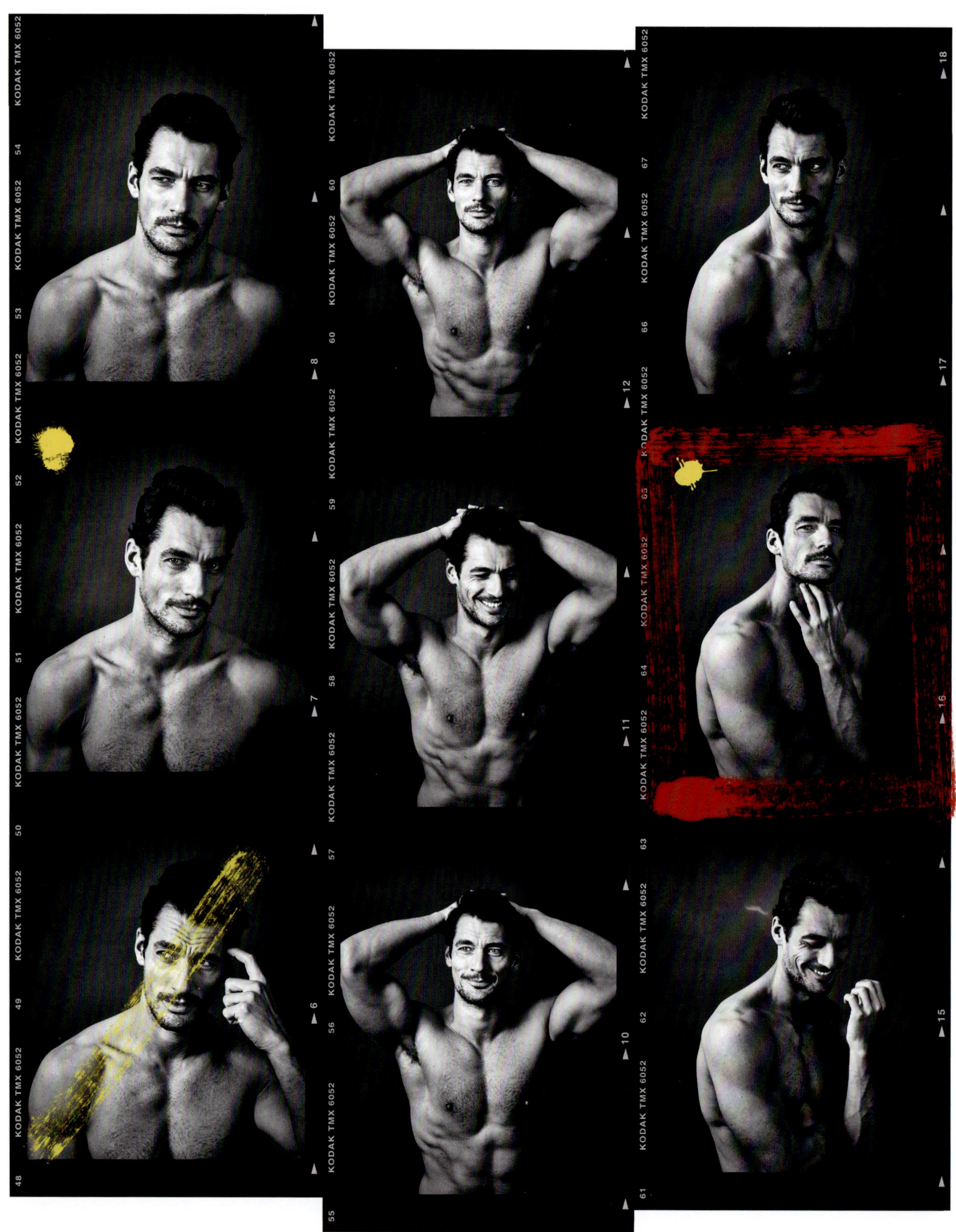
KODAK TMX 6052

David Gandy

I shot David in Flemings Mayfair. Being a model, David not me, it was a very easy shoot. He turned up in a three-piece suit as if he had come straight from a business meeting. He looked fab but I thought, 'he is known for his body', so I asked him to disrobe. Most models don't even blink when you ask them to get naked, and David was the same. I tried to light him with more shadow, so it didn't look like a 'model shot' and I think between us we arrived at the perfect balance.

David Oyelowo

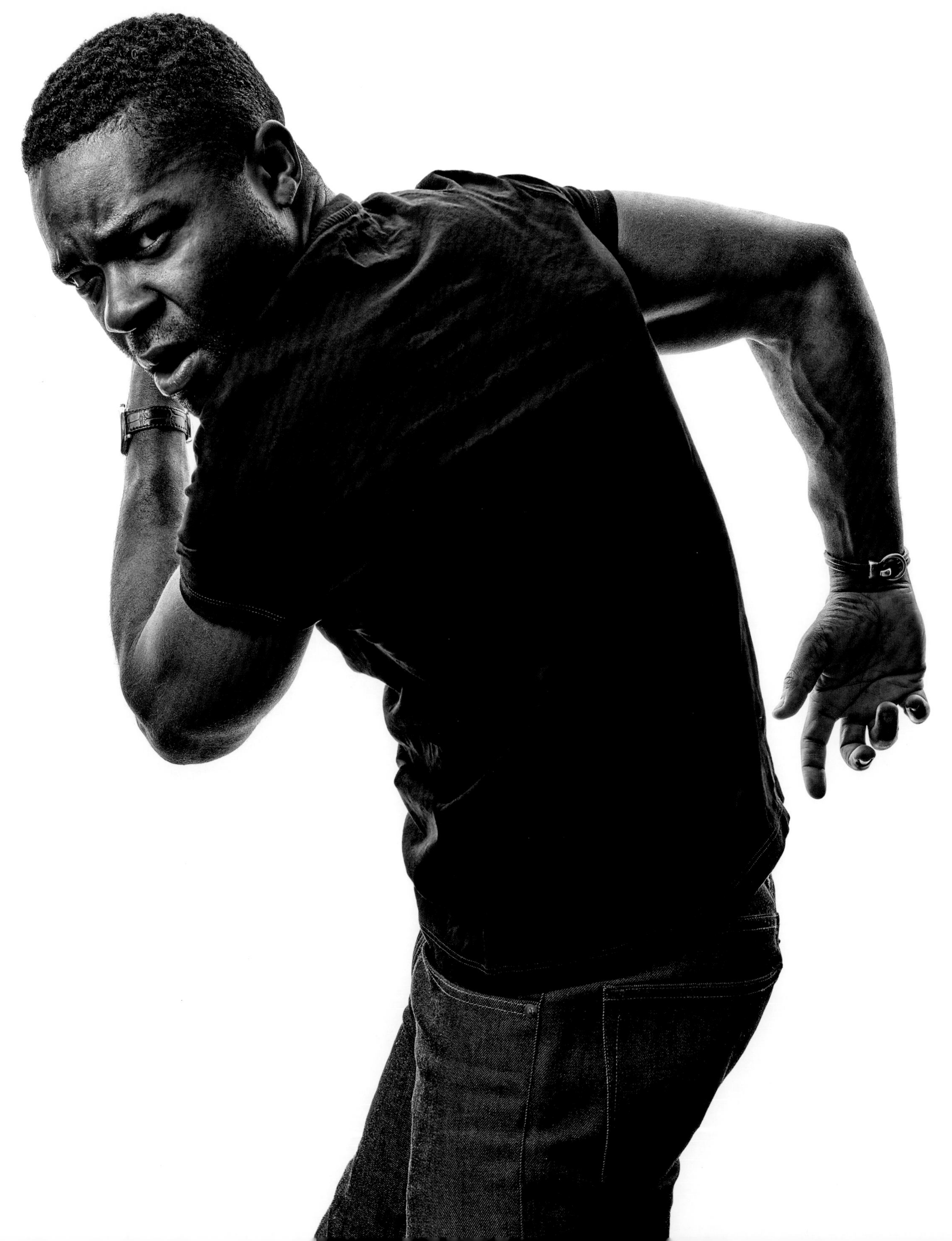

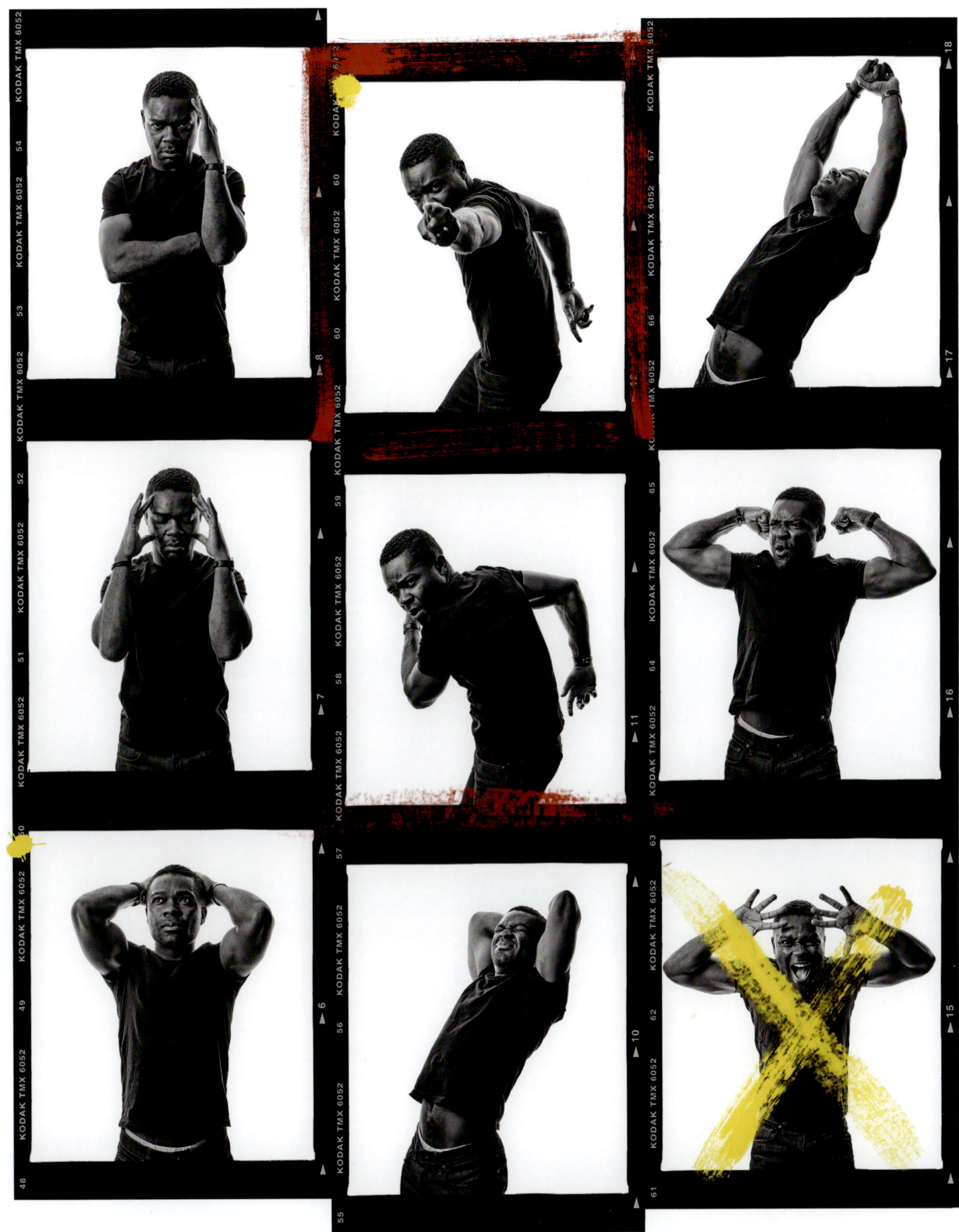
KODAK TMX 6052

Dita Von Teese

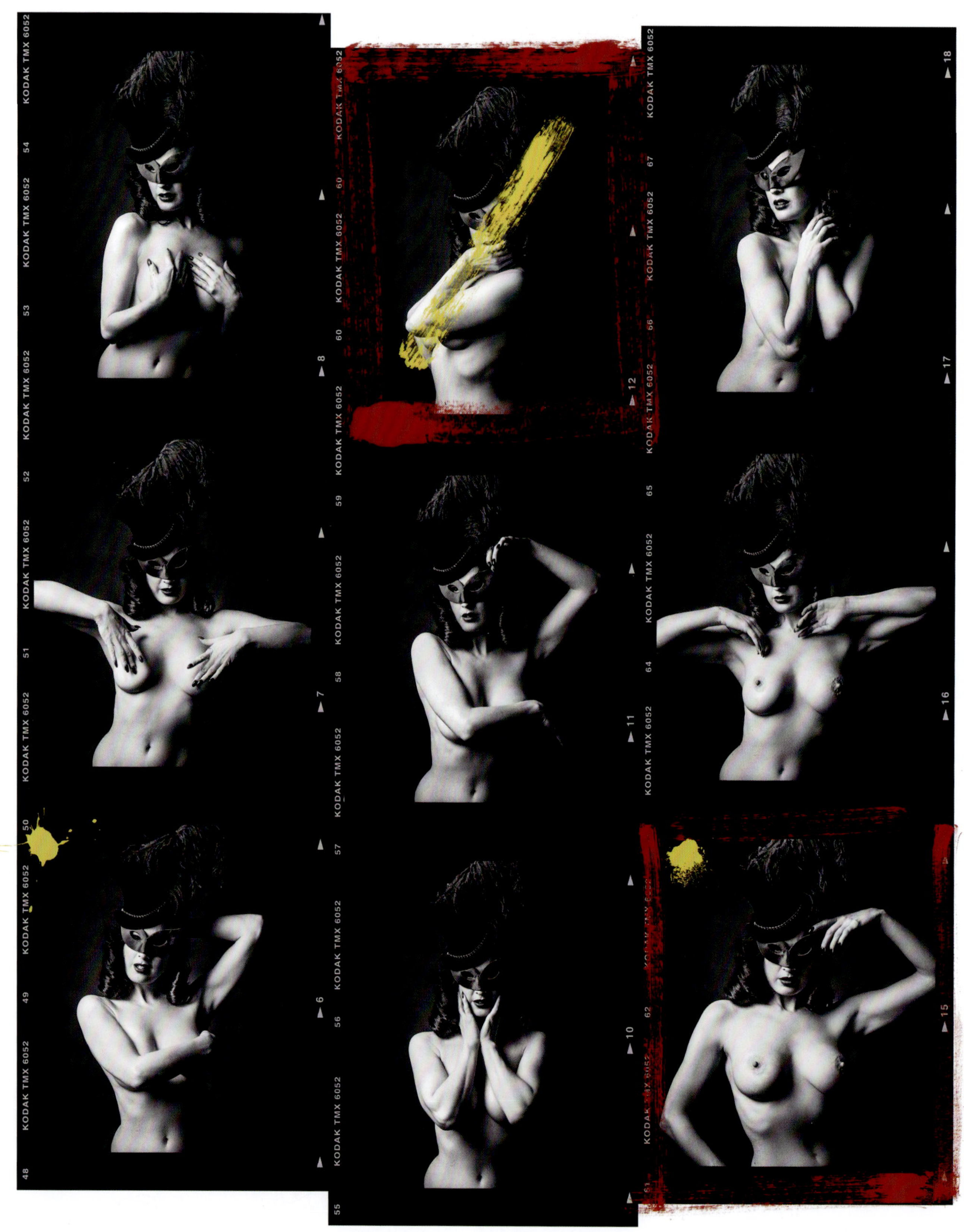

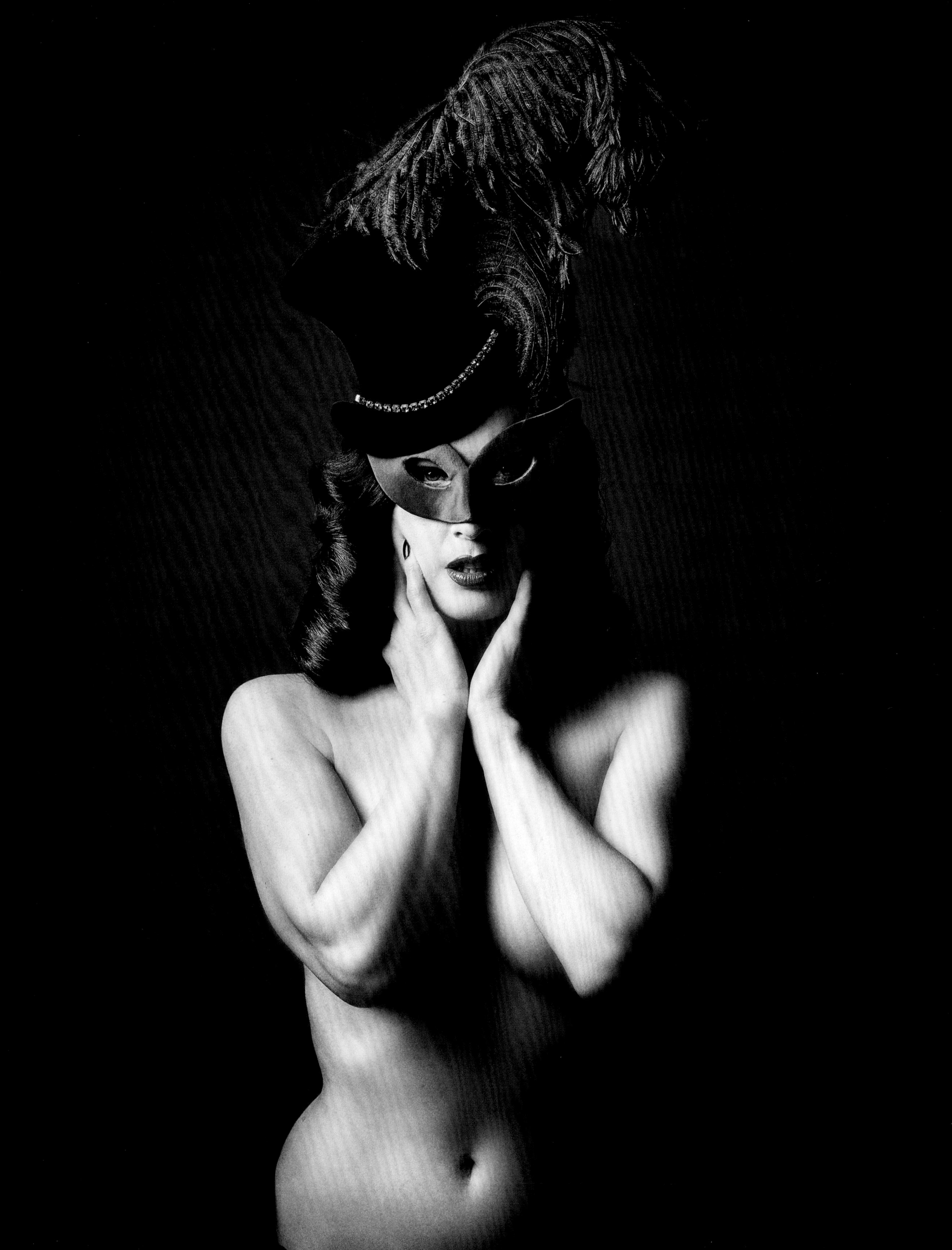

Dolly Parton

In this day and age the word 'icon' is bandied around far too easily. BUT if there was only ever one person whose head fitted this specific hat, it would be the phenomenal Dolly.

Dolly was in the UK doing some gigs and I was invited to shoot her on the afternoon before she did her sound checks. I was all set up and ready when there was a hefty knock on the door and a whole gaggle of people walked in and began busying themselves... doing what, I have no idea. Then, in an almost biblical entrance, Dolly glided in. There is nothing not to love about Ms P. If there was a checklist of what makes the perfect person, my Sharpie® would run out of ink making all the ticks for Dolly. She could see that I was not that happy with all the people milling around, so she said with a lovely twang in her voice "It's OK, y'all can go and leave me and Andy to it." She then took my hand in hers and gave me a huge radiant smile... It was at that point that the world melted away and I think at some point I took some shots; but I don't really remember.

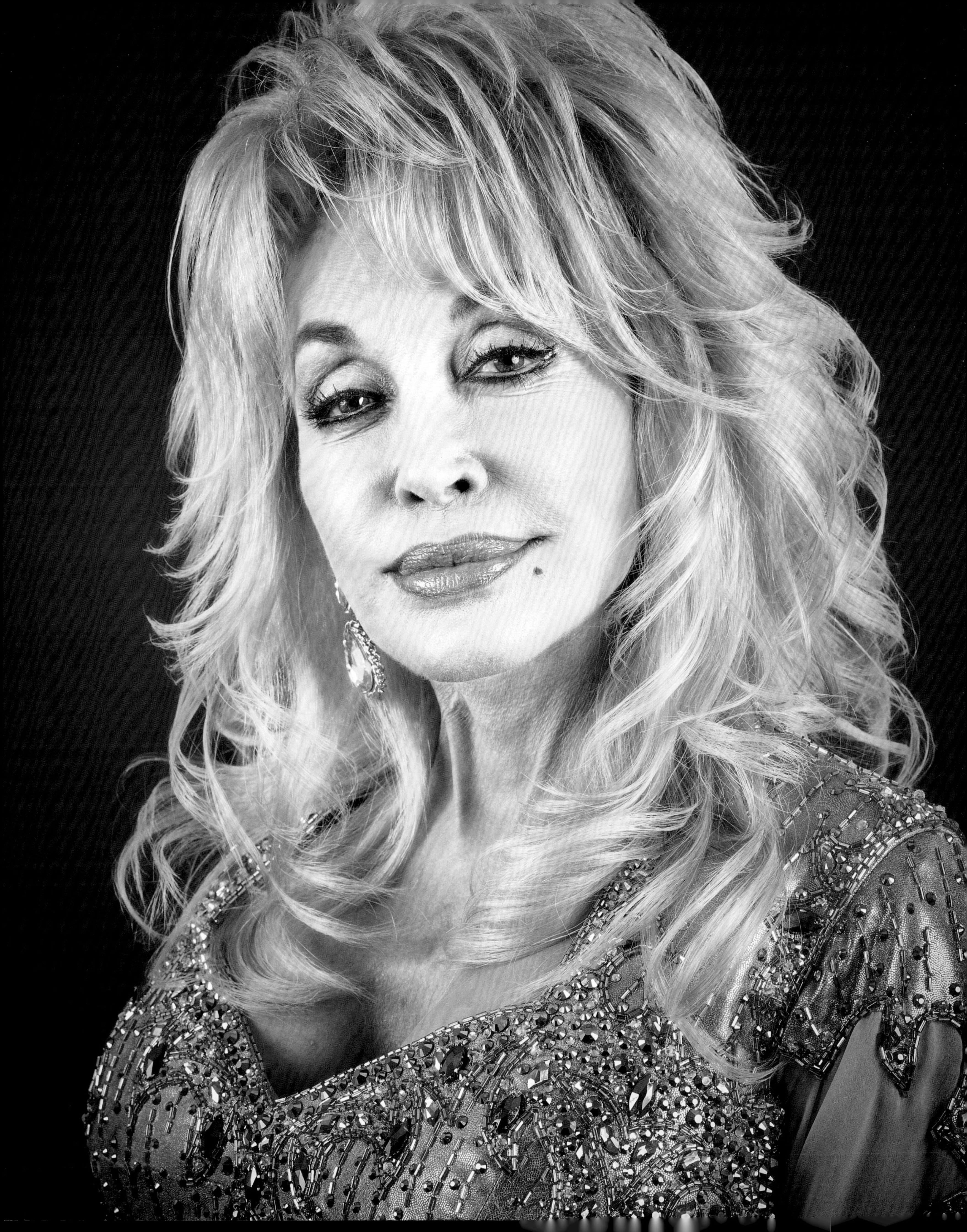

Dustin Hoffman

I shot Dustin in his office in Los Angeles. He is a businessman through and through, and everyone says he is a pain in the ass because he is always right, no matter what. All the way through the shoot, he was dictating a script over his shoulder to his daughter. I was lucky to get any shots in which he has his mouth shut. Half way through, I suggested we do a series of shots with him taking his shirt off, and although I was expecting a negative response, Dustin started to disrobe. During this striptease, I quipped: "Mr Hoffman are you trying to seduce me?"... it was a hilarious shoot!

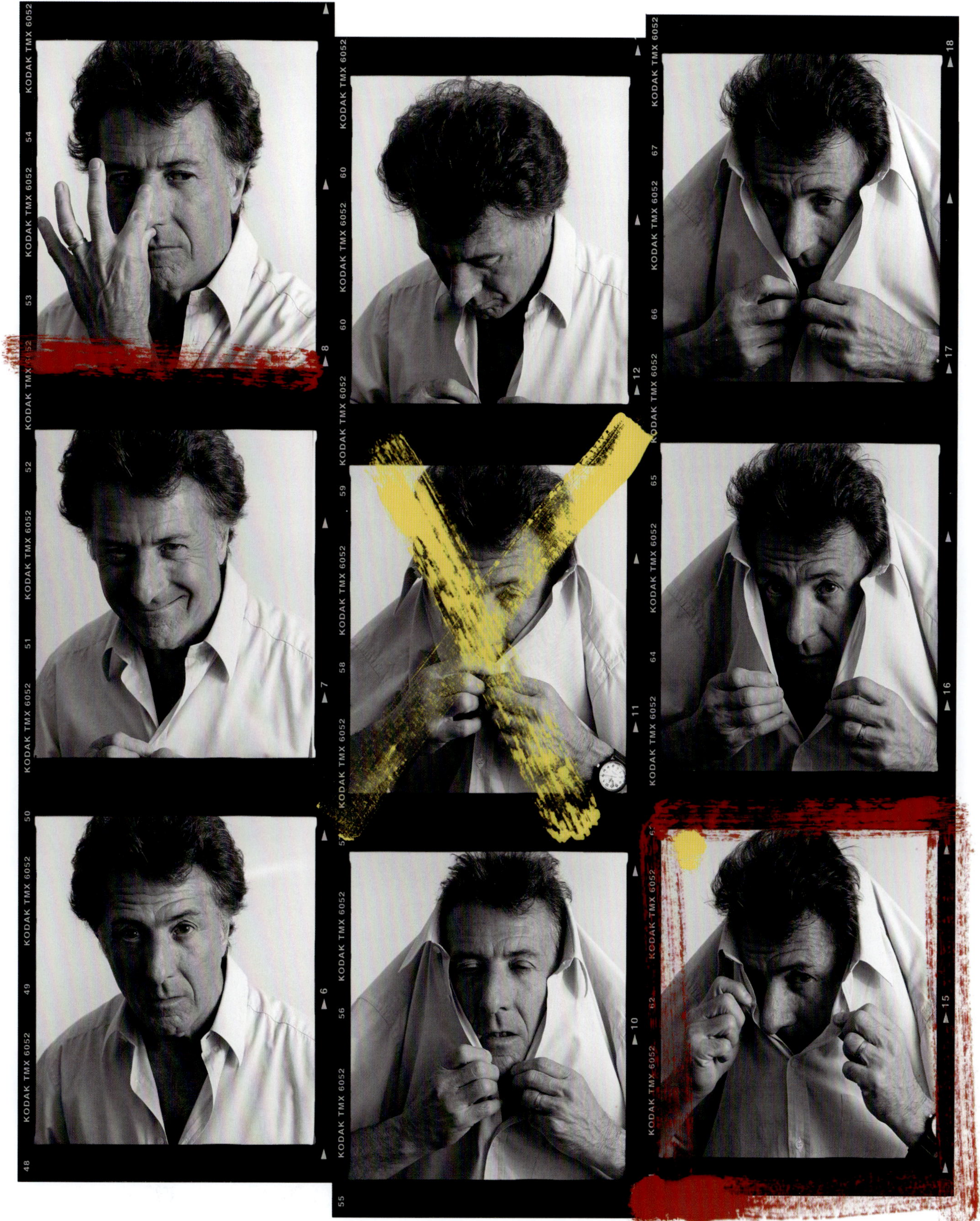

Eddie Redmayne

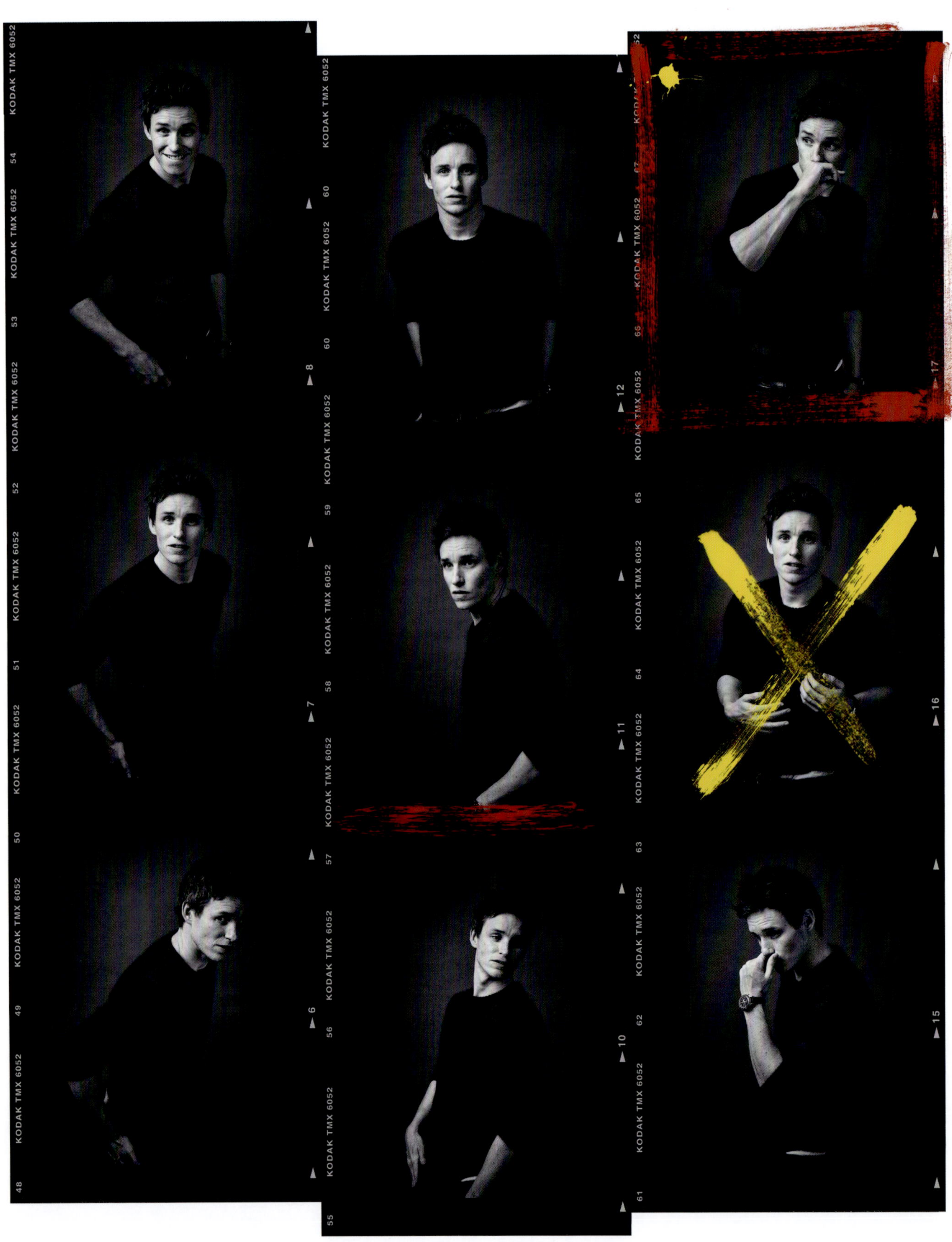

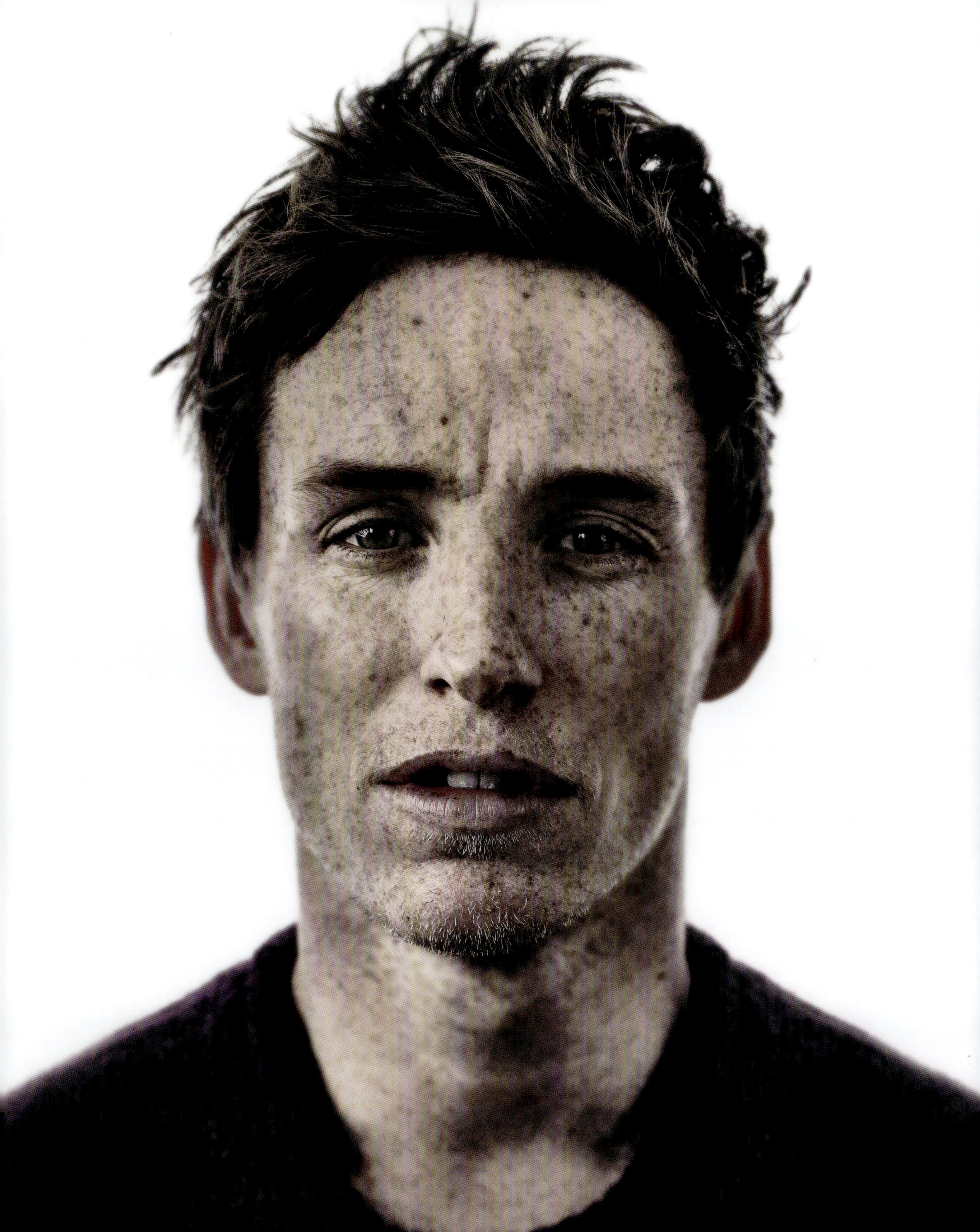

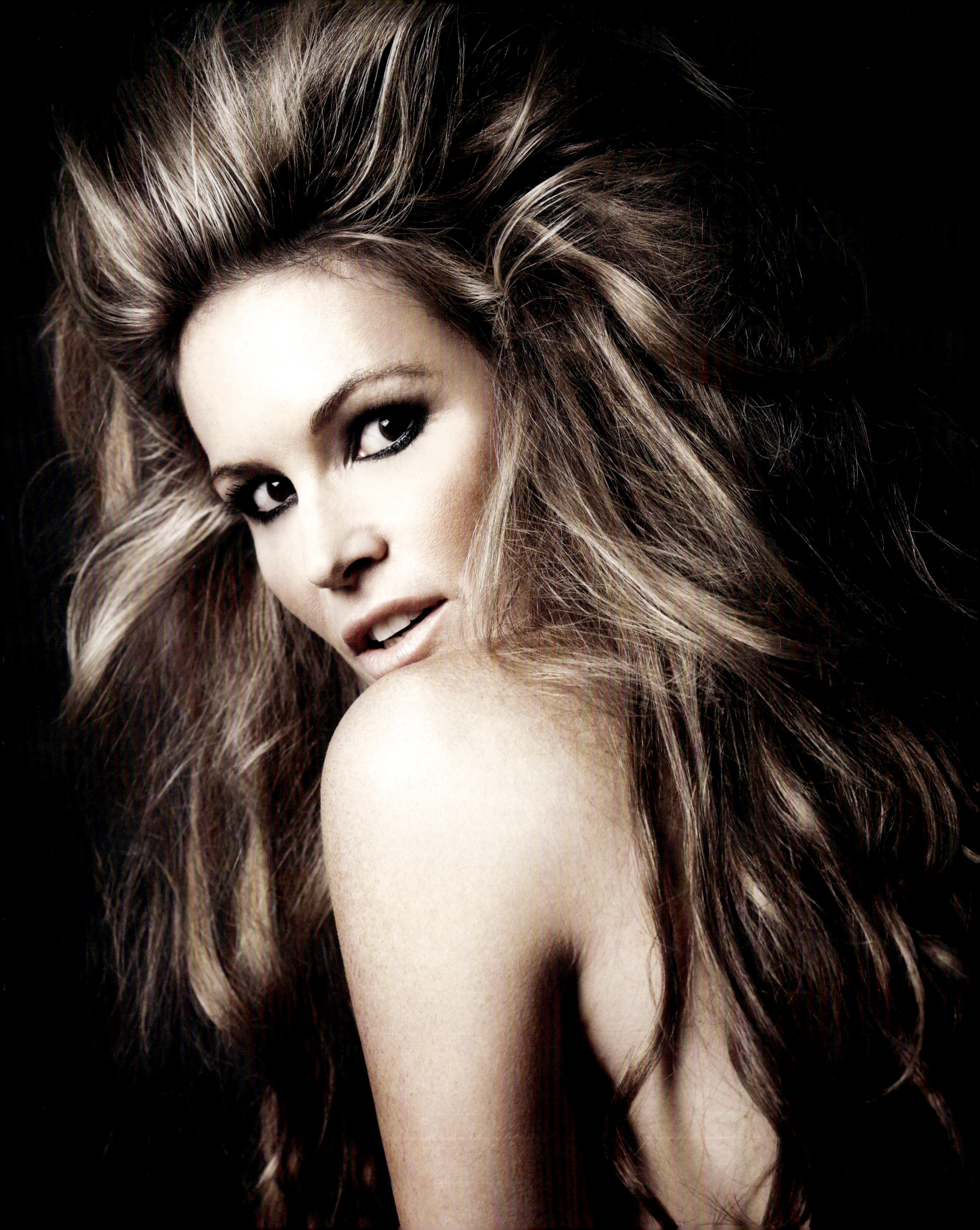

Elle Macpherson

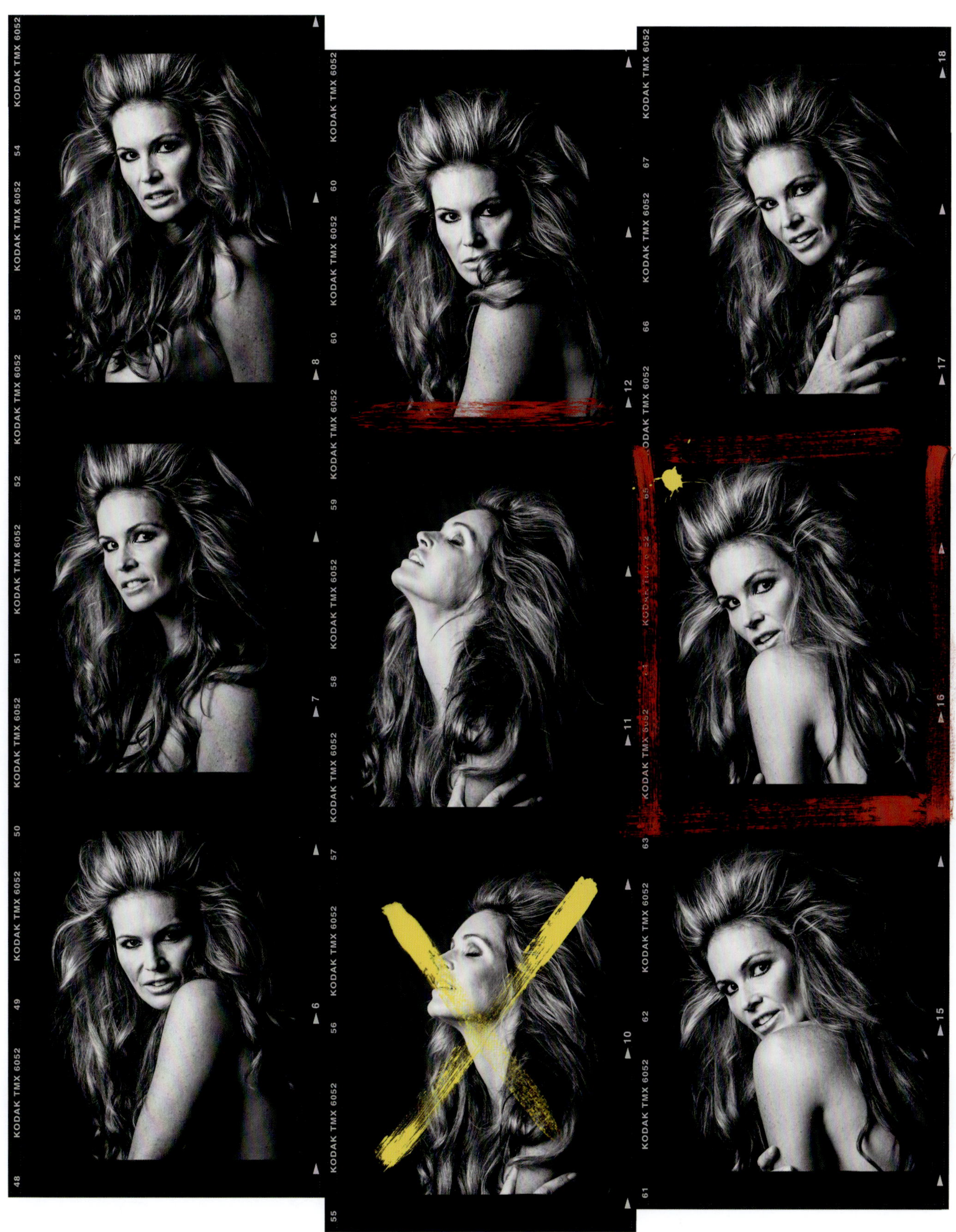

Elton John

For the first two decades of my career I only shot actors, as I am a huge movie buff. But when the option of having a shoot with music royalty came along, I was a bit overjoyed. Although I have been a fan of Elton John's music for quite sometime, it is his attitude that I think is fabulous. Anyone who phones their manager in London from New York on a gusty day and tells him to 'turn down the wind' absolutely deserves to be put on a podium and saluted. Our shoot was scheduled to take place in Lyon during his tour, meaning a lovely eight-hour drive through the glorious vistas of France. I set up my studio in the green-room before the show. Twenty minutes before curtain up, Elton breezed into my room. I knew he was not a fan of being photographed so I was prepared for a quick iconic-style portrait – just two or three shots. I was so happy when he started goofing around and being silly! There was an instant connection between us and his humour is infectious.

After the shoot, and having packed up all my equipment ready for the return home, I sat on my car bonnet, in the warm evening air, and listened to two or three songs before I hit the 'Yellow Brick Road' back to Blighty.

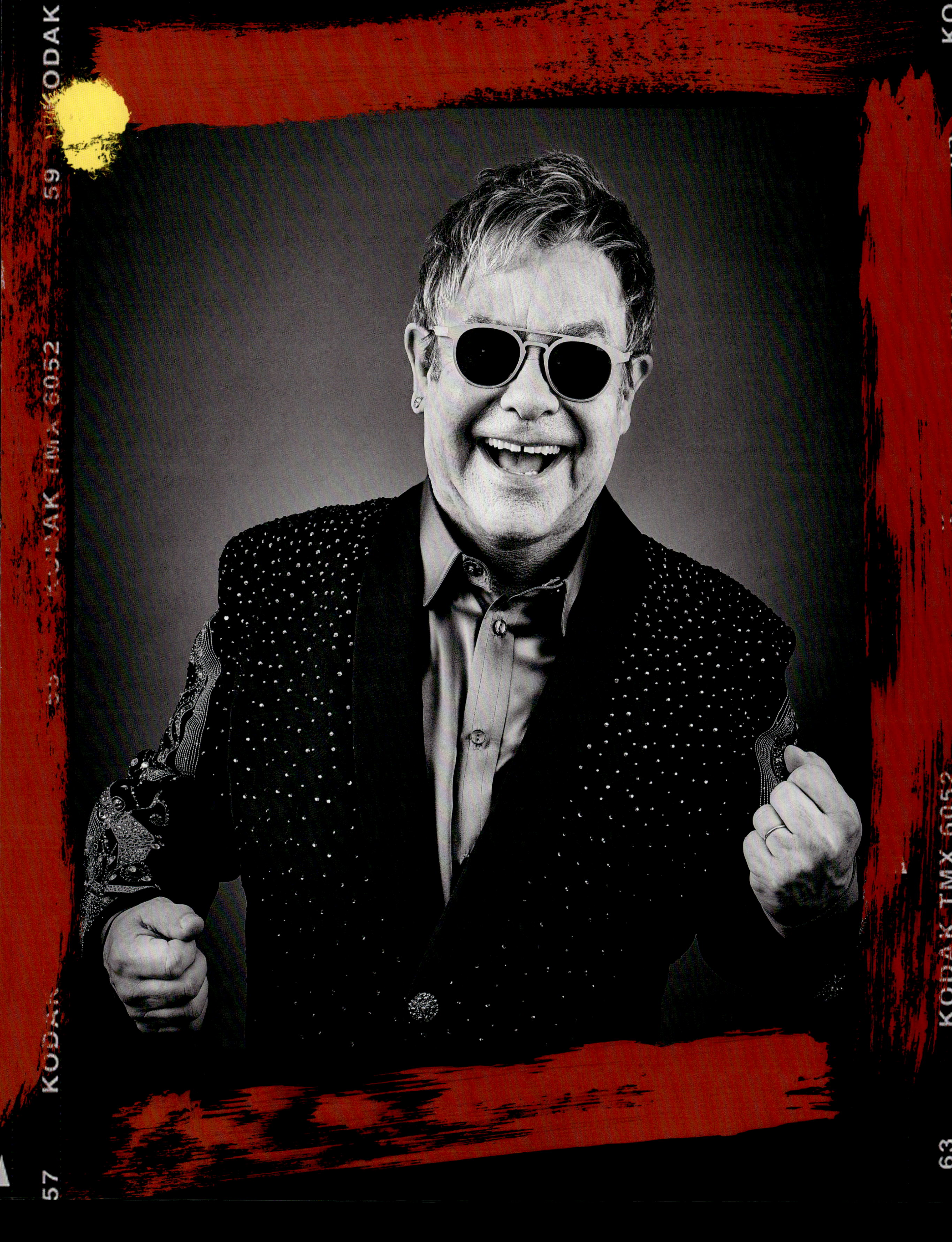
KODAK
59
KODAK TMX 6052
KODAK
57
KODAK TMX 6052
63

Elvis Costello

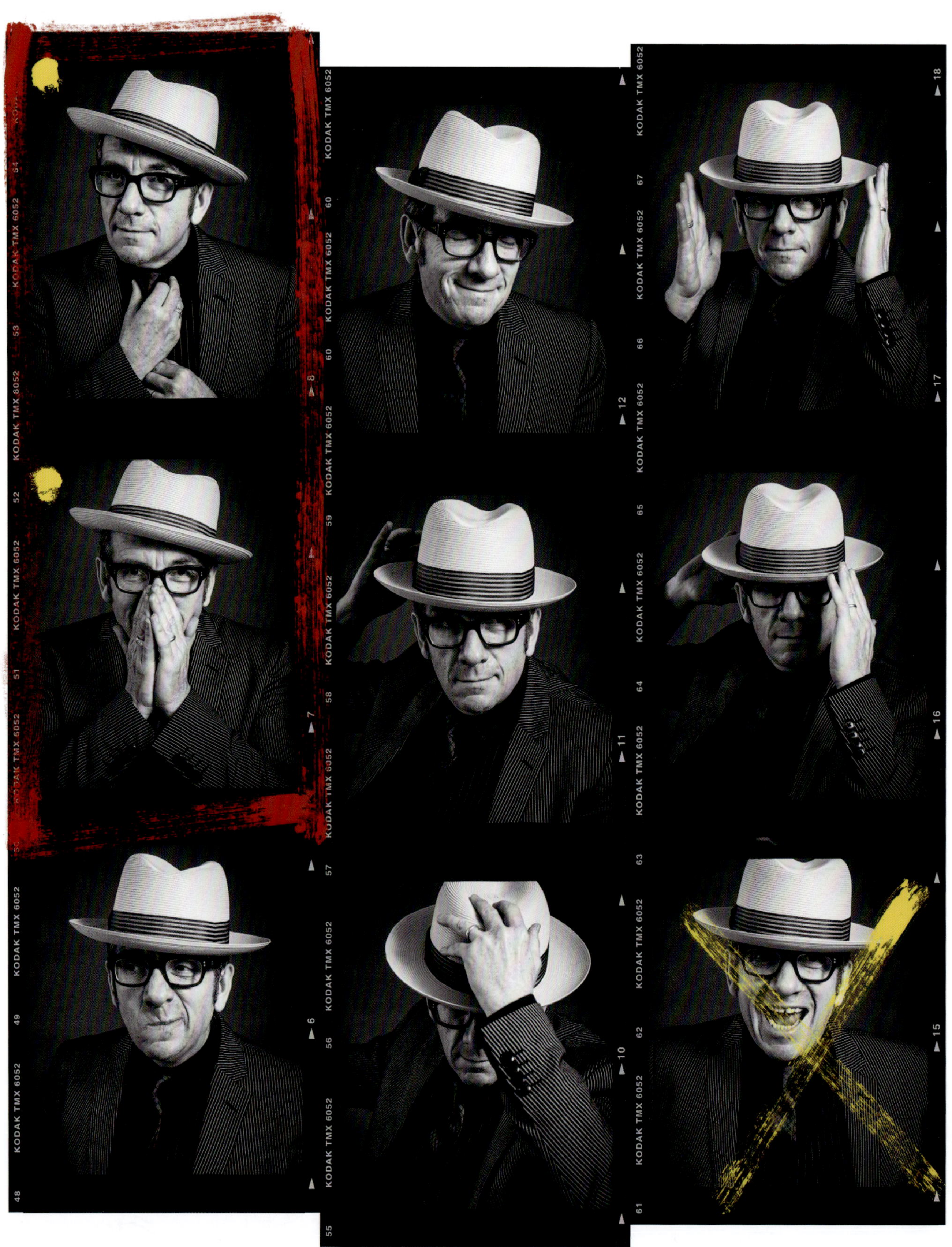

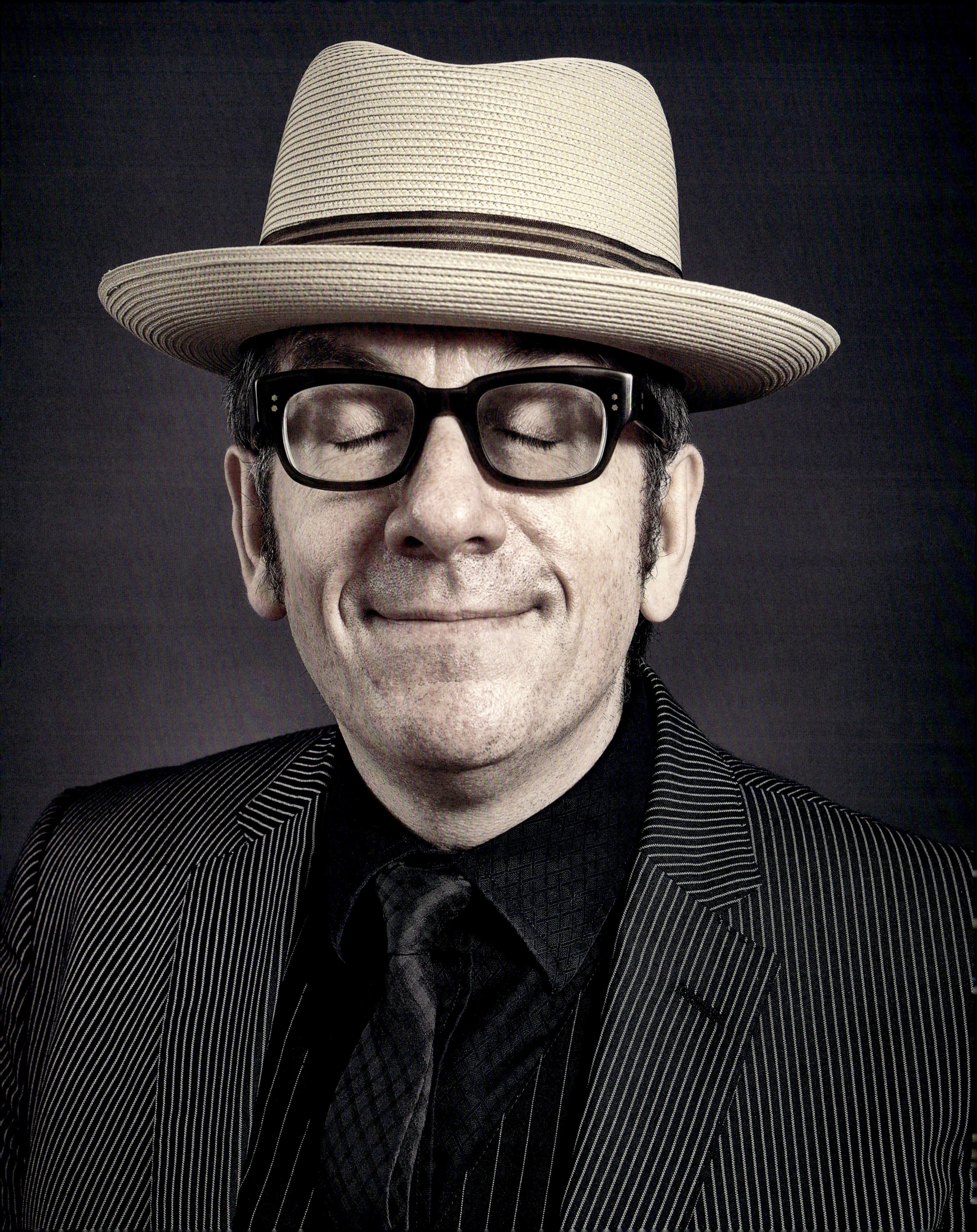

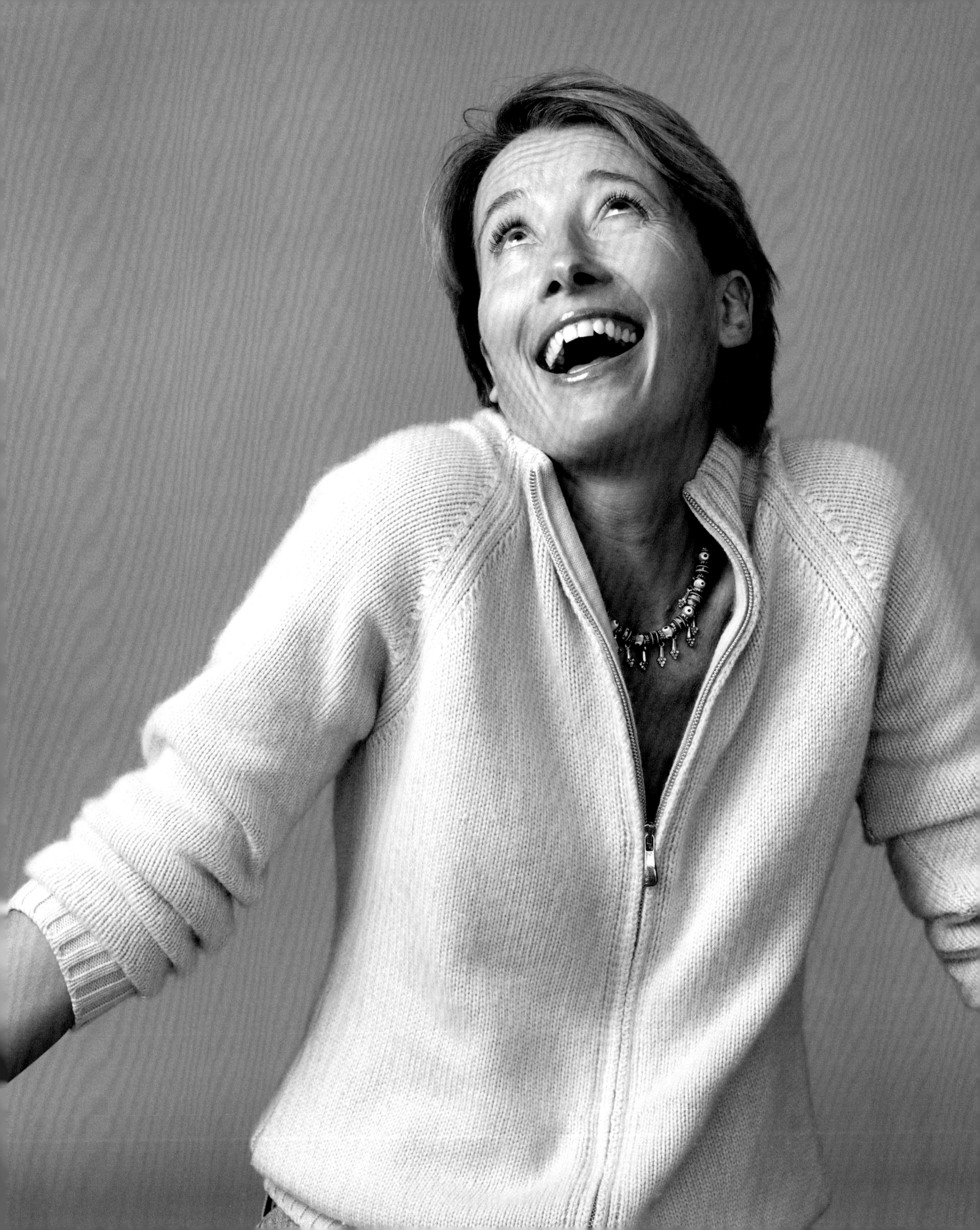

Emma Thompson

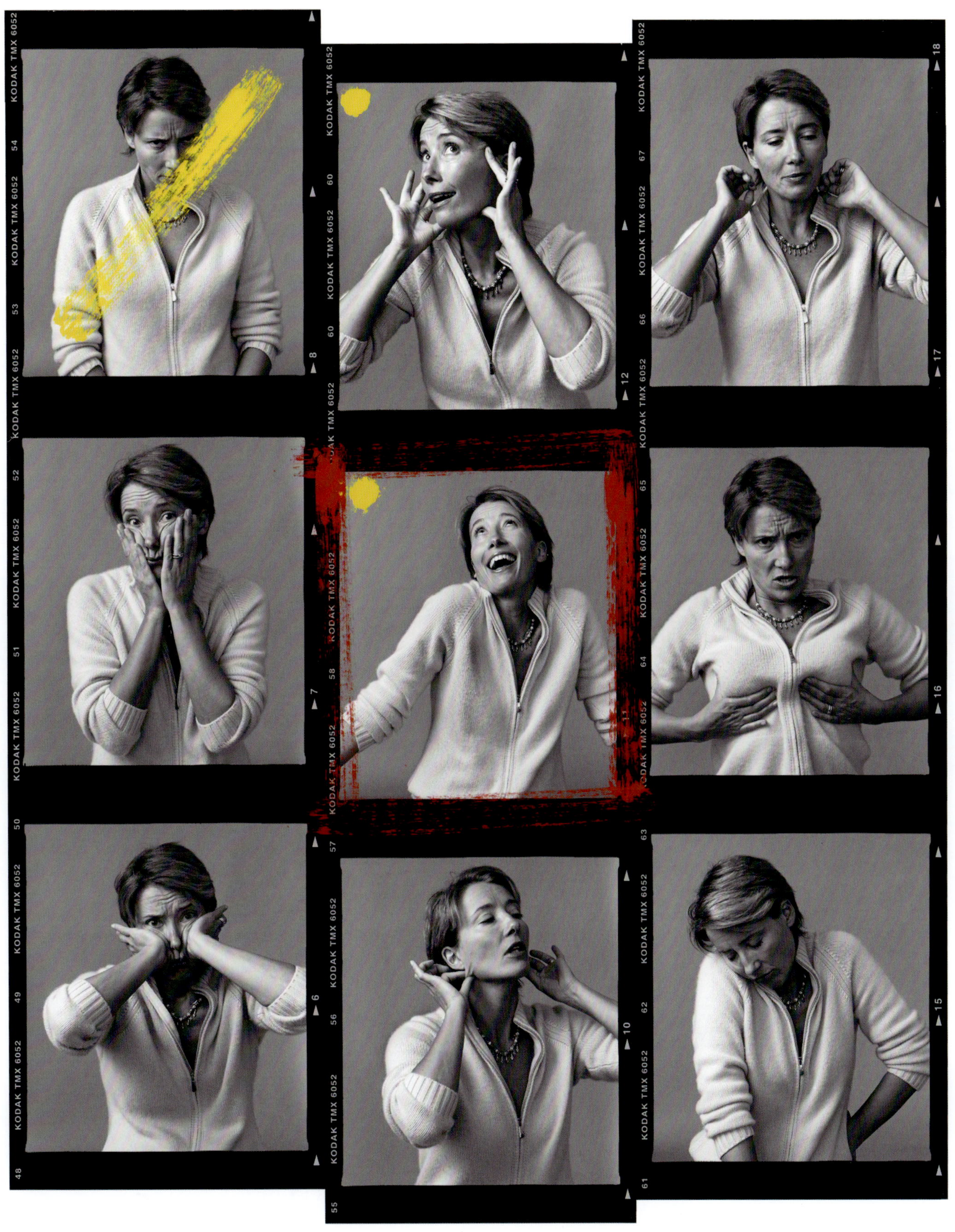

Gary Barlow

I shot Gary in Flemings Mayfair. It was a nice quick shoot as we both knew what we wanted. I wanted a nice quirky portrait, and Gary wanted it over quickly. So, we set up and the northern gurning began. In under five minutes we had more shots than we needed and we both left happy.

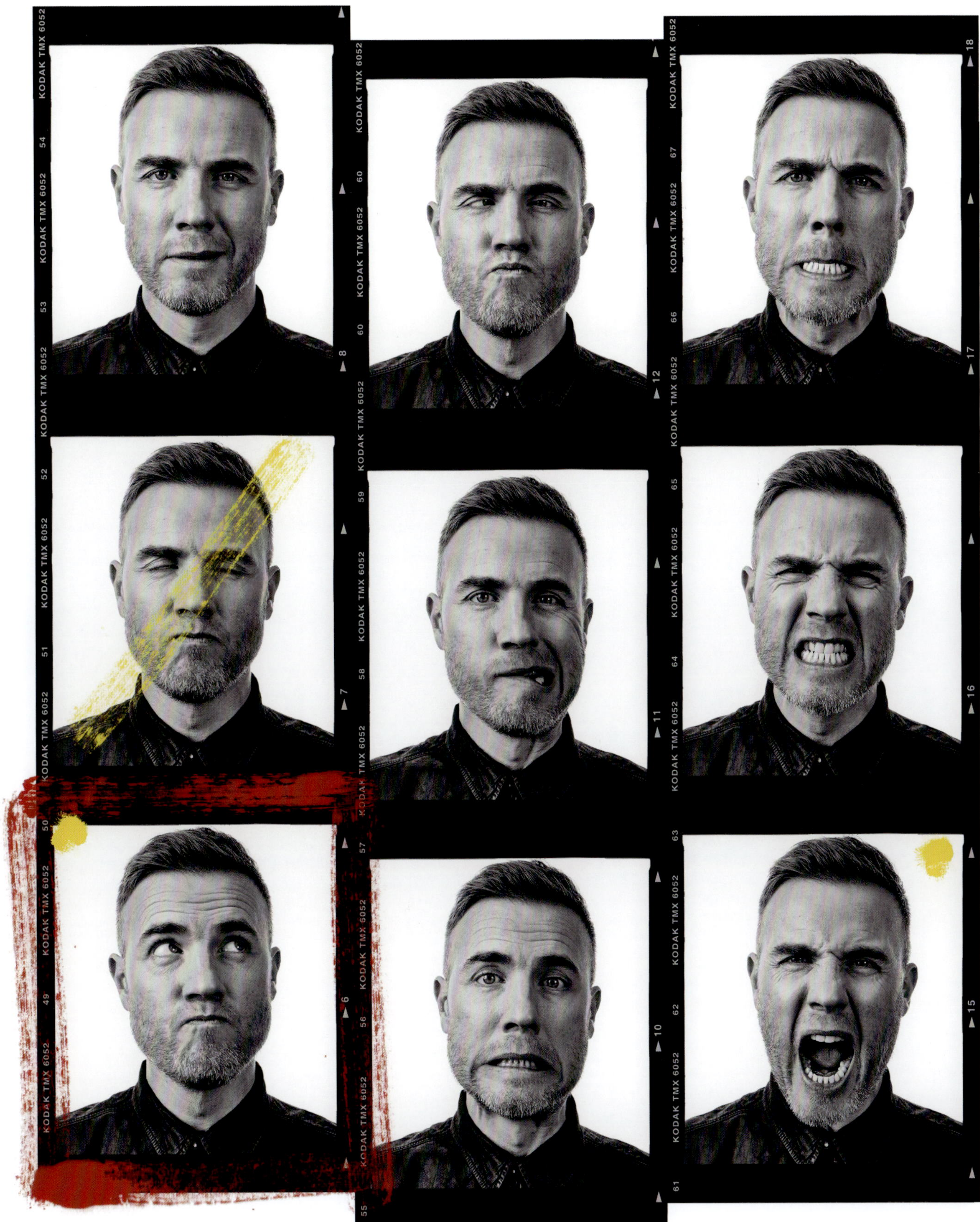

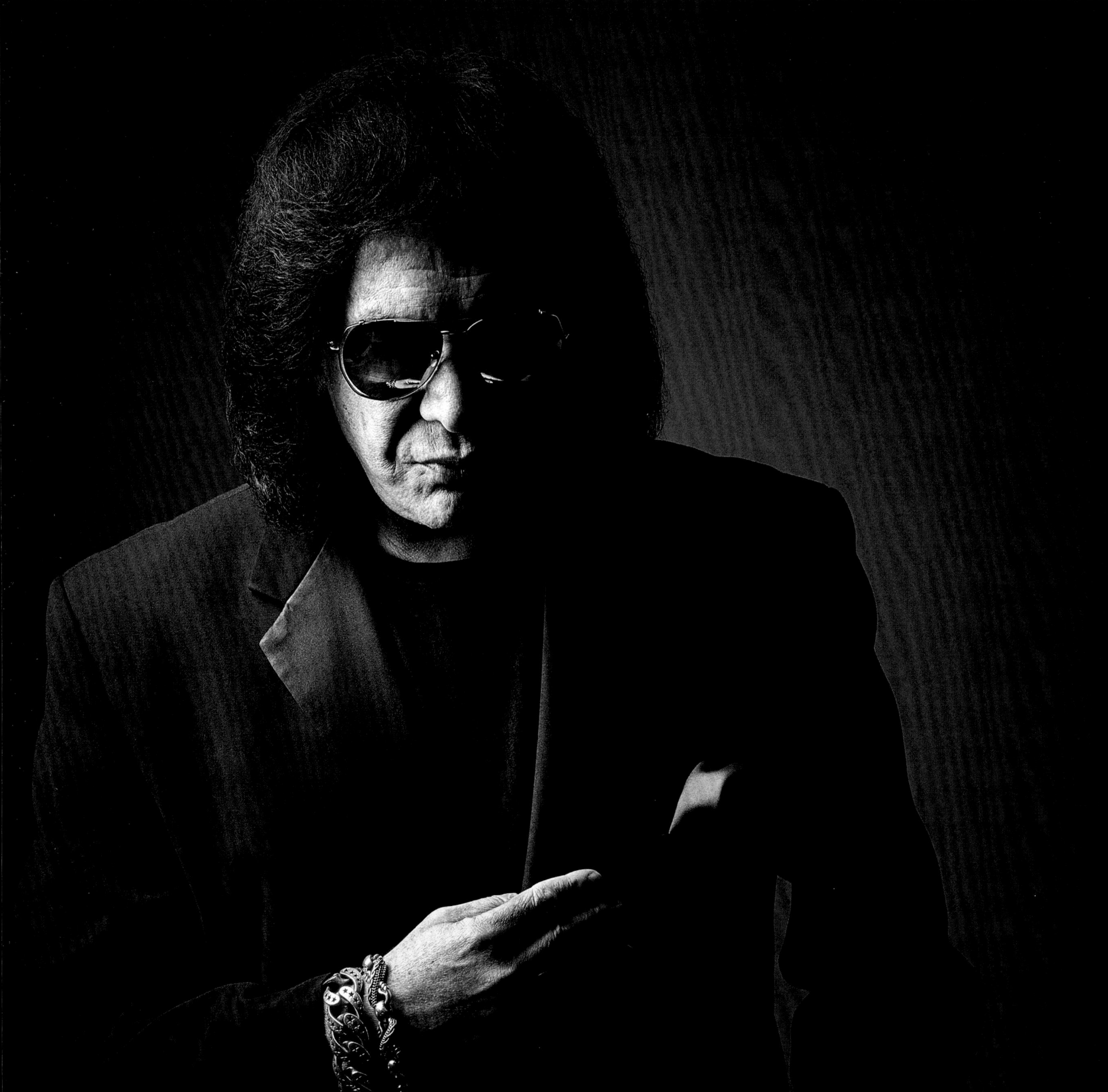

Gene Simmons

A picture, they say, is worth a thousand words.

Andy Gotts has been able to capture the stories, emotions and images of some of the most iconic figures on the planet. And only with pictures. The unguarded, unedited and unfiltered photos of these amazing people give us further insight into who they may really be. A contact sheet is pure art in the rawest form, which tells the story of the photo shoot, that moment in time.

It takes a great photographer to be able to convince someone to let their guard down, be vulnerable and, yes, often silly.

I'm proud to have been given the opportunity to say a few words about Andy. His subjects are the ones that often get the acclaim. Andy, behind the lens, doesn't get the acclaim he deserves.

With this amazing book, you will see why Andy is as much a star as his subjects.

May I have your autograph, please?

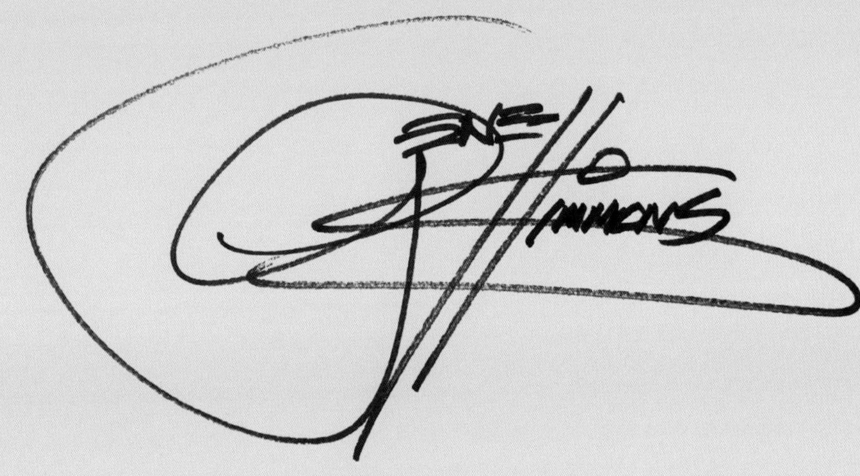

"A CONTACT SHEET IS PURE ART IN THE RAWEST FORM, WHICH TELLS THE STORY OF THE PHOTO SHOOT, THAT MOMENT IN TIME."

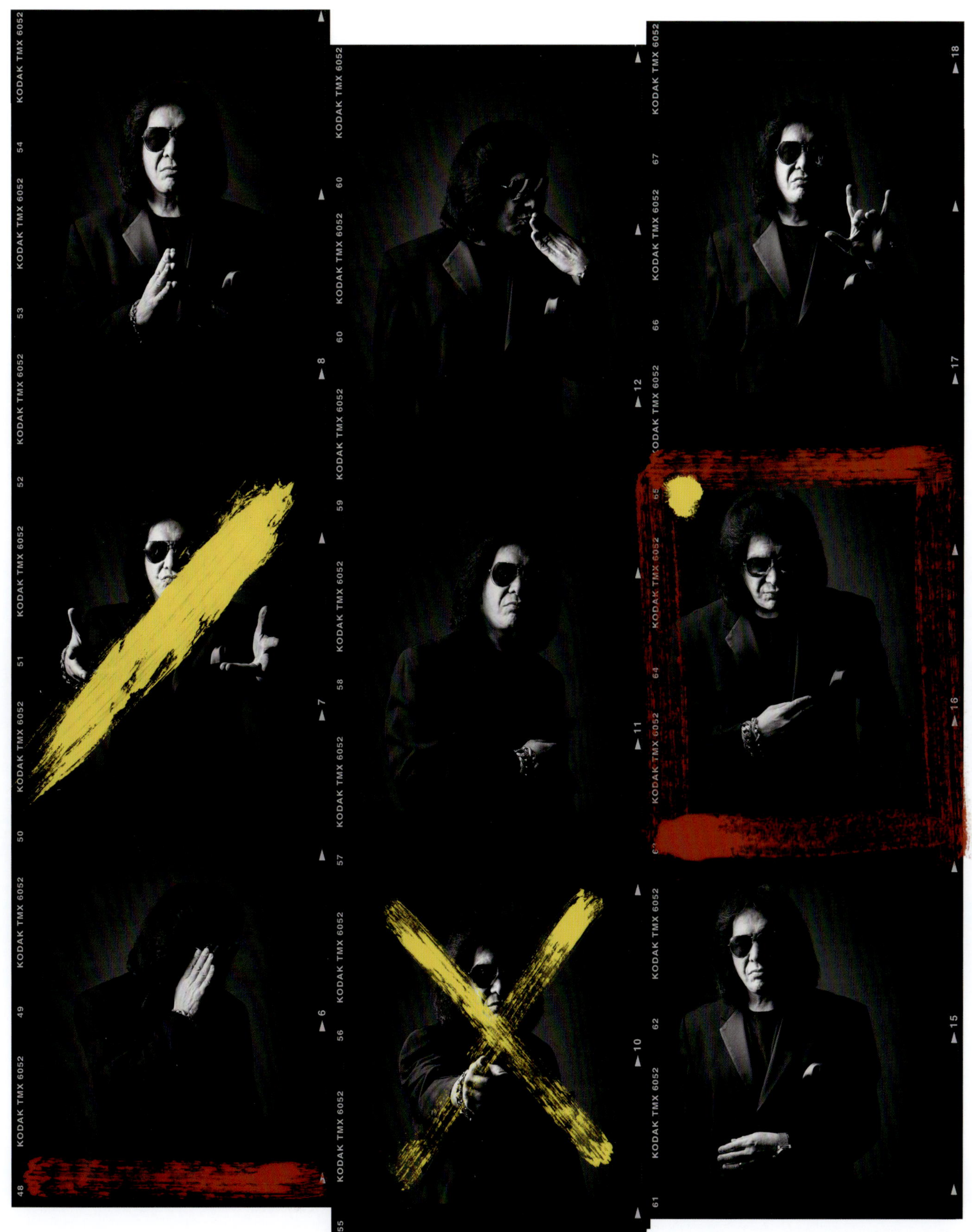

George Clooney

I shot George at his beautiful Lake Como residence. When I arrived, breakfast was being served on the veranda. It seemed more like a five-star hotel then a private house. After breakfast, George disappeared to find a space which had a plain white wall for the shoot. I had to manoeuvre my equipment around three obese (live) ducks in the hallway. But my tripod hit his bookshelf and a very large World Atlas dislodged from the shelf and plummeted onto a duck. In a panic – and not knowing what to do with an unconscious duck – I kicked it behind the bookshelf. George soon re-emerged wearing a pirate's hat, which he had worn at a dinner party the previous night. When I pointed out what a fool he looked, he started roaring with laughter – there was my pic! Not long after the shoot, there was a muffled quack from behind the bookshelf and a dazed duck waddled out. I let out a nervous giggle.

I found George, as you can imagine, a very charismatic man and you get the impression that he is very quickly in tune with anyone he's engaging with. He has this unique ability, whilst in his company, to make you feel as if, for that moment in time, you are the most important person in his life.

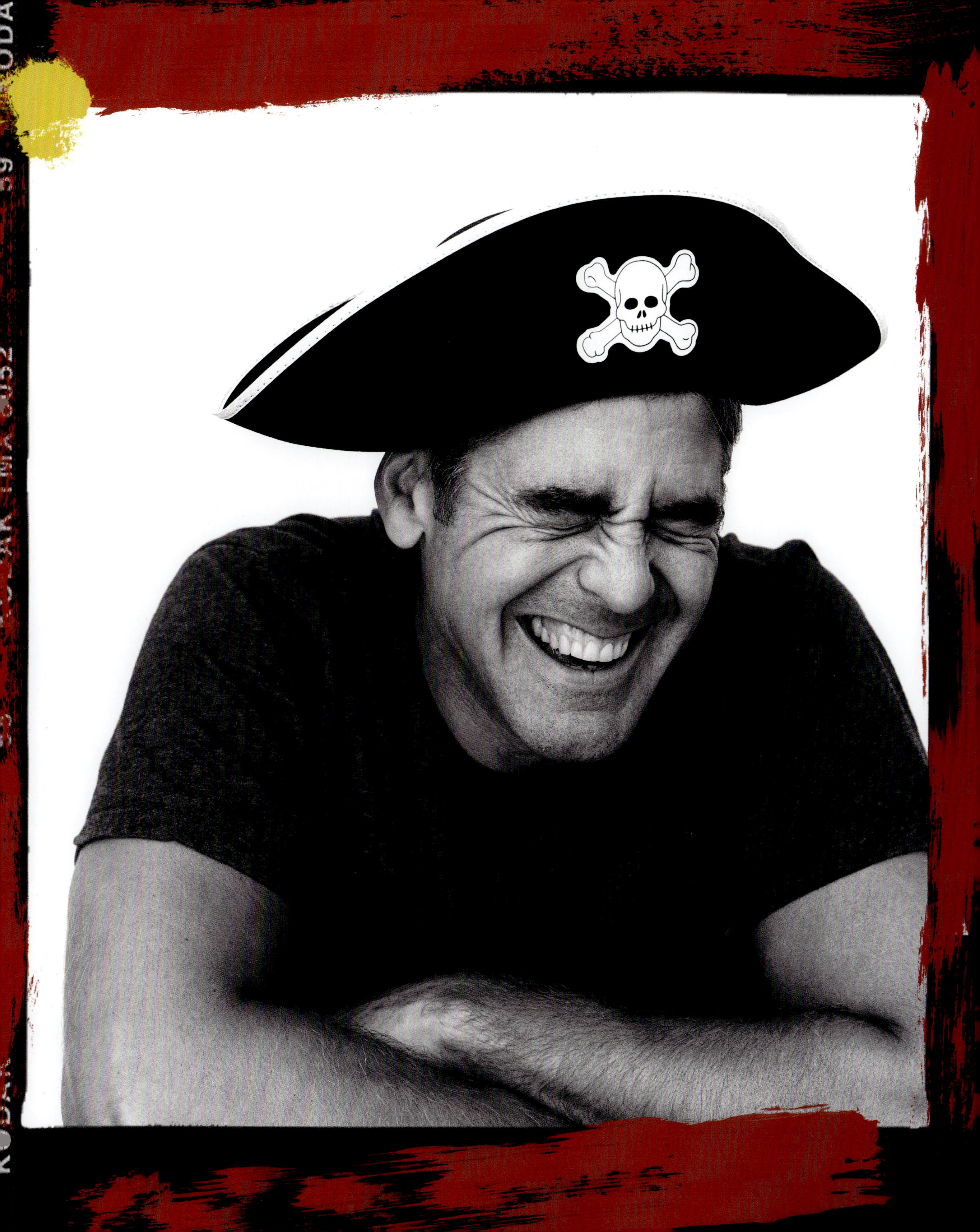

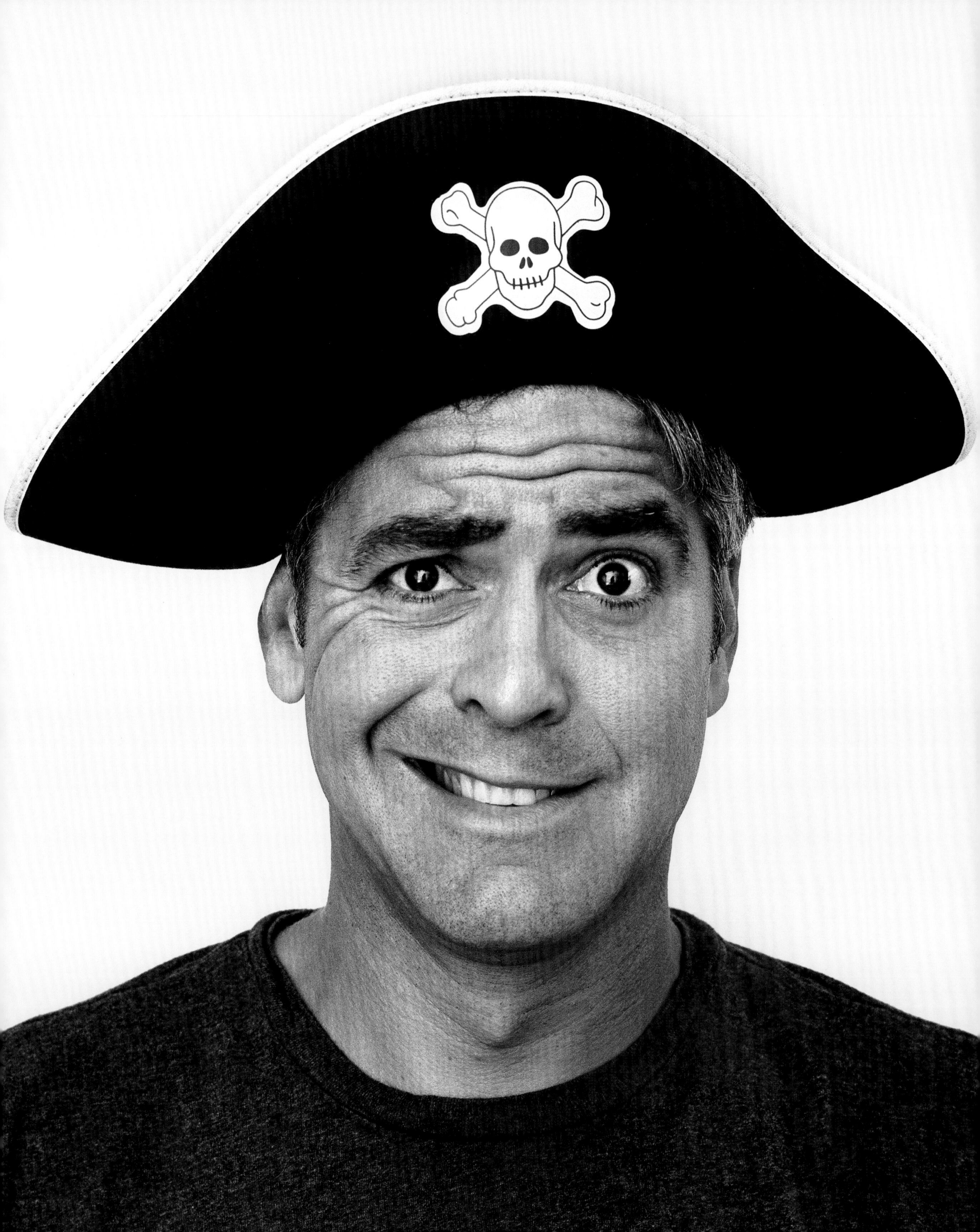

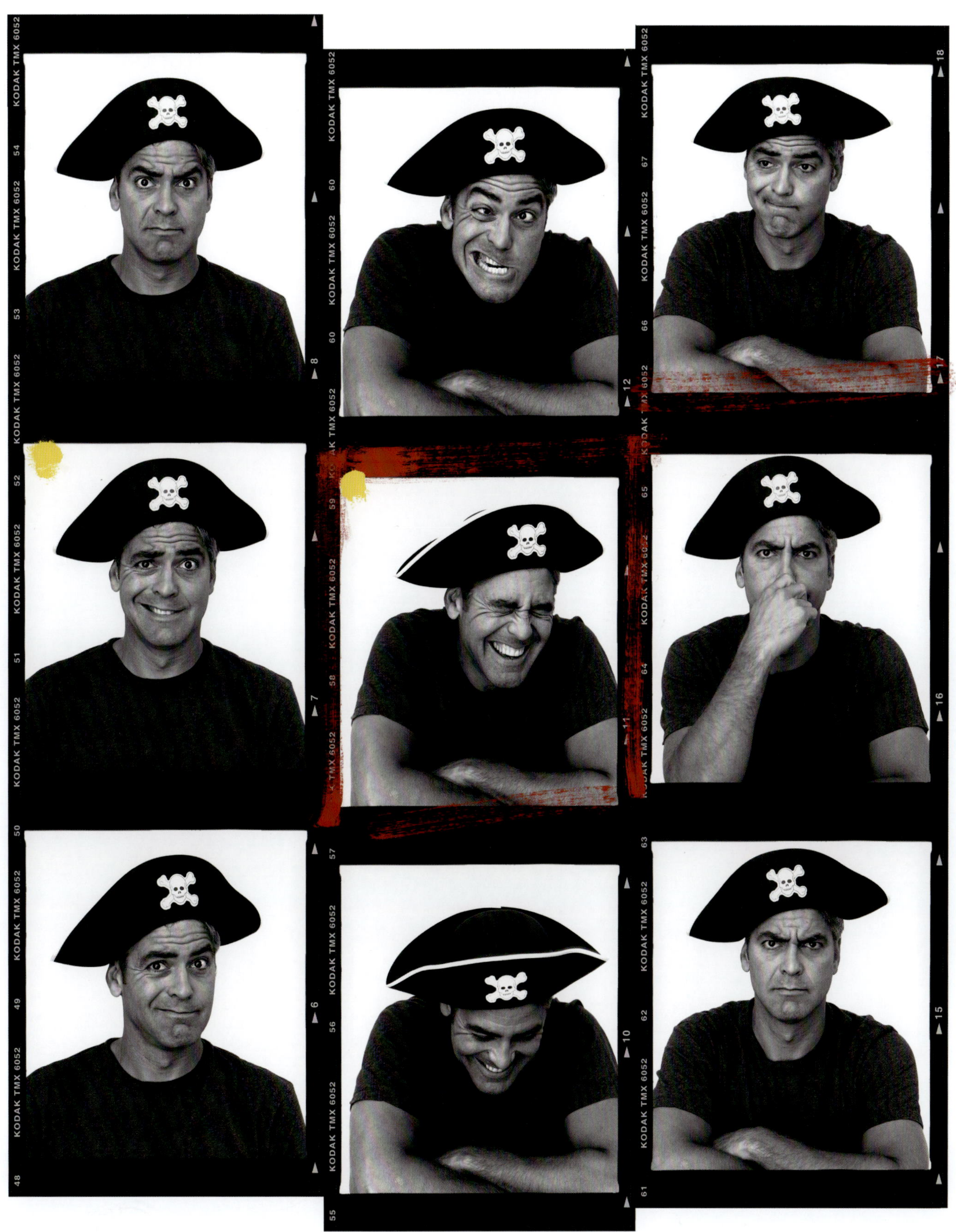

Gwyneth Paltrow

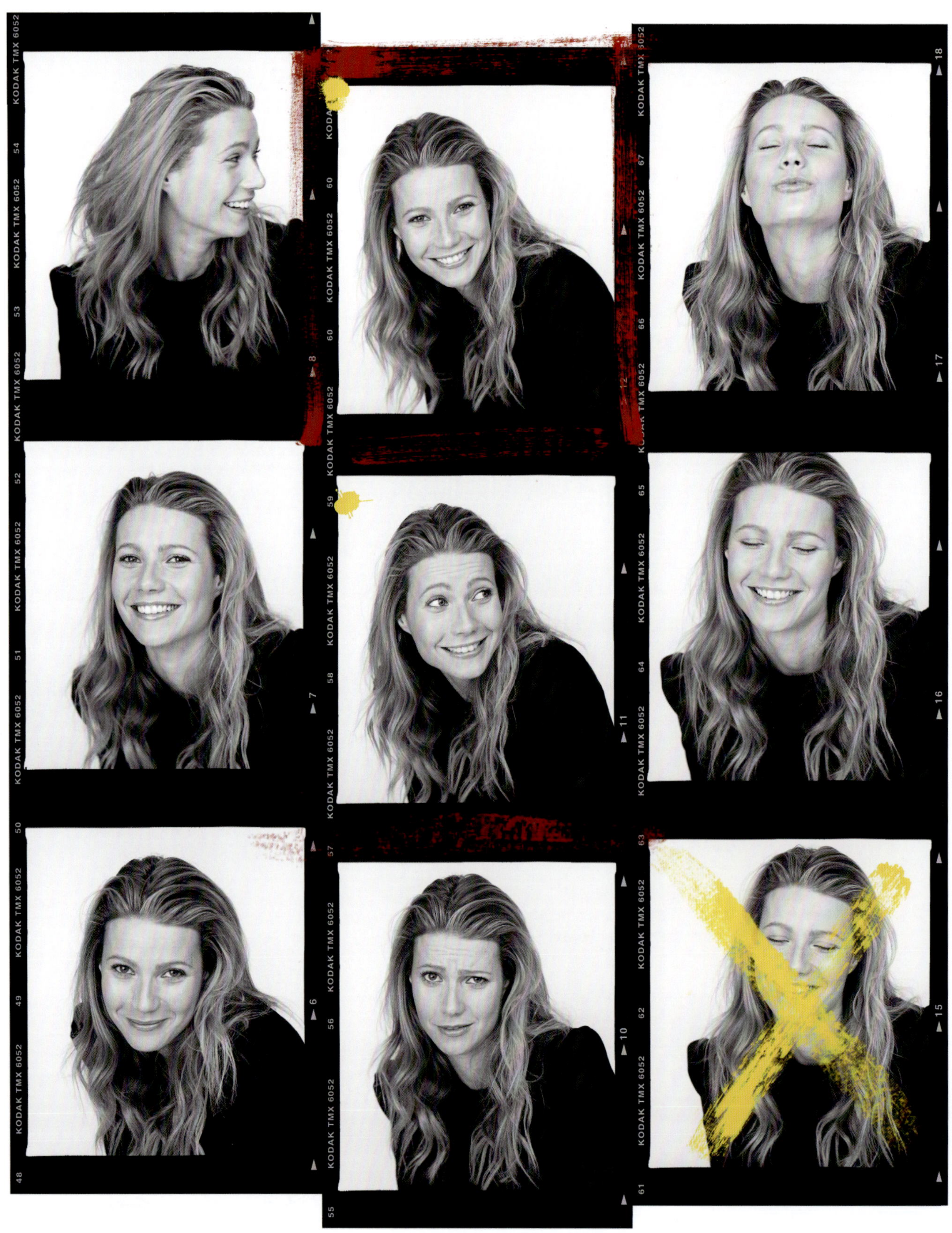

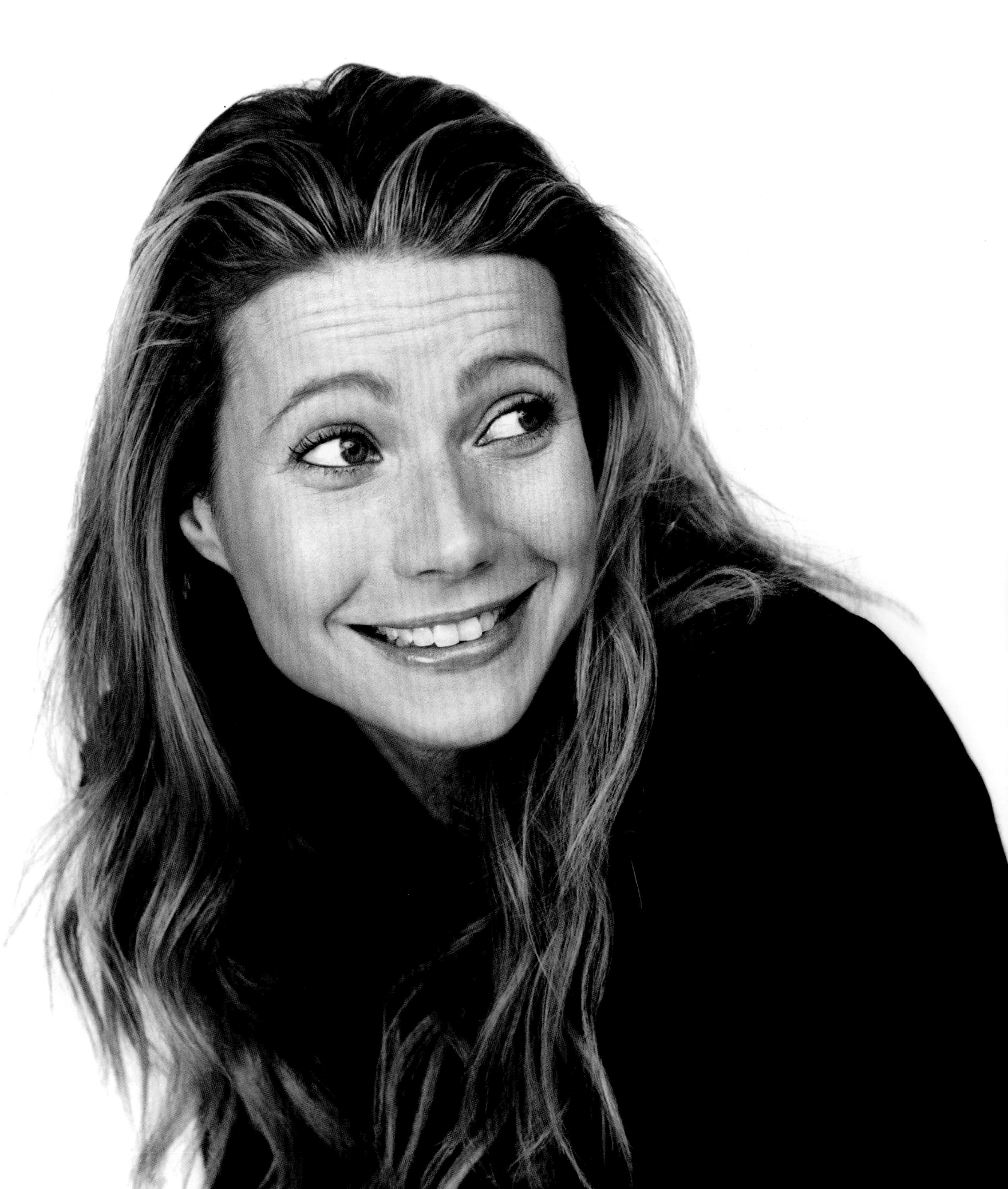

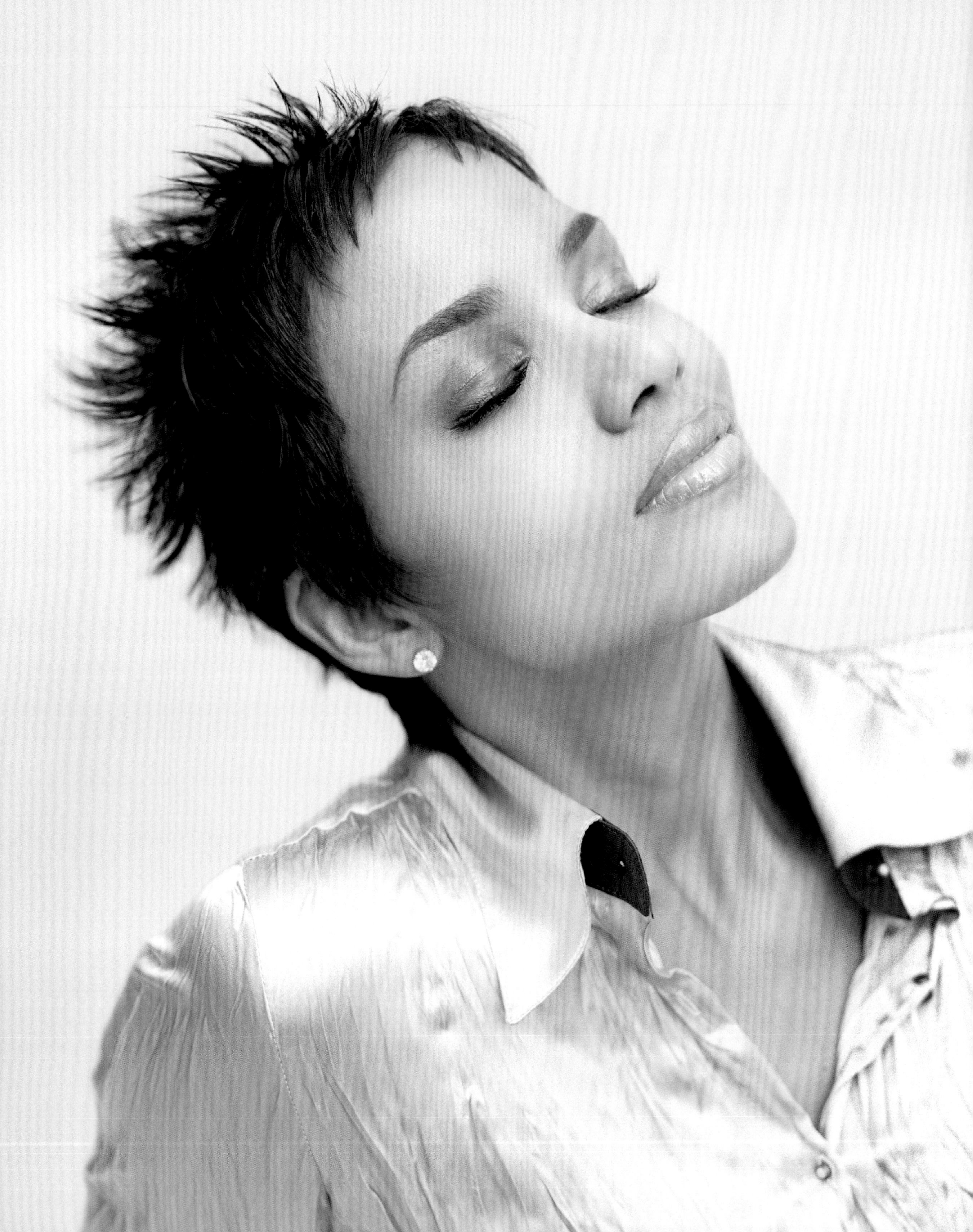

Halle Berry

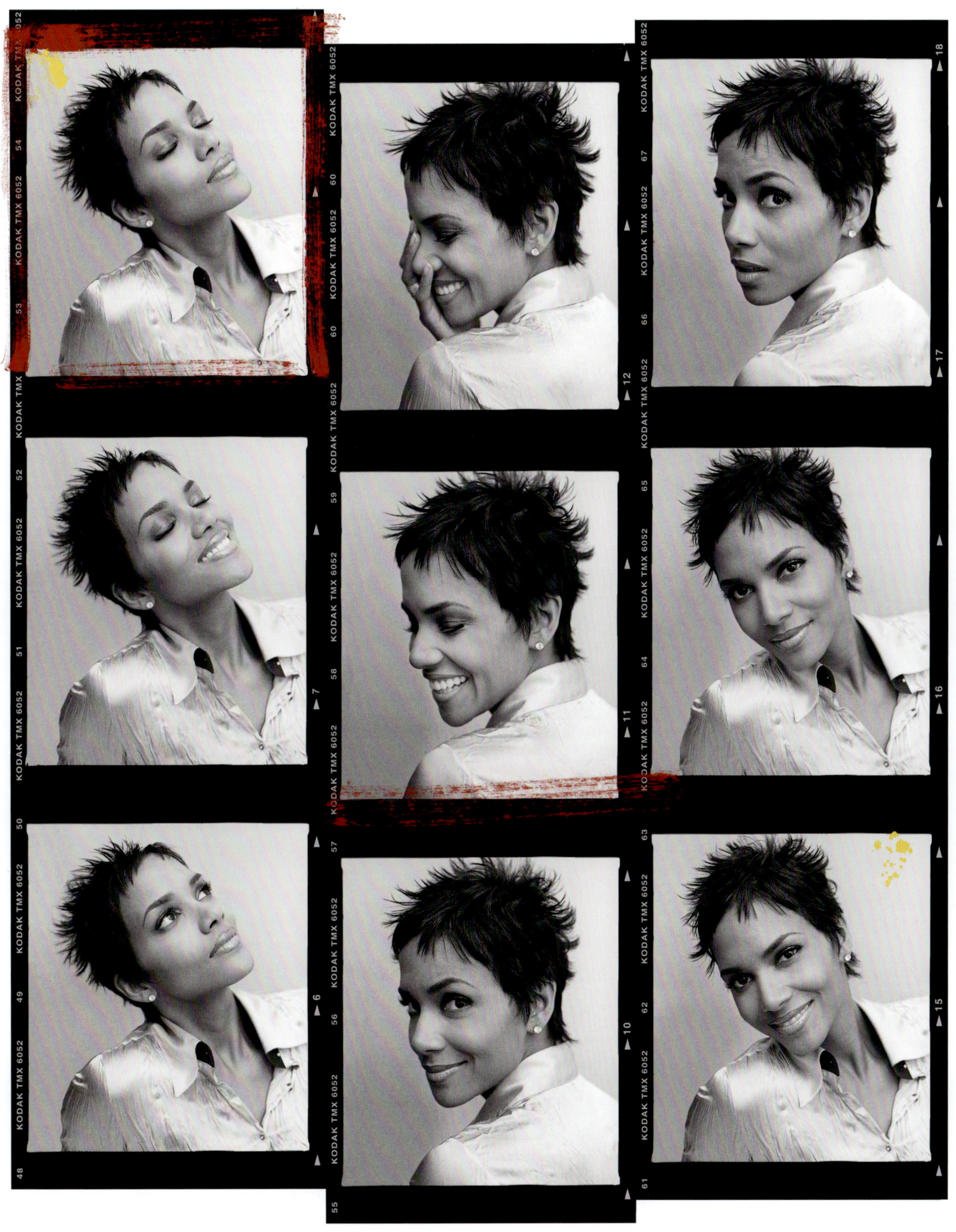

Harrison Ford

I shot Harrison at the Flemings Mayfair hotel. I had been warned many times, by many people to 'be careful of Harrison', as he was apparently grumpy at photo shoots or interviews. I never pay much attention to these comments as people's moods change all the time, and I must state that I am not always a glowing example of politeness, so I had no preconceptions before he arrived.

Harrison was just wrapping *Star Wars: The Force Awakens*, so I was expecting a small entourage to appear with him, but no. There was a little knock at my door and there stood this silver-haired man in a black coat and sunglasses asking if I was expecting him. He came in and started talking in an excited manner as he was going to see some vintage aircraft that afternoon. So, with my listed knowledge of WWII craft, we muddled through a lovely long chat, then began the shoot. We got on like a house on fire. I joked with him: "I was told you were a moody bastard", which he though was hilarious.

At the end of the shoot I suggested we do some funny face goofy shoots. Harrison looked at me with a beaming smile and said, "Andy, in all my years I have never been asked to mess around in shots, people think I'm an ass!" With that, he burst into a multitude of hilarious contorted faces, and without doubt 'The Force' was with me that day!

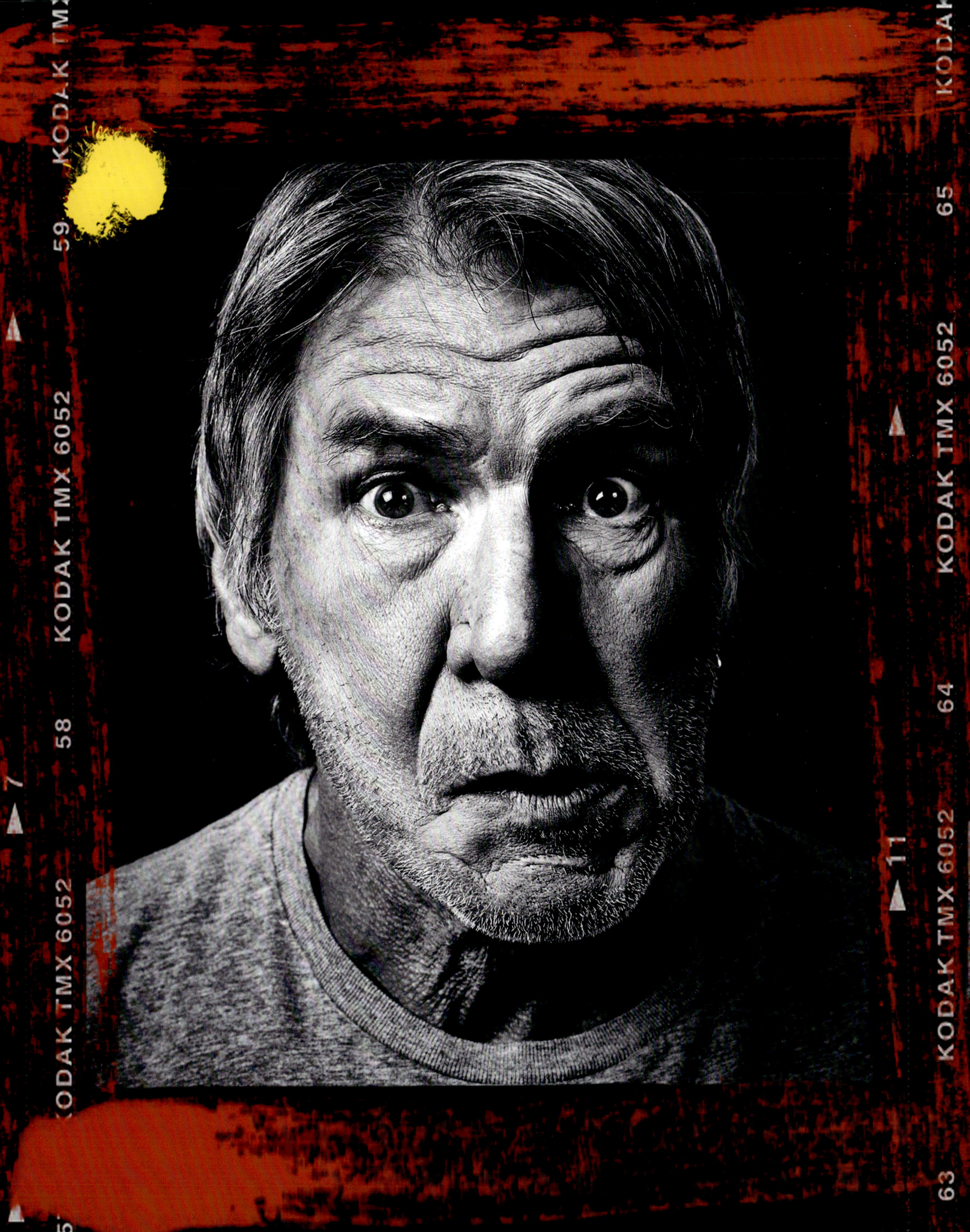

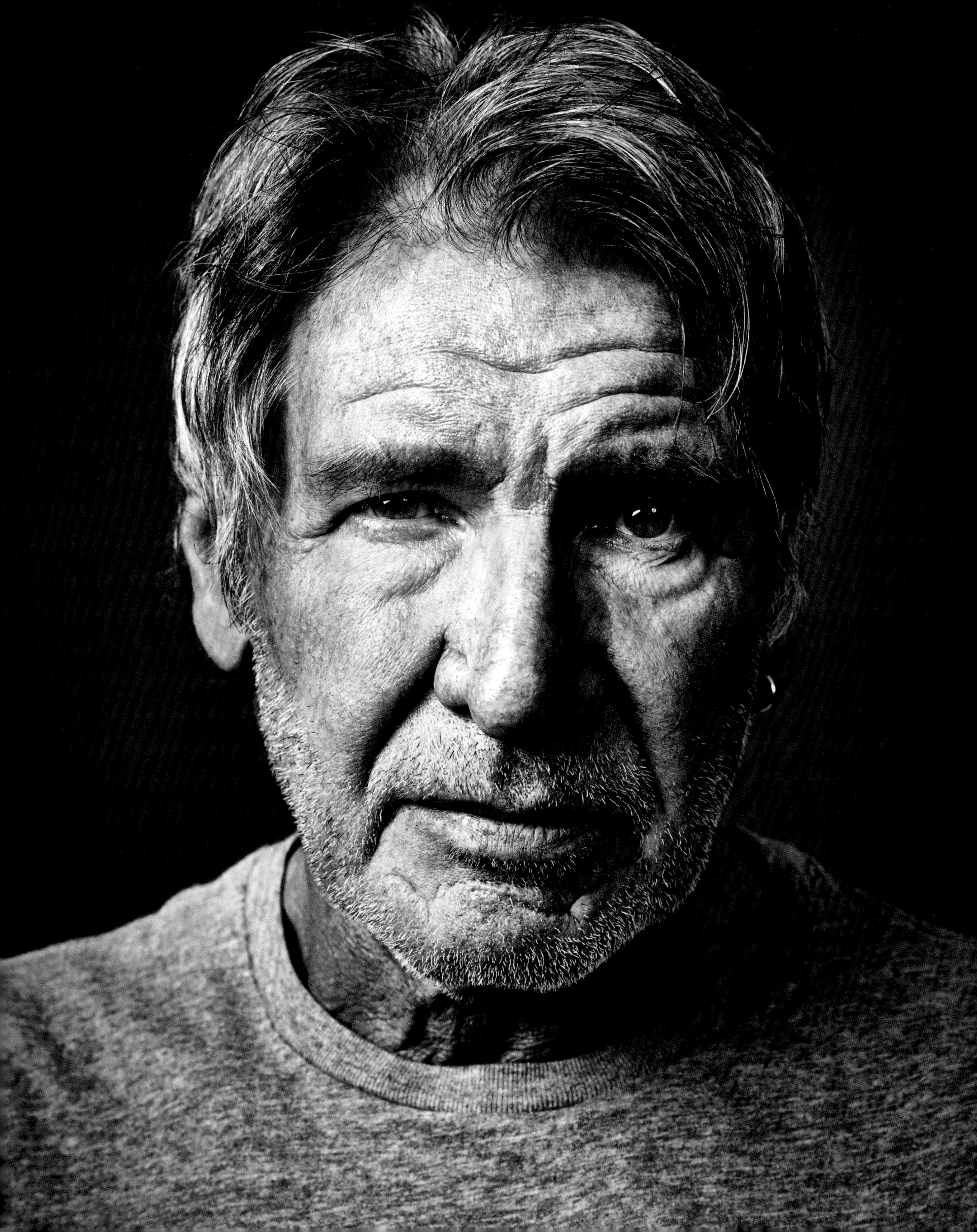

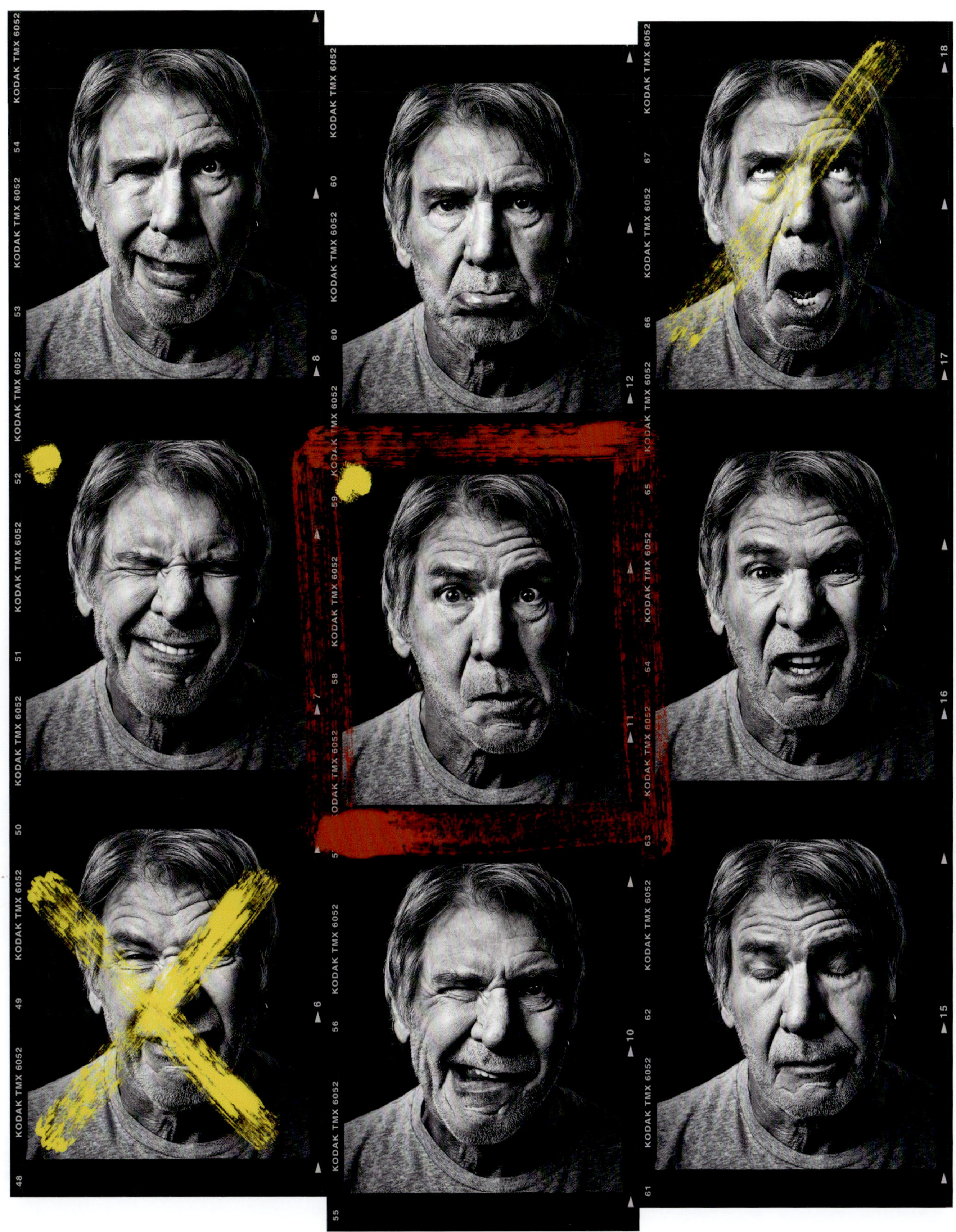

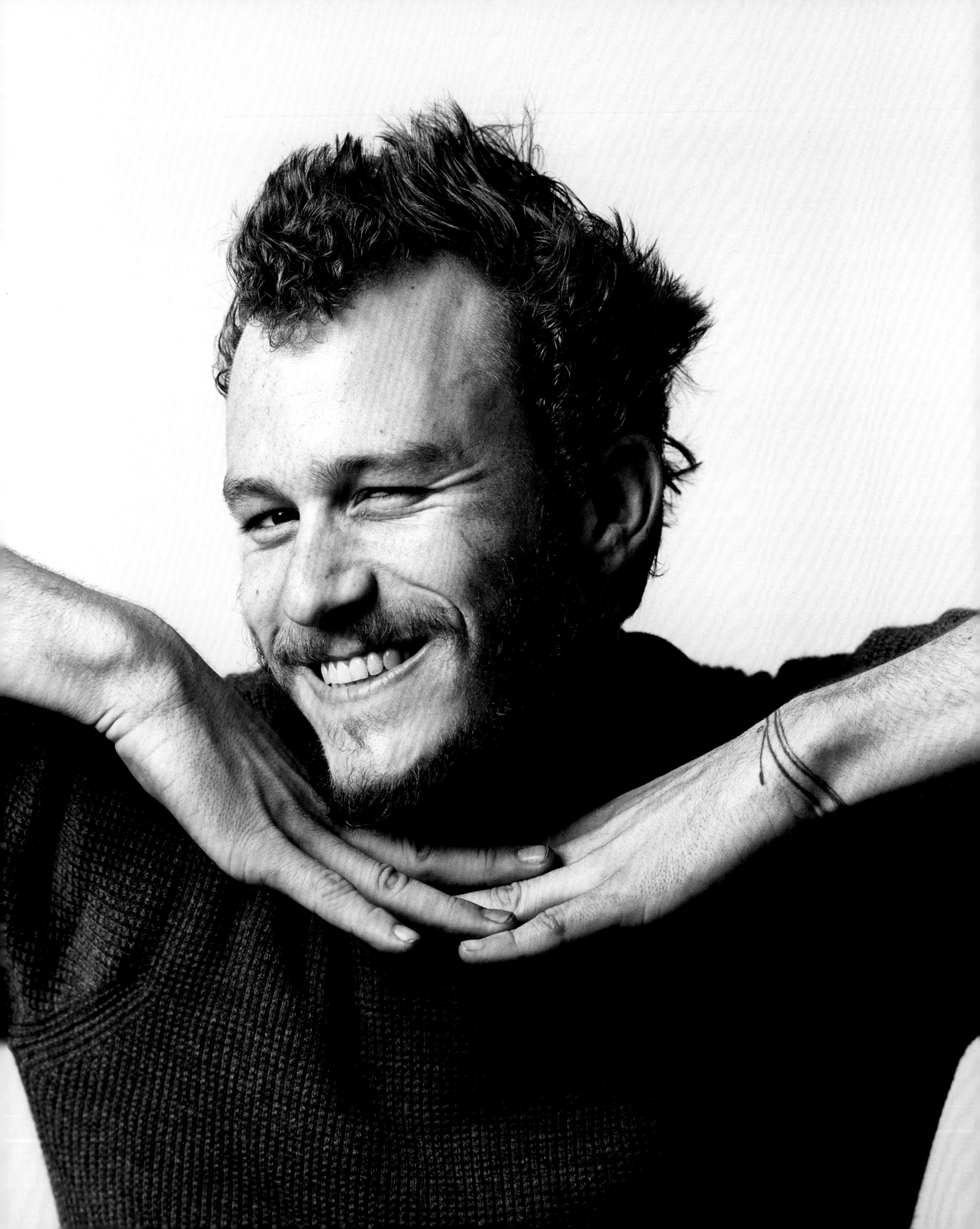

Heath Ledger

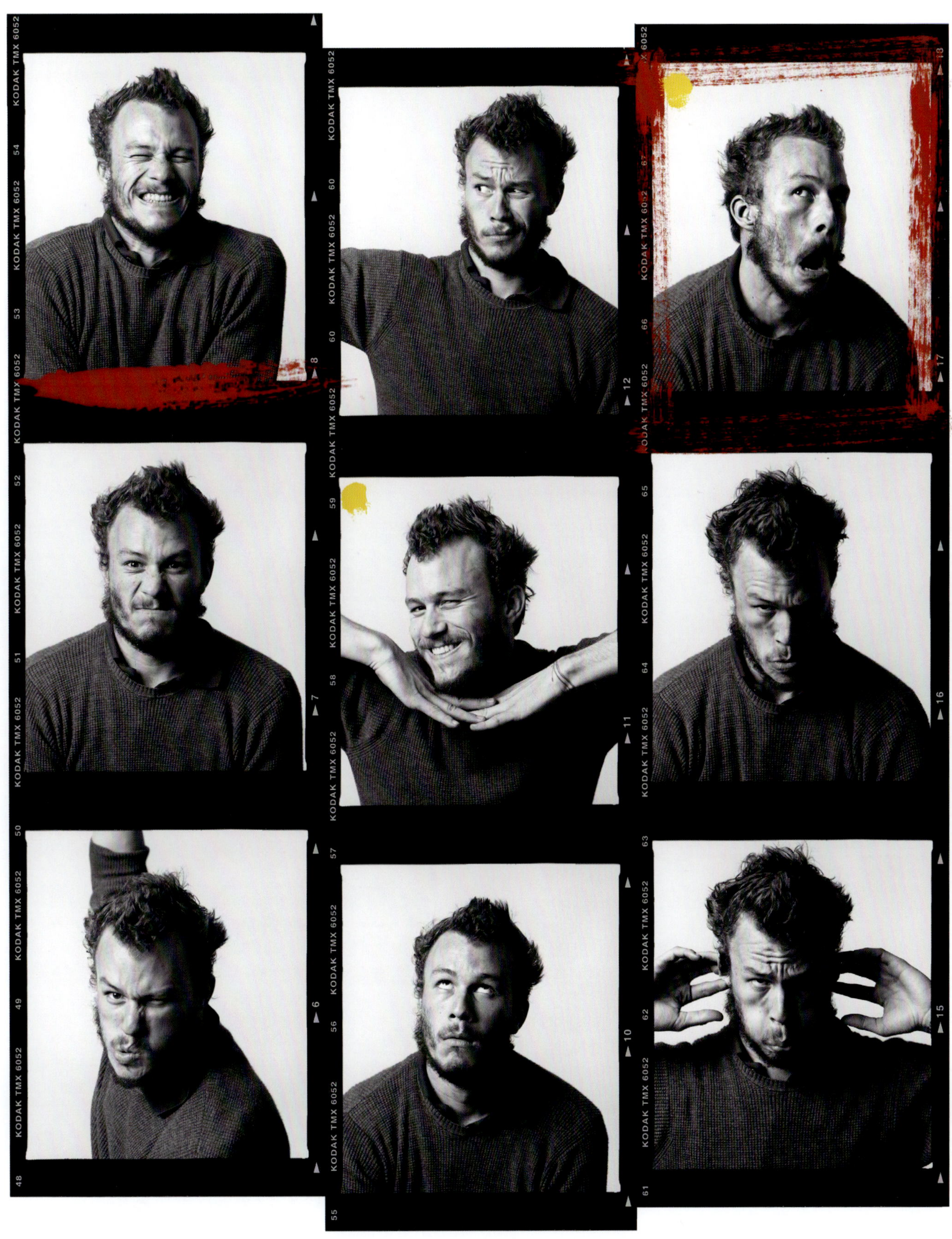

Helen Mirren

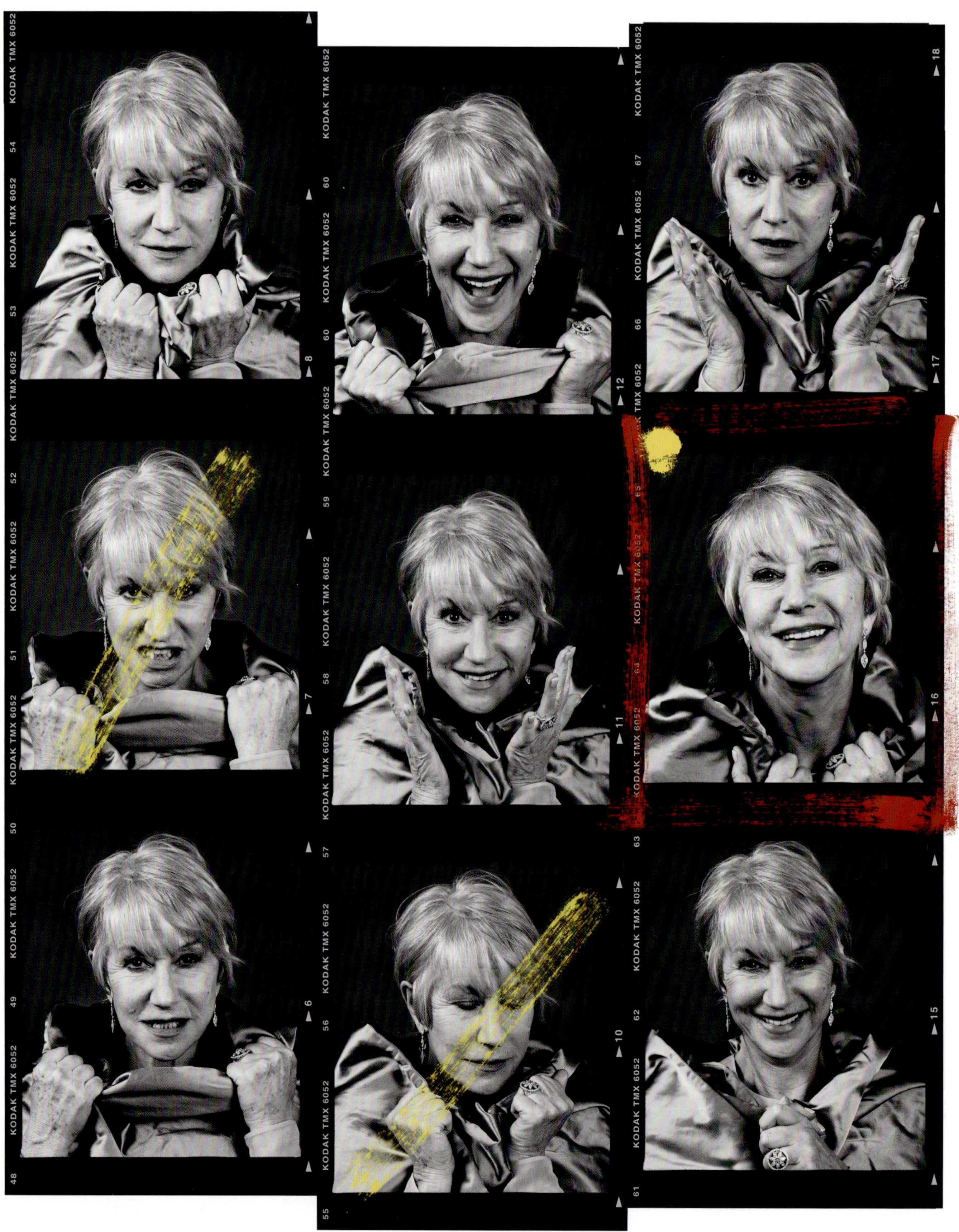

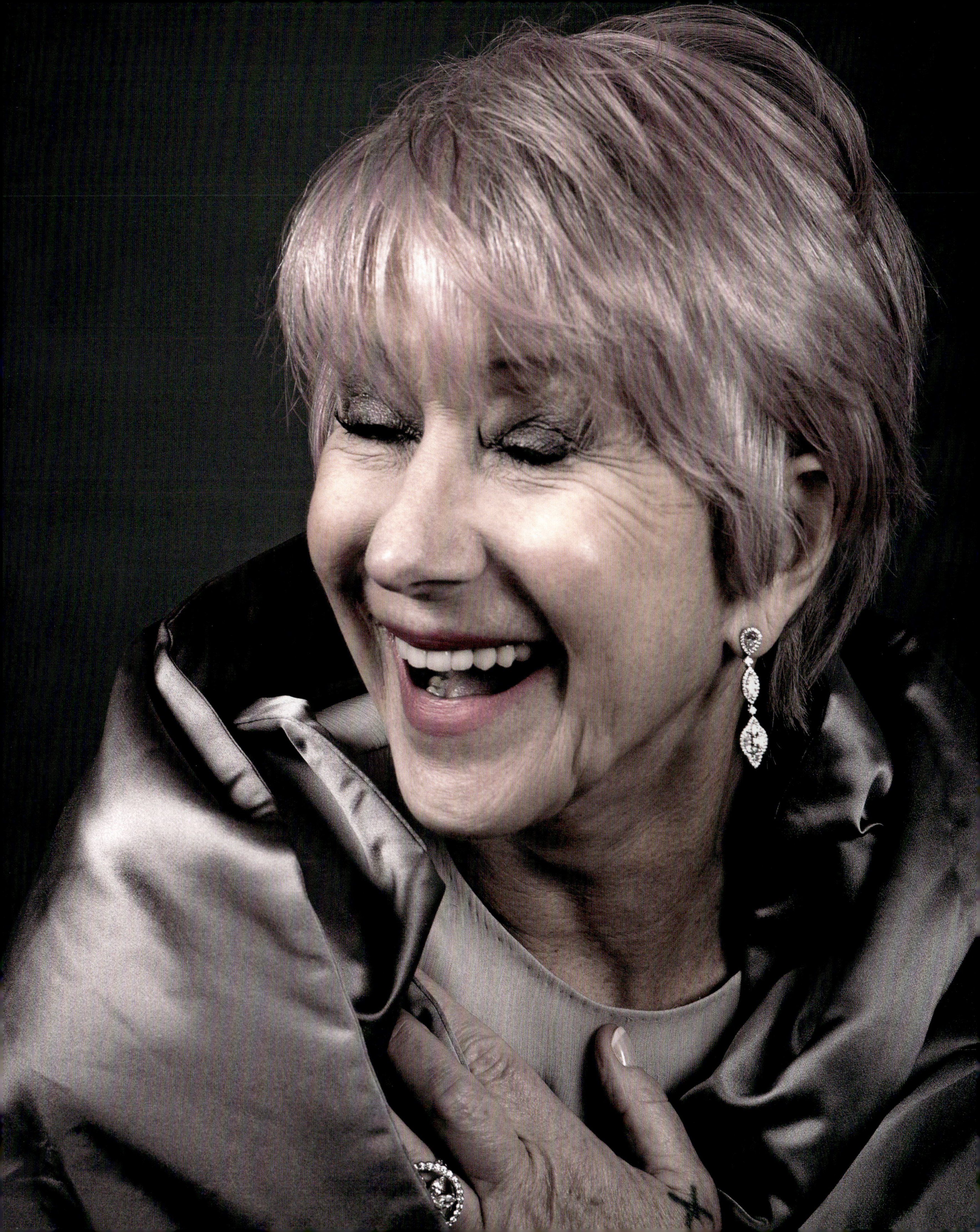

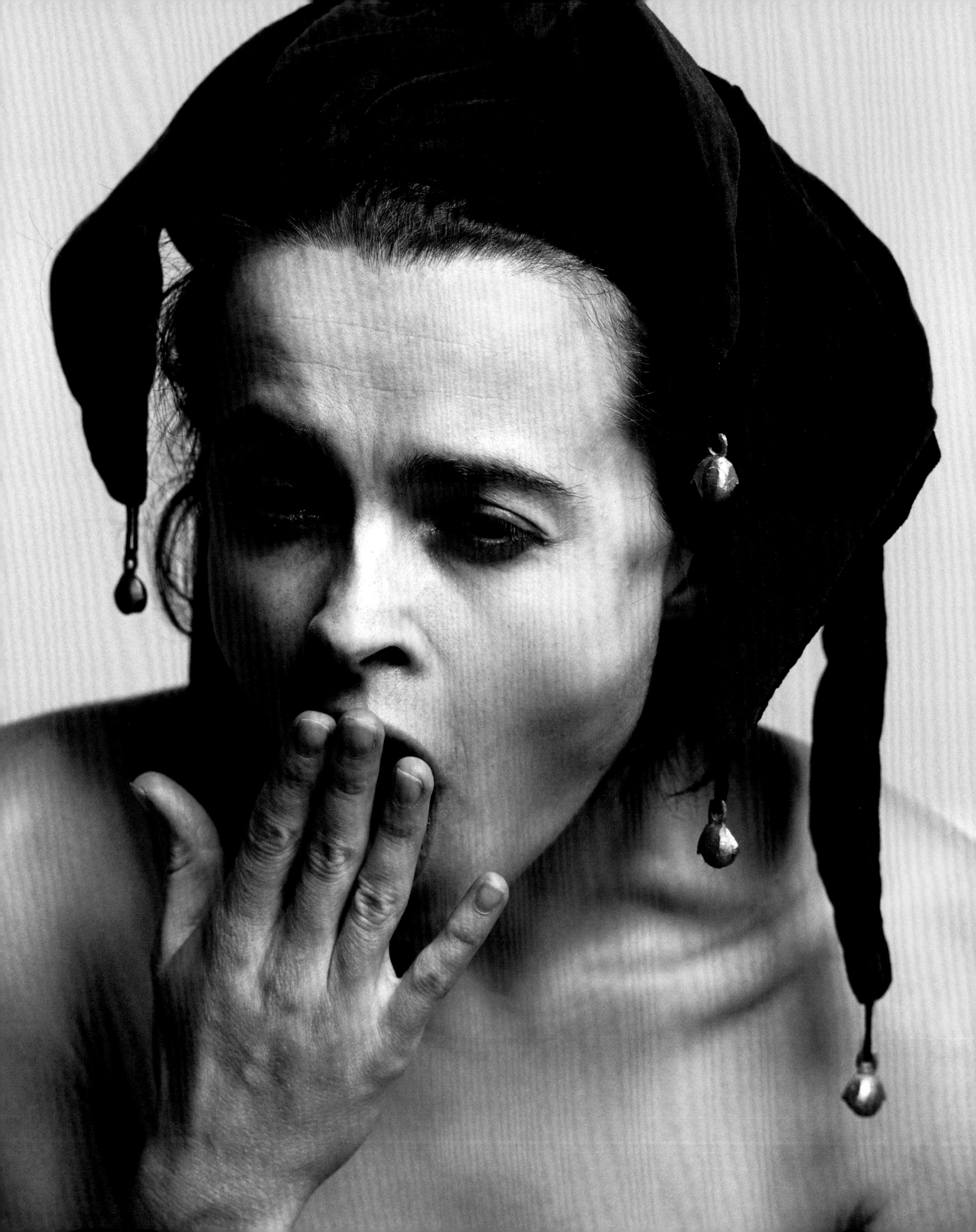

Helena Bonham Carter

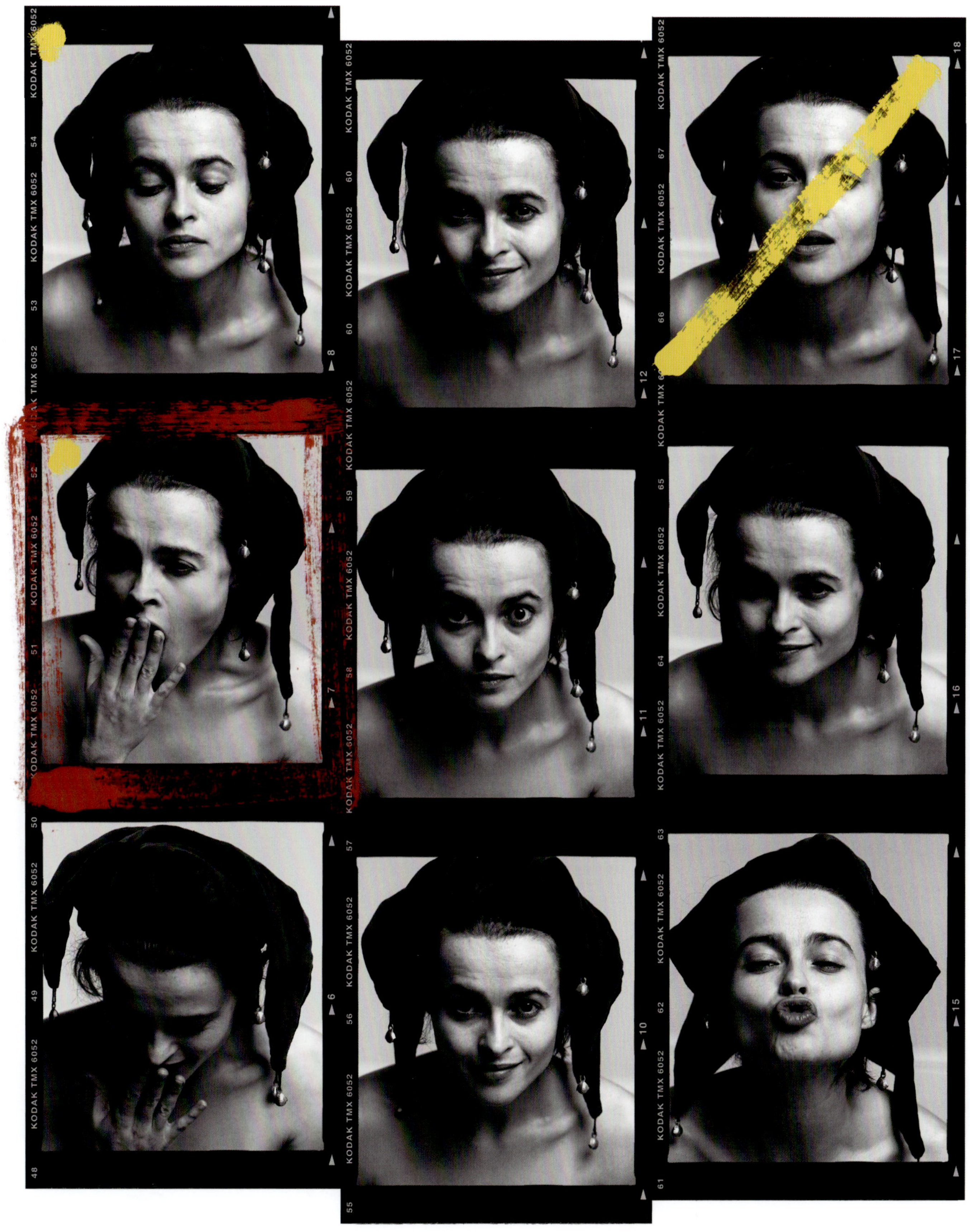

Hugh Grant

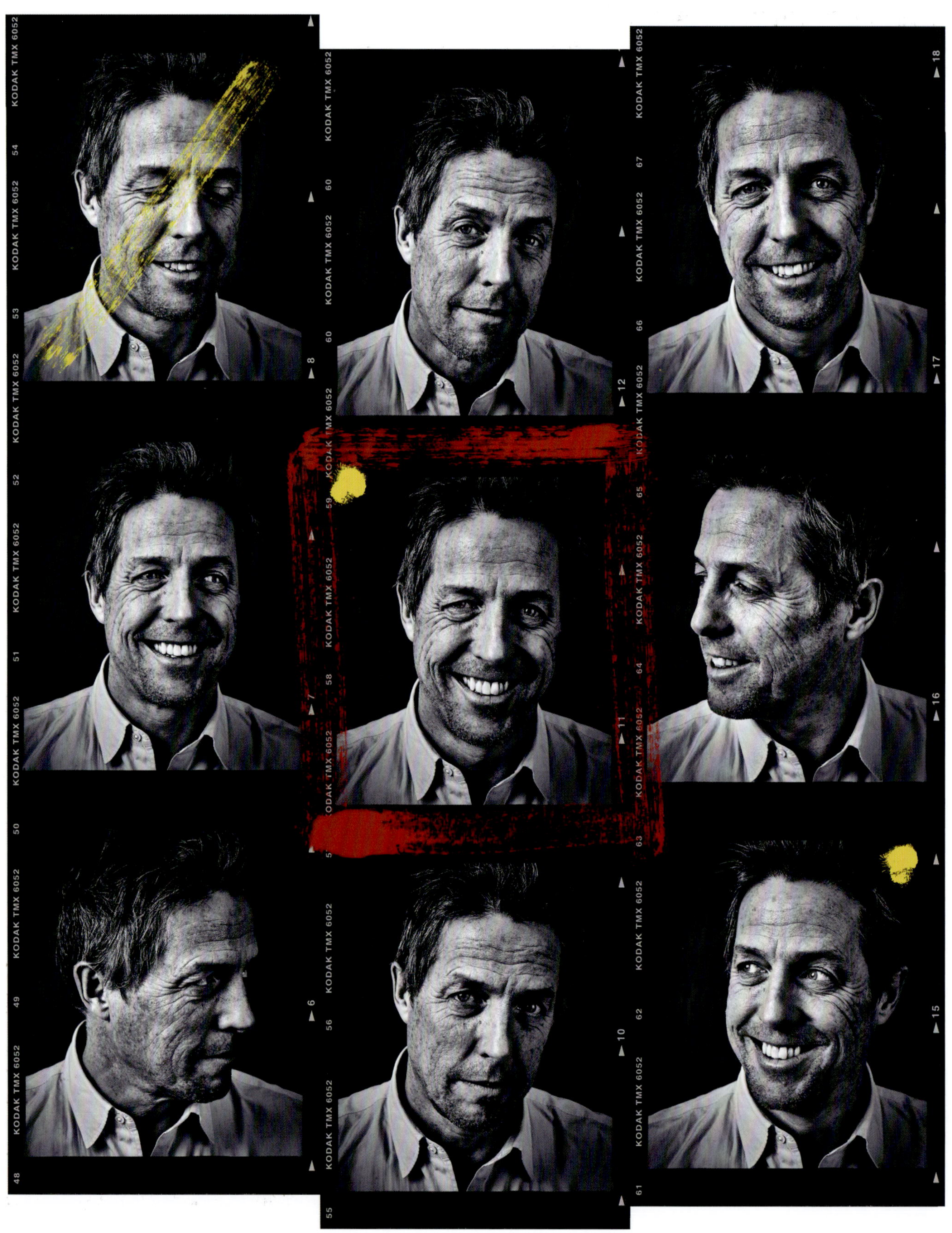

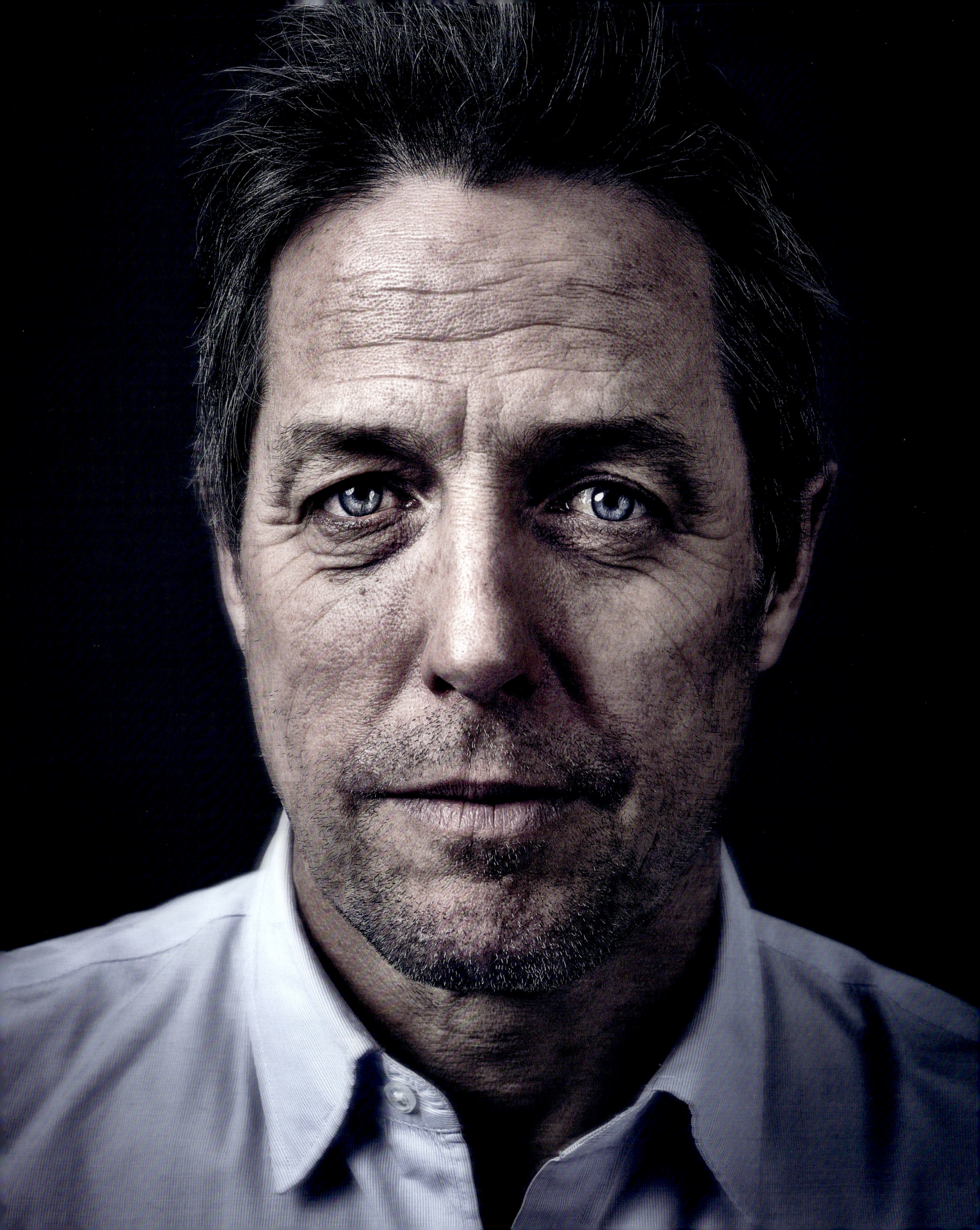

Ian McKellen

Have you ever heard of Samuel Dunseith McKellen?

Towards the end of the nineteenth century he invented one of the first portable cameras that was patented, though I think its success was overtaken by Kodak, etc.

This new book featuring these splendid photographic contact sheets is a beautiful treat for the eyes. But forgive me if I don't provide an introduction or in-depth insight into the artistry, as masterful as it is, I don't share my ancestor's expertise.

Do keep on capturing human nature in your inimitable fashion.

All best wishes,

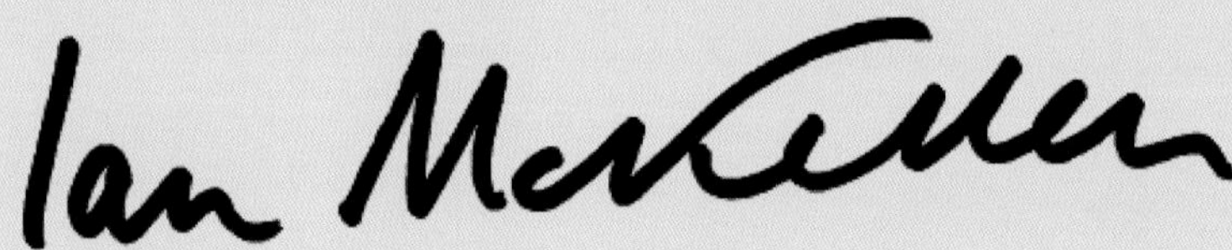

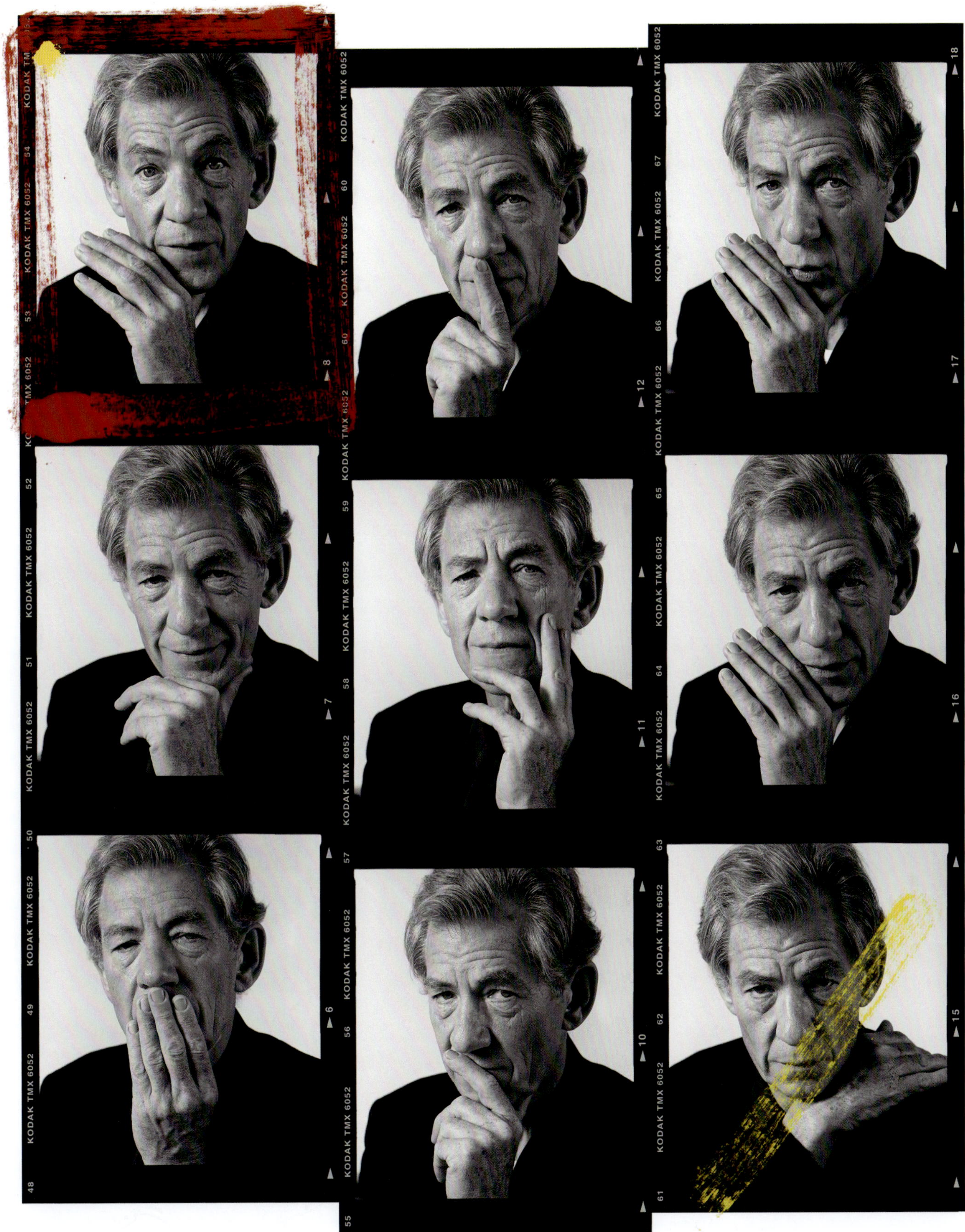

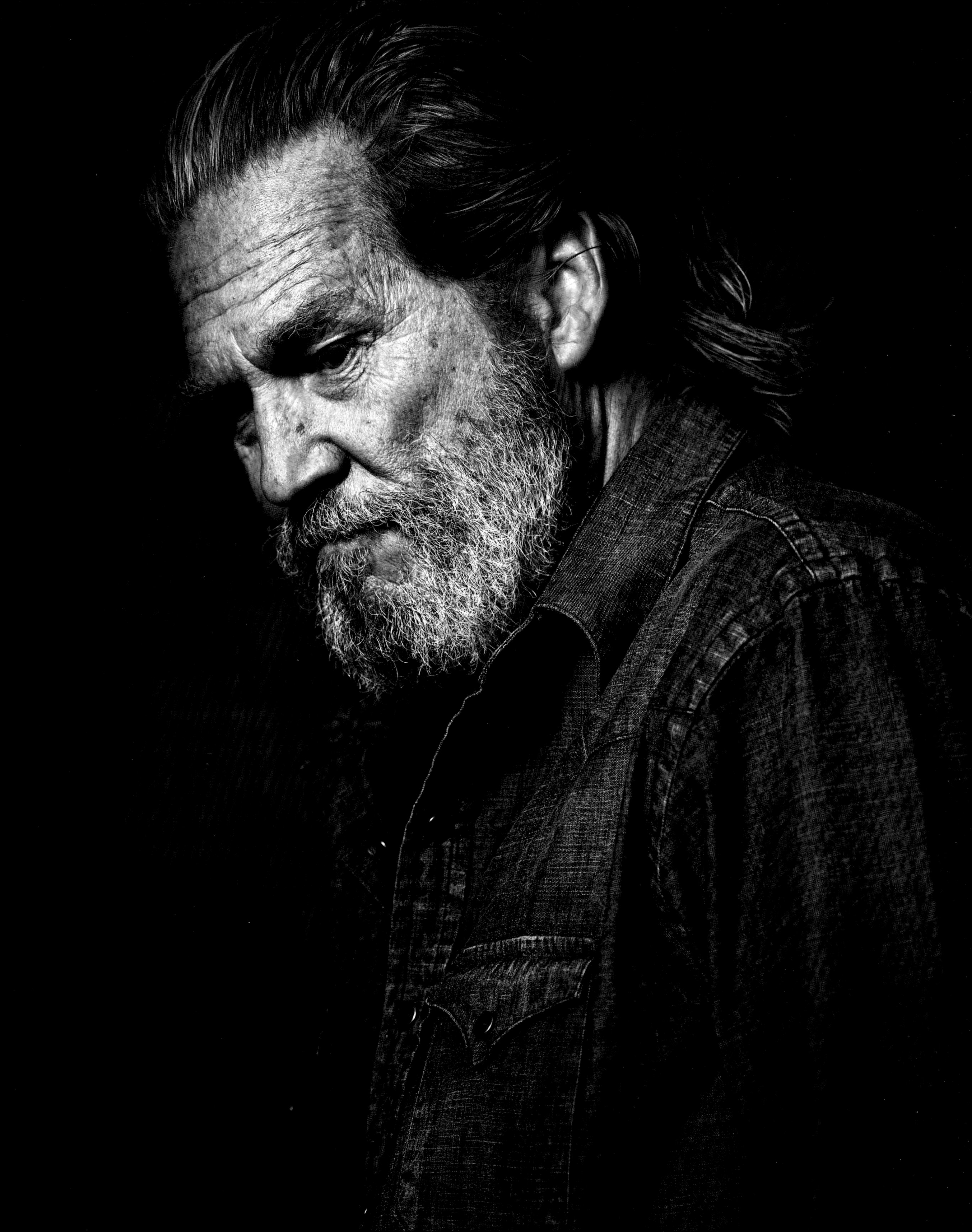

Jeff Bridges

Andy Gotts – what a brilliant career over a span of many moons, over 30 years to be exact. He captures the personality of his subject in an original and unmistakable style all his own; arty, moody, playful, ethereal and piercing all at once.

Here, Andy gives us a peek under the photographer's hood to see his process. Being a photographer myself, I love the surprise of seeing a contact sheet for the first time. You never know what you're going to get, as someone said once. You may have high expectations. You have those when making movies, too. And, every once in a while, those expectations get exceeded. To be a part of that is something wonderful, something special and something Andy knows all about.

Photography is a passion of mine. It always has been. Way back when I was living with my folks I would borrow my father's Nikon and even set up a darkroom in the bathroom. With tinfoil on the windows and the red light, the whole concept of time goes out of the window.

In downtime when on set I am usually seen with my Widelux camera in hand, looking to see what I can capture in my lens before the bellow of "ACTION" from the director.

I remember fondly the shoot I had with Andy. A few days before I had won the Academy Award for *Crazy Heart* and I was planning a new movie in New Mexico. My head was everywhere – on the immense high of the award win and trying to mentally pack for the next few weeks on set.

We shot at my home here in Montecito. Andy had set up and was ready to shoot in the blink of the eye; I was actually astounded with the speed, just how quick he was. The atmosphere was so laid back and chilled, just like I had known this dude for 30 years. I sat back and let the shoot wash over me like the warm waves in Malibu. He captured 'me'.

Thanks for the memories man.

"HE CAPTURES THE PERSONALITY OF HIS SUBJECT IN AN ORIGINAL AND UNMISTAKABLE STYLE ALL HIS OWN."

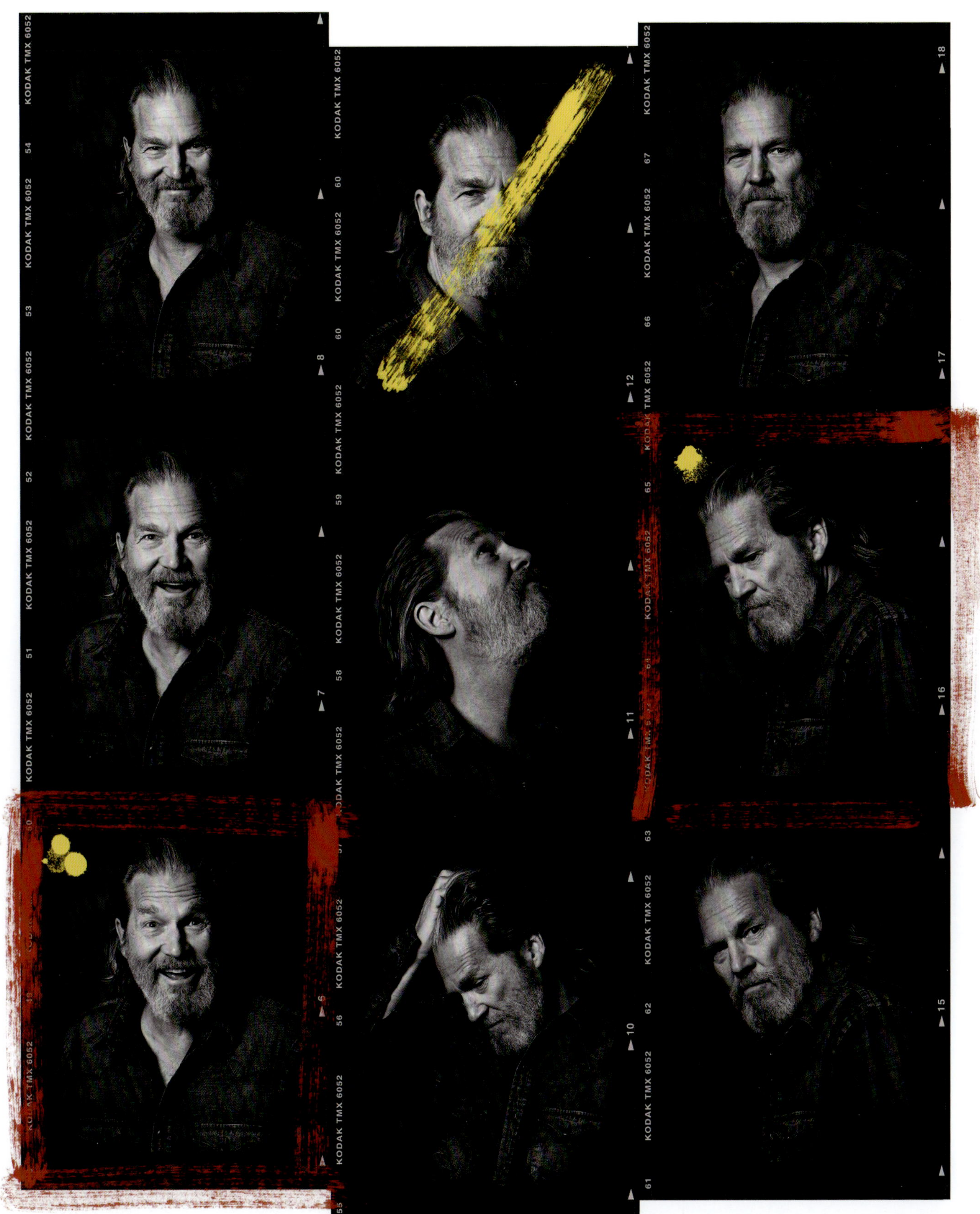
KODAK TMX 6052

Joan Collins

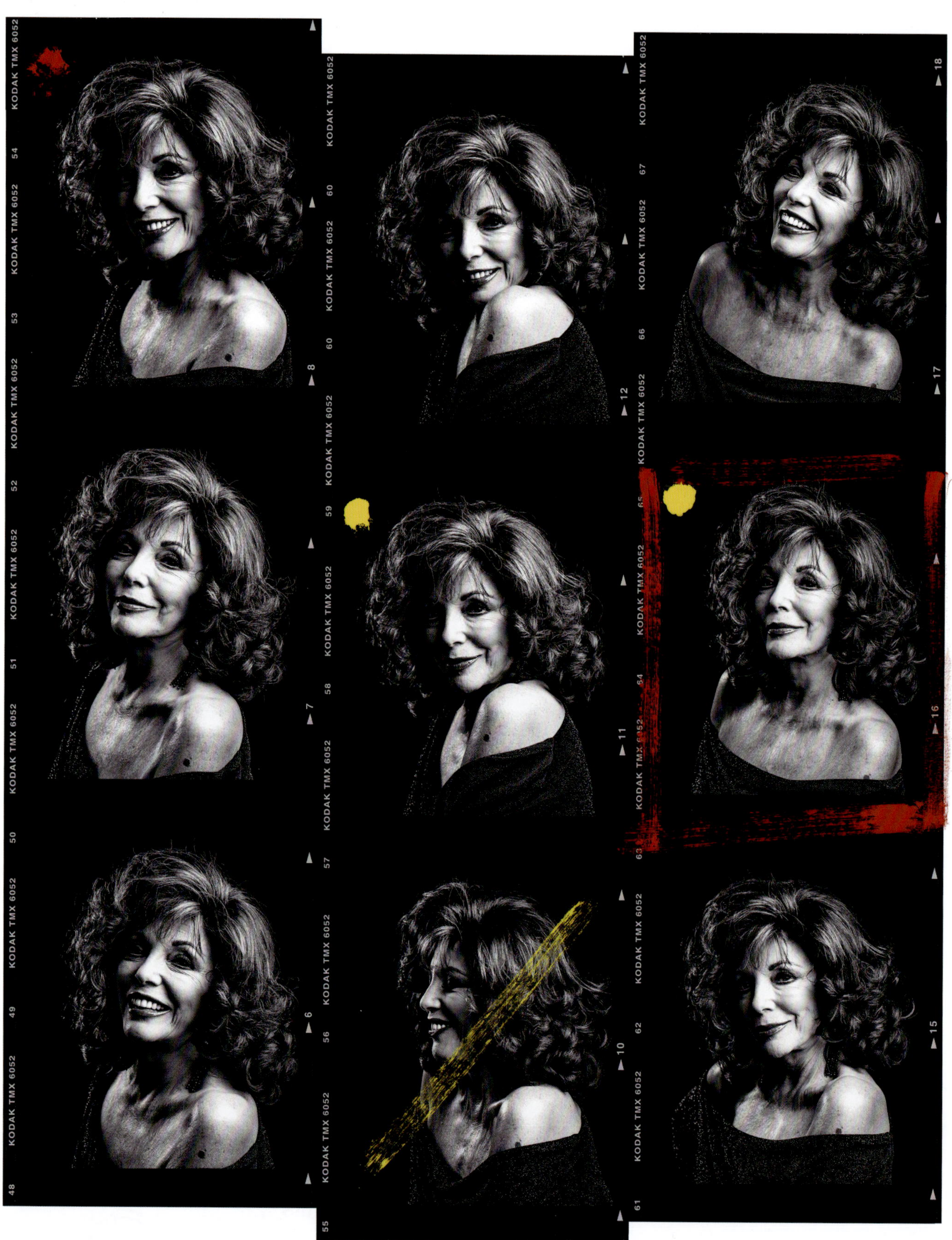

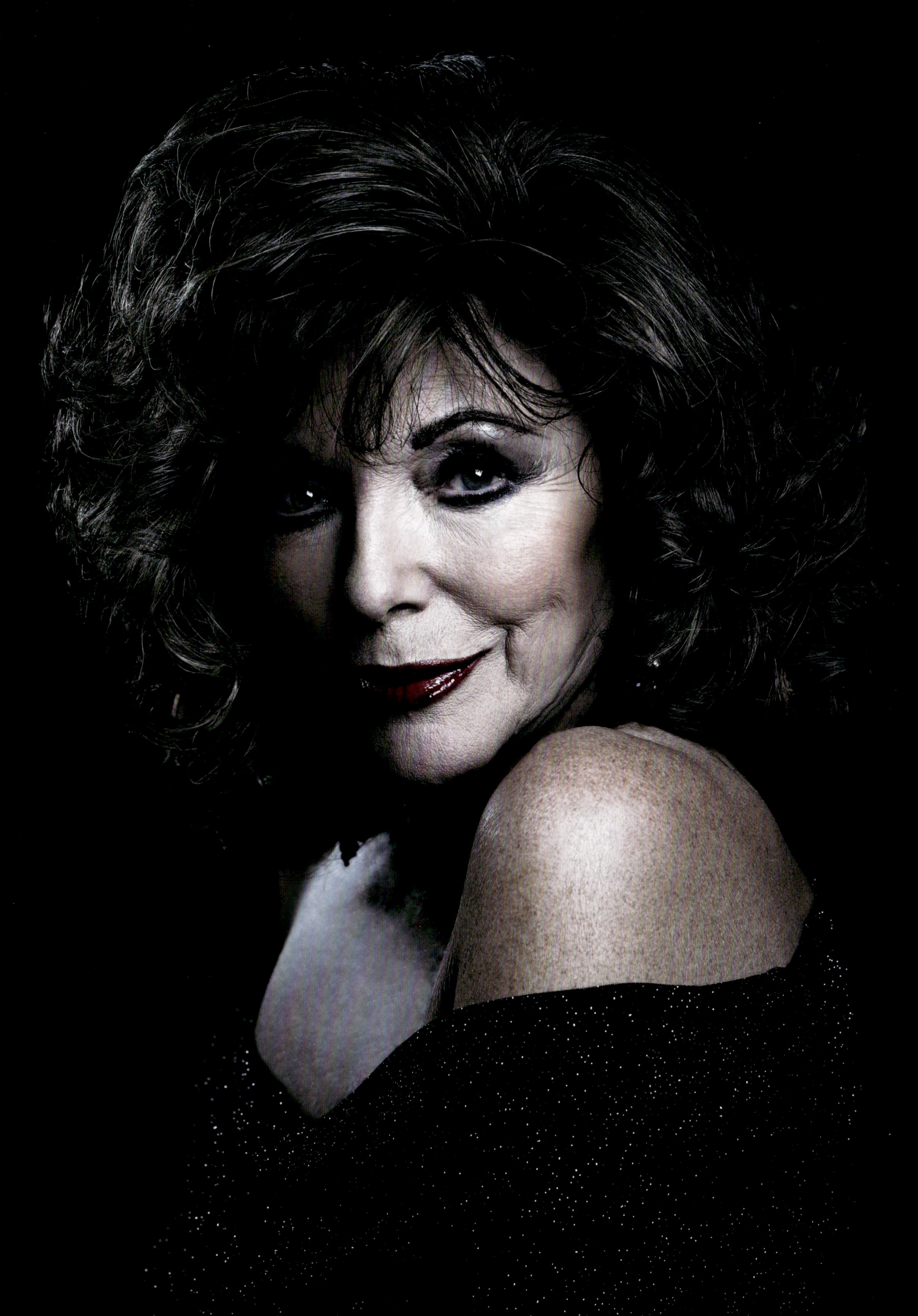

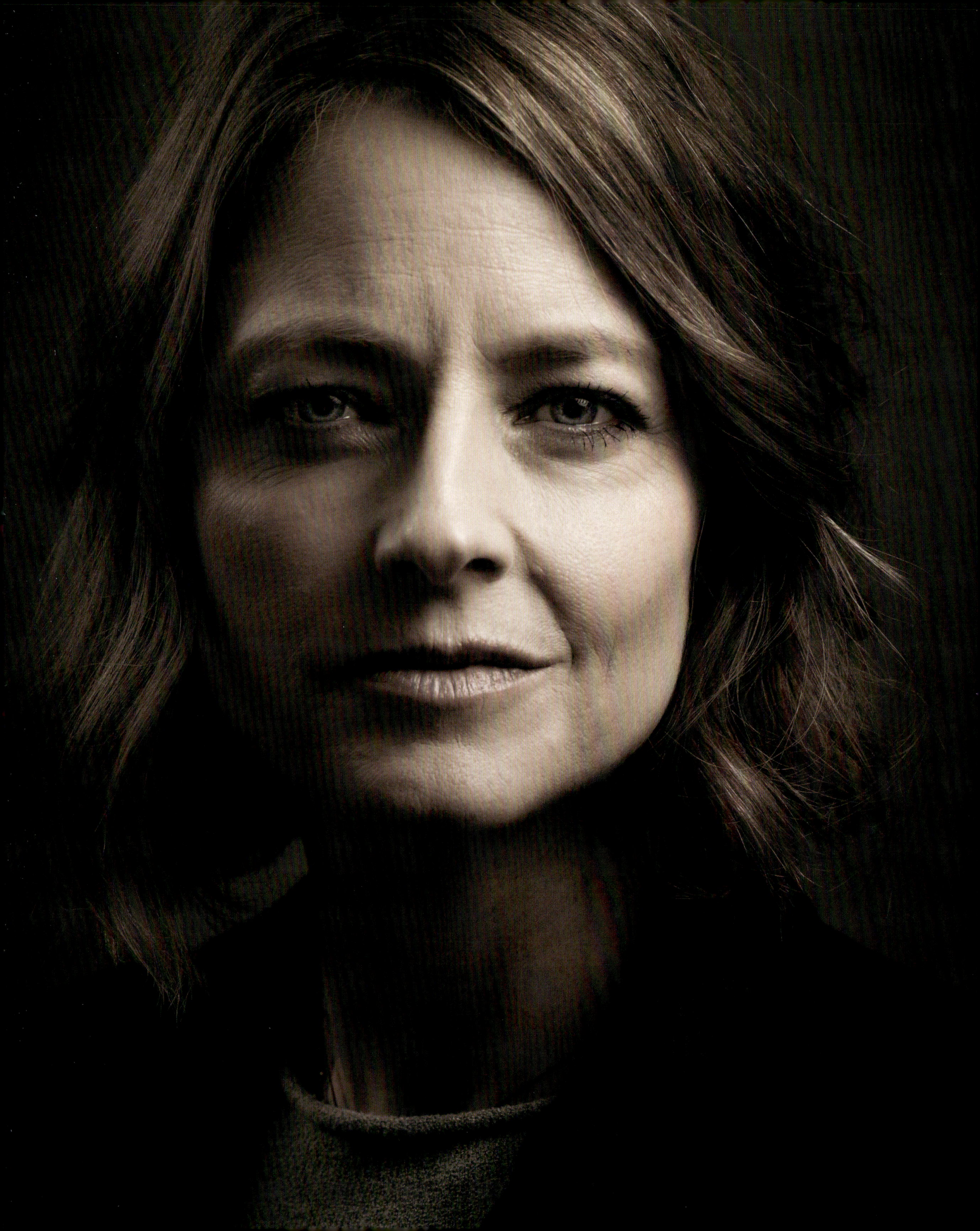

Jodie Foster

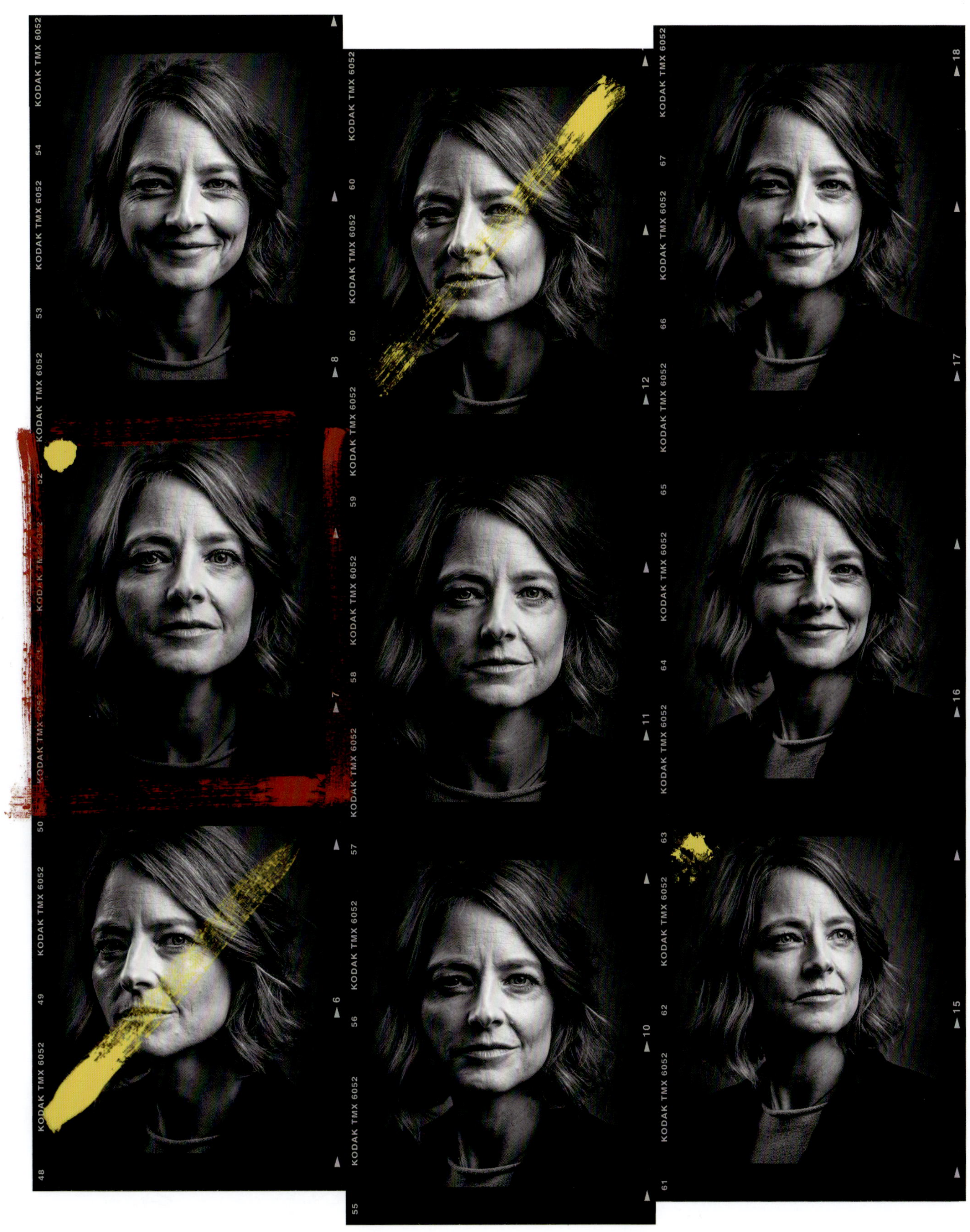

John Hurt

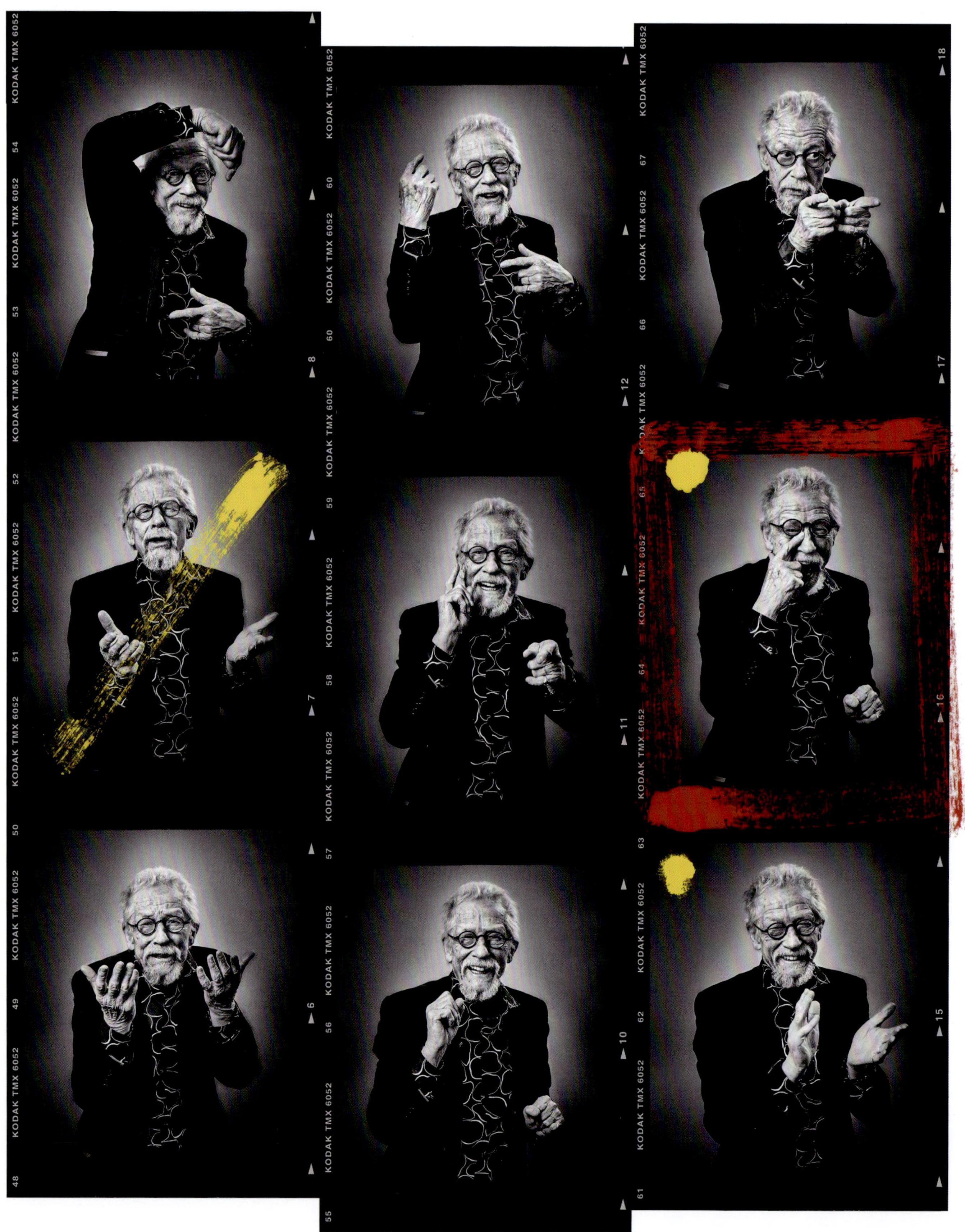

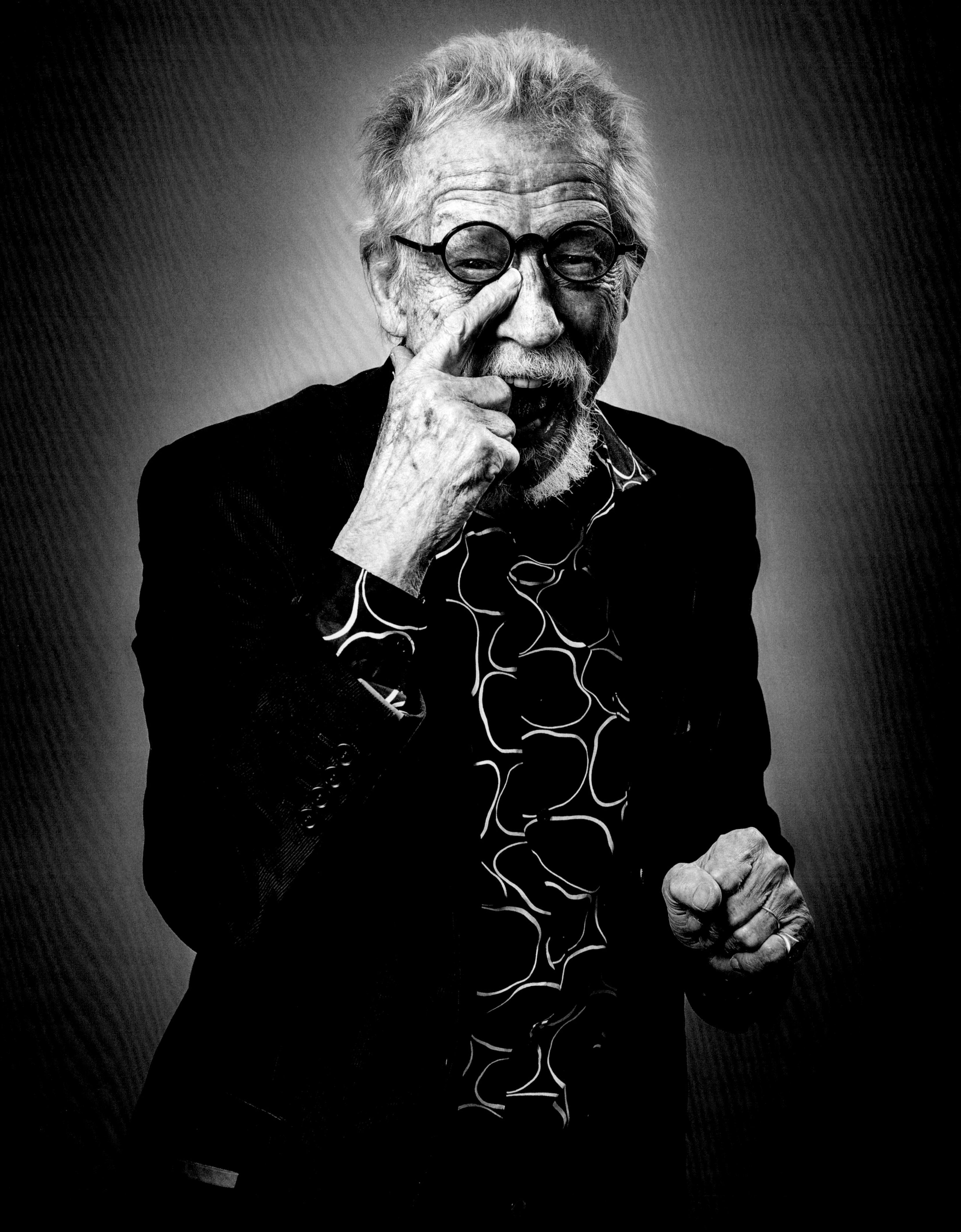

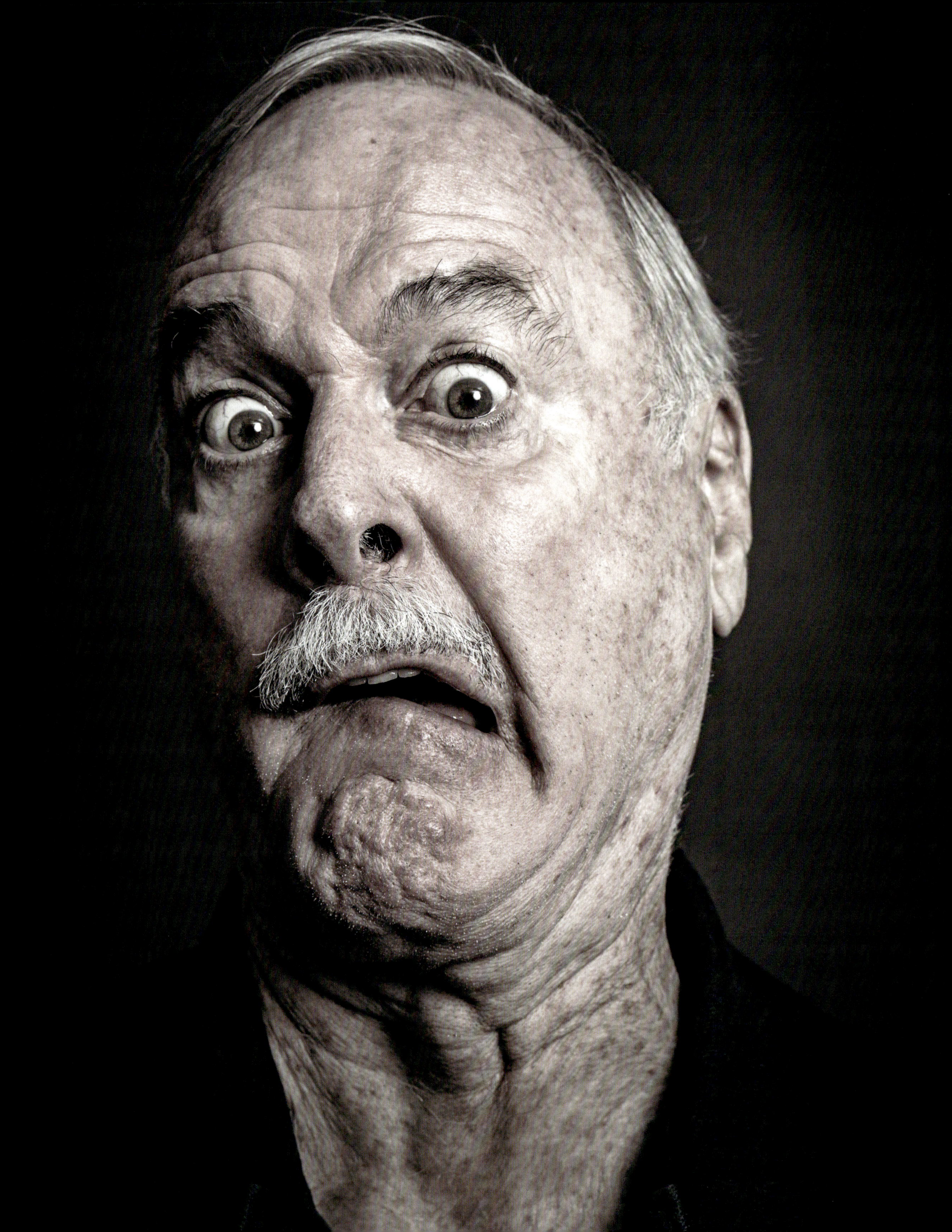

John Cleese

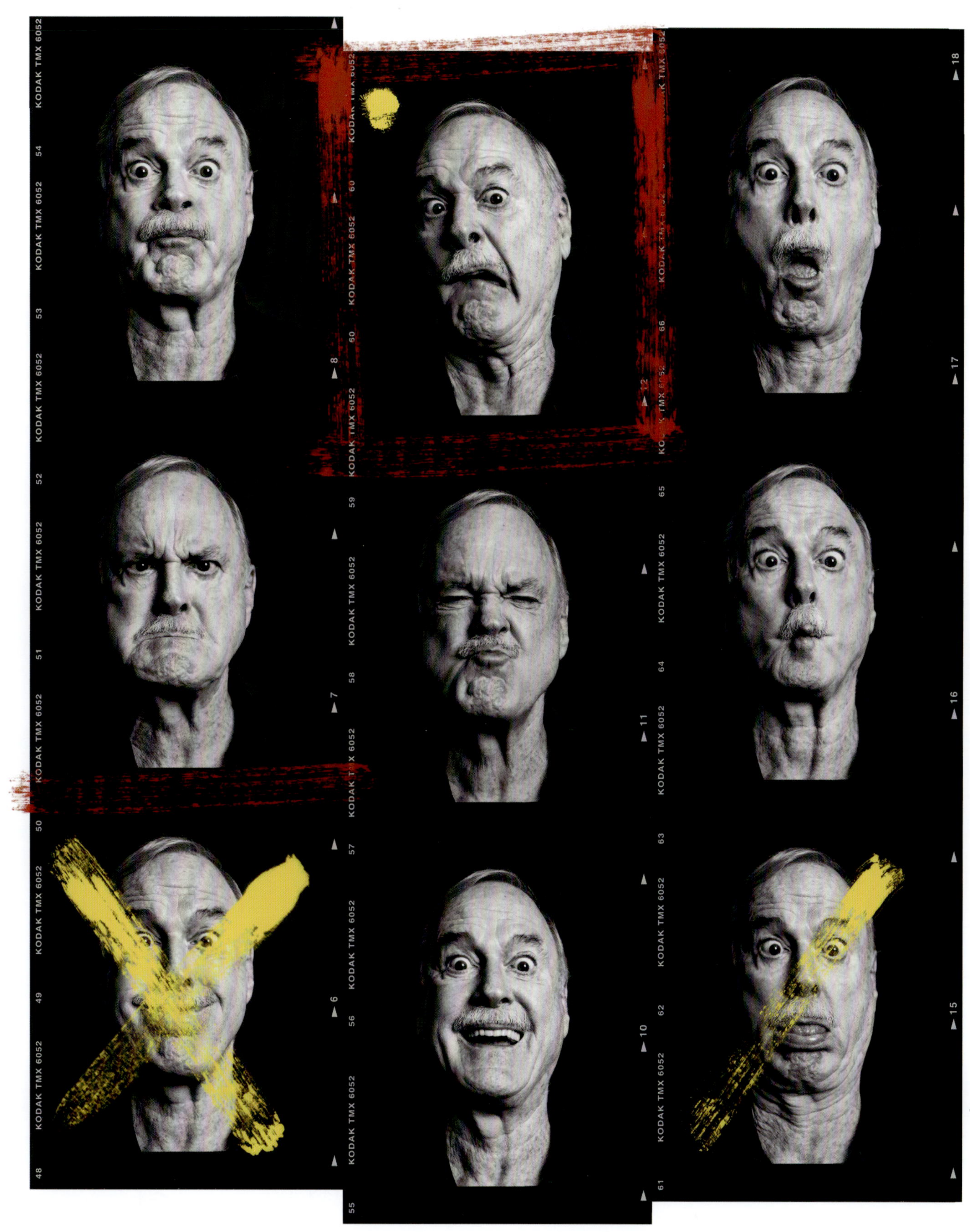

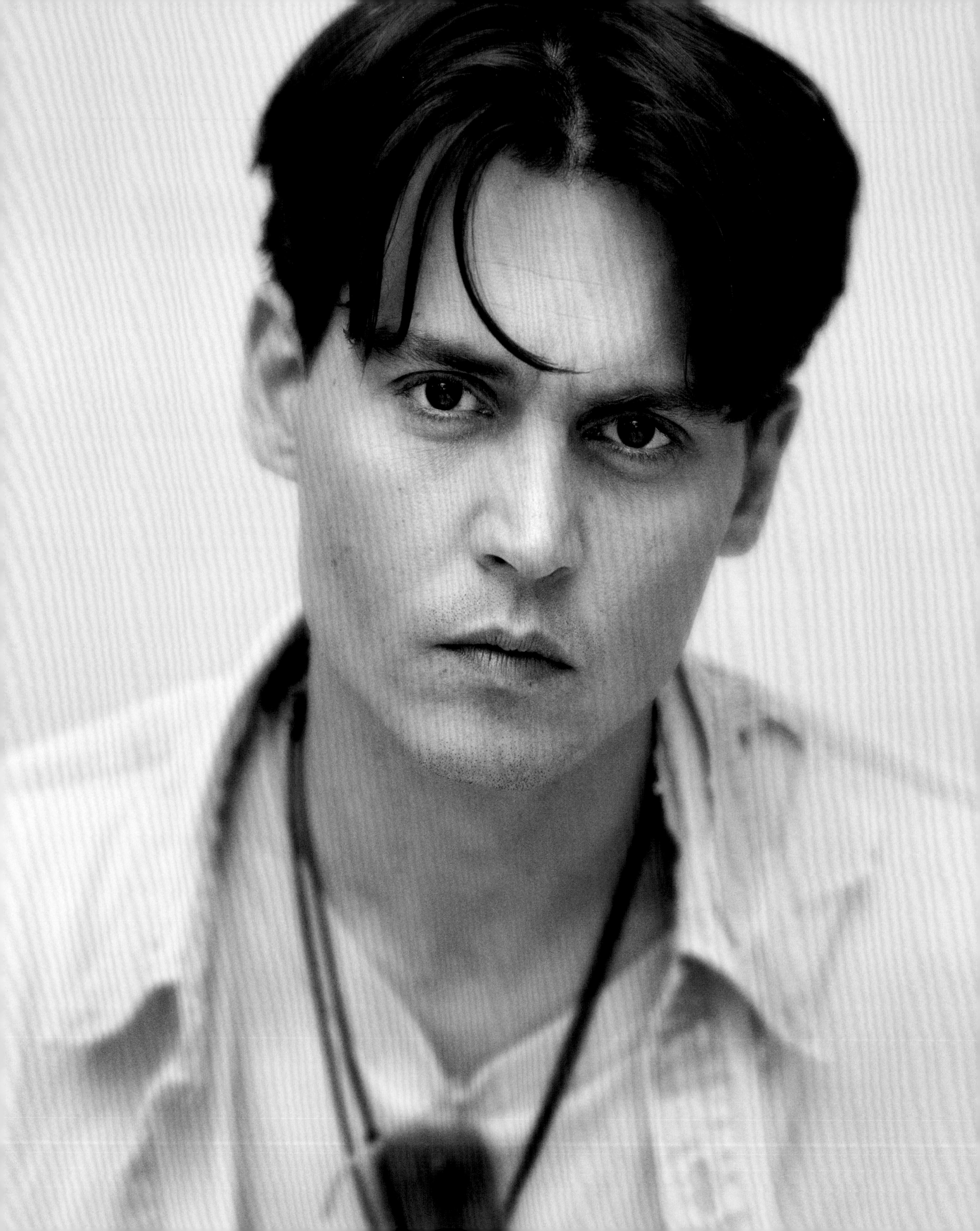

Johnny Depp

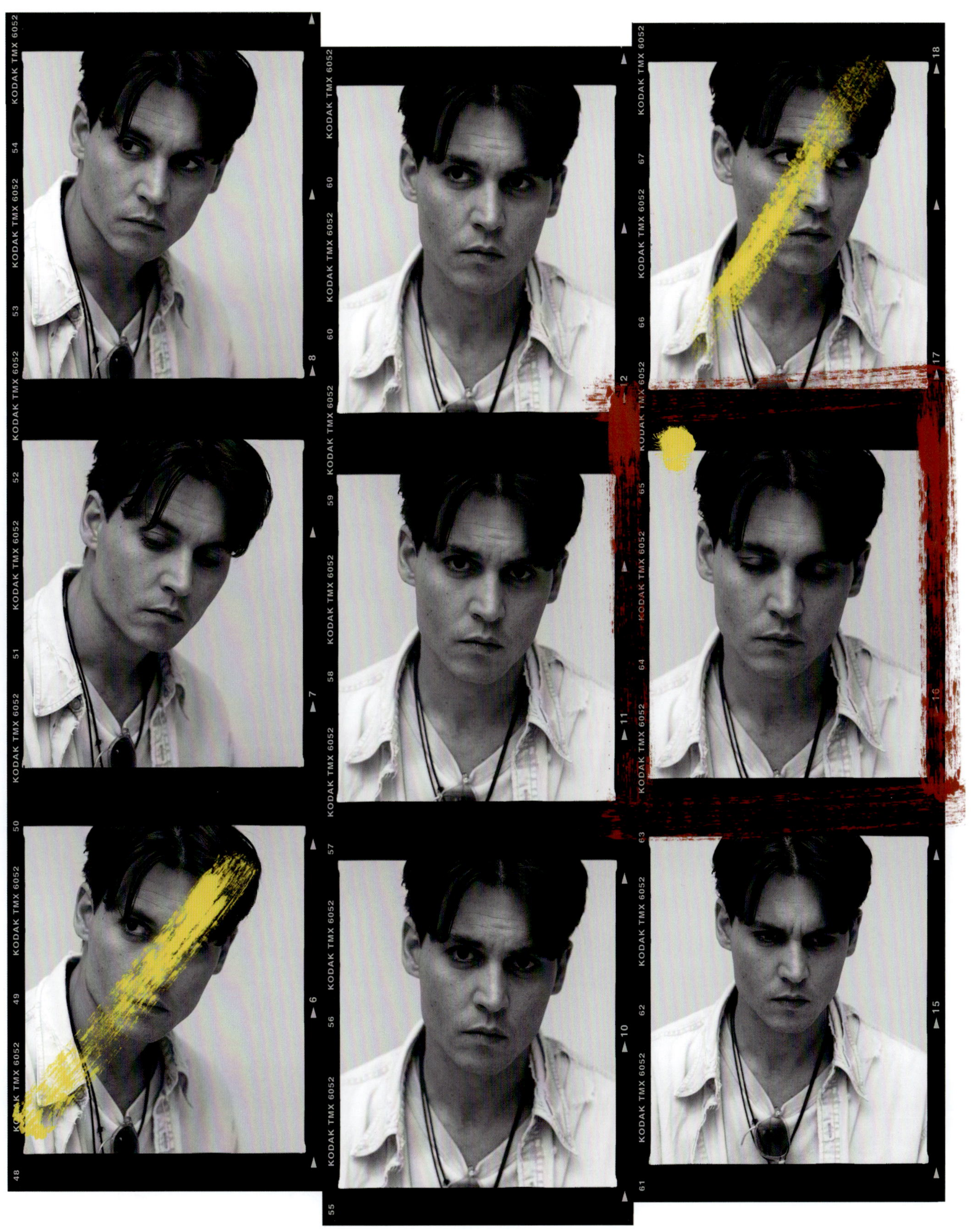

Jude Law

I met with Jude in a rehearsal room for a play that he was in called *Doctor Faustus*. When actors play a role, they often inhabit their character, so Jude arrived as the Doctor. We got more of the Doctor than Jude that day and I feel with Jude it's easier for him to play a part than for him to give away much of himself. The main observation I did make about Jude was that he was very conscious about how he looked, especially his thinning hair. However generally I came away not knowing who Jude was, just that he wasn't the Doctor.

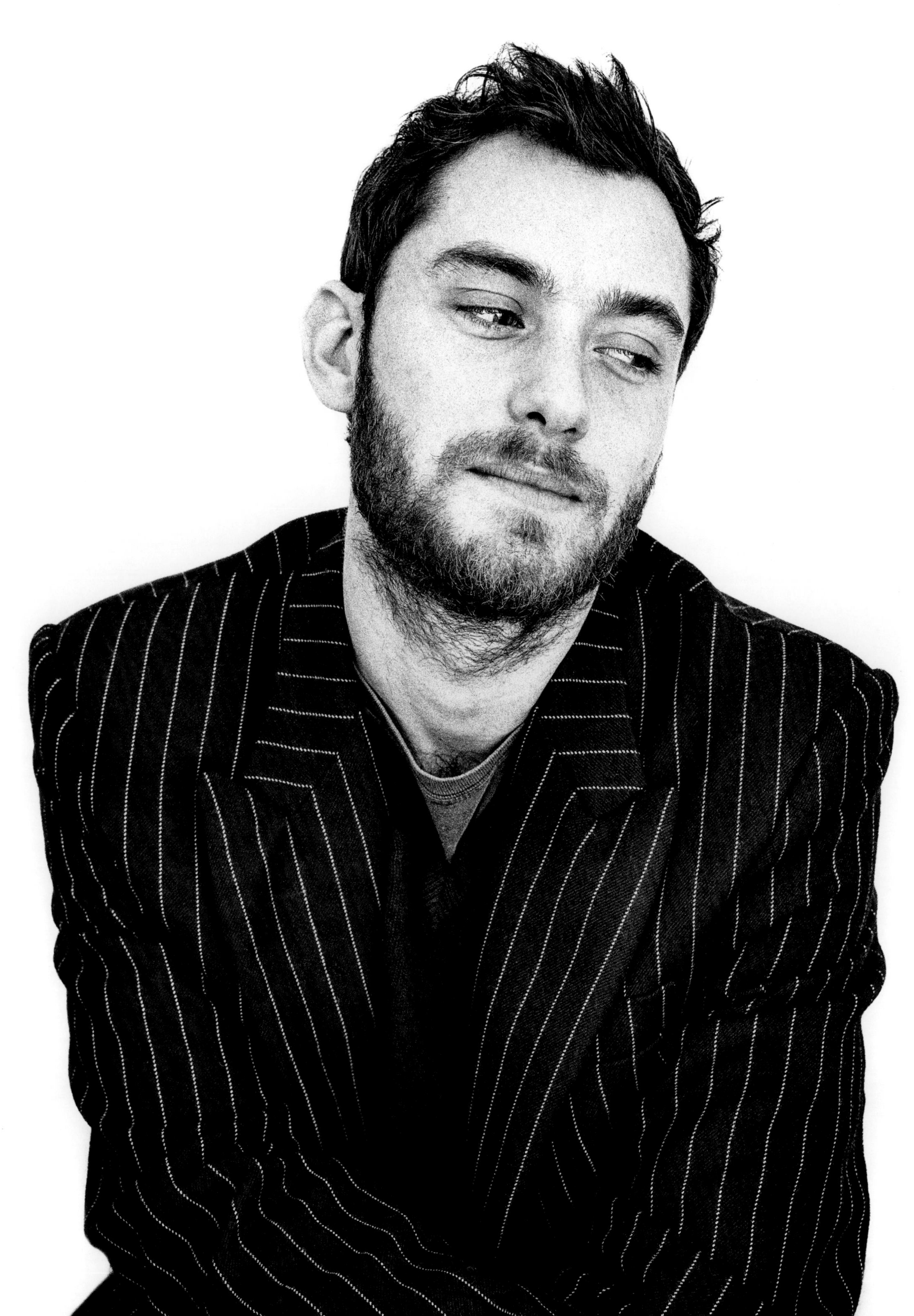

Judi Dench

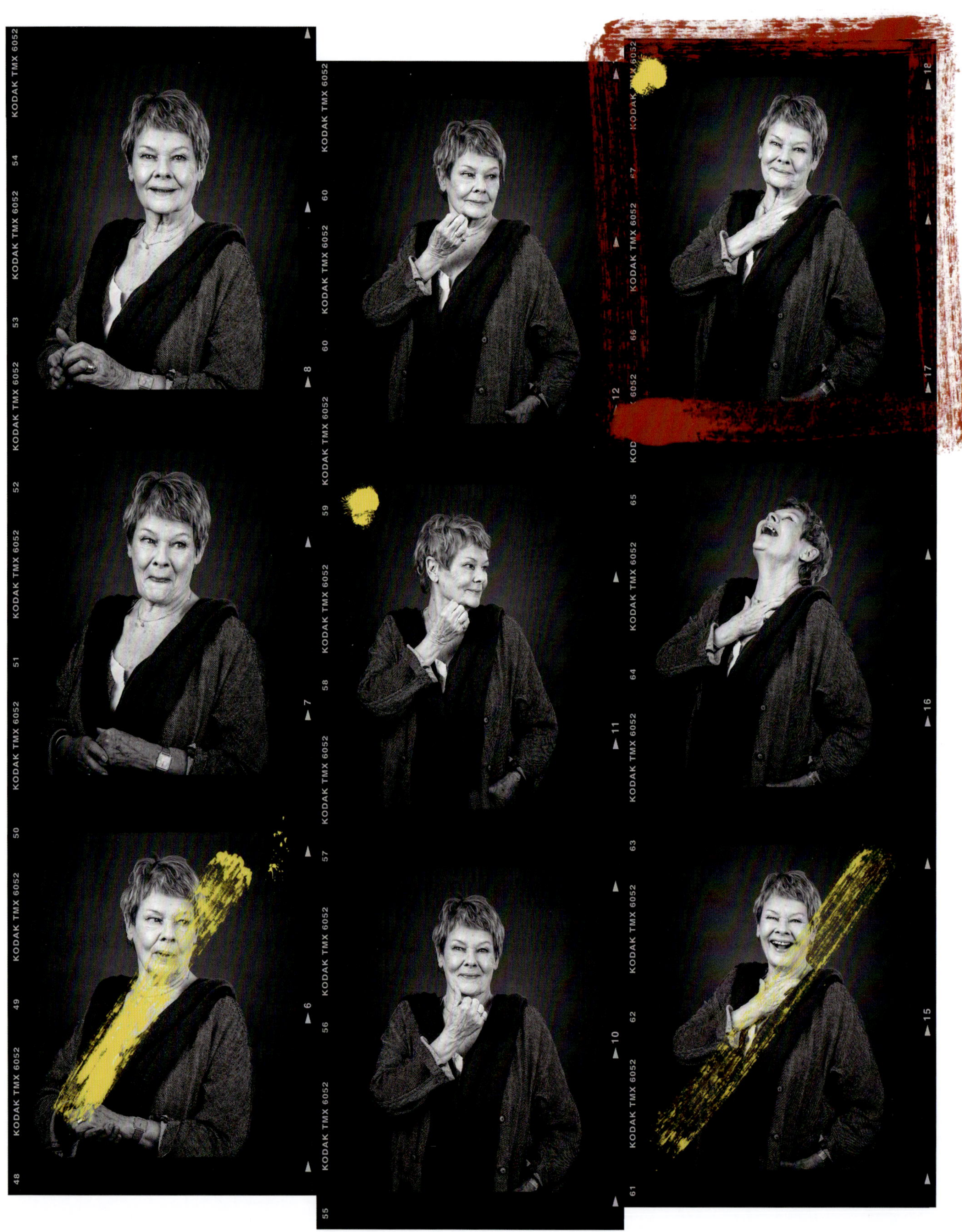

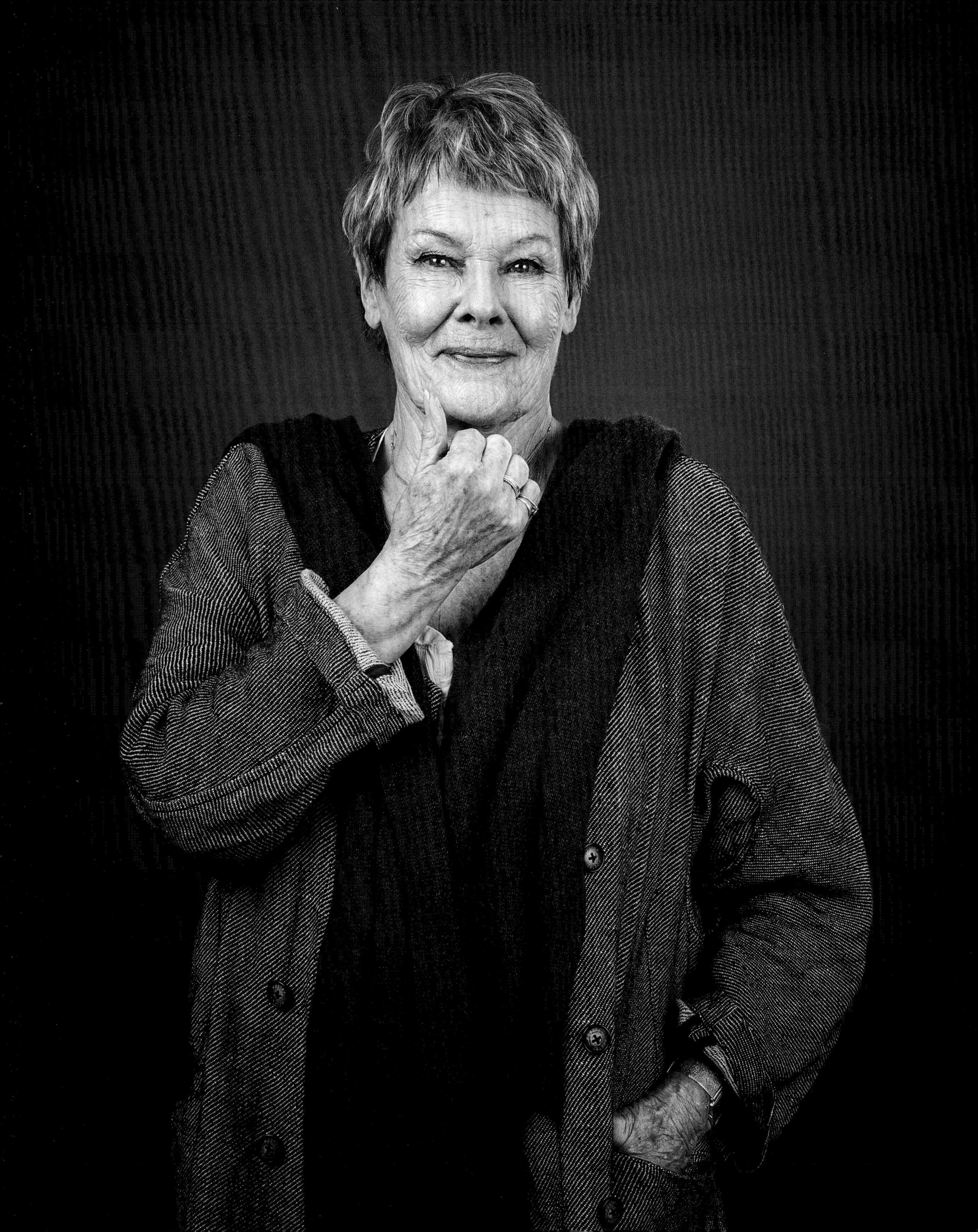

Julia Roberts

I shot Julia at Elstree Studios while she was filming *Closer*. I remember when I initially called Julia's publicist, Marcy, she told me Julia never did these sorts of projects; so I was a little surprised the very next day when she called back saying Julia had agreed to take part. The shoot was originally arranged for New York, but her schedule changed and it was decided that it would be better to wait until she was in London. I had never been to Elstree before and it was a bizarre place. You looked in one direction and you saw Albert Square from *Eastenders*, and in the other direction you had the *Big Brother* house. I was informed I would not have much time with Julia, about 10-15 minutes as she was doing a makeup test for the film, so I erected two backgrounds: a white one for a fashion-style shot and a black one for a more classic shot. Julia came in and started to instantly mother me ... asking if I was warm enough and did I want a cup of tea or anything. But she was very gracious and she really helped me to get some good shots – such as flicking her head around to give her hair movement, as I didn't have a wind machine.

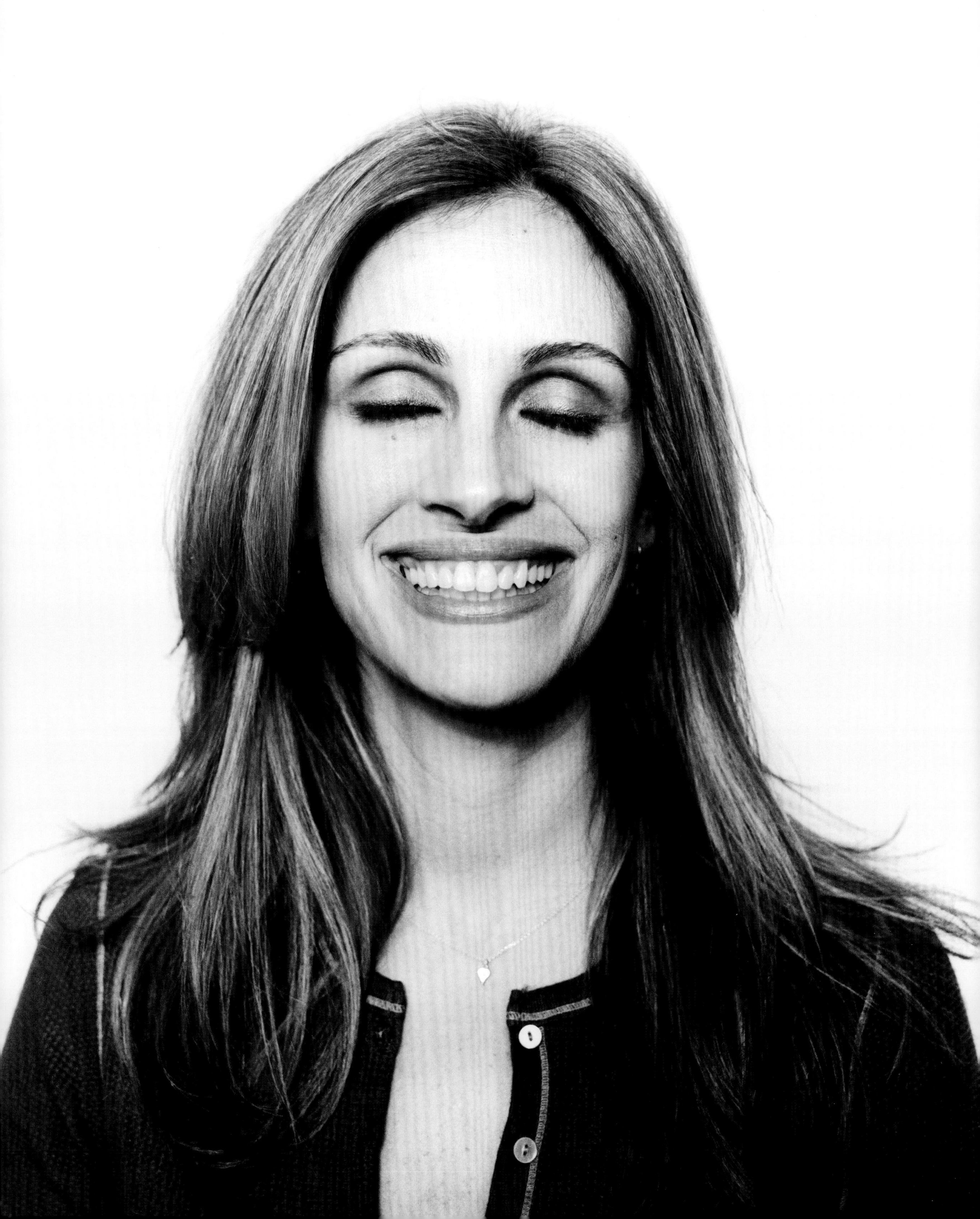

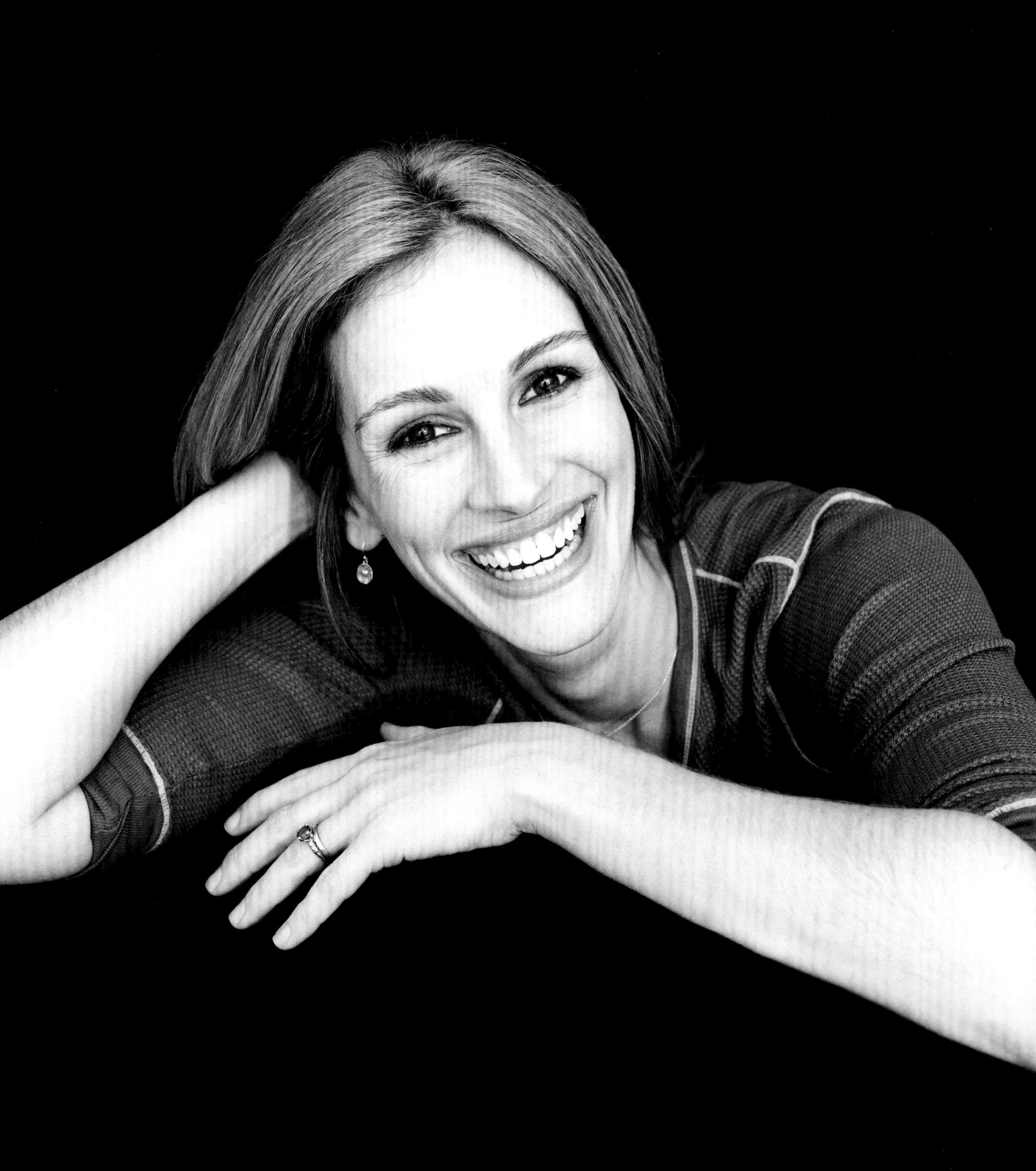

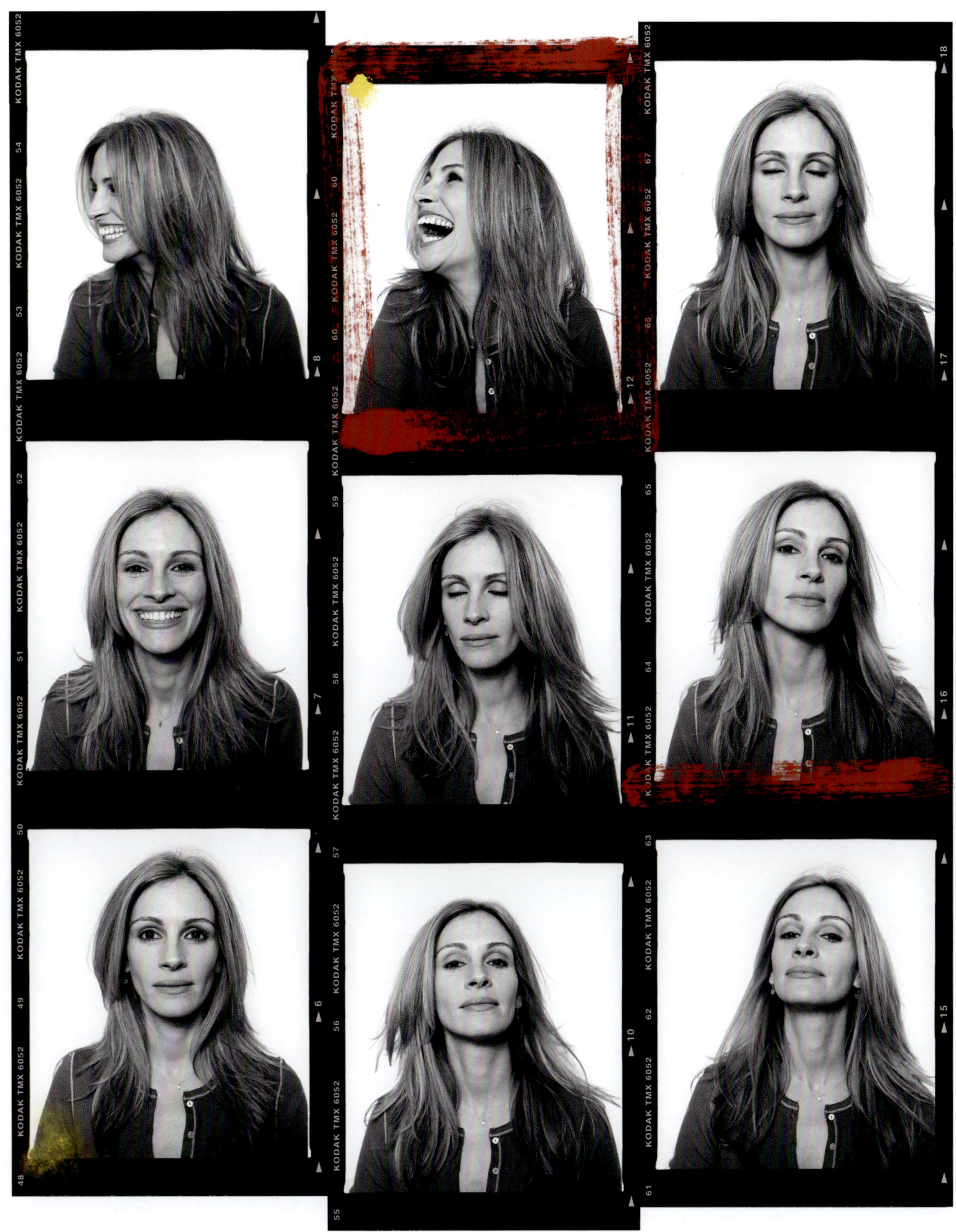
KODAK TMX 6052

Kate Moss

I wanted Kate's image to be more of a portrait than a fashion shoot. I don't think people realise how important Kate Moss is and what she has done for the art scene. She is a muse for every artist. If you do not have her in your arsenal you are missing out. There are some supermodels who act like supermodels. Kate Moss acts like Kate Moss. Kate is everything you want her to be. She answers the door to her house with a glass of wine in one hand and cigarette in another. She sits down on the sofa and tells rude stories about her mates. I wanted the focus of my shoot to be on her and not what she was wearing. She isn't that attractive in person but she just takes an incredible photo. People believe it's those with symmetry in their faces that take the best photos. I believe it is combination of elements, the right lens, the image set up and the right face. Kate has a broad face with uneven eyes. Her face is odd-looking but she knows her angles and with the right camera and photographer she takes iconic images. The common factor when shooting all models is their impatience on a set and without fail they will all say at some point "I'm sure you've got it by now".

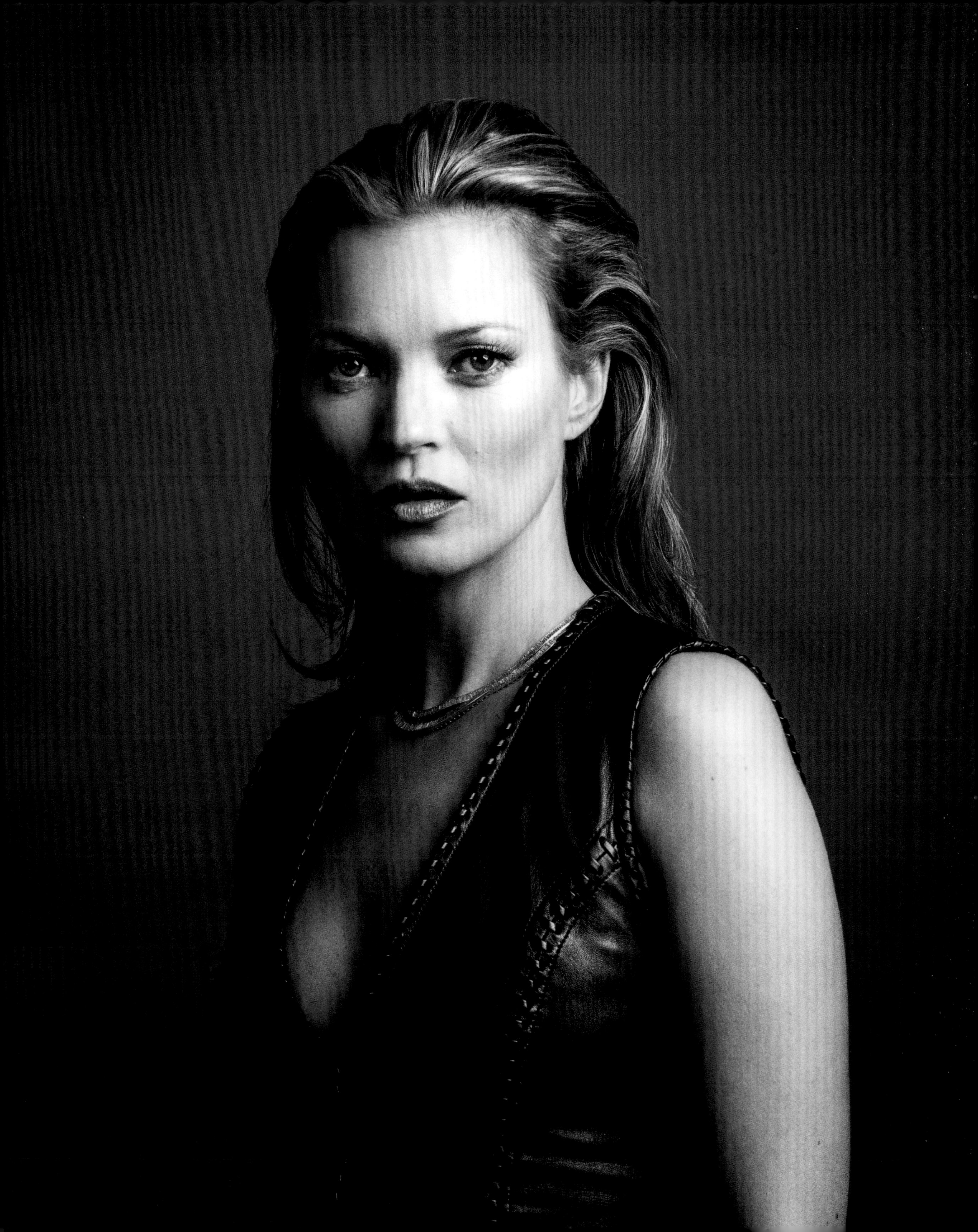

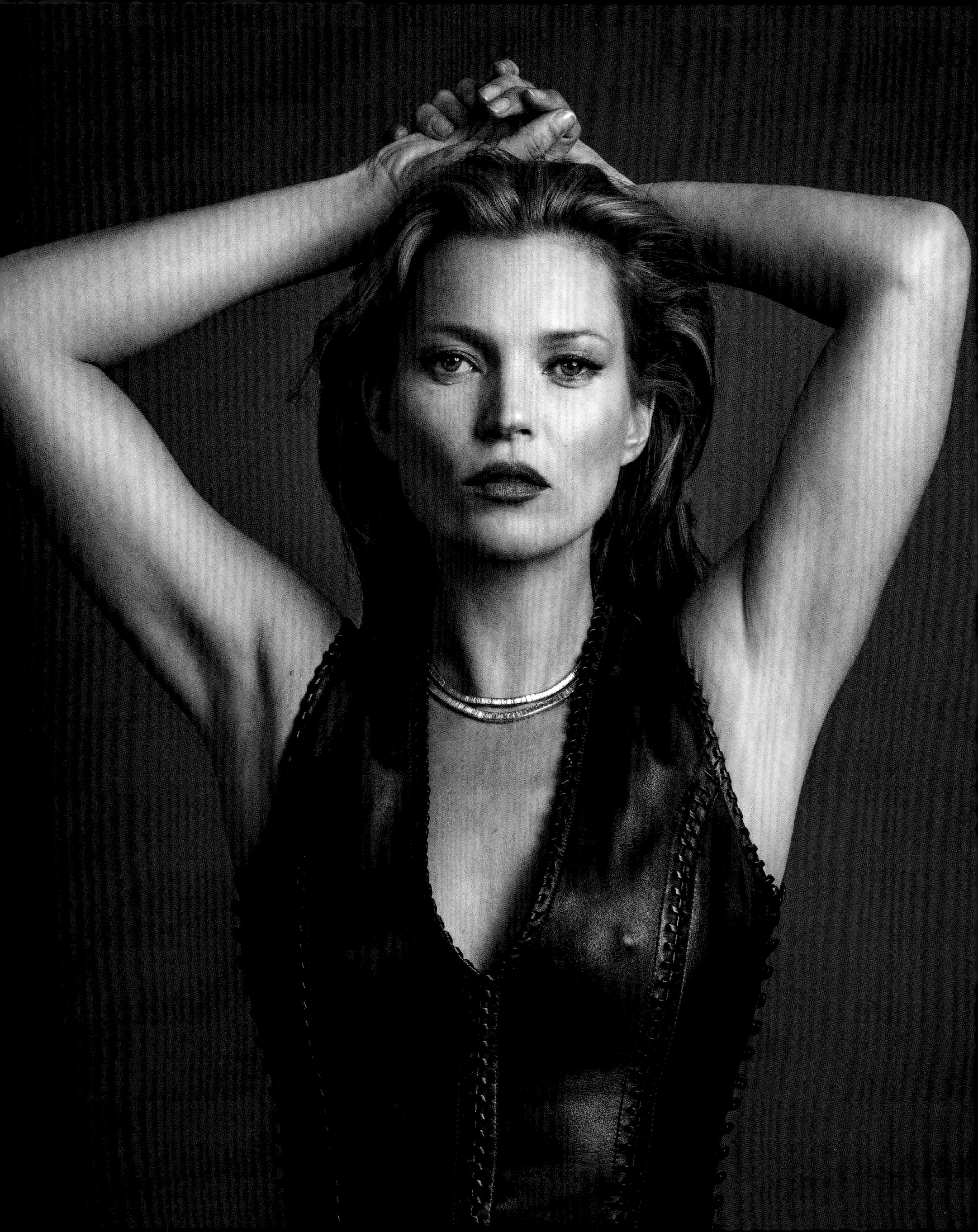

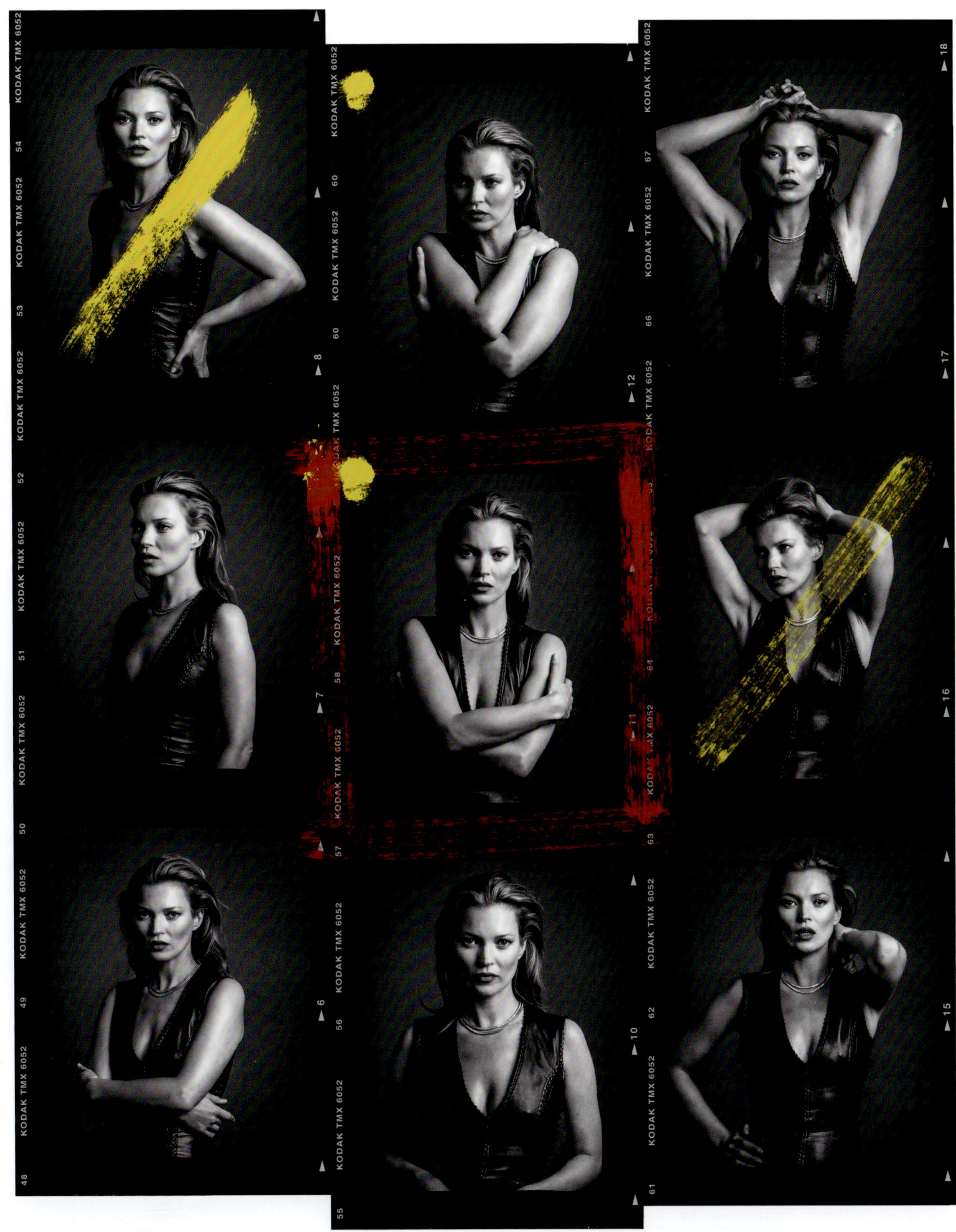
KODAK TMX 6052

Kate Winslet

Photography has been a blessing in my life. Not just because I have the pleasure of creating some lovely images and meeting many exceptional people; but now and again, I meet someone that becomes a friend ... and this is the case with Kate. Over the years, I have shot Kate sooooo many times its untrue.

This specific contact sheet I love, as Kate was in such a good place and on cloud nine in life. She was eight and a half months pregnant with her son, Bear. Kate was so happy and playful, and we laughed throughout the unplanned shoot. When I look at these shots, I can see our beautiful friendship reflected in them.

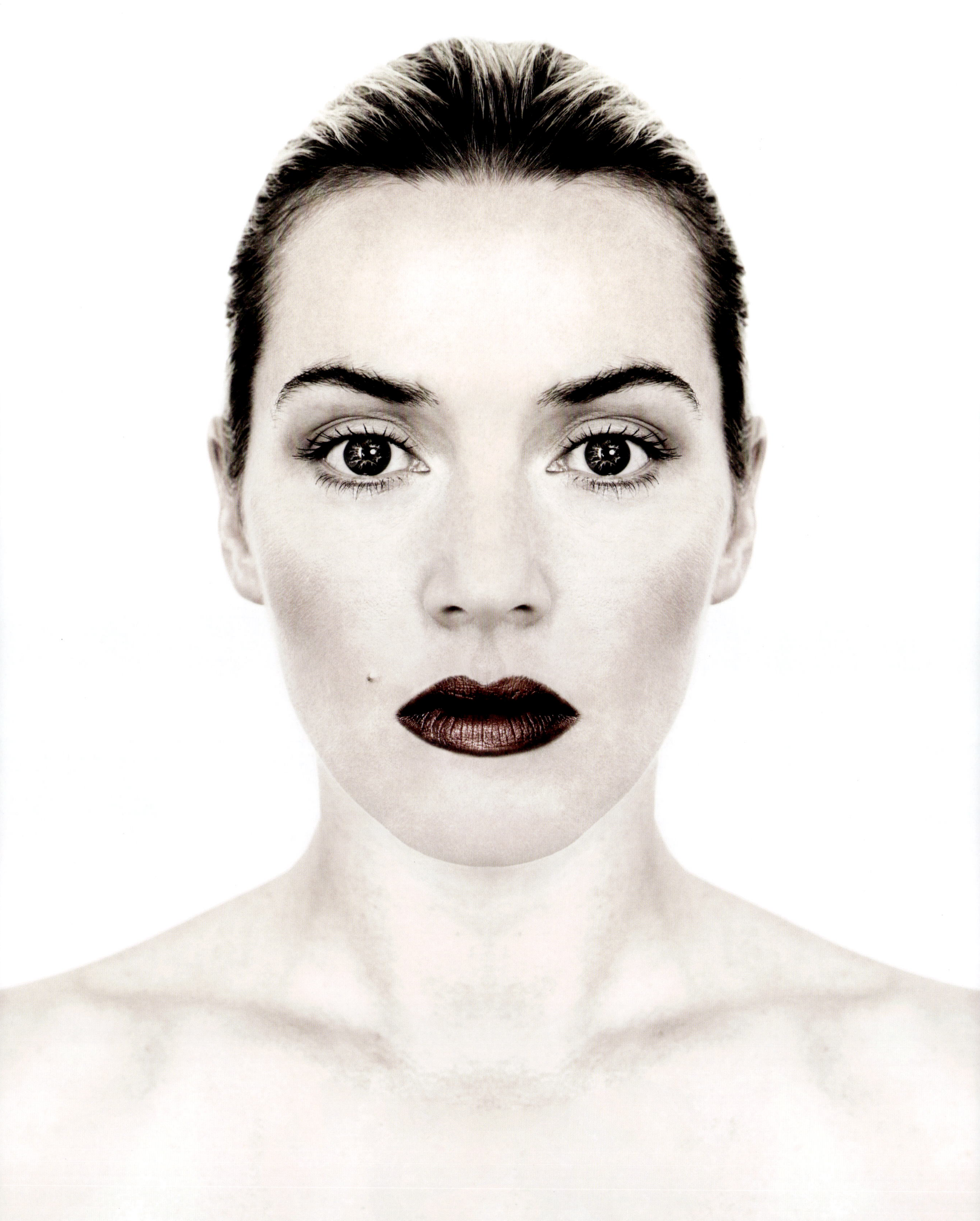

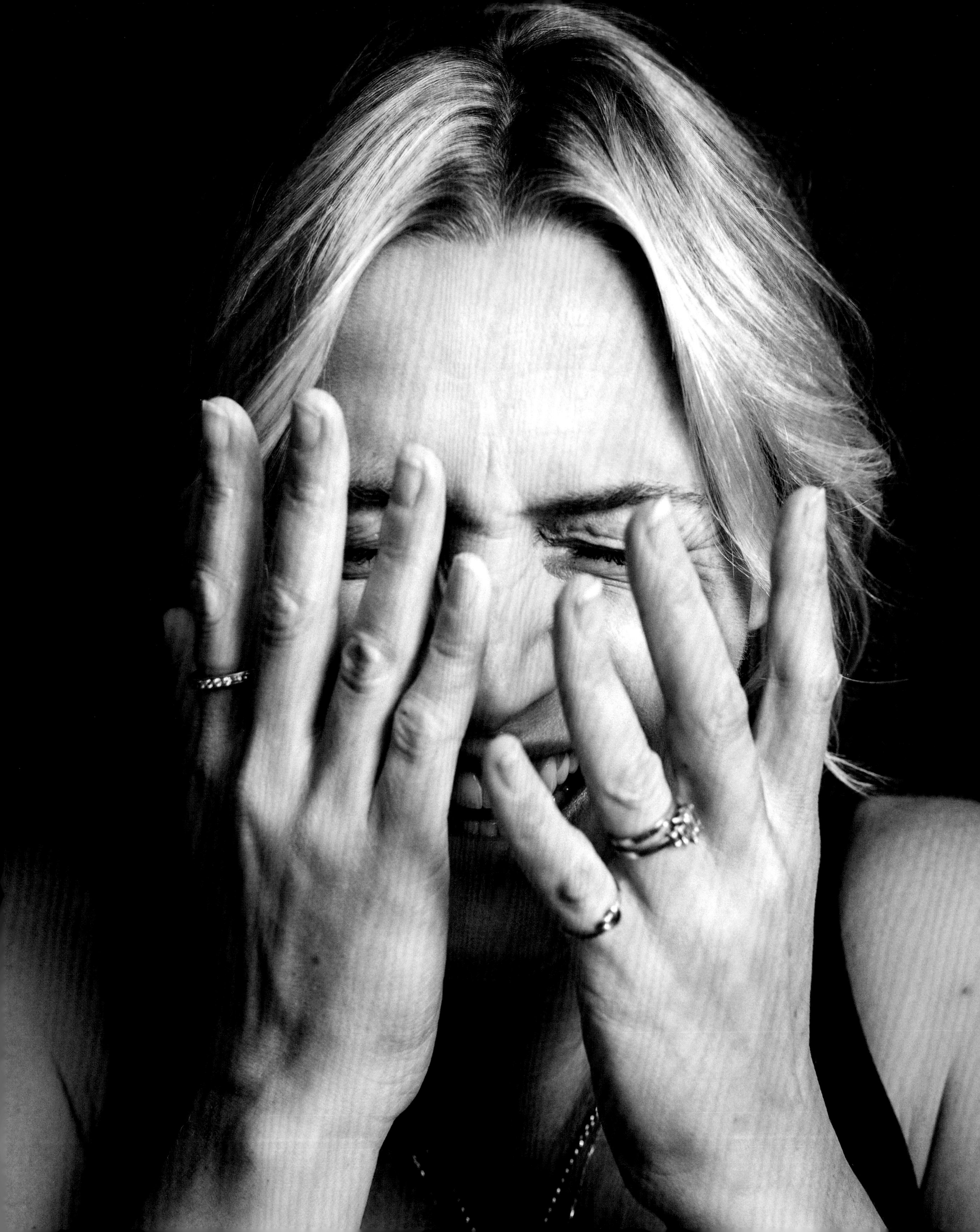

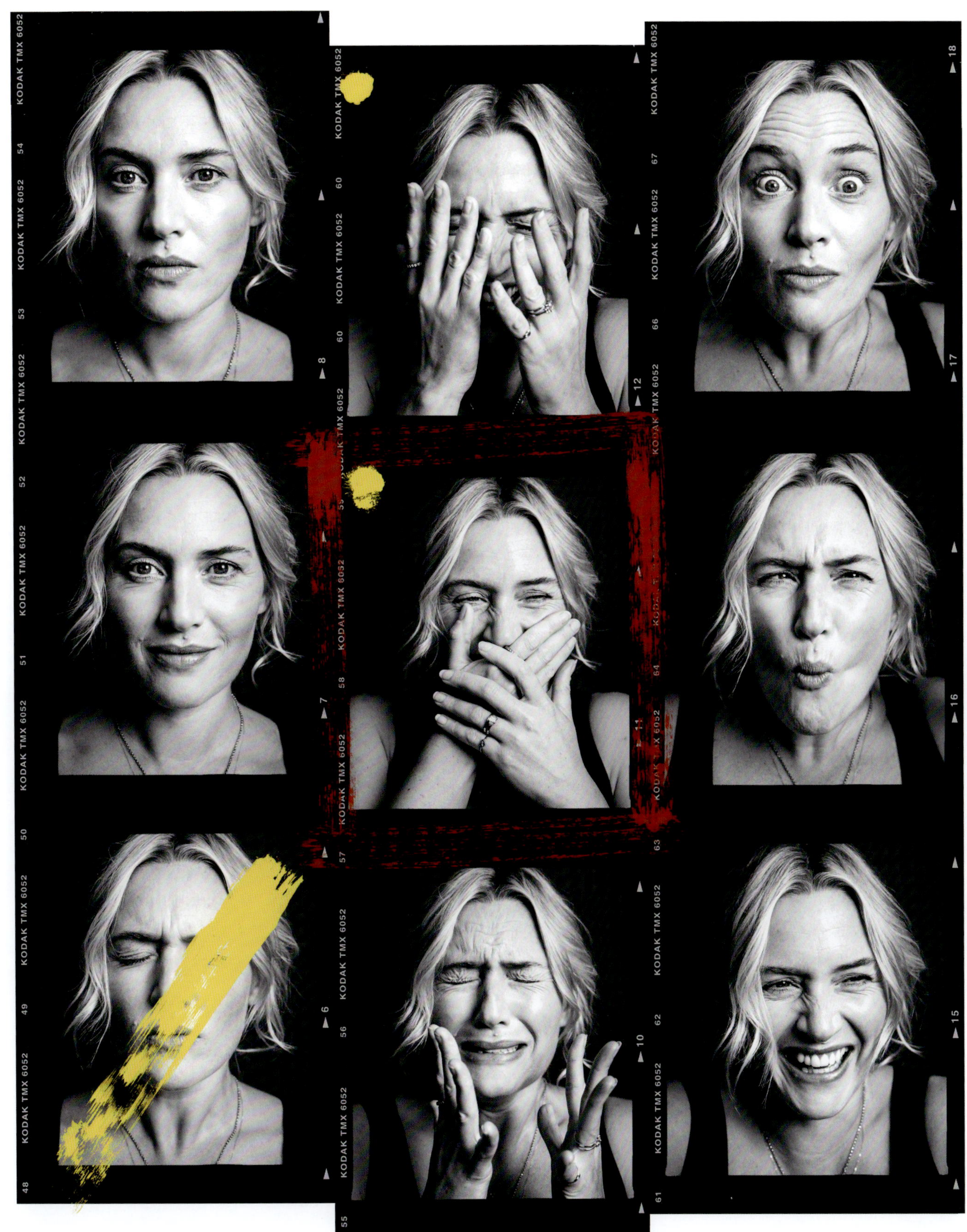
KODAK TMX 6052

Keira Knightley

I shot Keira in London and I was a little shocked when she turned up to the shoot, and this was due to the juxtaposition between the US- and UK-based actresses. If had done the shoot with a nineteen-year-old American starlet, I have no doubt she would have had at least one or two chaperones with her, but this was not the case with Keira. She bounded across the foyer of the Savoy, on her own, with a big grin on her face. It was like a breath of fresh air during the shoot, and to say Keira was 'wise beyond her years' would be an understatement. On a separate note, she has been one of the youngest people I have shot.

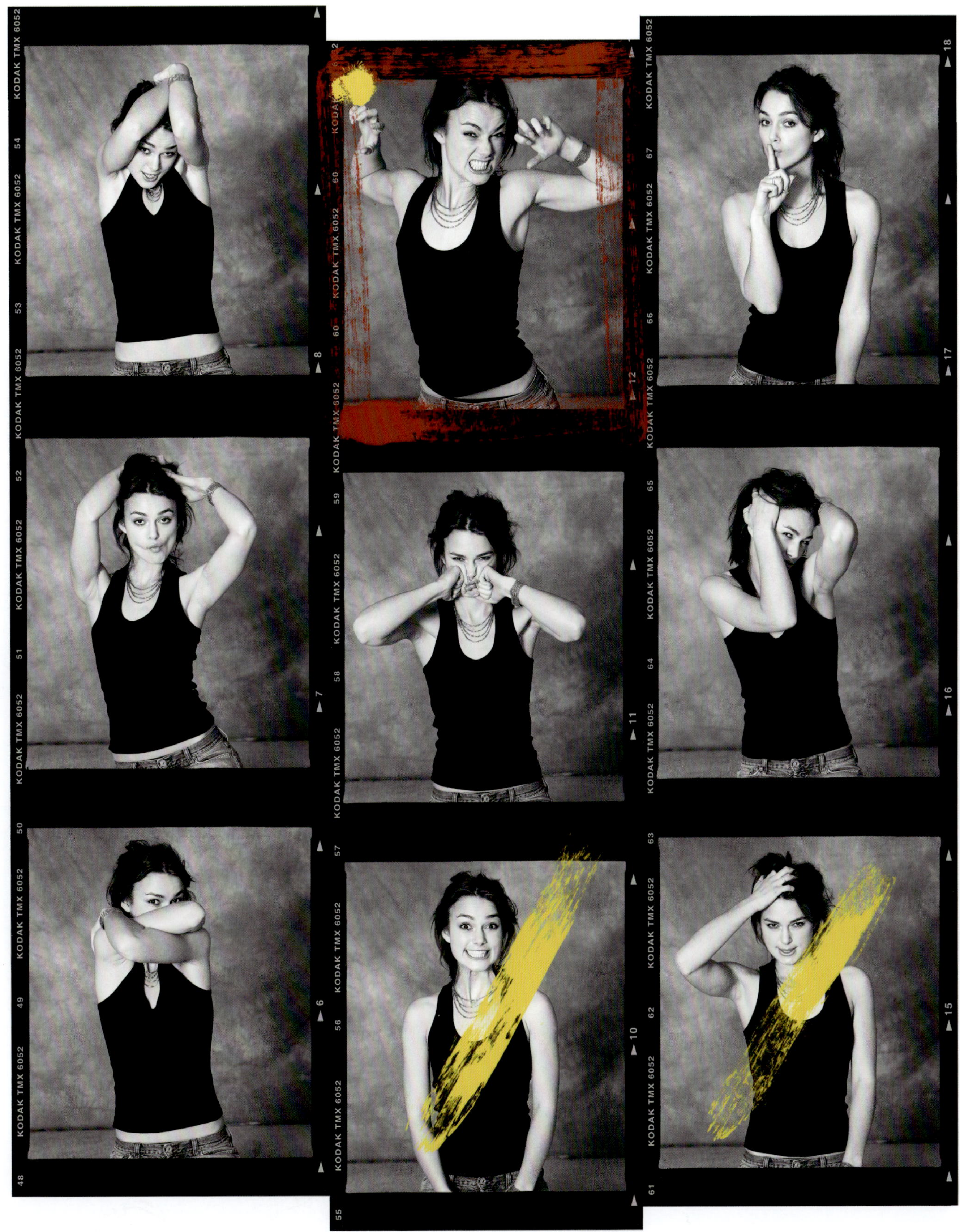

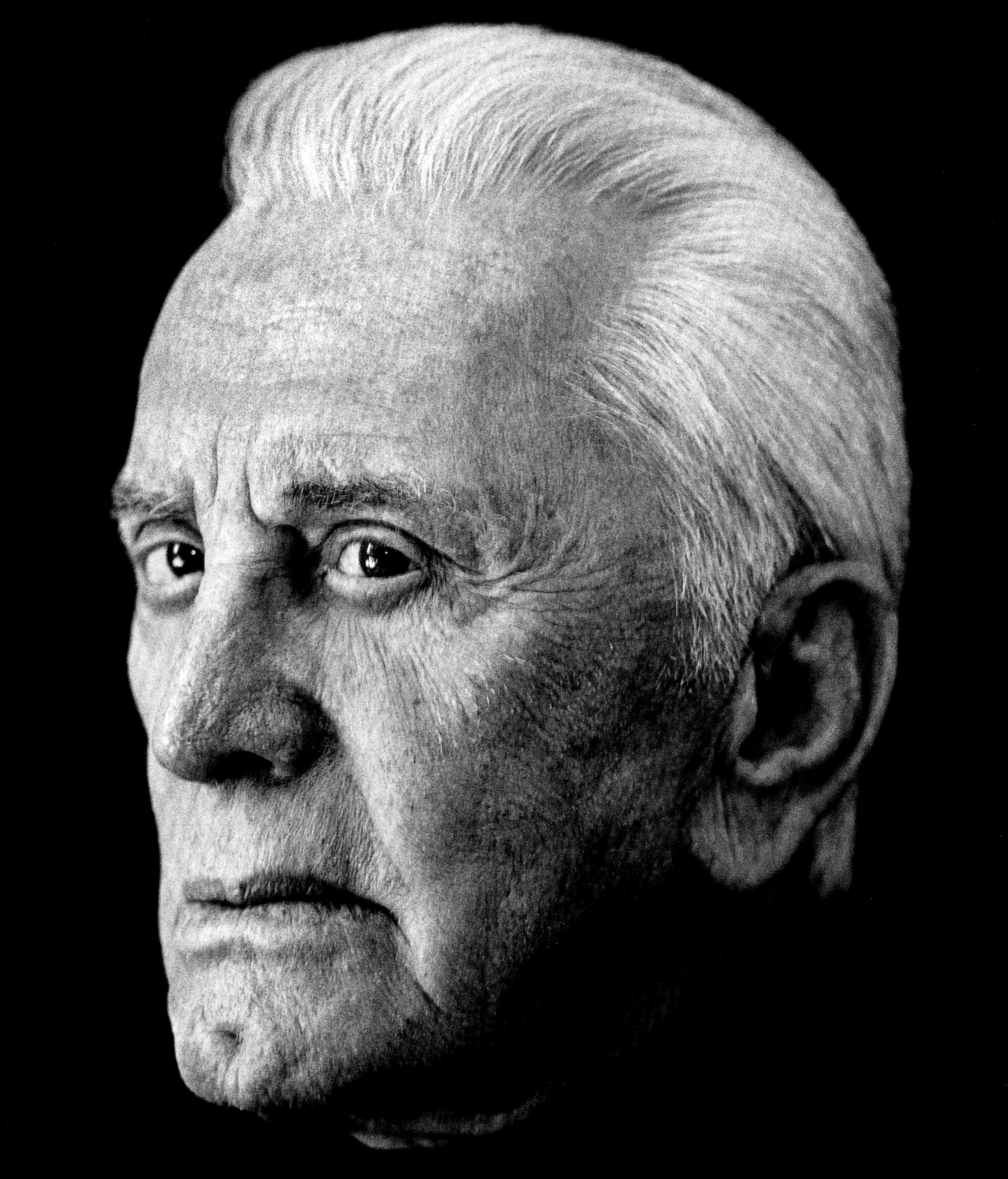

Kirk Douglas

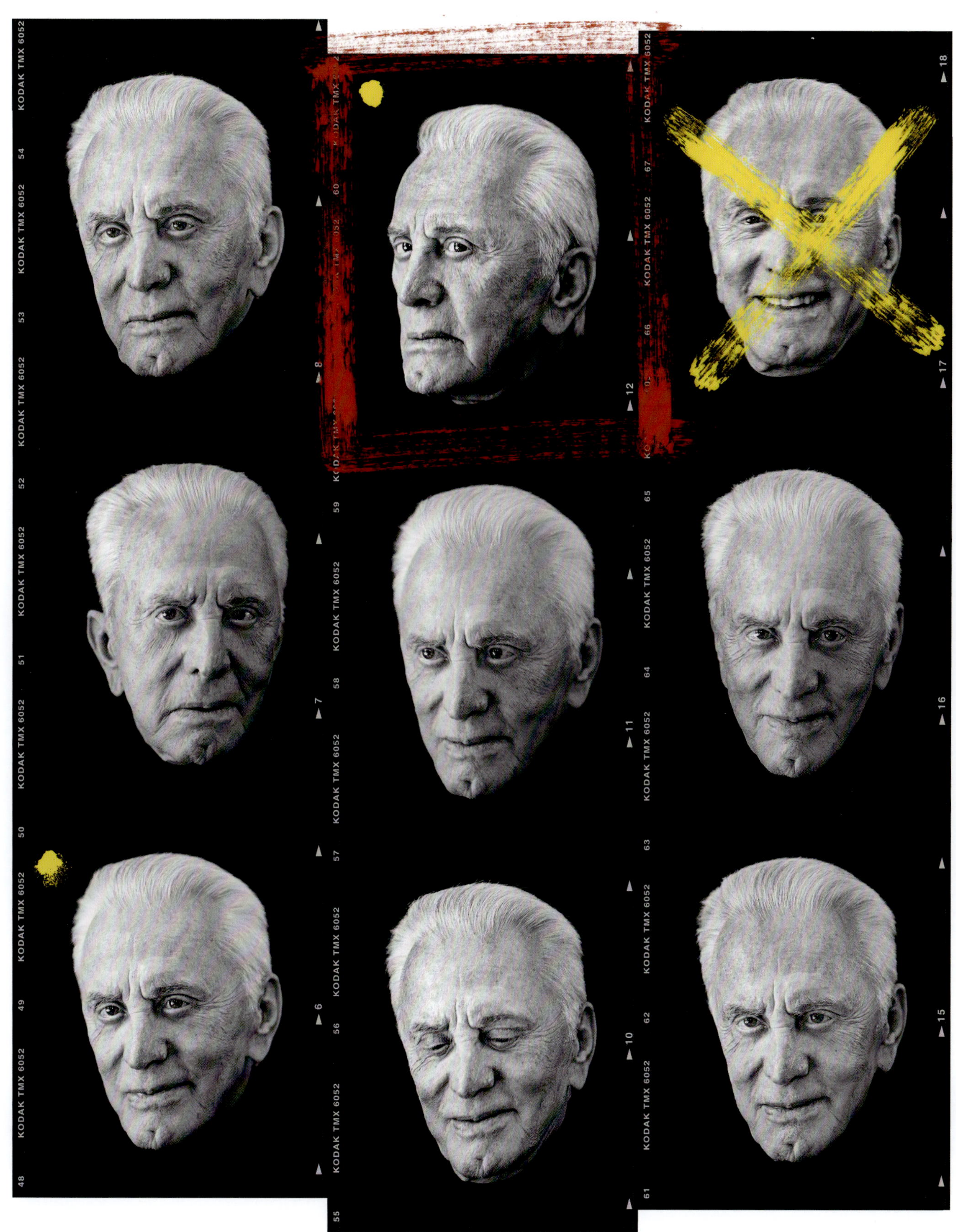

Lauren Bacall

Ms Bacall lived in the famous Dakota Building in NY, made infamous for the killing of John Lennon on the steps outside. Due to this fact, photography and filming are not allowed in the building at all. I was told I would have to disguise my equipment and go to the building under the guise of being a friend stopping by for a visit. I took the minimal amount of equipment and packed it into two small bags, to enable me to take a close-up head and shoulders portrait and climbed the stairs to her apartment. Owing to a double hip operation, Ms Bacall was not able to manoeuvre far, so I suggested that I set up where she was sitting and just used a piece of black velvet as a backdrop. Ms Bacall entertained me with stories of Bogie, Katharine Hepburn and Spencer Tracy, whilst chain-smoking and eating pistachio nuts. When I was ready to do a lighting test, I just asked her to look at the camera and I took one shot. And it was this one shot that turned out to be my favourite, a non-smiling, totally naked and stripped-back portrait.

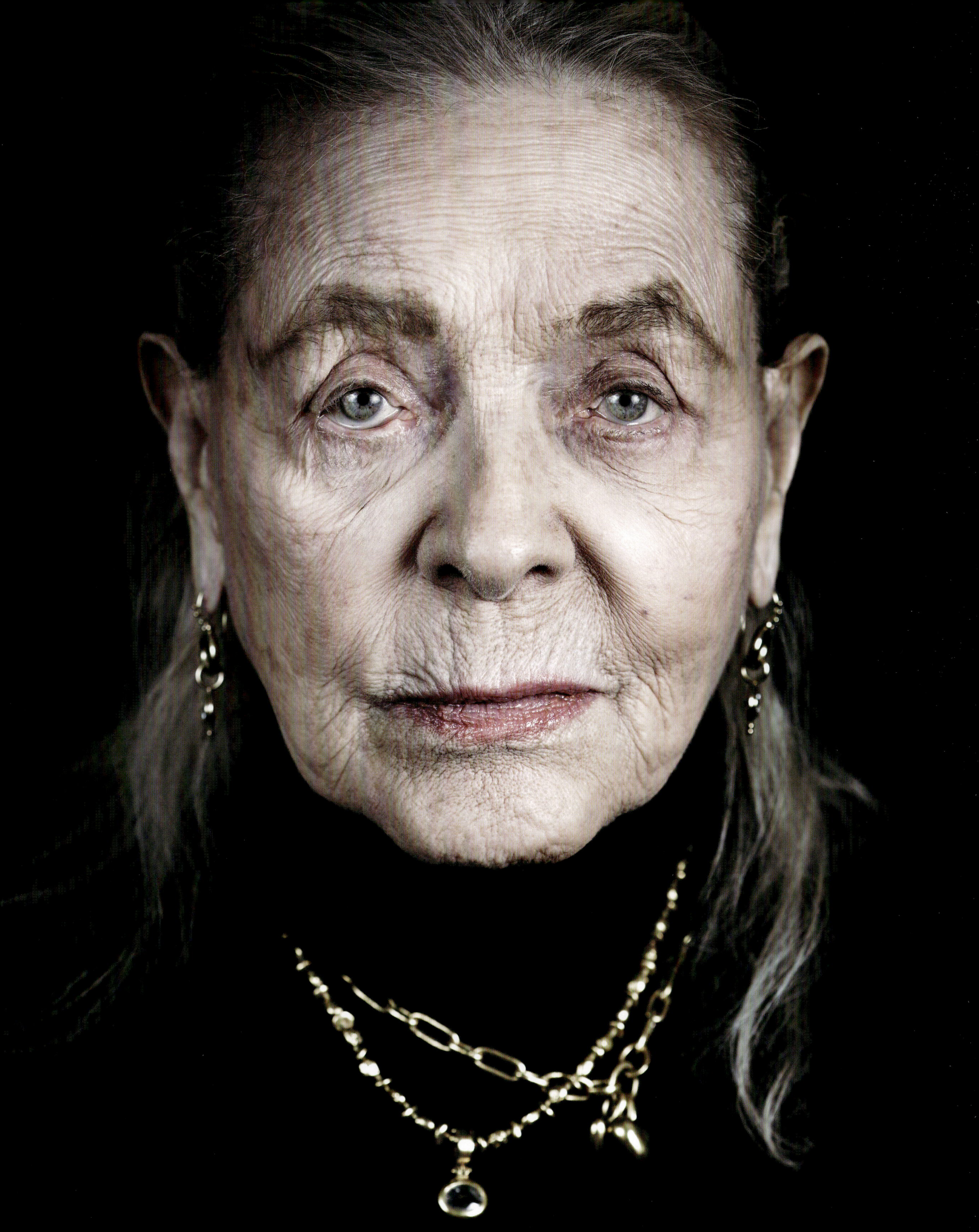

Lester Piggott

You can count on the toes of Long John Silver how many sports people I have ever shot. My forte has always been actors, with the occasional musician thrown in. But for some reason this idea of a portrait of Lester popped into my head and I found it very funny. I was actually very surprised when I told him the idea and he found it as funny as I did. The only difficult part was getting him to wear the helmet, as this was one of his original ones and the inside had started falling out. But, with the use of a staple gun and a couple of straws we managed to forge something that would balance on his noggin for a few minutes to get the shot. It was like a comedy sketch, with Lester moaning about trying to fix the helmet and my shouting "But no-one will know it's you without it!", which we both found very funny, and we ended up giggling like naughty school boys.

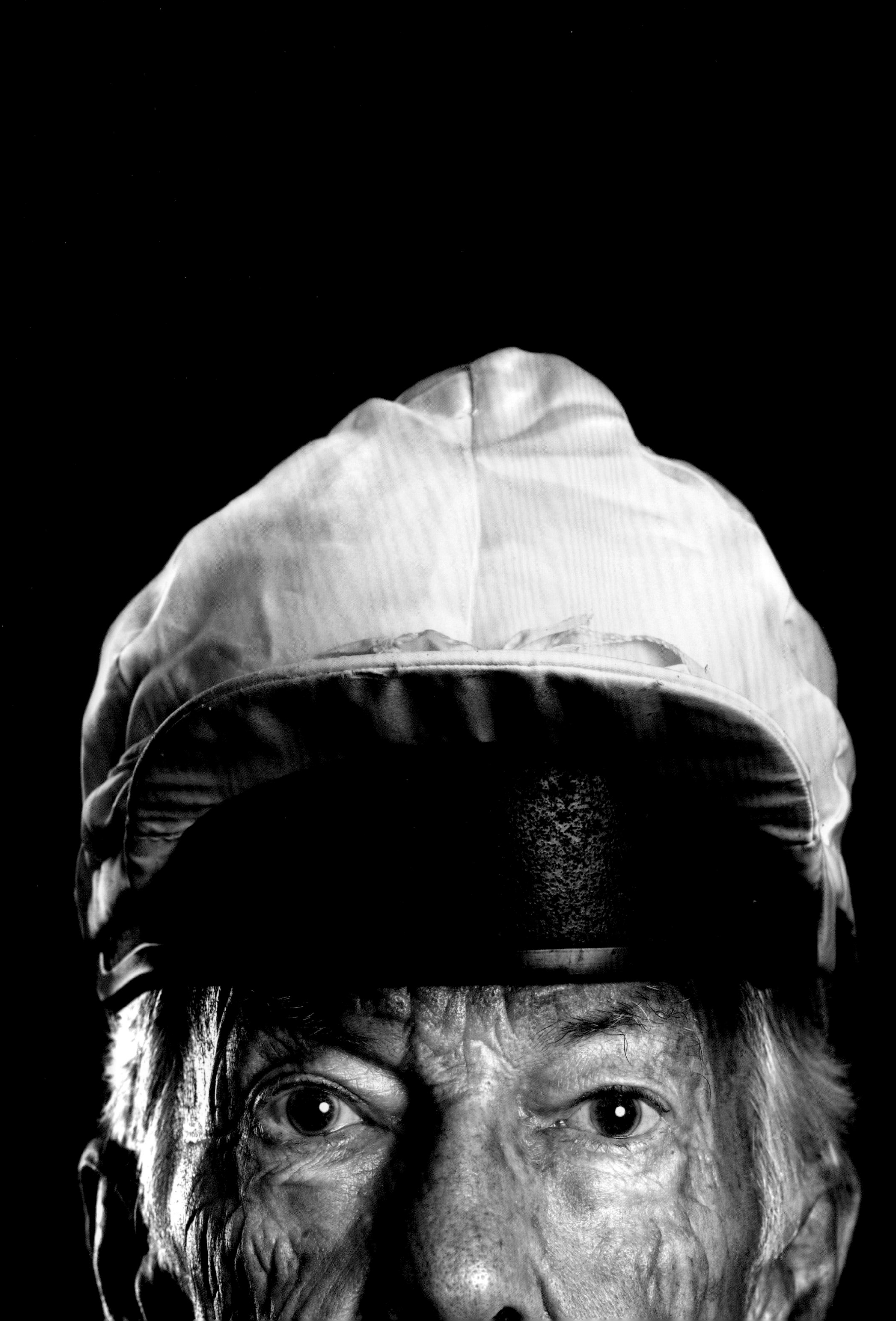

Lily James

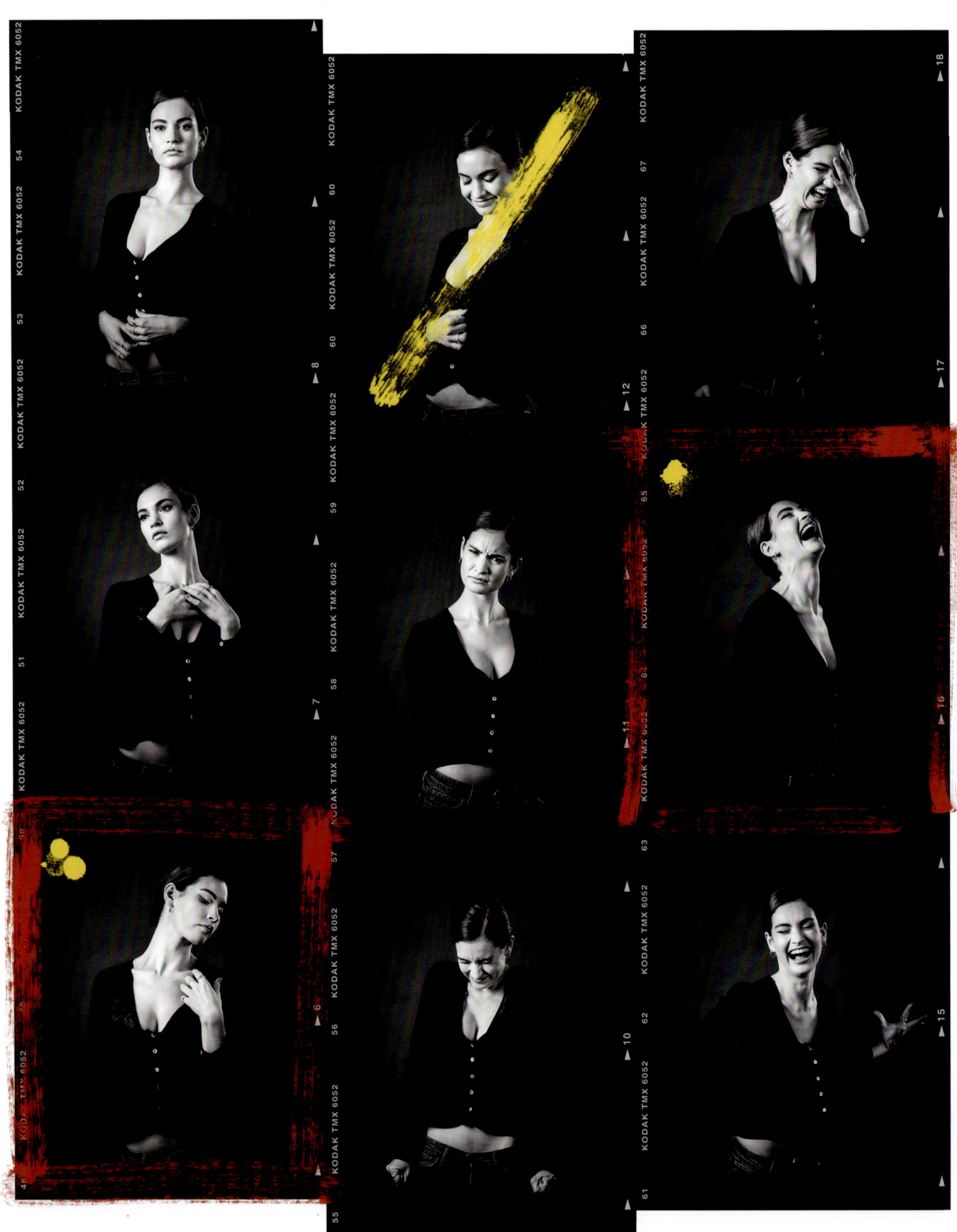

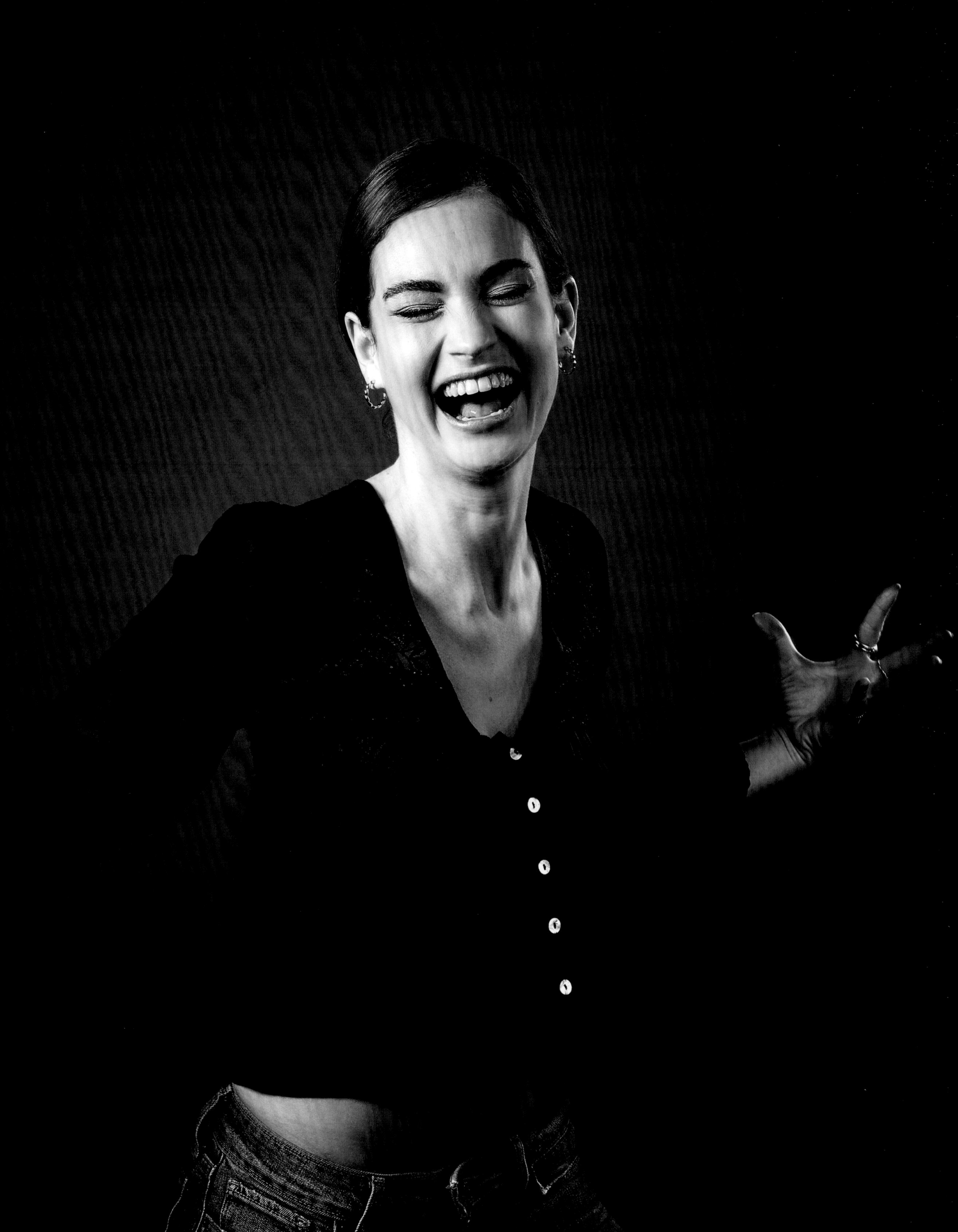

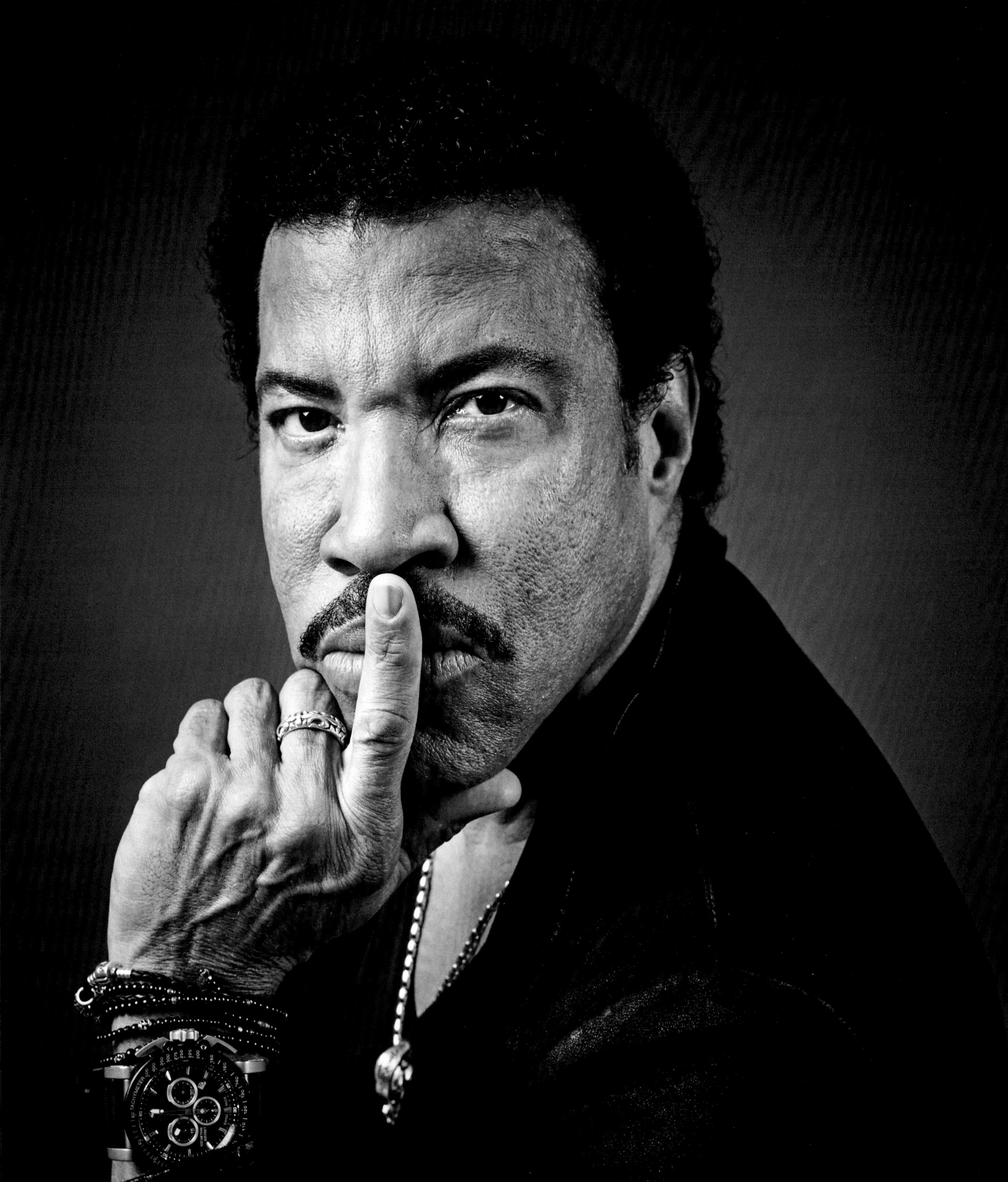
TACHYMETER

Lionel Richie

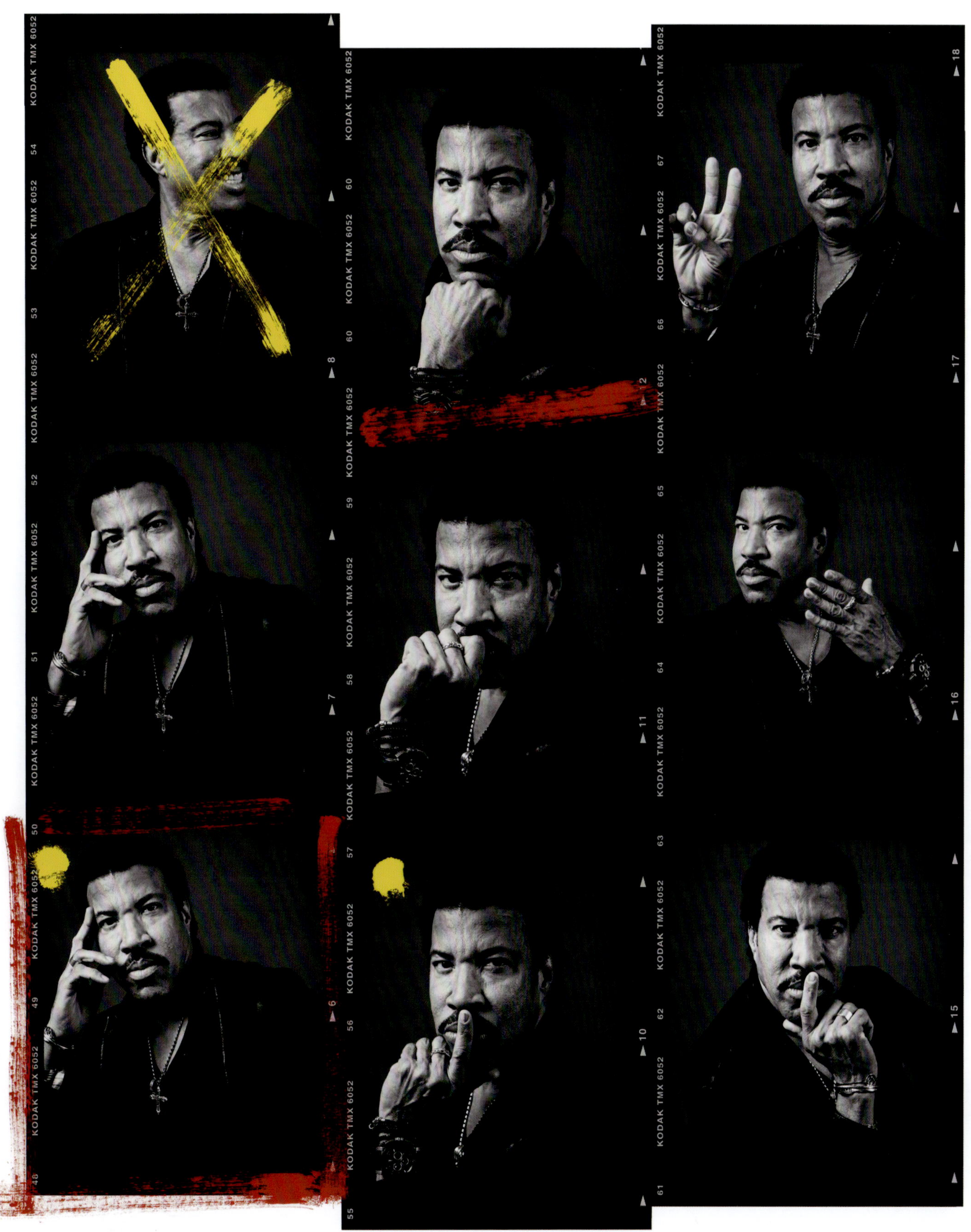

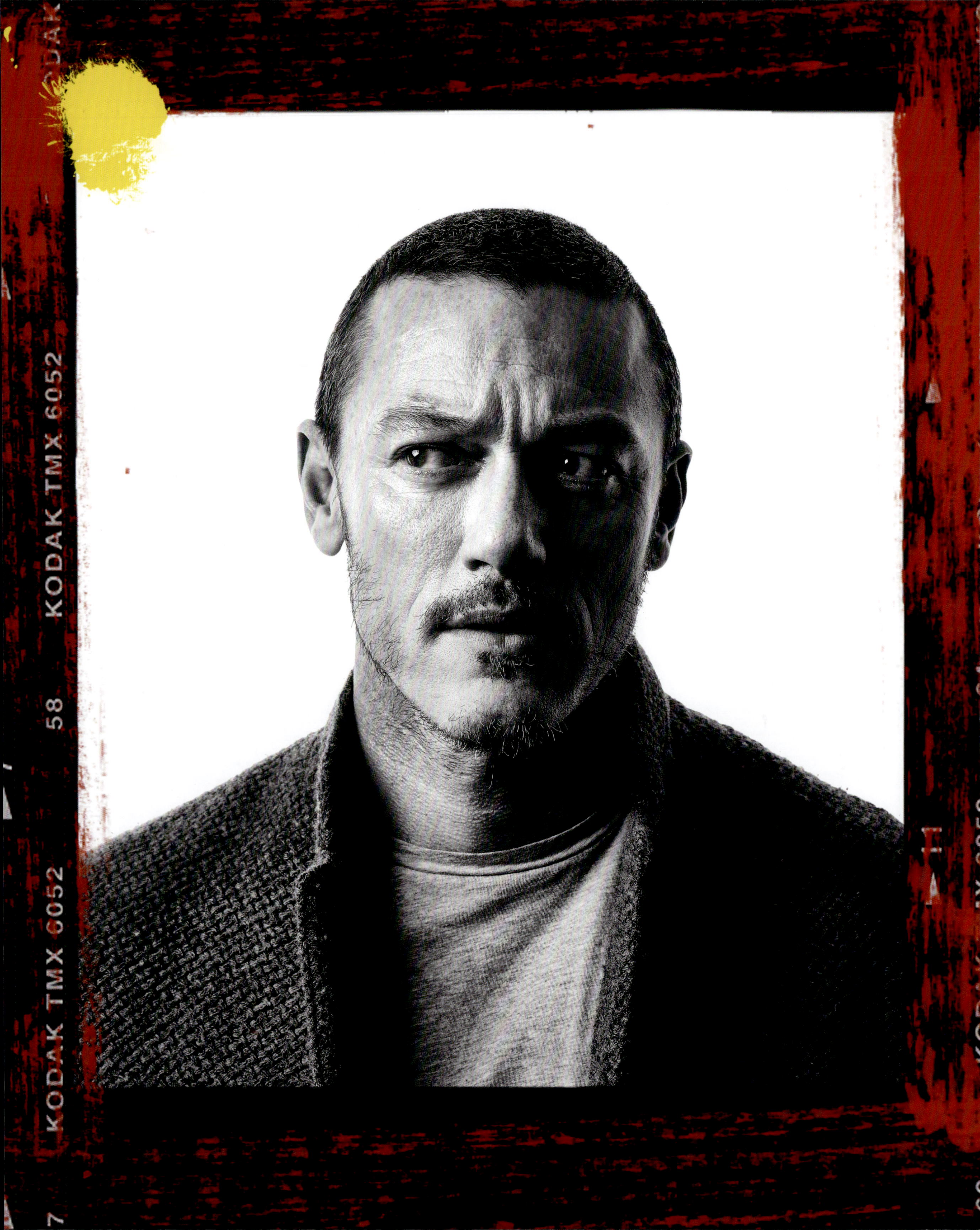

KODAK TMX 6052

58

KODAK TMX 6052

7

Luke Evans

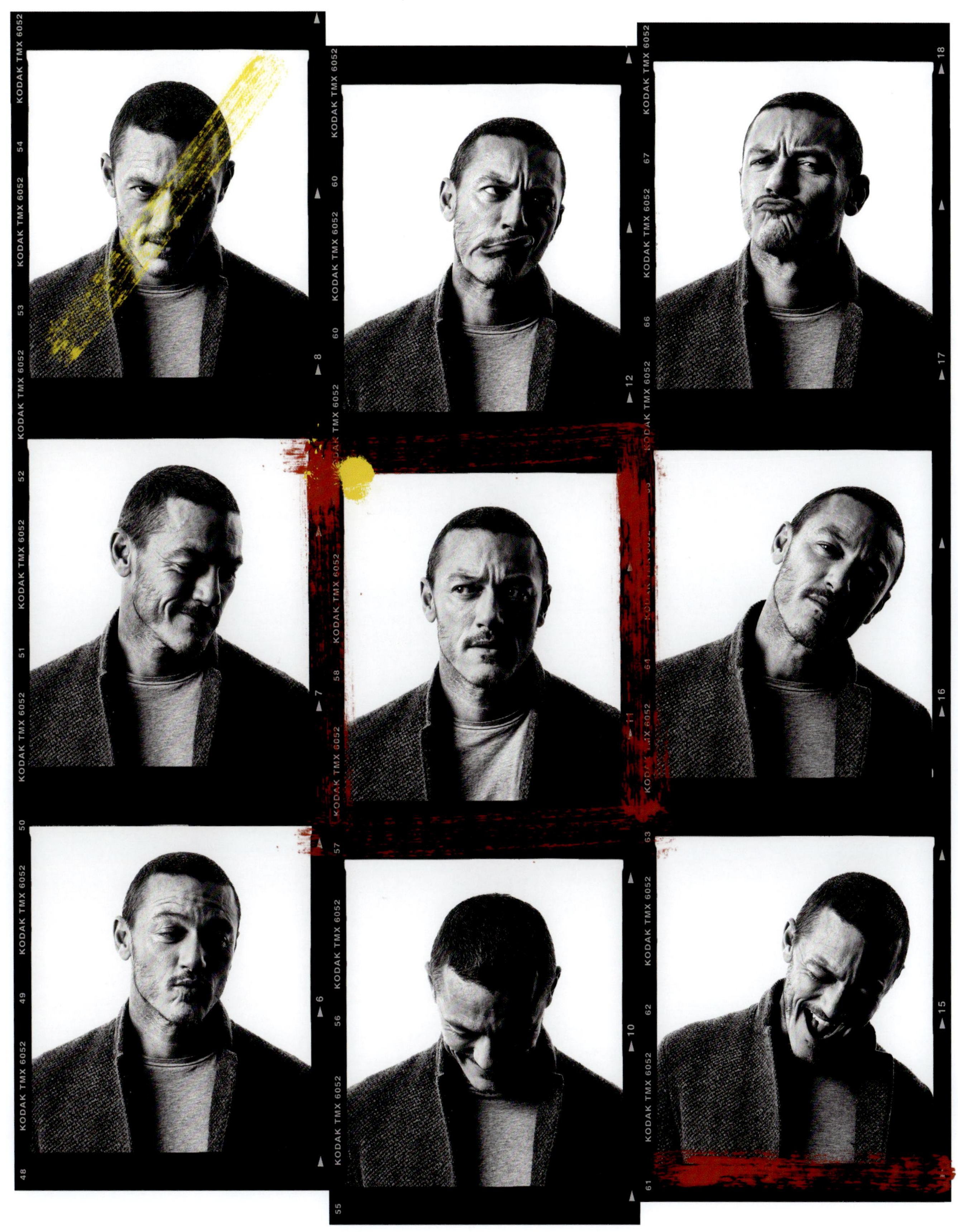

Marion Cotillard

My shoot with Marion was at the BAFTA dinner after the awards ceremony. I had a little studio set up and there were a small number of actors I was shooting that evening. They all arrived at the same moment and I had a wonderful time shooting Marion, Helen Mirren, Daniel Day-Lewis and Christoph Waltz. Daniel shouted heckling remarks during the shoot, which everyone found very amusing, and made the 'Little Sparrow' giggle a few times.

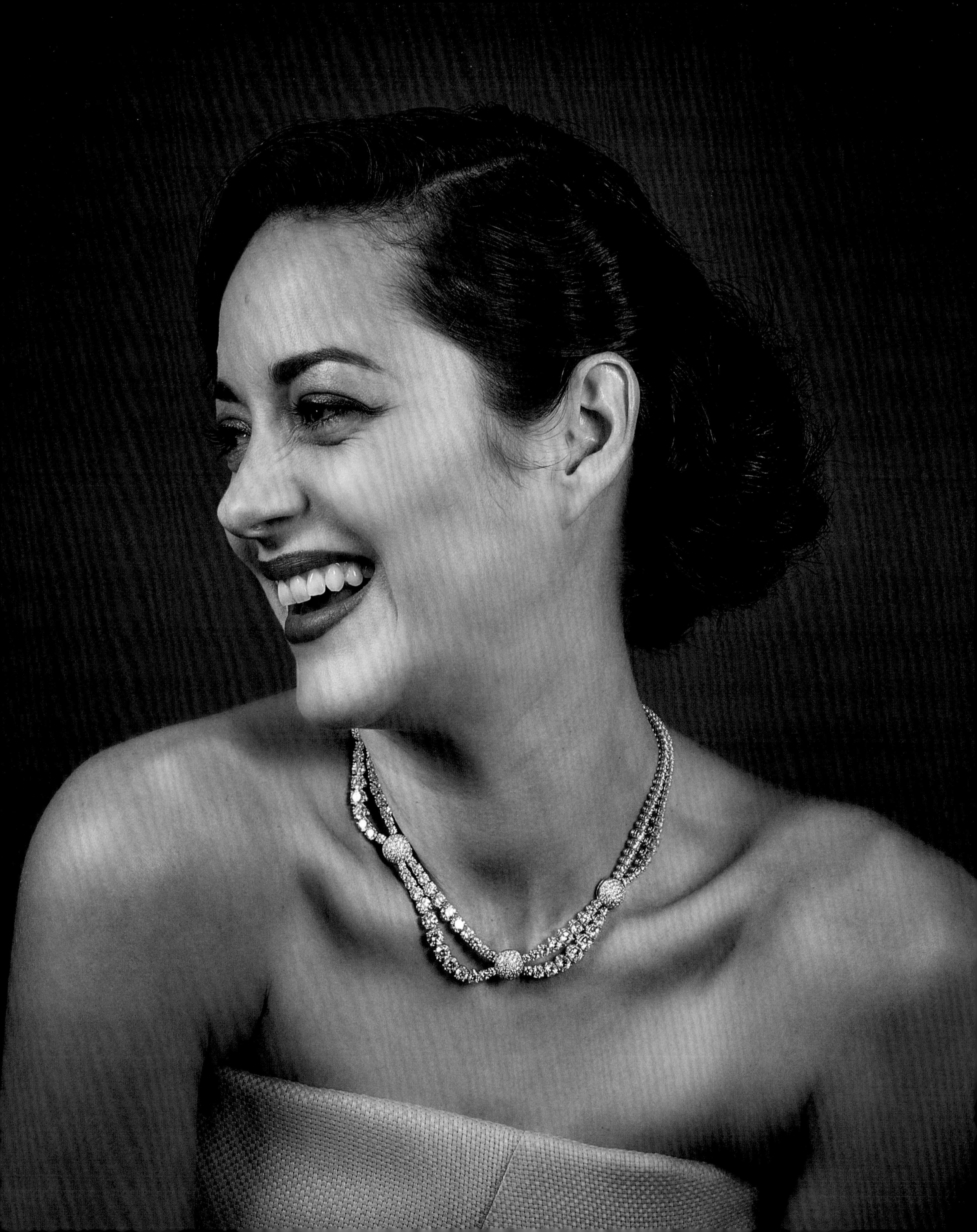

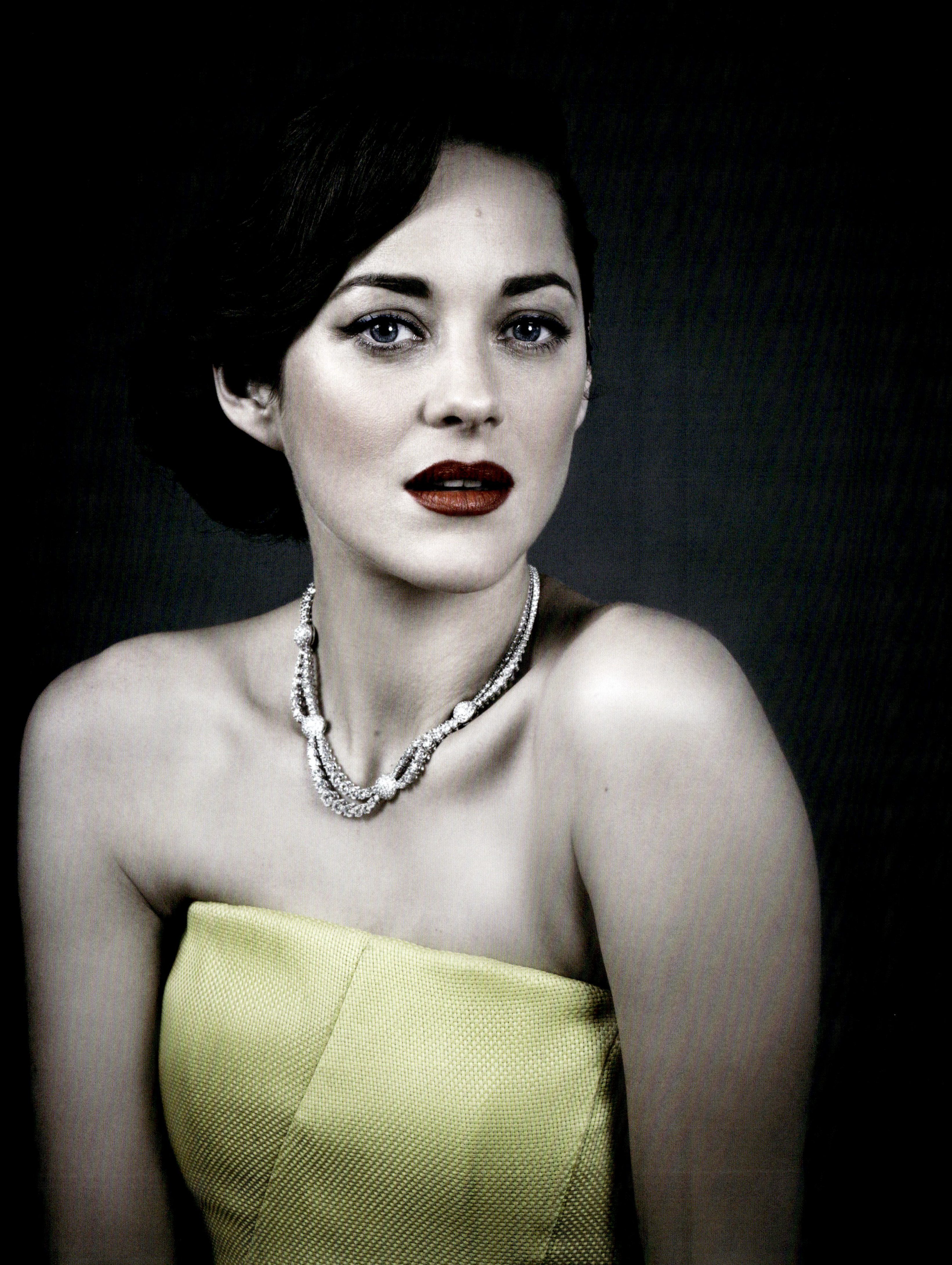

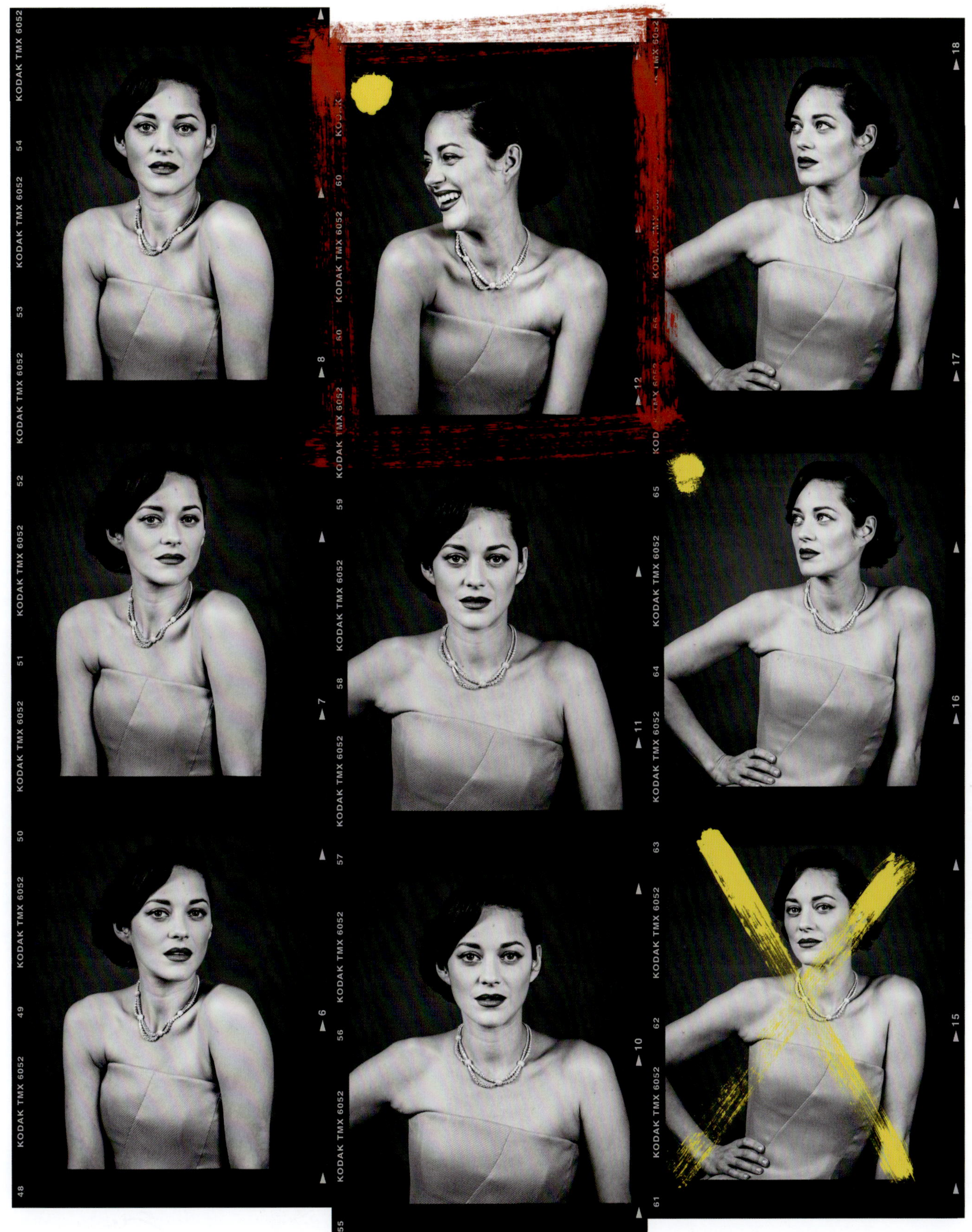

Mark Hamill

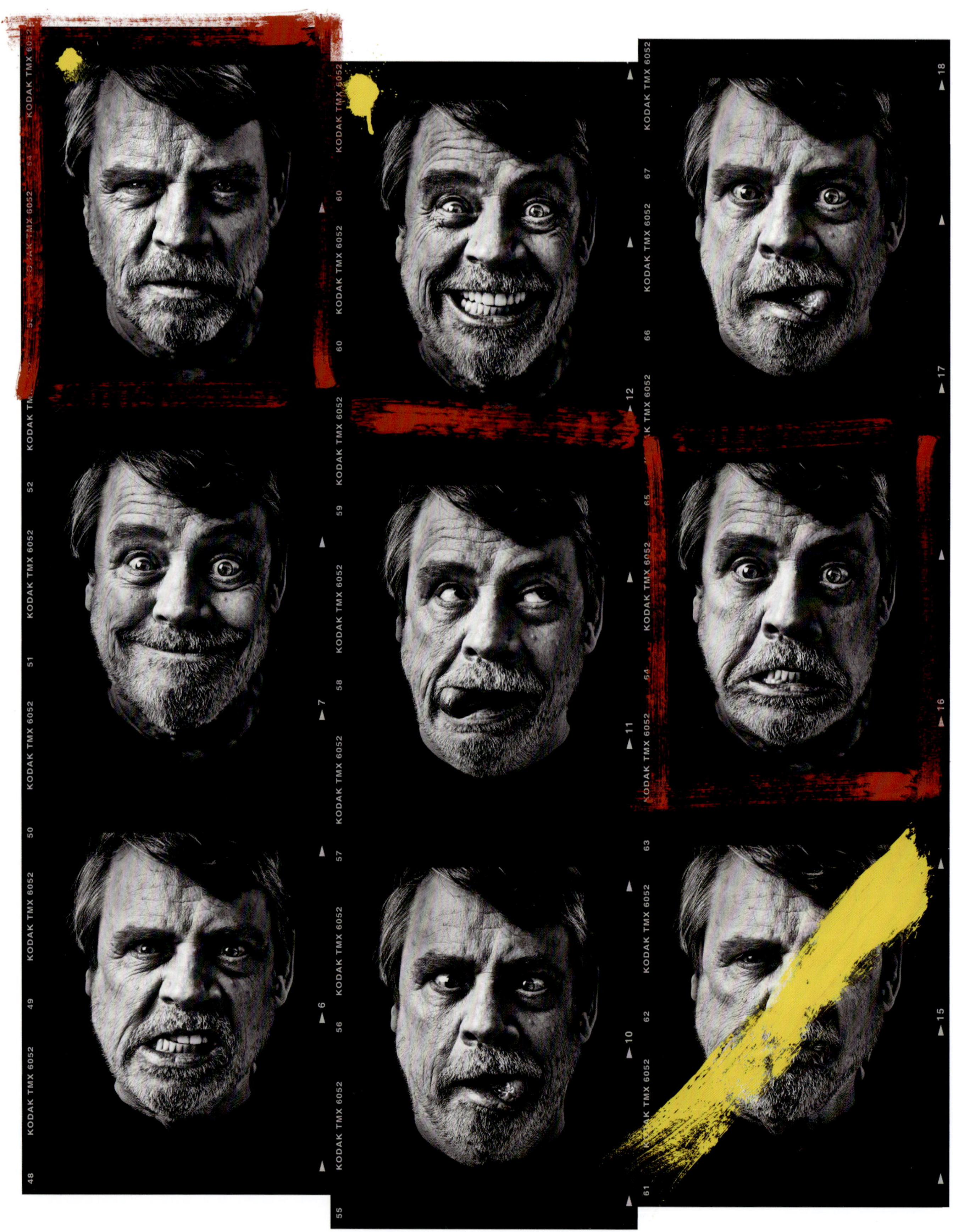

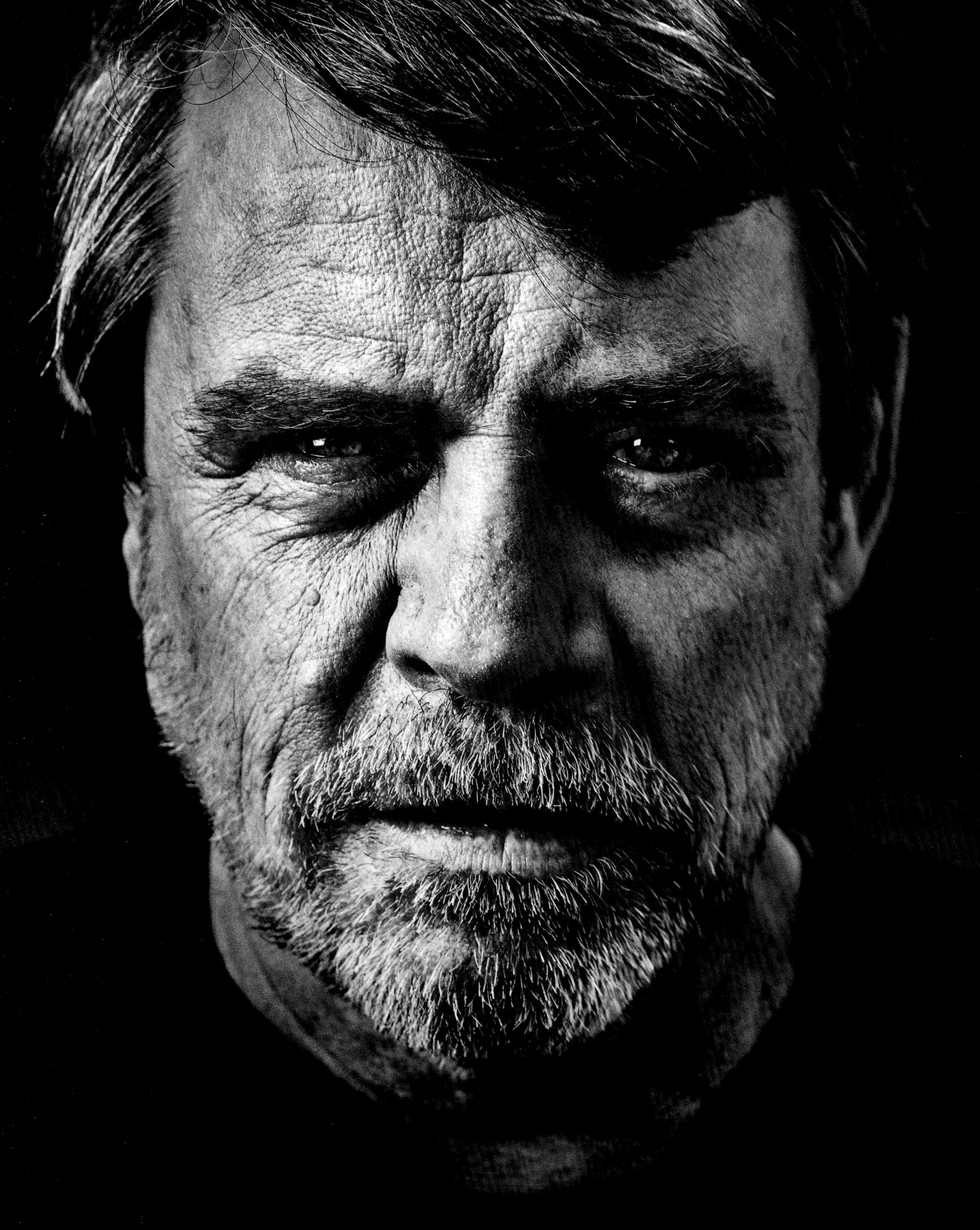

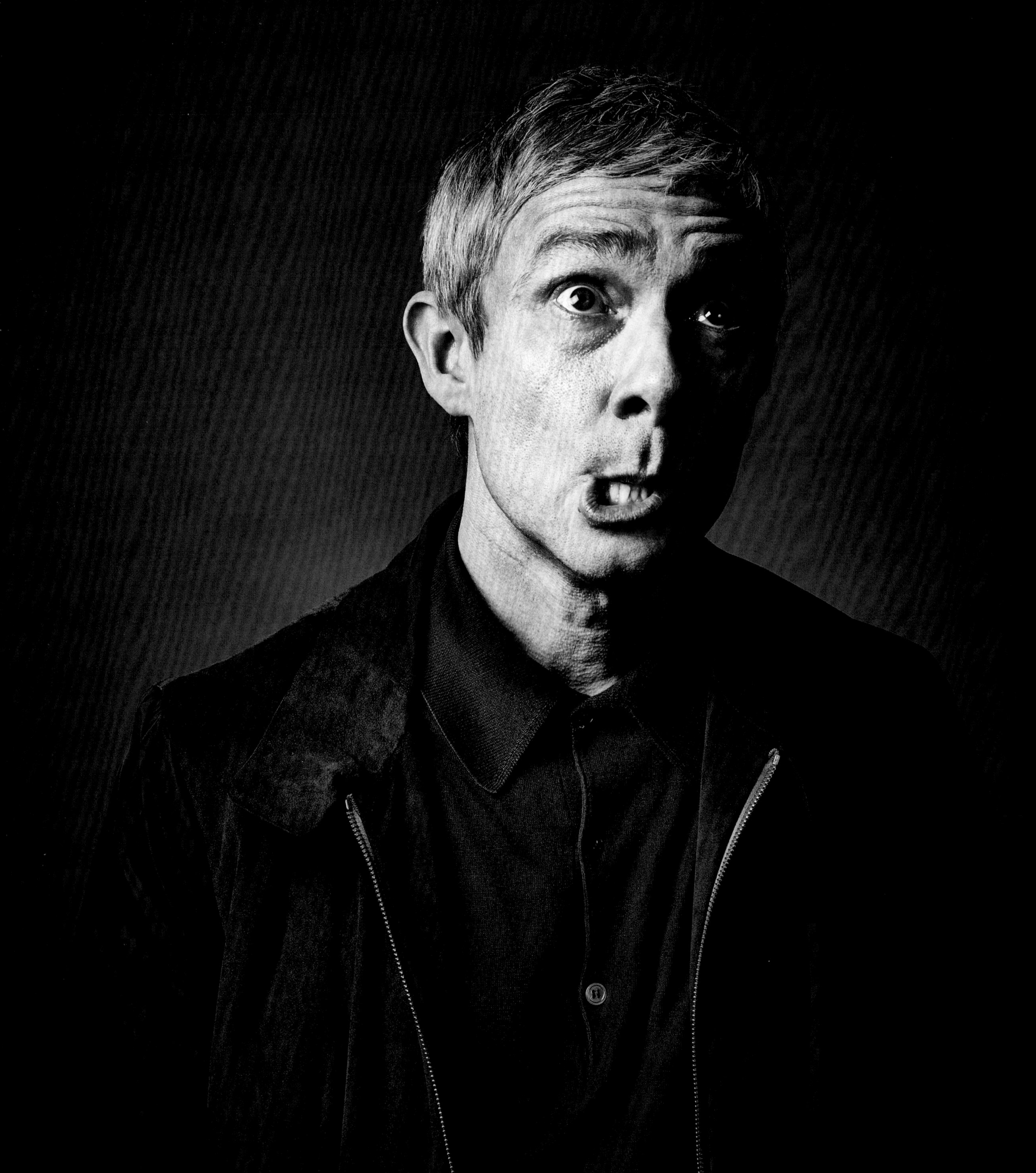

Martin Freeman

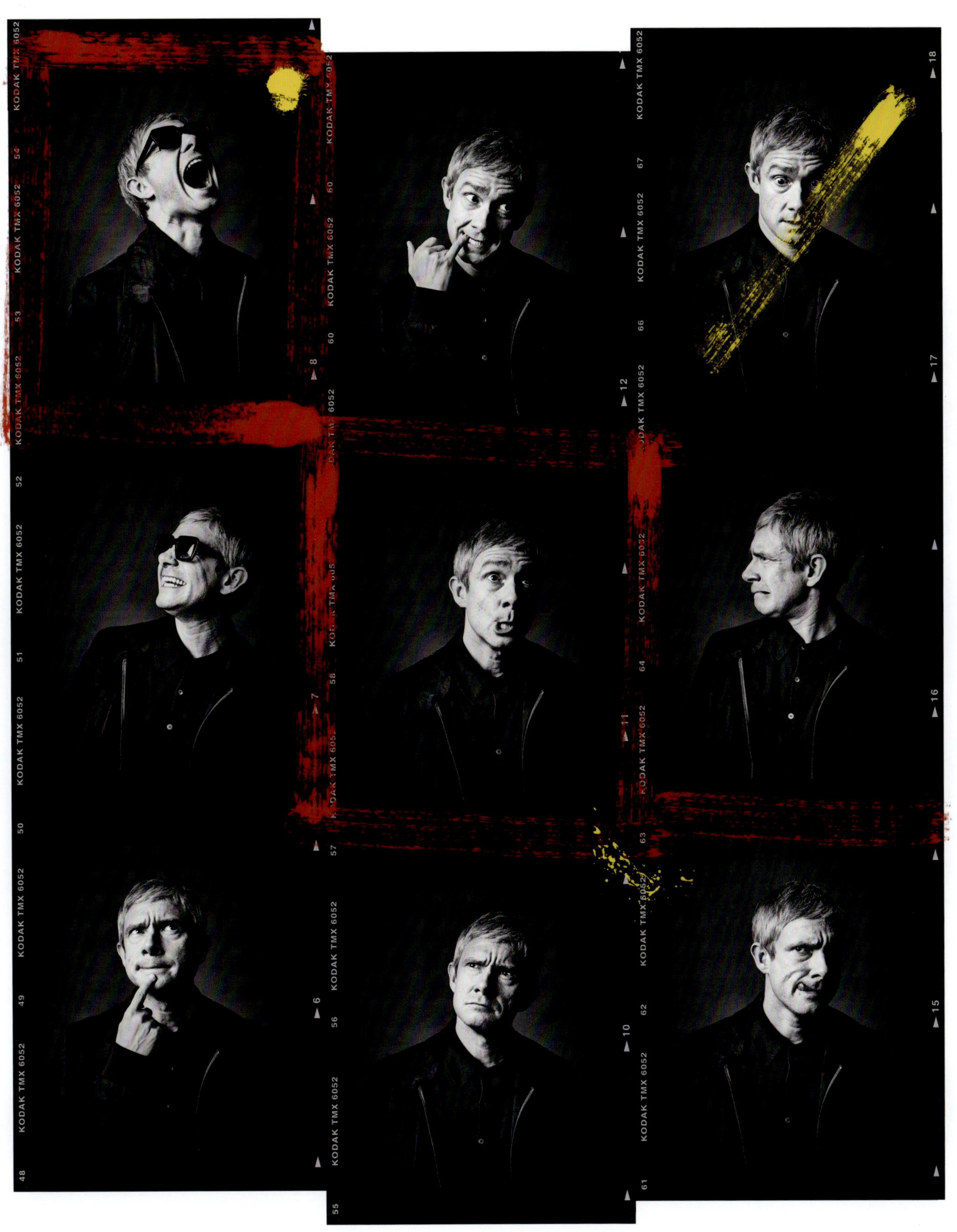

Matt Damon

Matt Damon is such a sweet guy, there is no other way to describe him. George Clooney arranged for me to shoot him for my Degrees project. The shoot was on the set of his Terry Gilliam movie *The Brothers Grimm*. Matt was filming *The Bourne Supremacy* and *The Brothers Grimm* simultaneously. When briefing Matt on the shoot, I asked for more Bourne than Grimm. For someone like Matt you don't even need the five reels you bring. I think a lot of this comes down to him being such a great communicator – you get what you want in three reels max. This was also a blessing because halfway through the shoot, Heath Ledger (his co-star in the movie) came bounding in. Heath did his best to distract Matt, but being the true pro, Matt got what we needed whilst still humouring his buddy. I then used to rest of my reels to shoot Heath and the two of them goofing around together, which was very special and memorable.

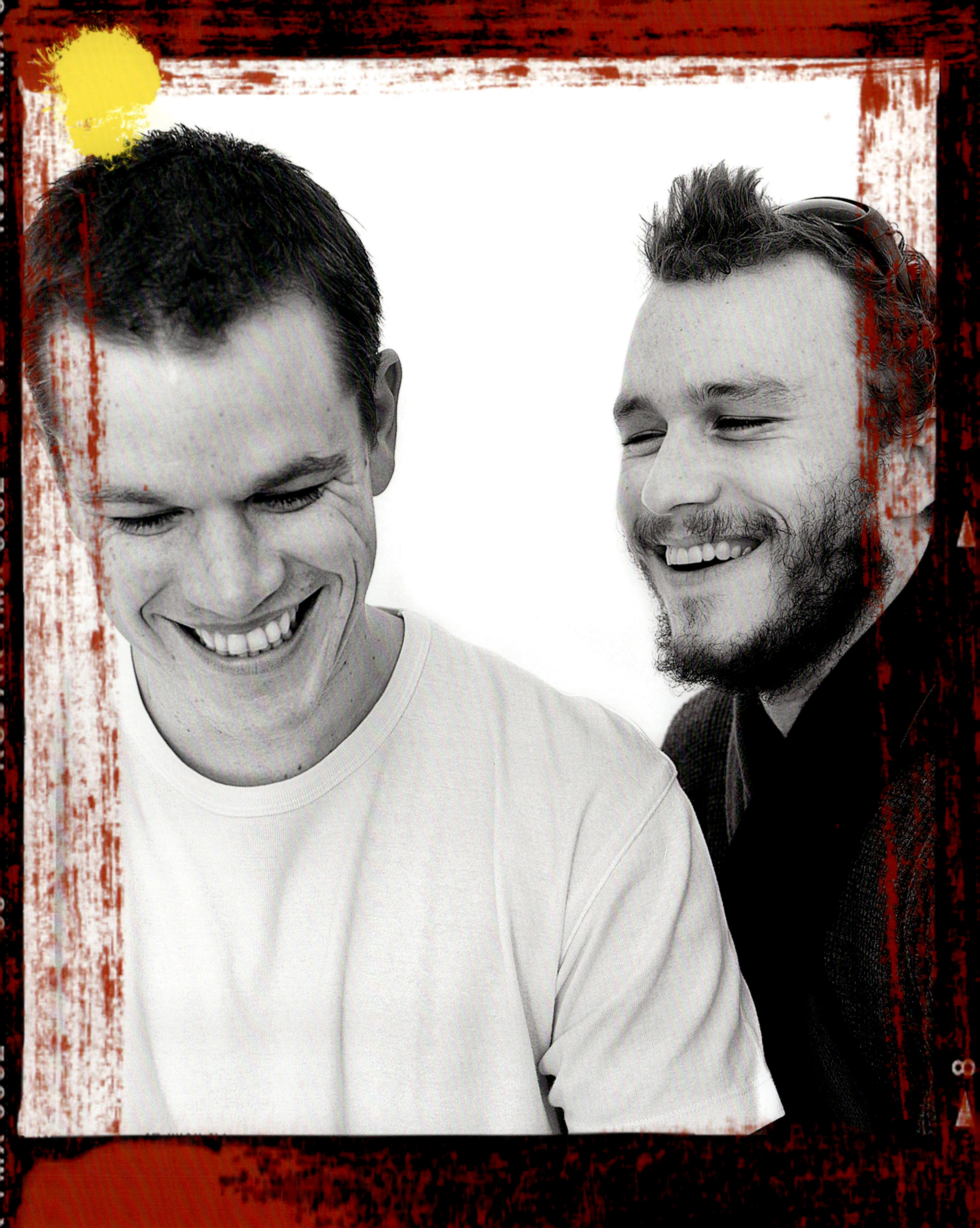

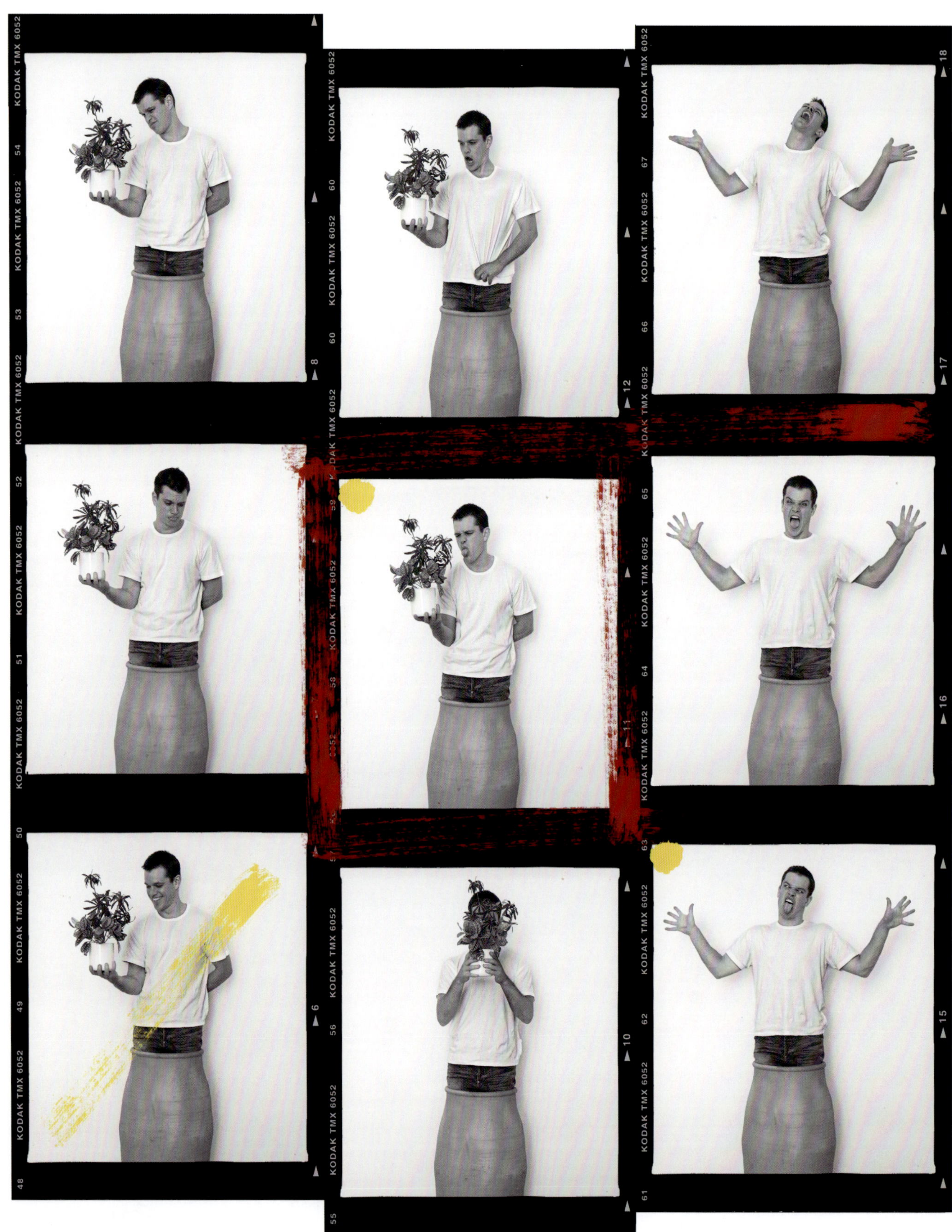

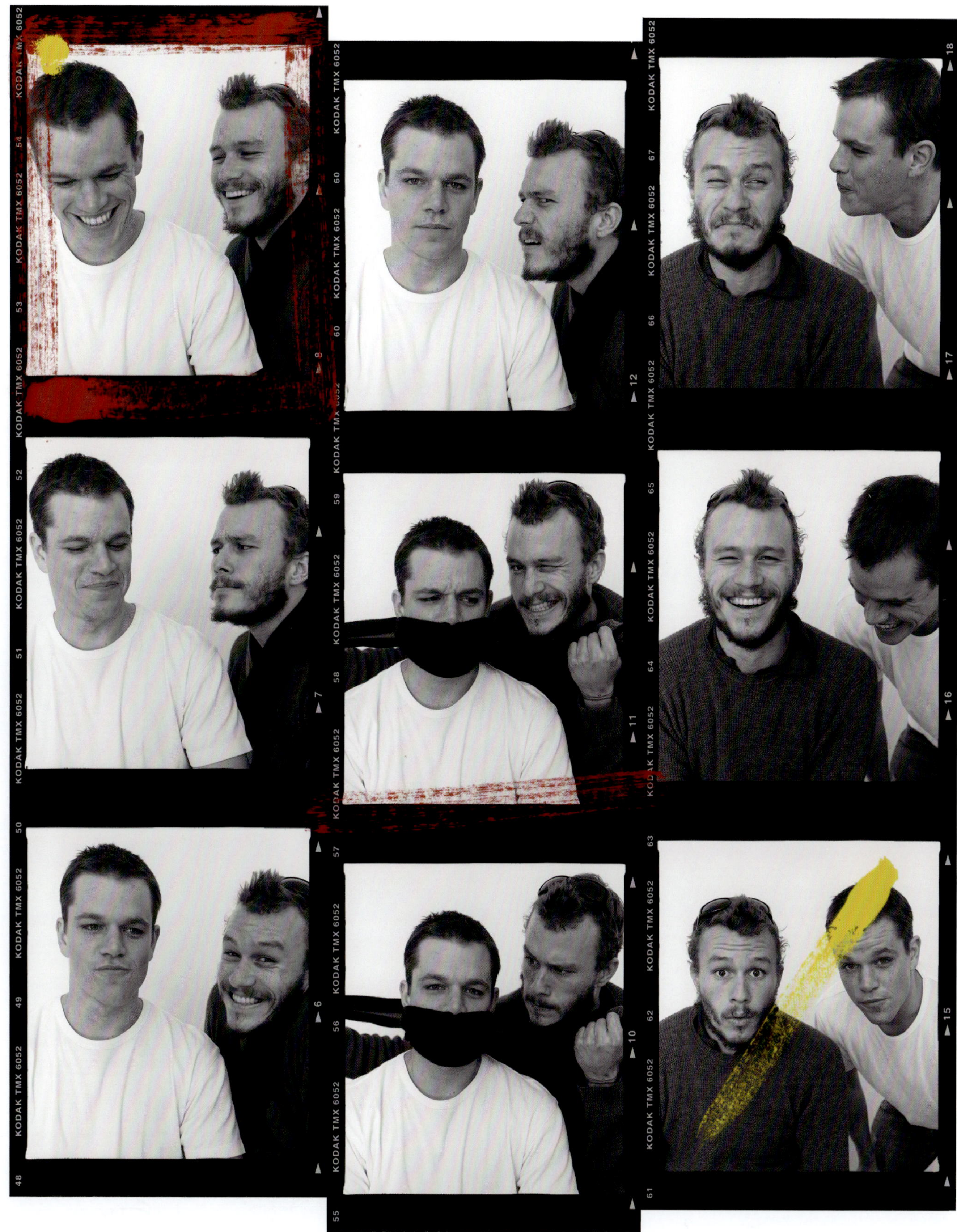

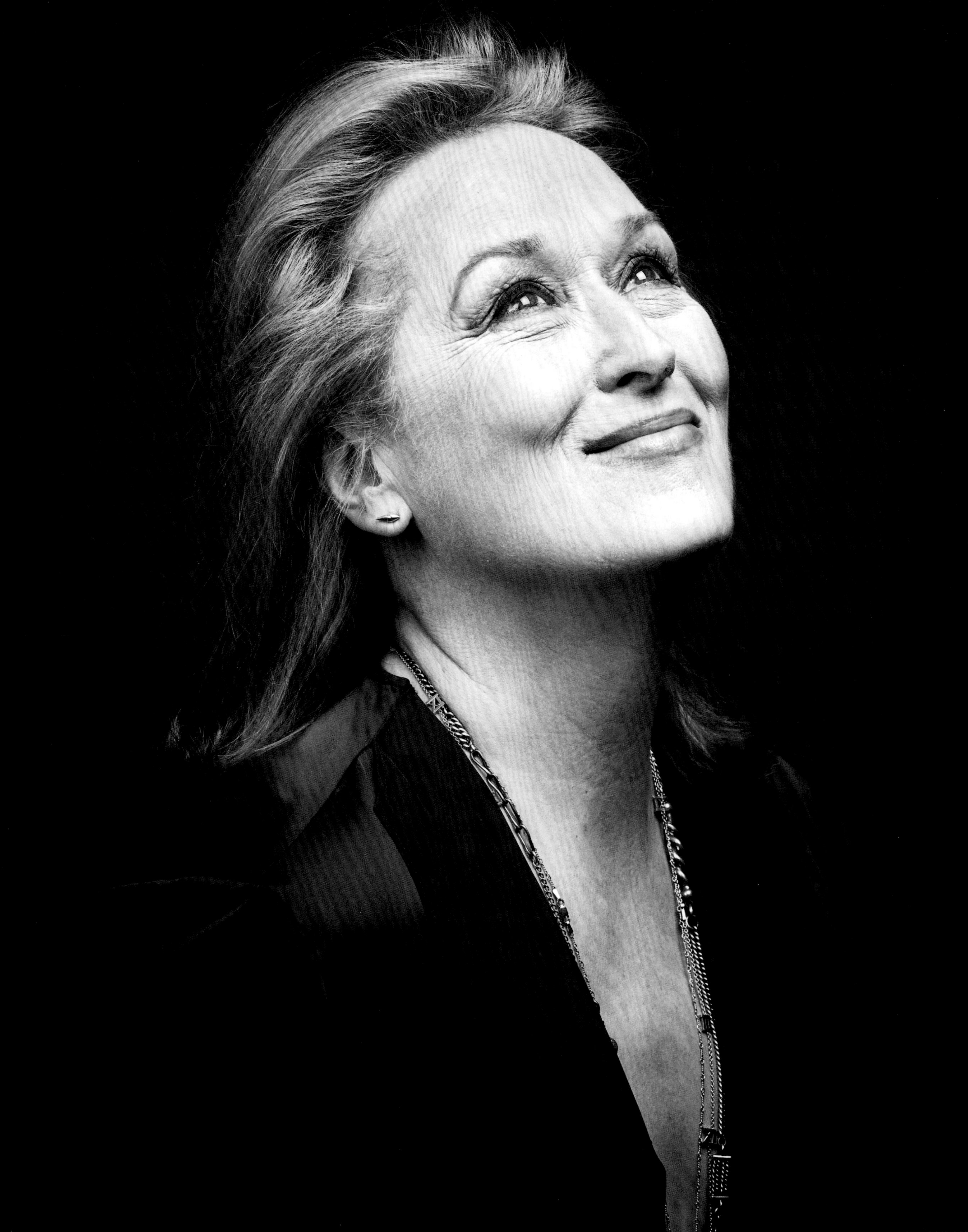

Meryl Streep

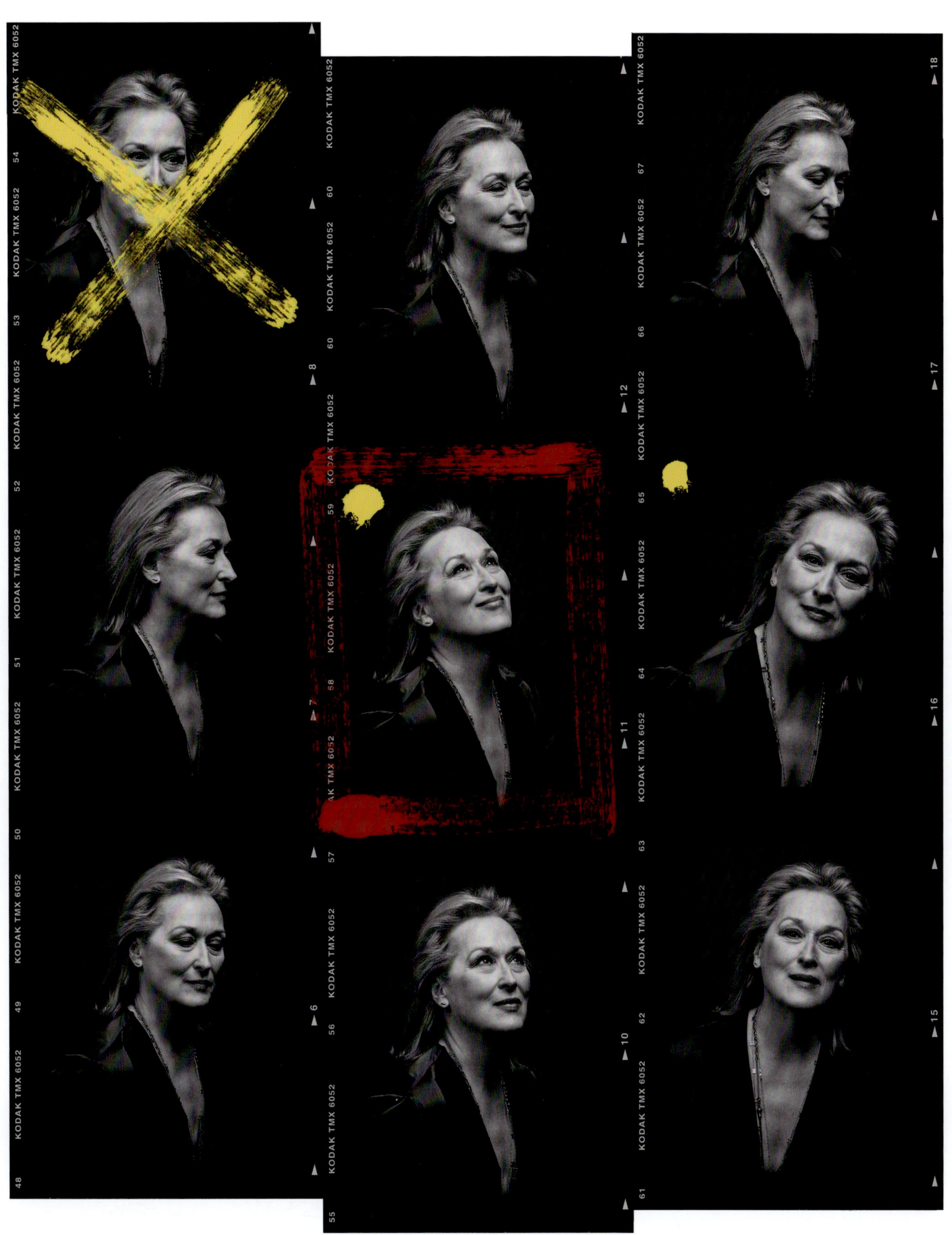

Michael Caine

Since the 1950s I have been photographed more times than you can shake a stick at, and by most of the famous photographers of the time. Some of the most well-known photos of me come from the 1960s, with one of the most iconic taken by David Bailey. The photograph is a straight-on shot. I am wearing a black suit and have my Yvan black-rimmed glasses on.

Over recent years I have been photographed by Andy Gotts a number of times. Each time has been fun and included many conversations about movies, as we are both movie buffs; we both try to outdo each other with our trivia knowledge.

One day my wife Shakira told me Andy was due to photograph me again for one of his projects. "He wants to do a photograph with a nod back to the 1960s, rather than a larking around shot", she said. I have been asked countless times to recreate the Bailey shot but I always shy away from these requests; why remake a classic? But I knew the shoot was going to be fun regardless.

On the day of the shoot I travelled to Andy in Mayfair. It is terrific to walk through that part of London; it feels very Dickensian, especially on cold, crisp mornings. Unbeknown to me Andy had phoned and asked Shakira to put my old Harry Palmer black-rimmed glasses in my coat pocket, so when I arrived at the shoot he knew I would be already prepared.

As soon as I put the glasses on, I was transformed back into my Harry Palmer mind-set, transported back to the swinging sixties. In this set of magnificent images, Andy revealed the grim side of me that no-one ever sees.

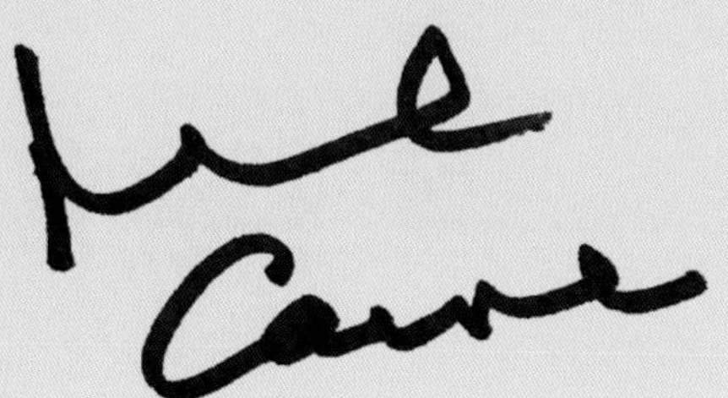

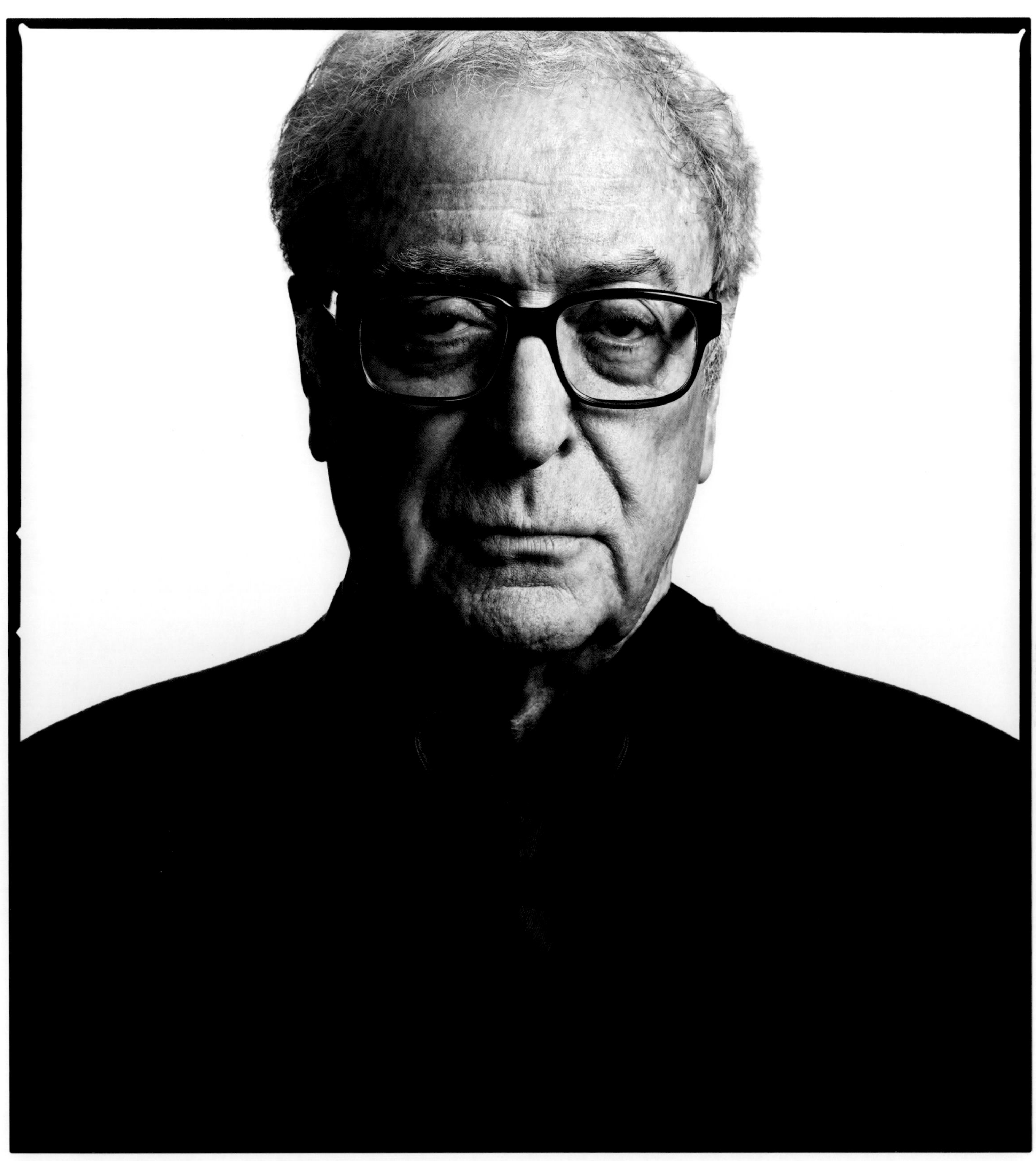

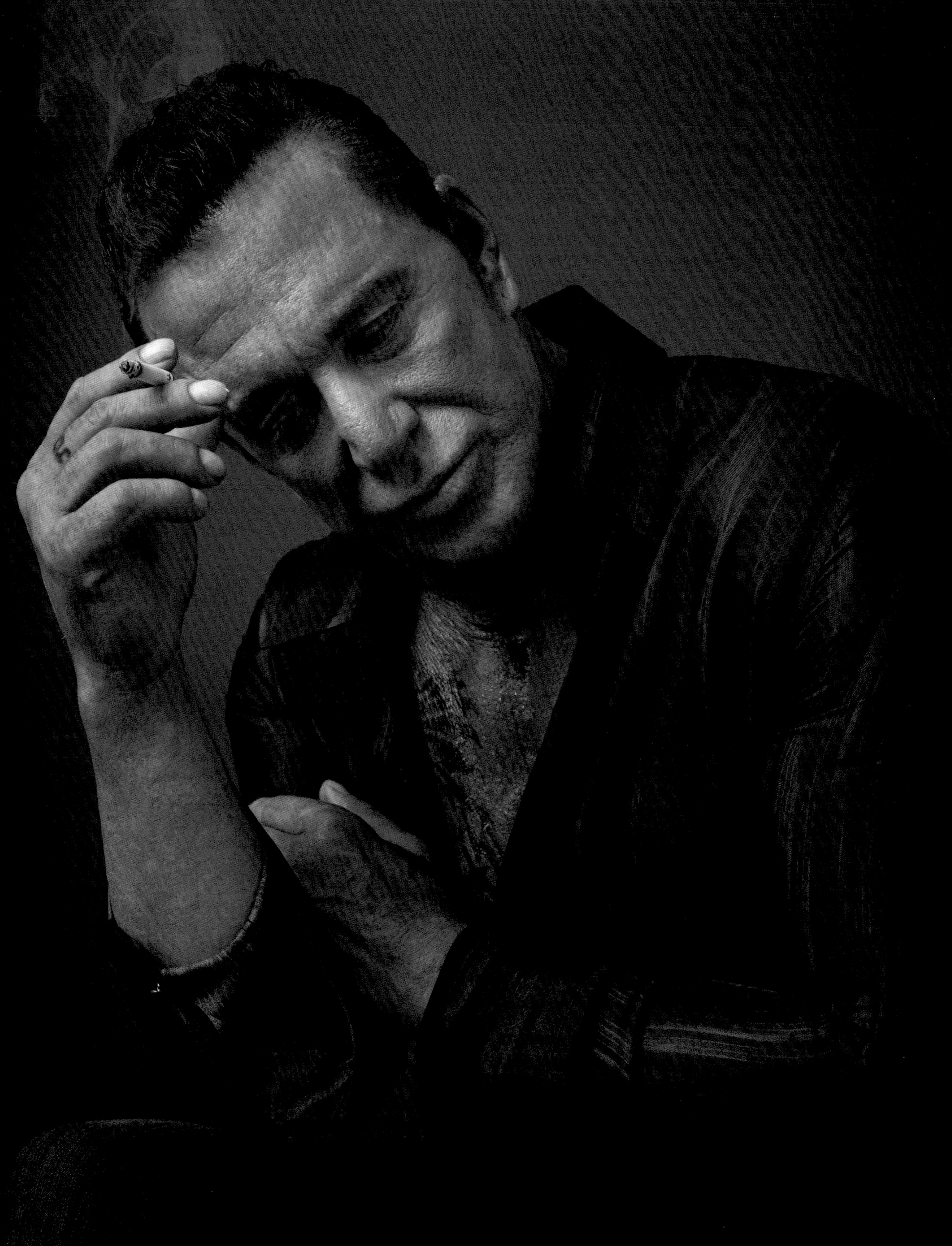

Mickey Rourke

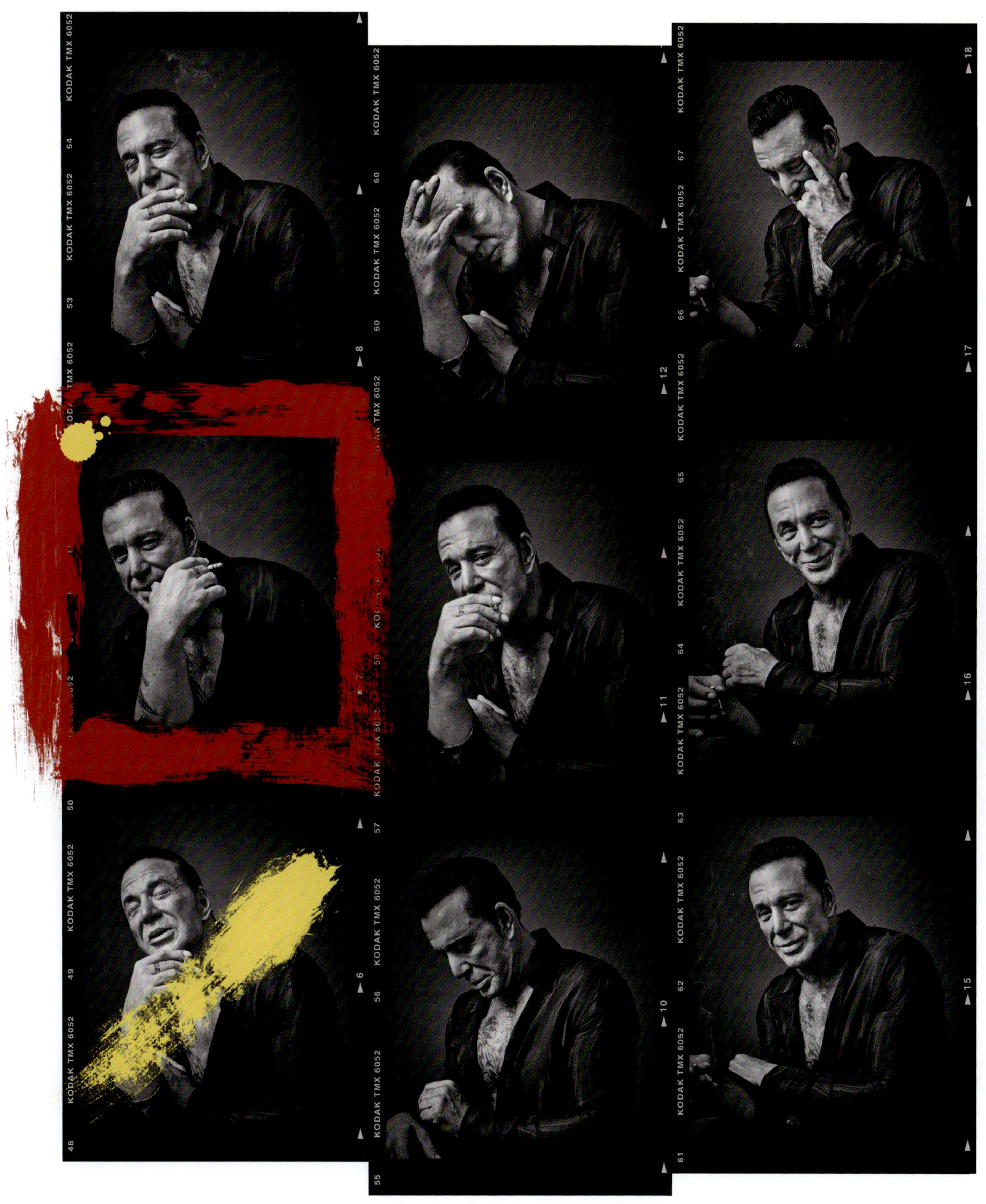

Monty Python

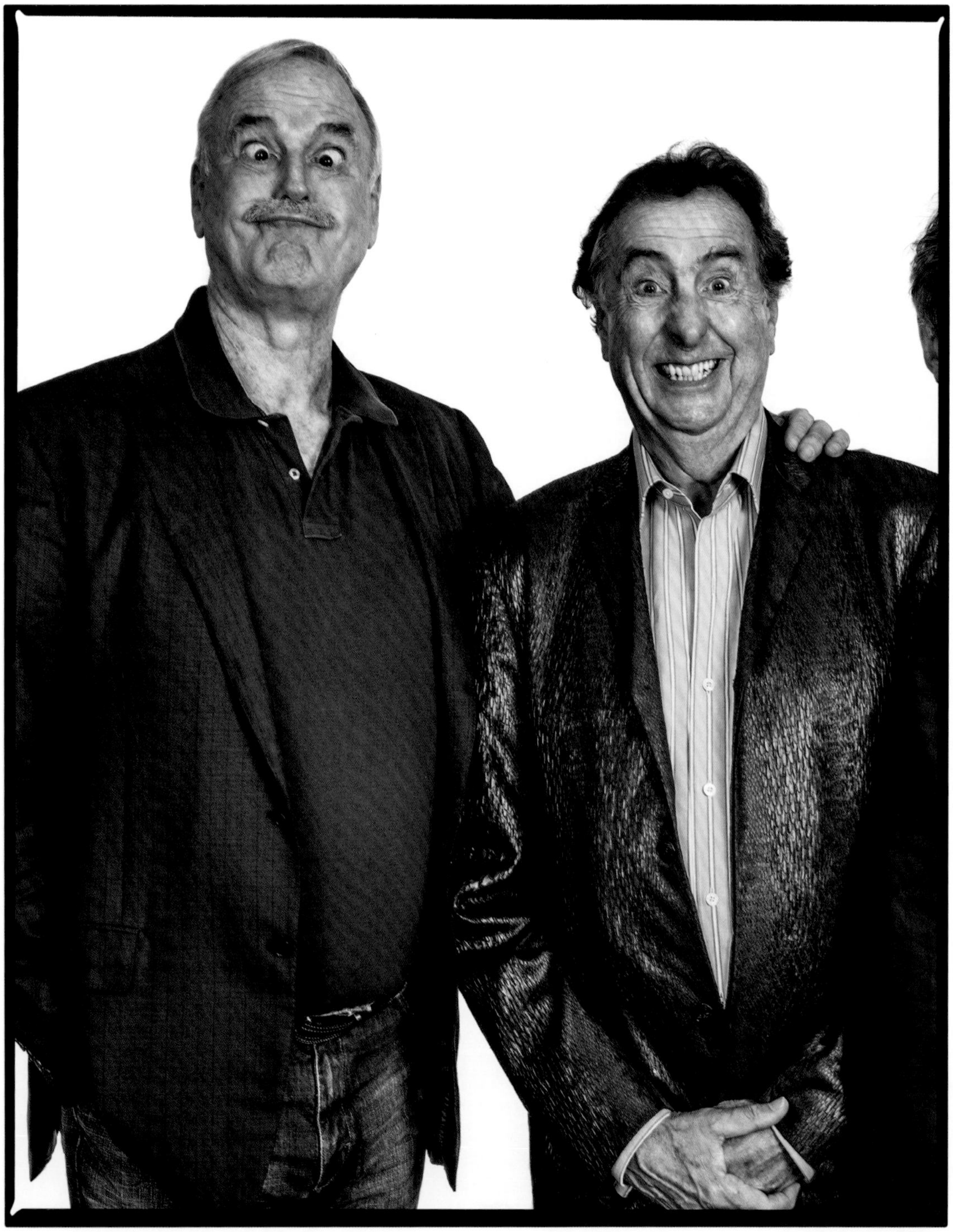

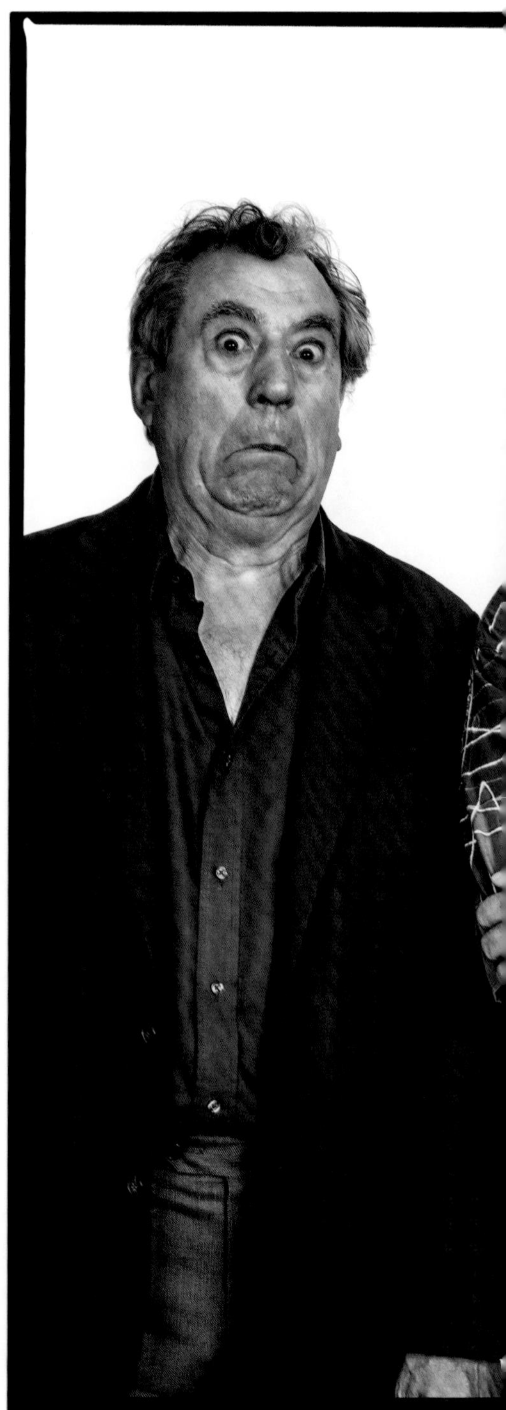

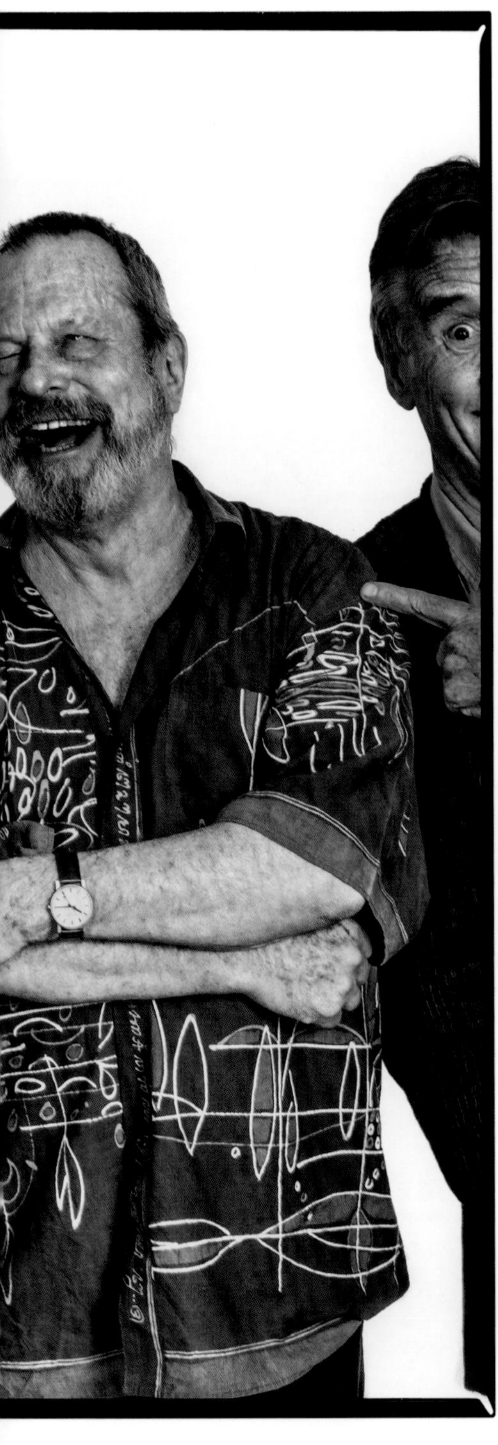

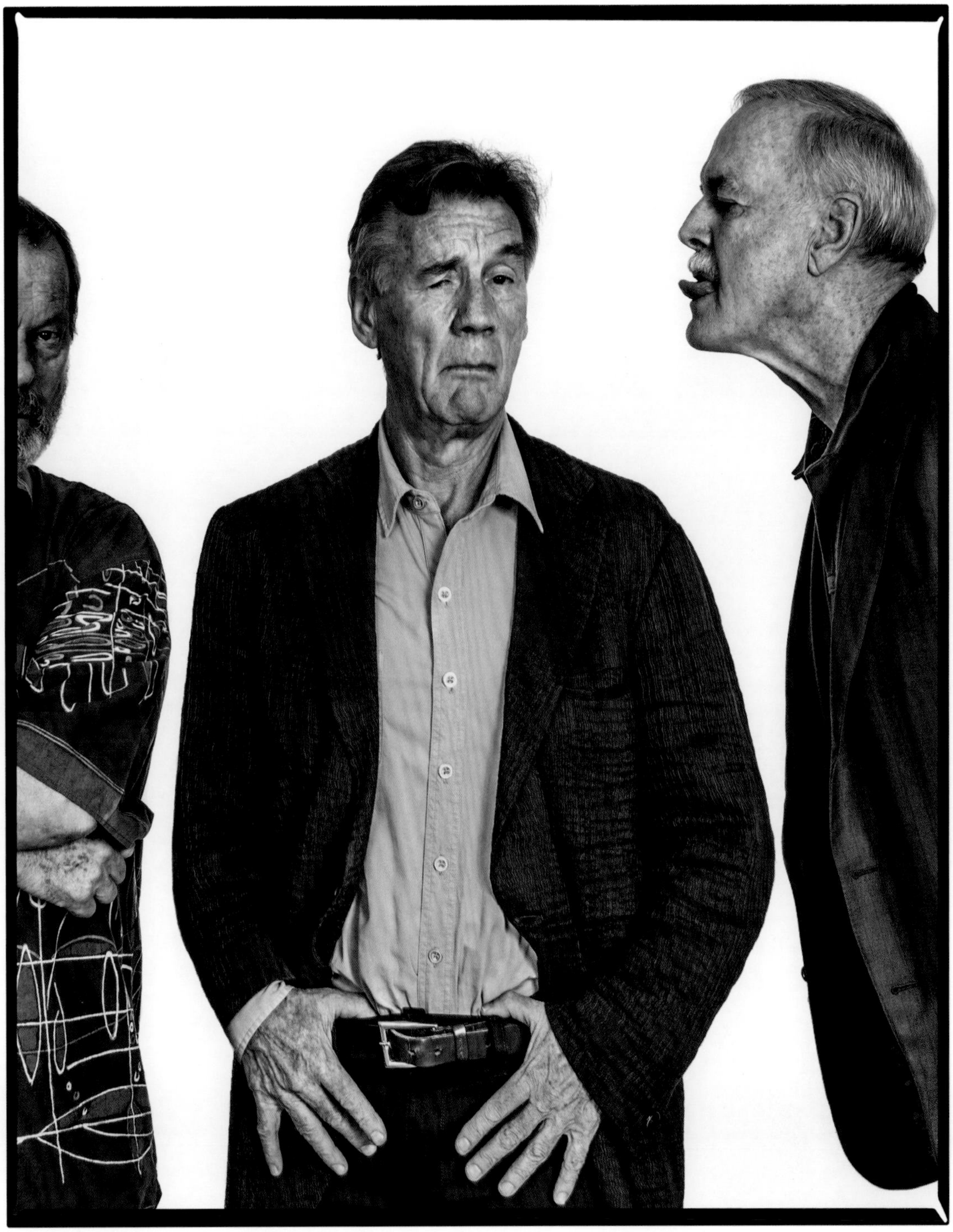

Morgan Freeman

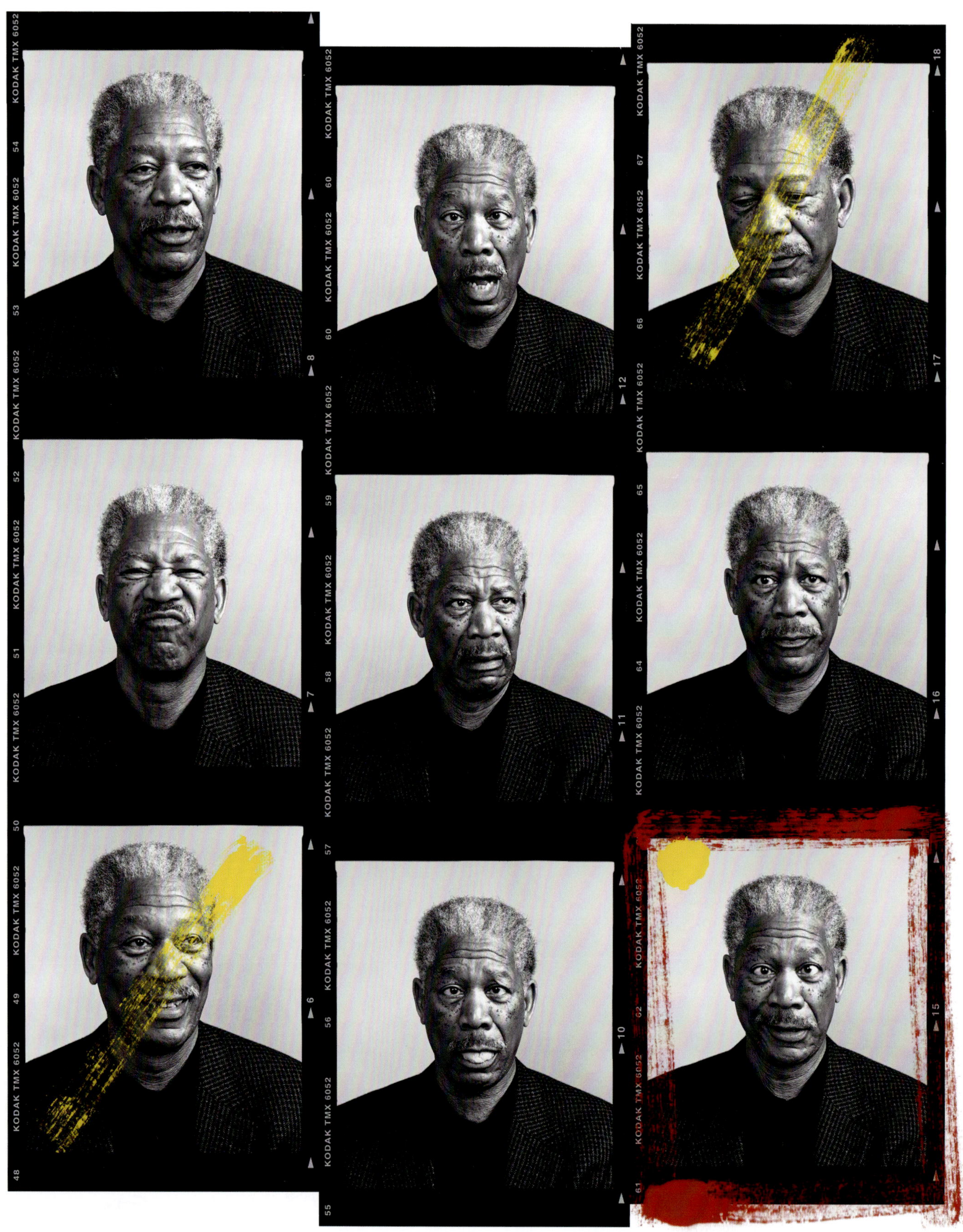

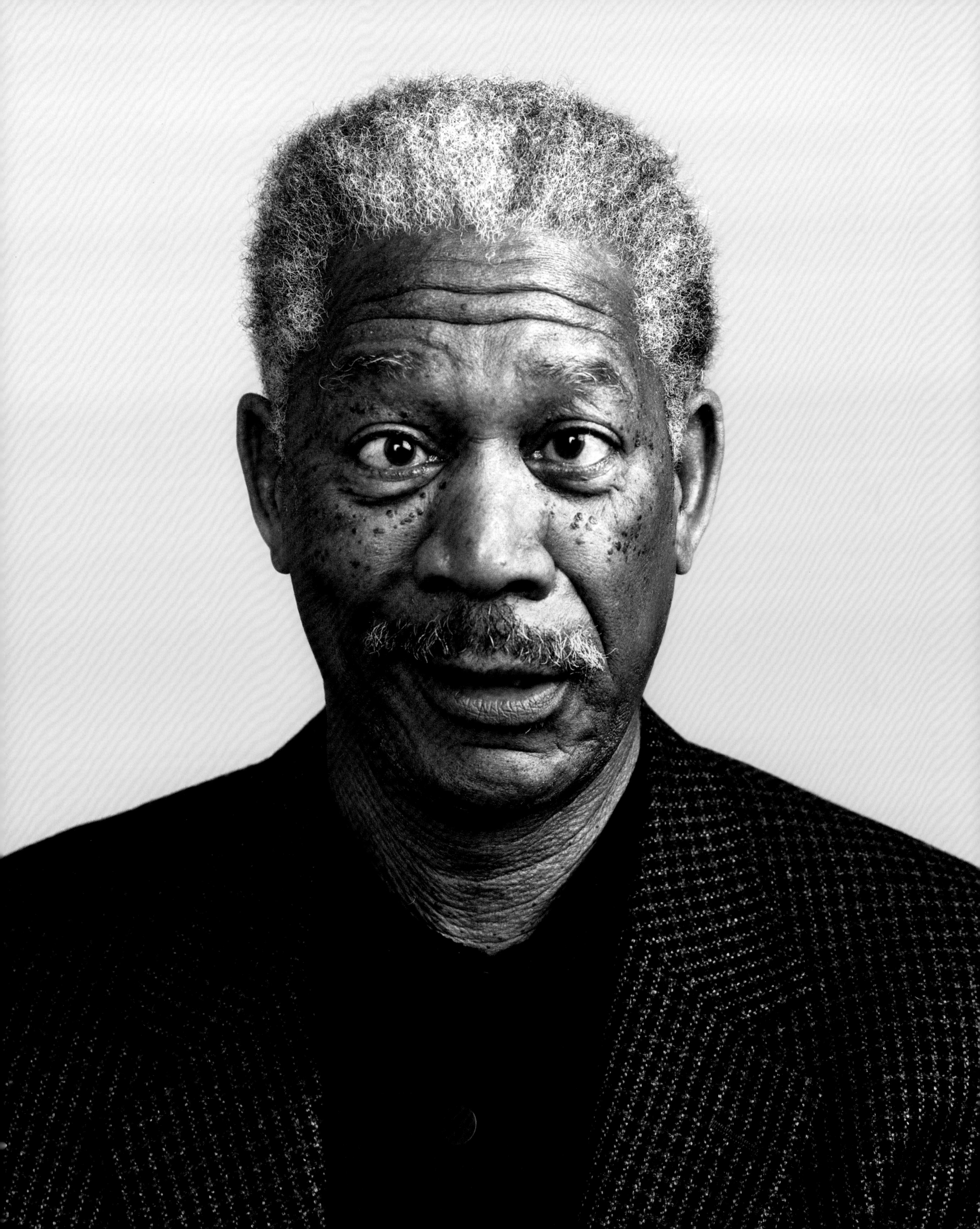

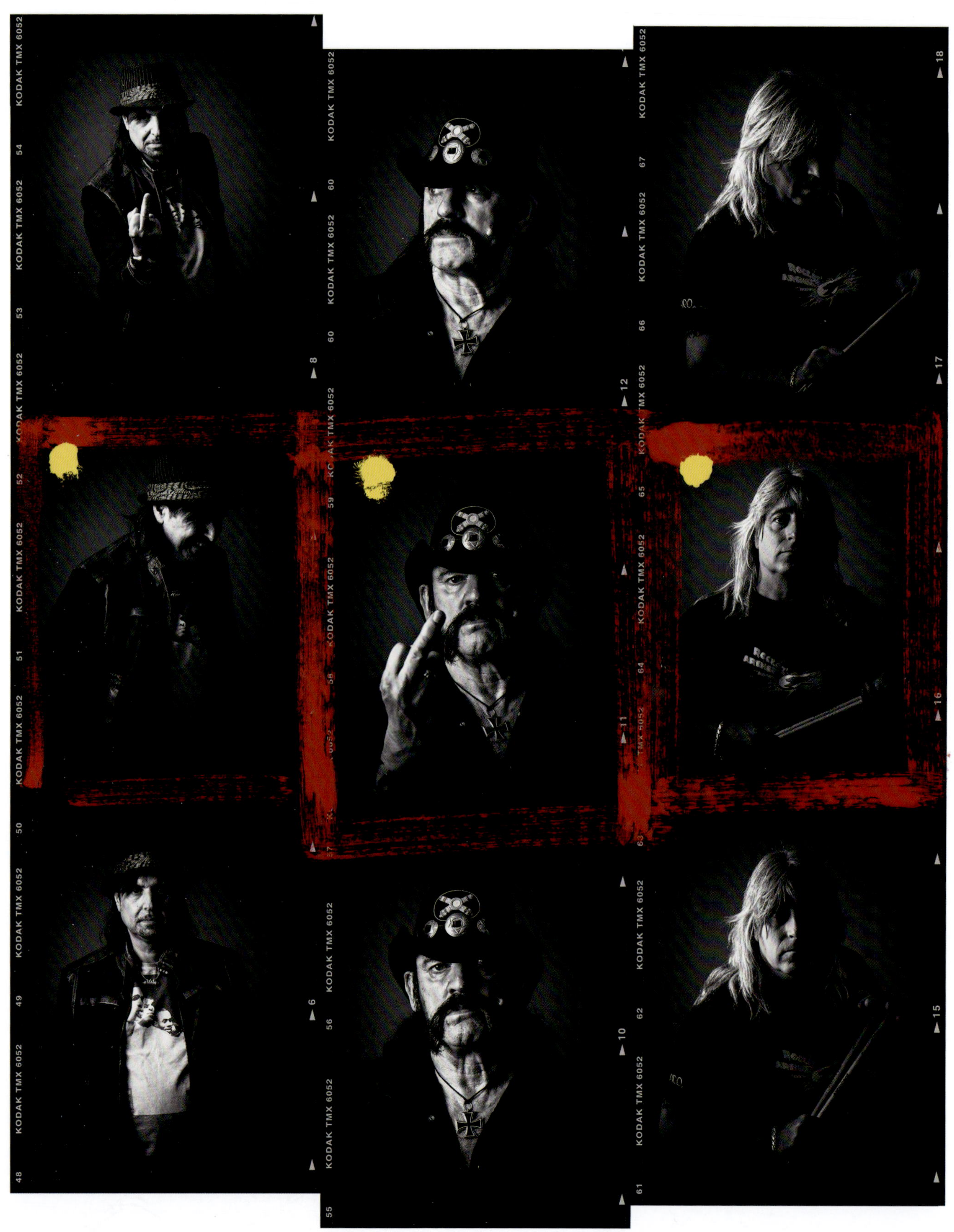

Motörhead

The shoot took place at the Music Bank studios in London. It was taken during rehearsals for a series of concerts the lads were going to do across Europe. There wasn't much space to do the shoot as every inch of the studios was filled with something, whether it was equipment, old rockers, barrels of beer, or cases of Jack Daniels. The only space I could find was inside the freight lift. After blasting out *The Ace of Spades* a couple of times, the guys came over. "I have done a few things in lifts over the years but never a f*cking photo-shoot", chuckled Lemmy. I am pleased I broke his photo/lift cherry; something else to add to my résumé.

Naomi Campbell

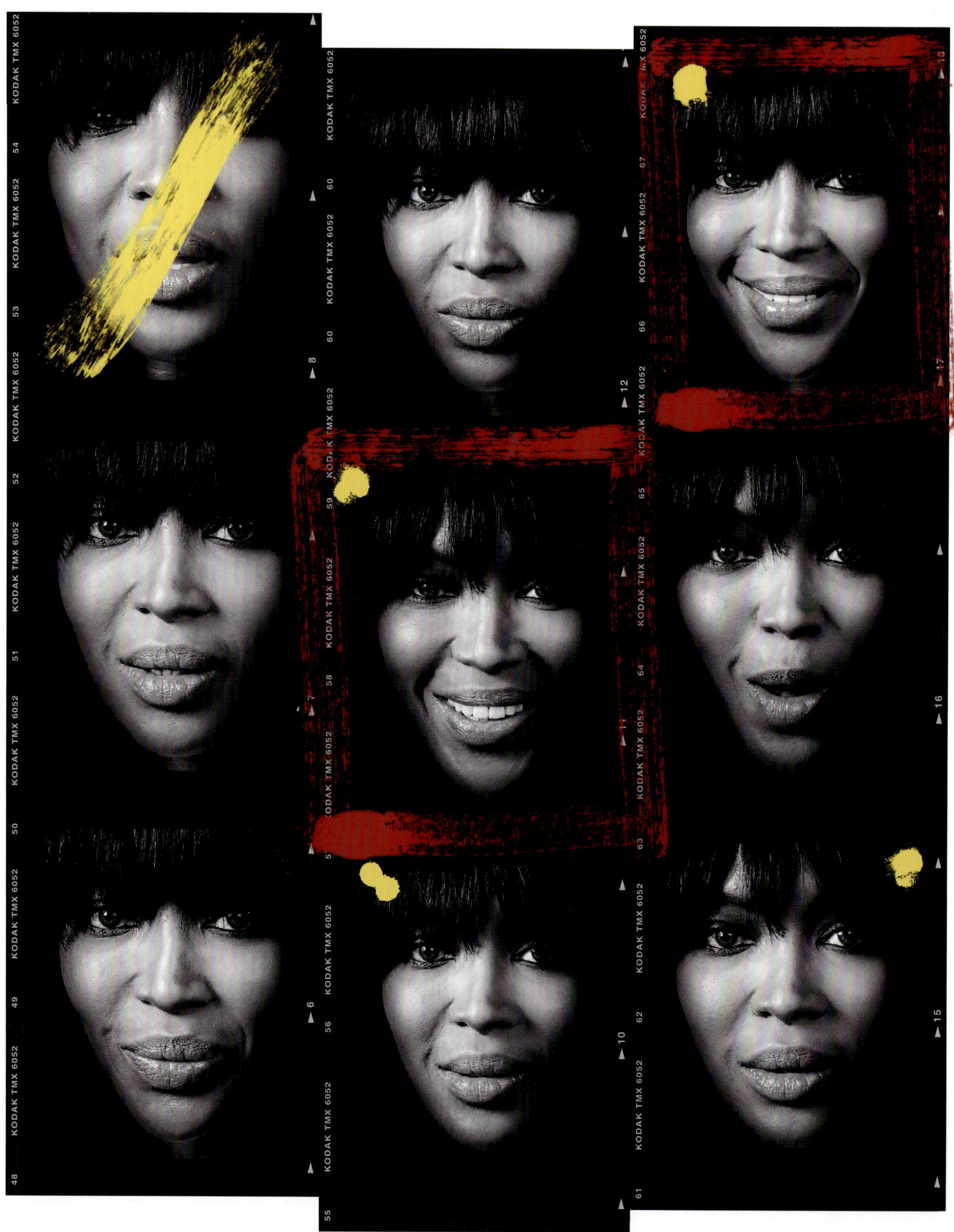

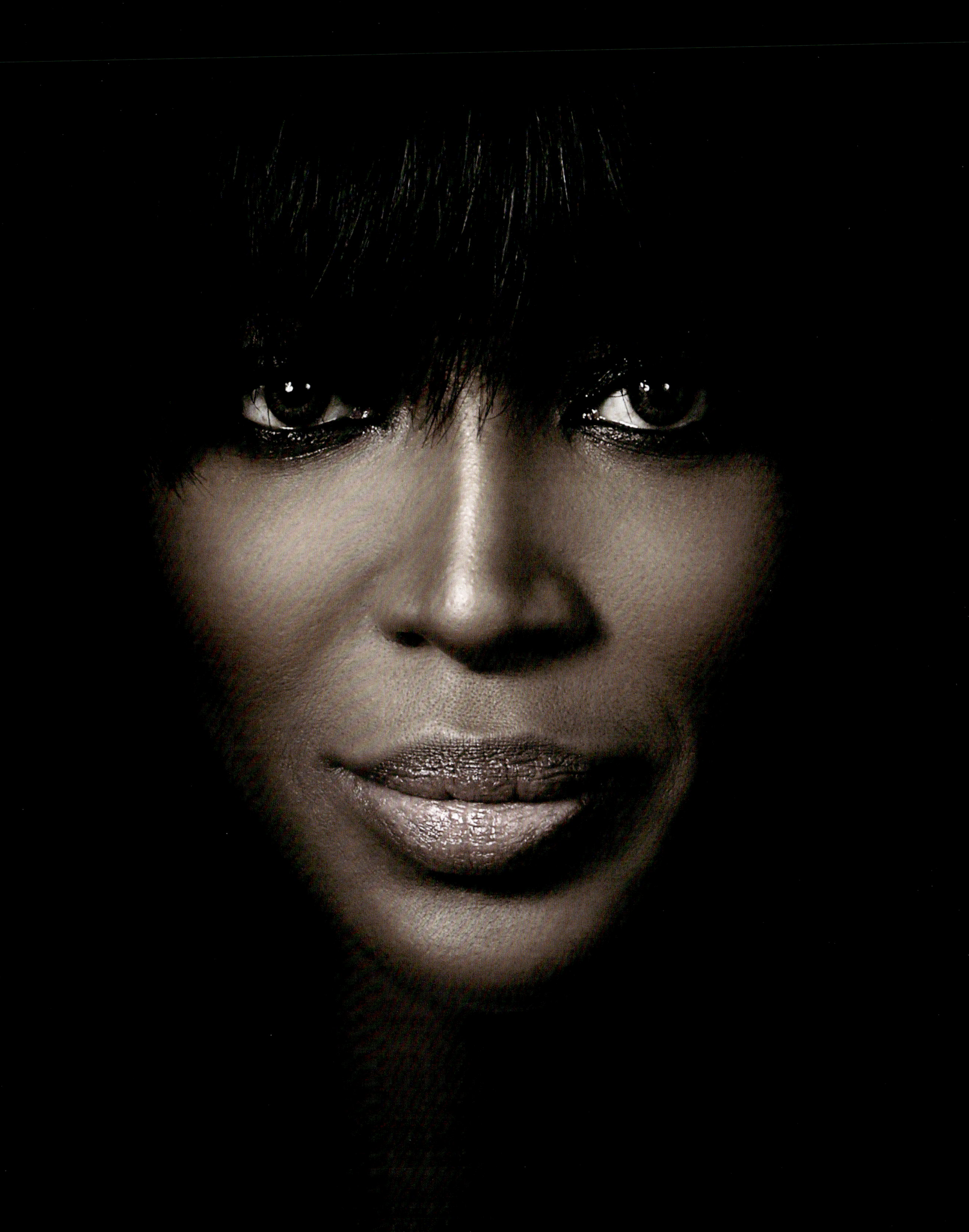

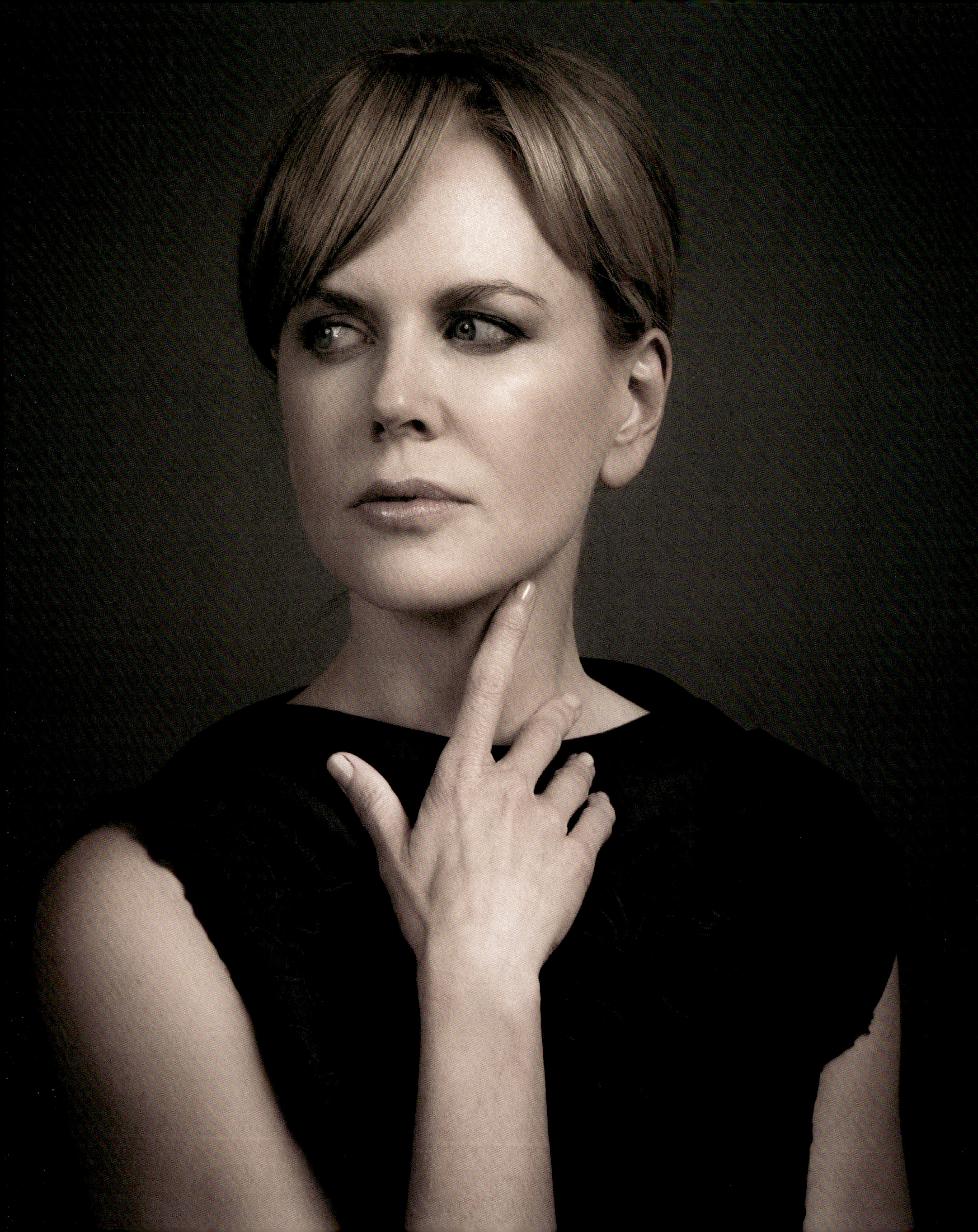

Nicole Kidman

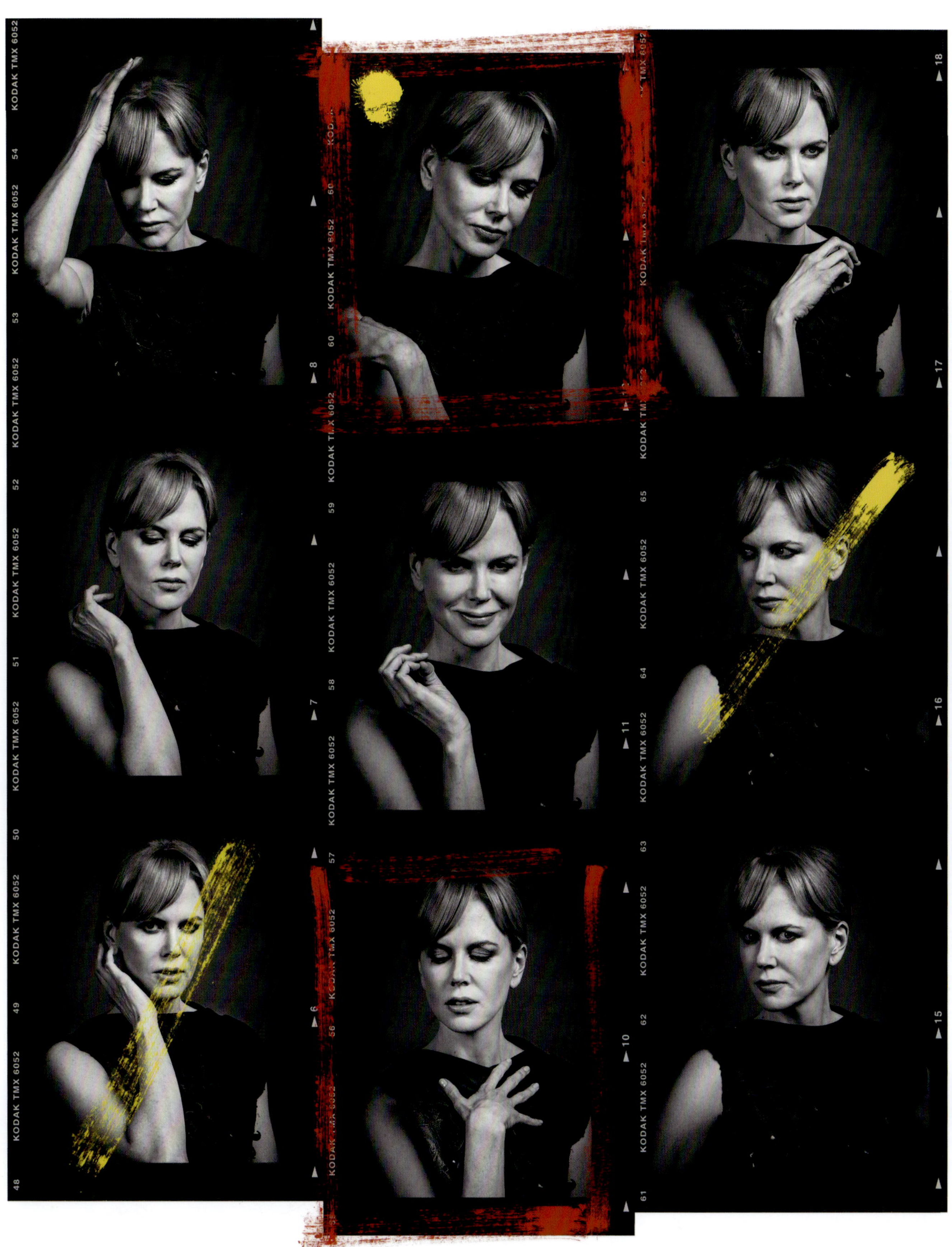

Nicole Scherzinger

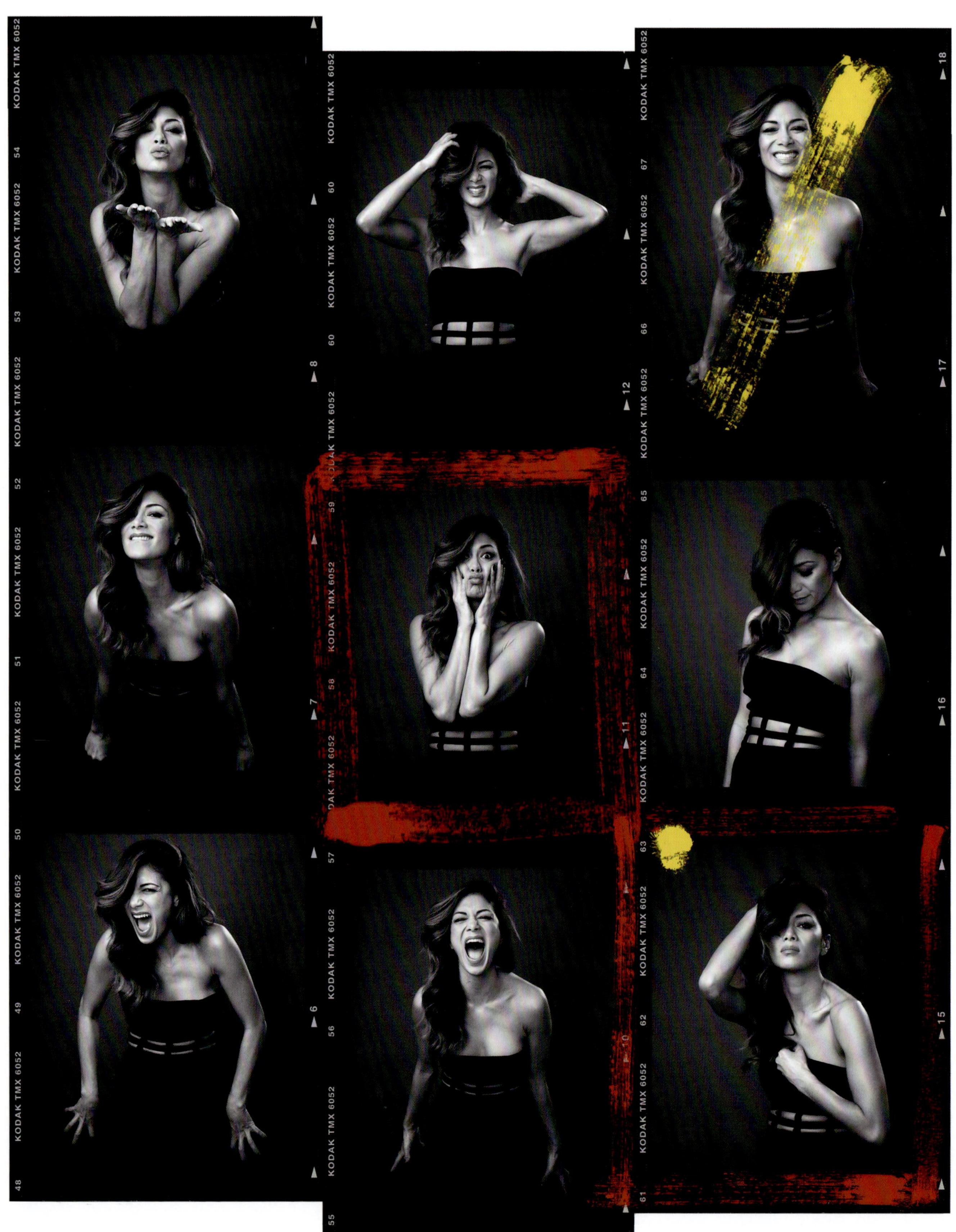

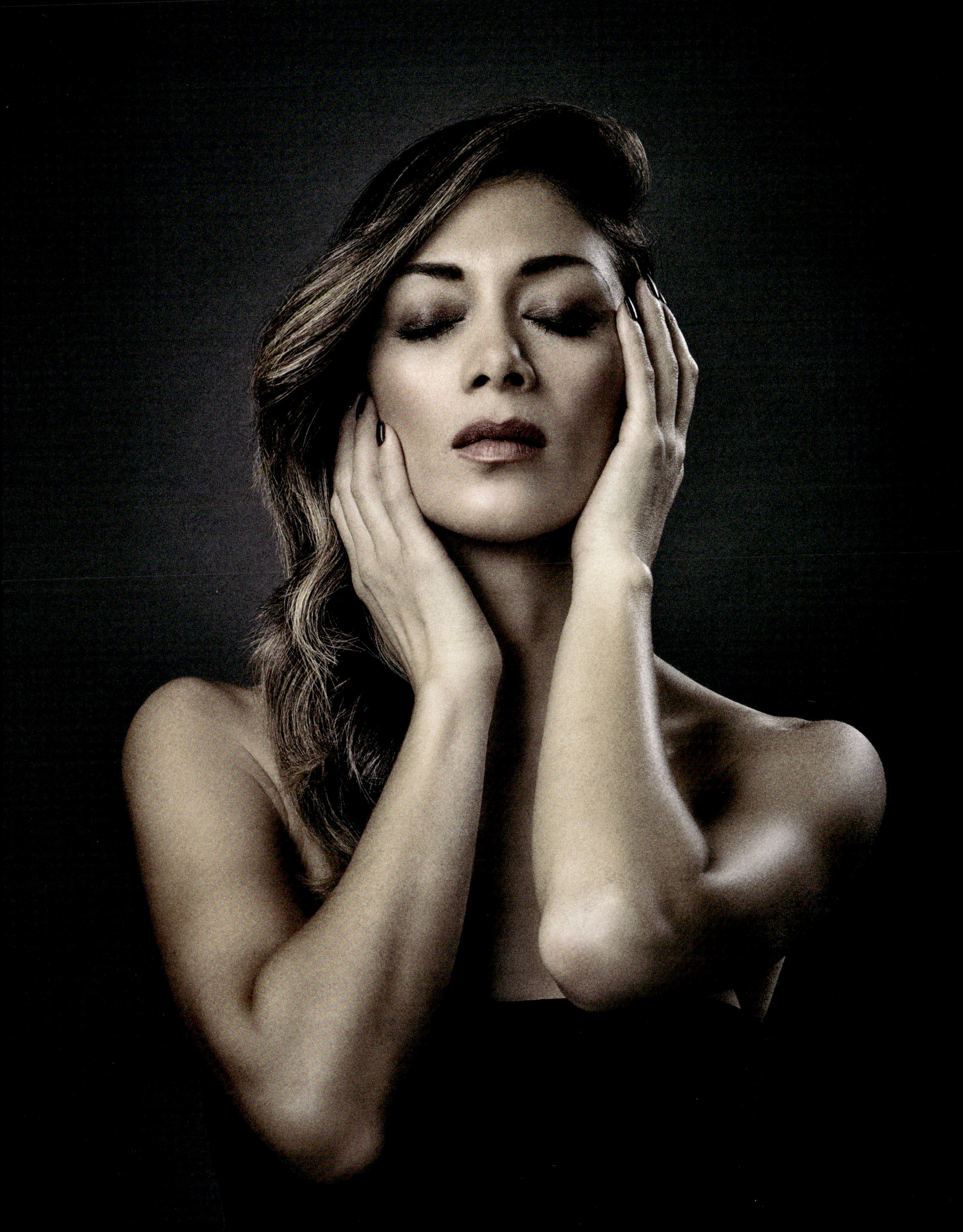

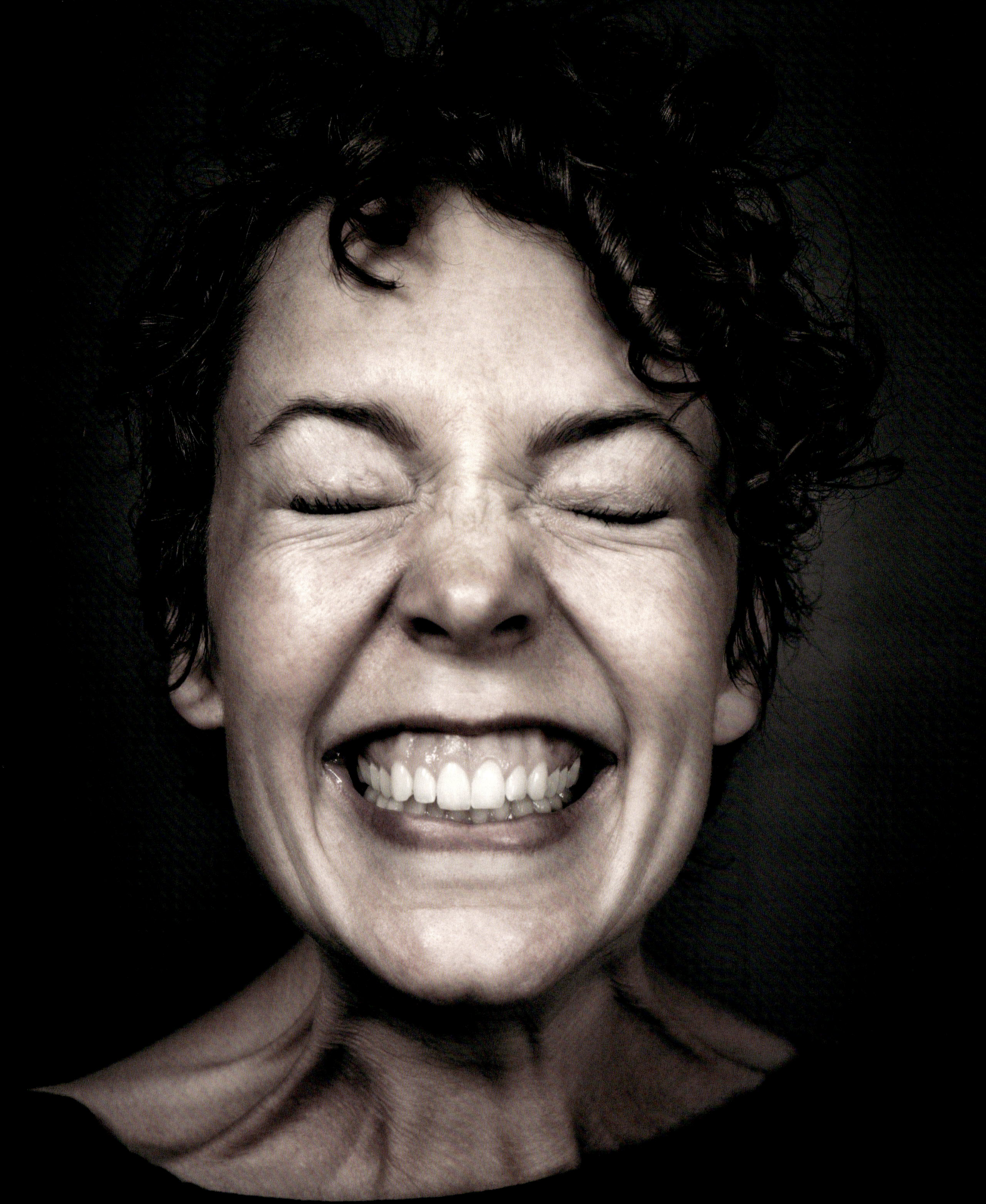

Olivia Colman

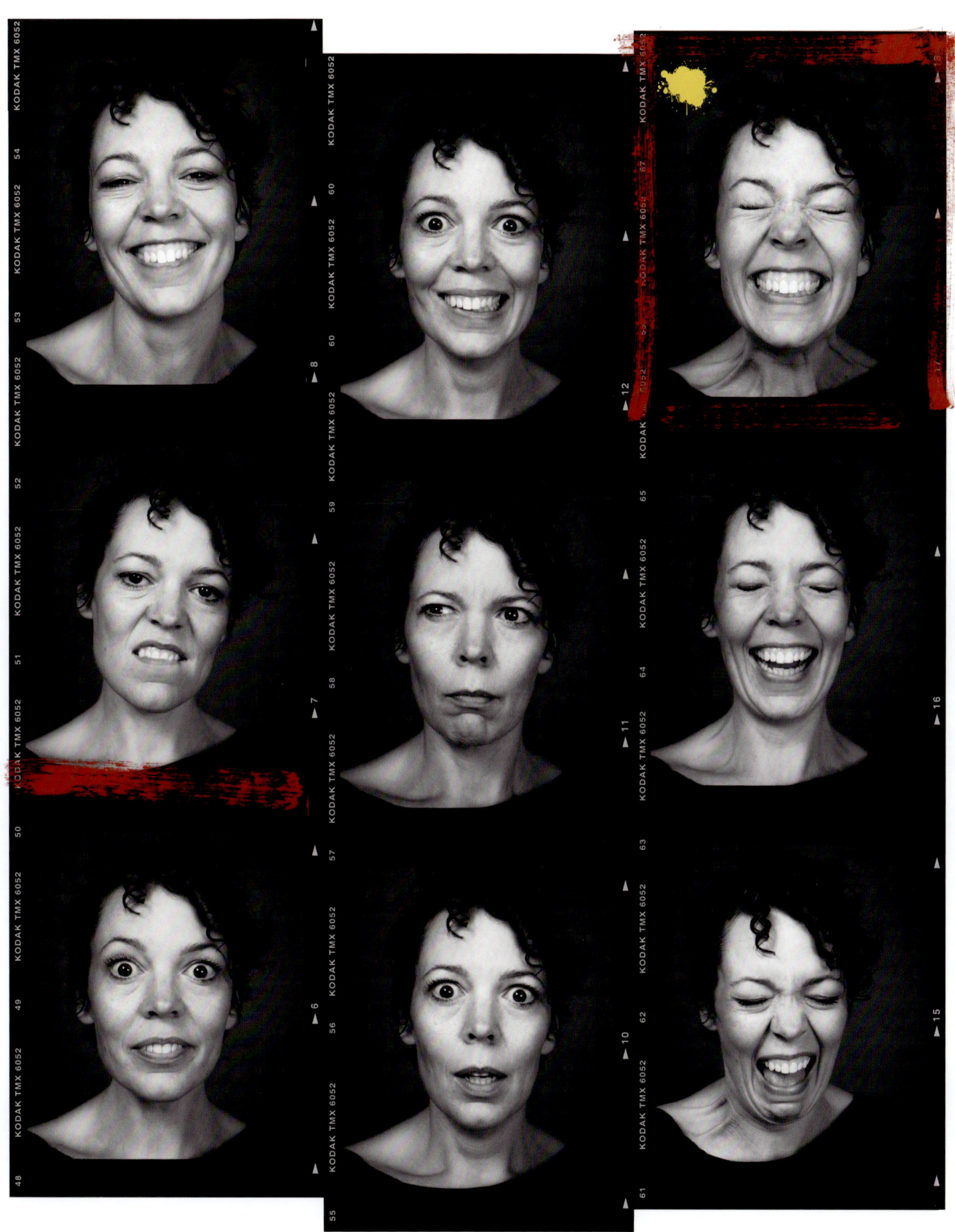

Orlando Bloom

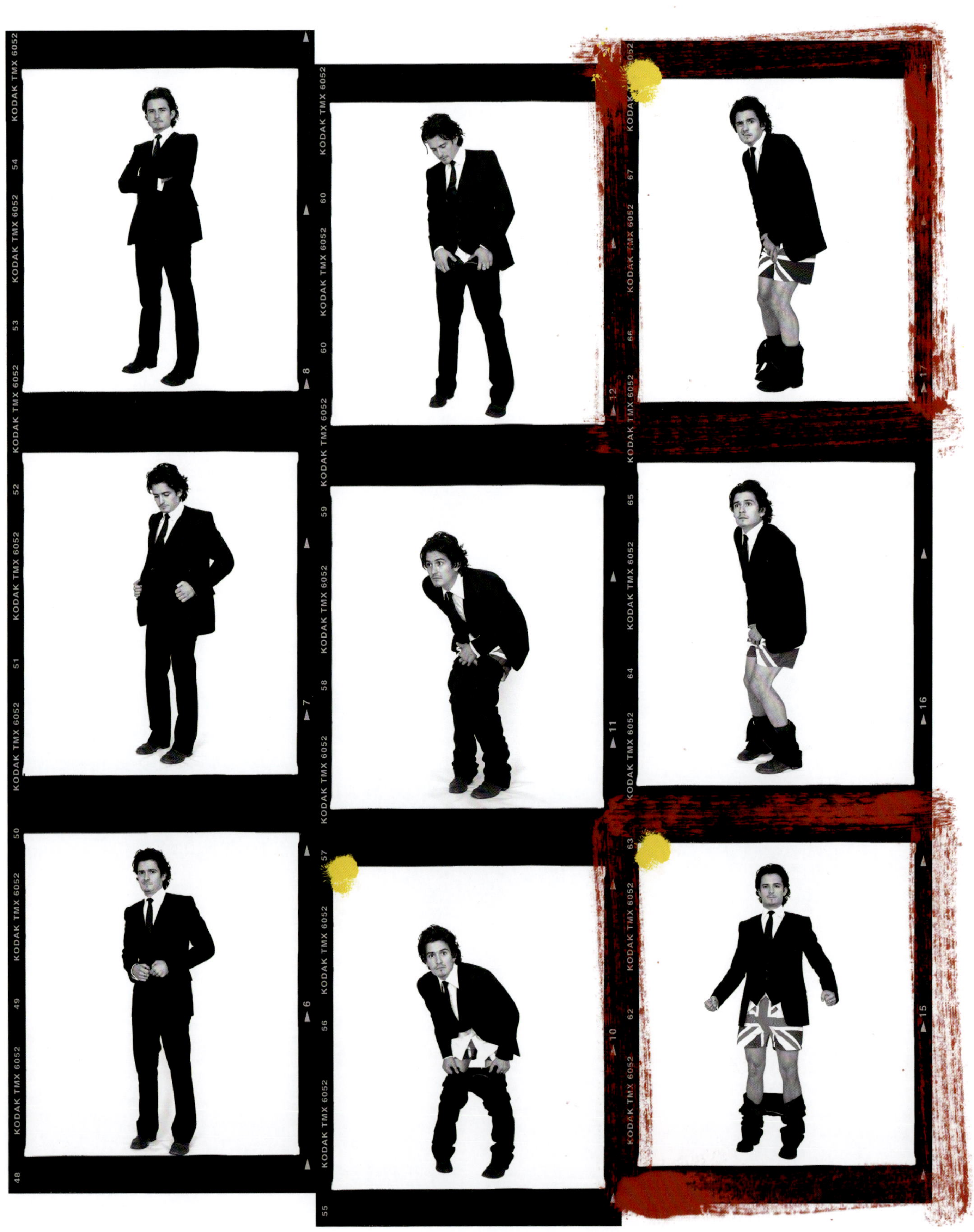

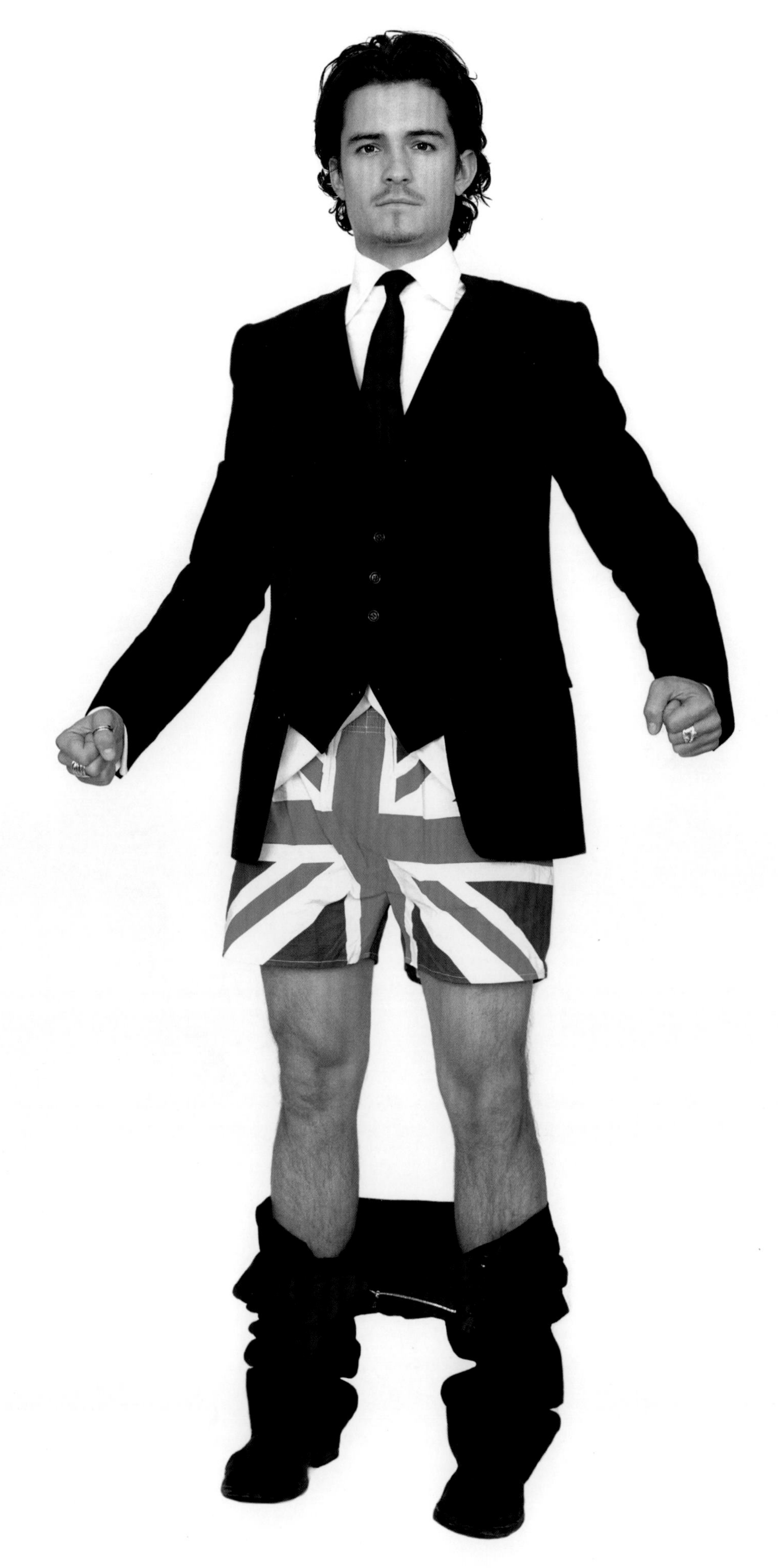

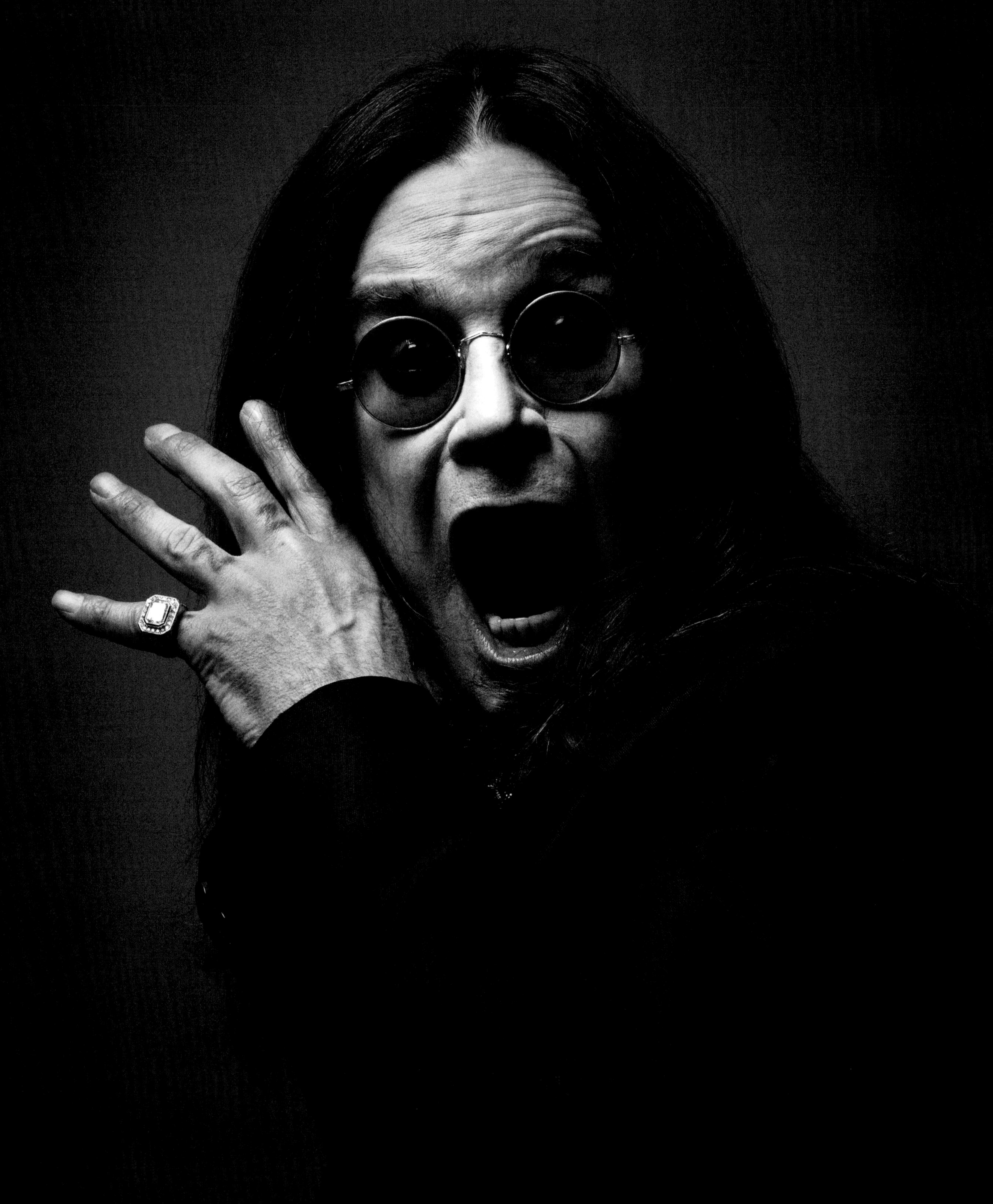

Ozzy Osbourne

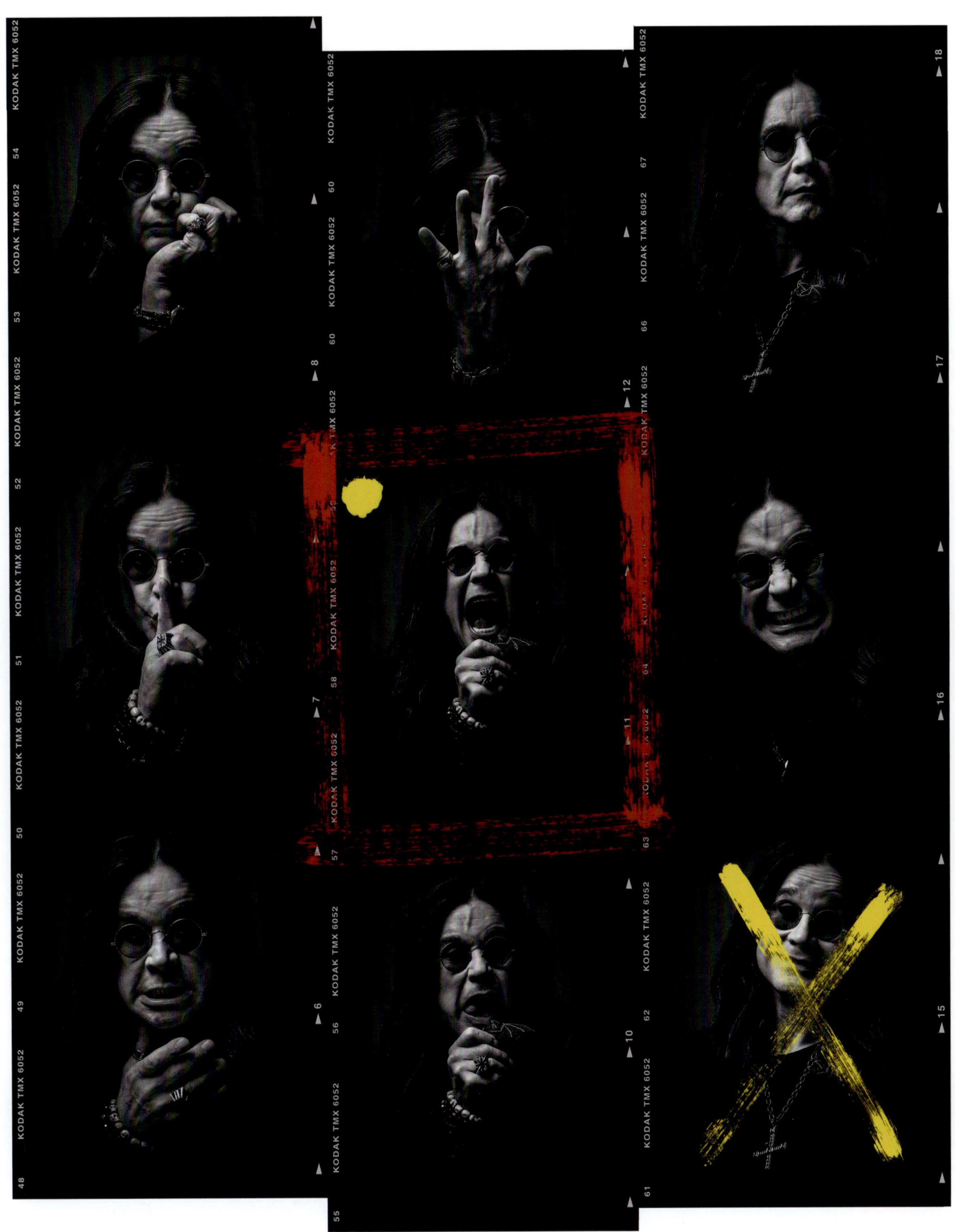

Paul Newman

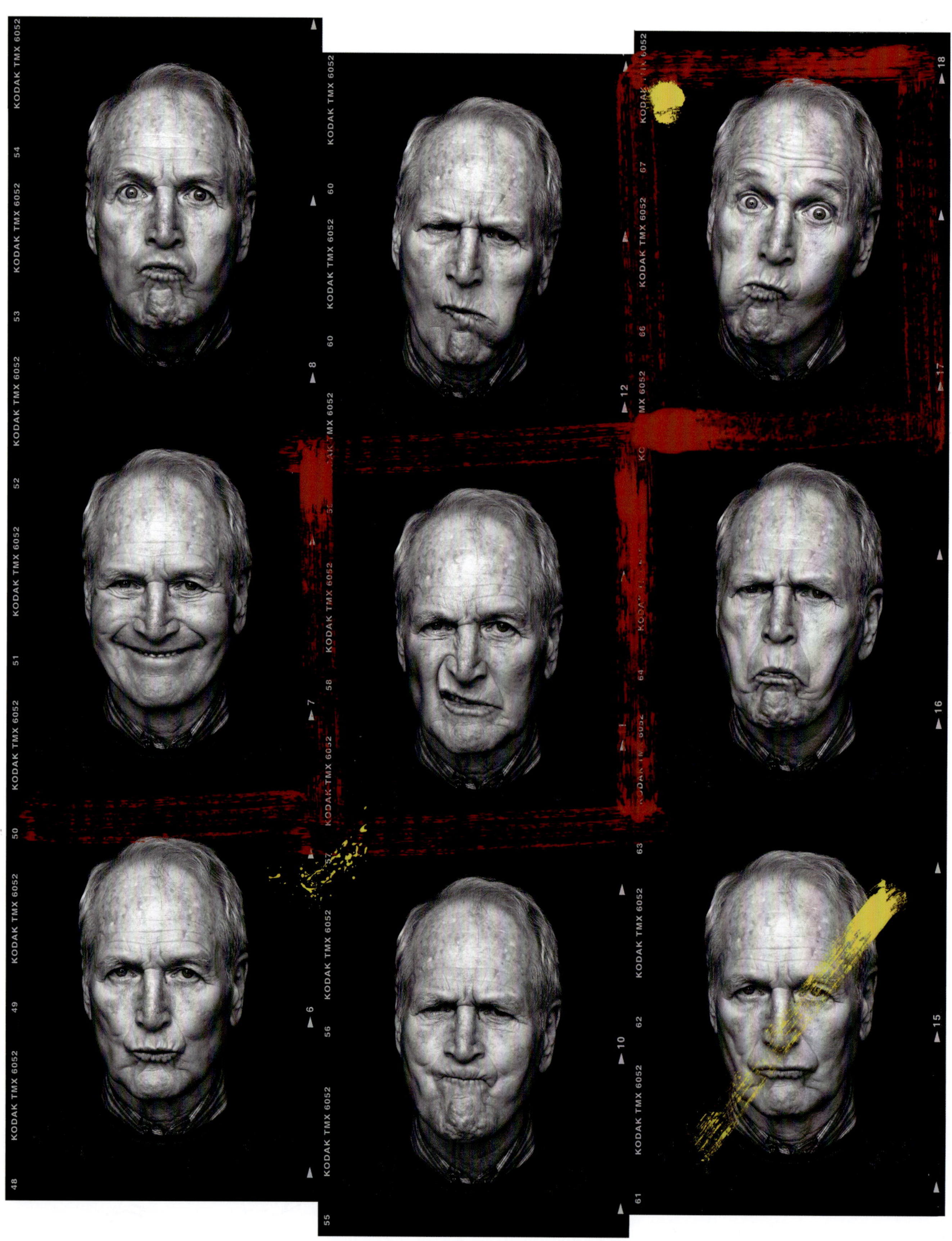

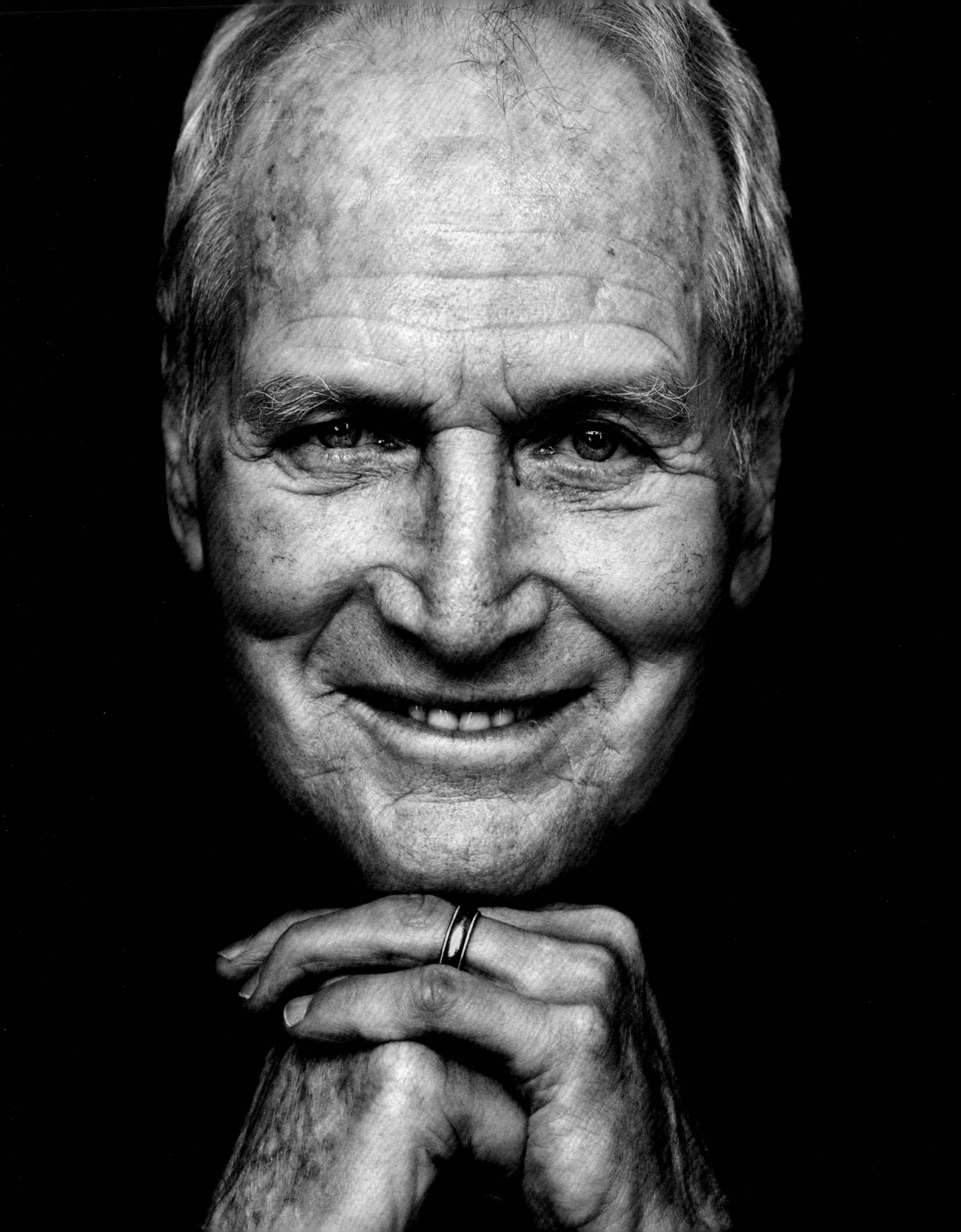

Penélope Cruz

Penélope was a dream and every inch as beautiful in the flesh as she is on film. I was all set up and ready to shoot at The Dorchester hotel, when Penelope arrived. I could hear muffled talking and laughing as she entered, and following her into the studio was her husband, the actor Javier Bardem. I had shot Javier before and we got on very well, so he wanted to come to the shoot to see me and say "Hi". My idea for Penelope was a sexy, brooding shot. But every time we started shooting, Javier kept making comments to her in Spanish. I've no idea what was said, but each time her cheeks flushed and she burst into hysterical laughter. I took the chance to take some fun shots during their banter, but when I wanted the brooding shots, I made Javier stand outside like a naughty schoolboy, which actually made her laugh more. Eventually I got the shot I was after.

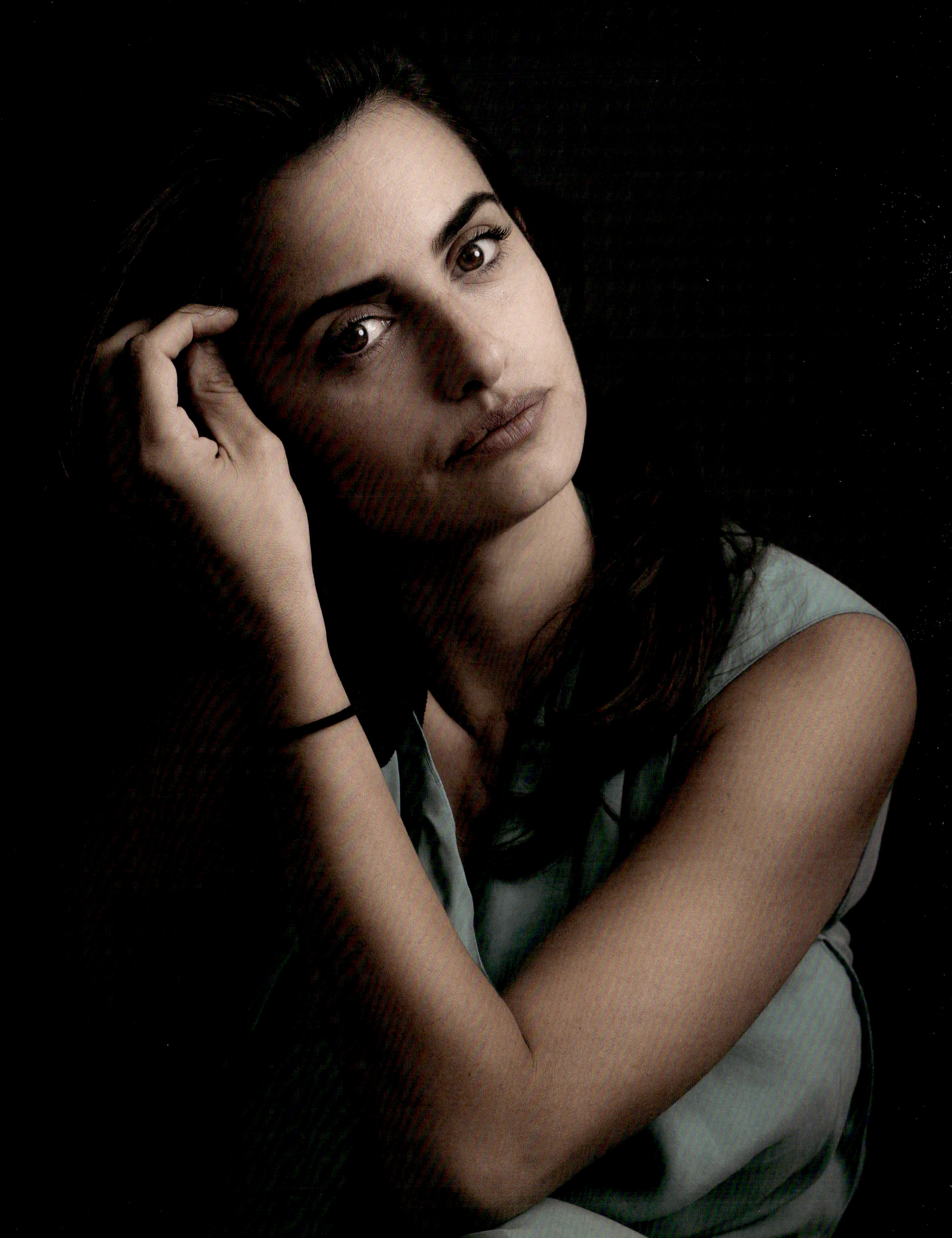

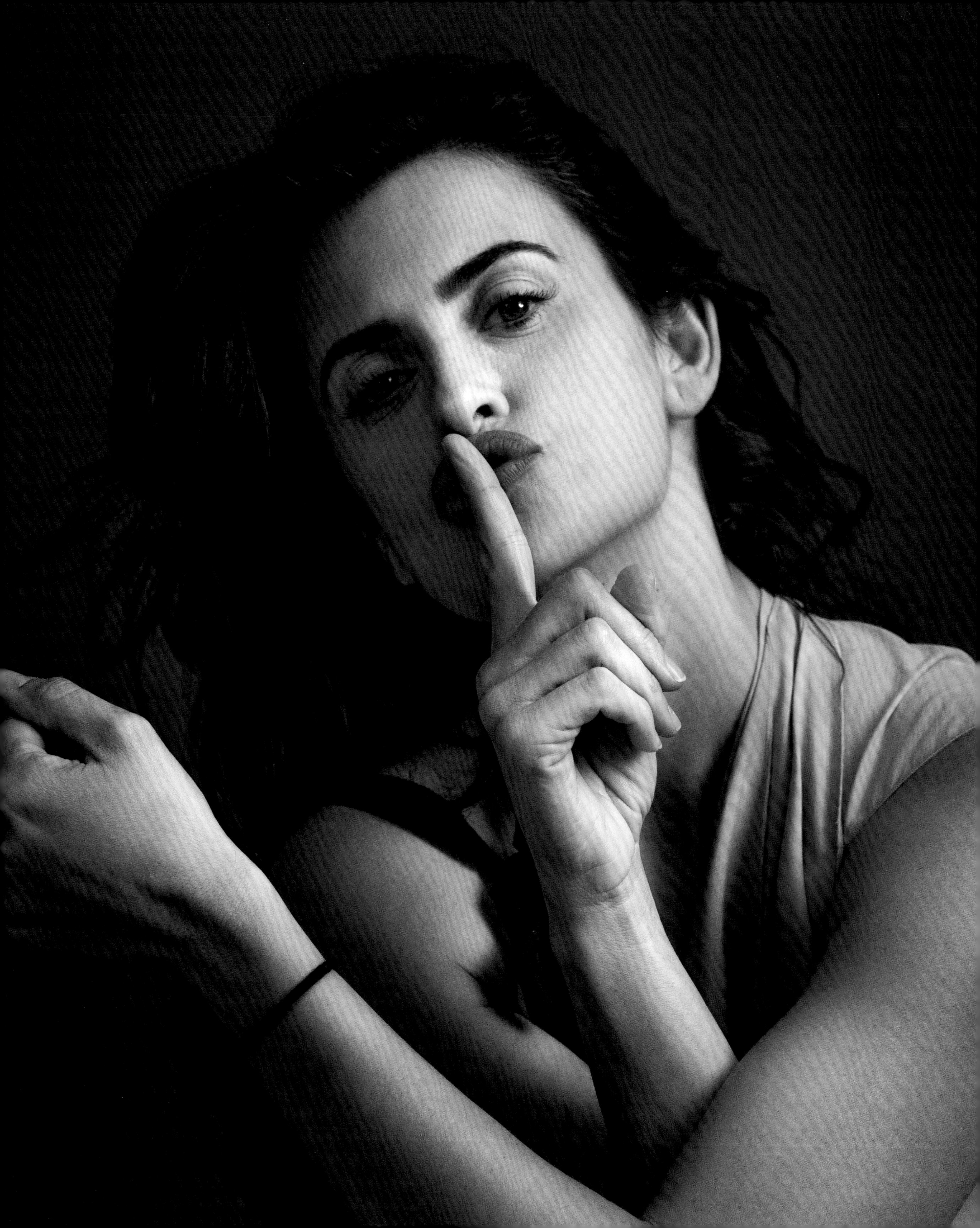

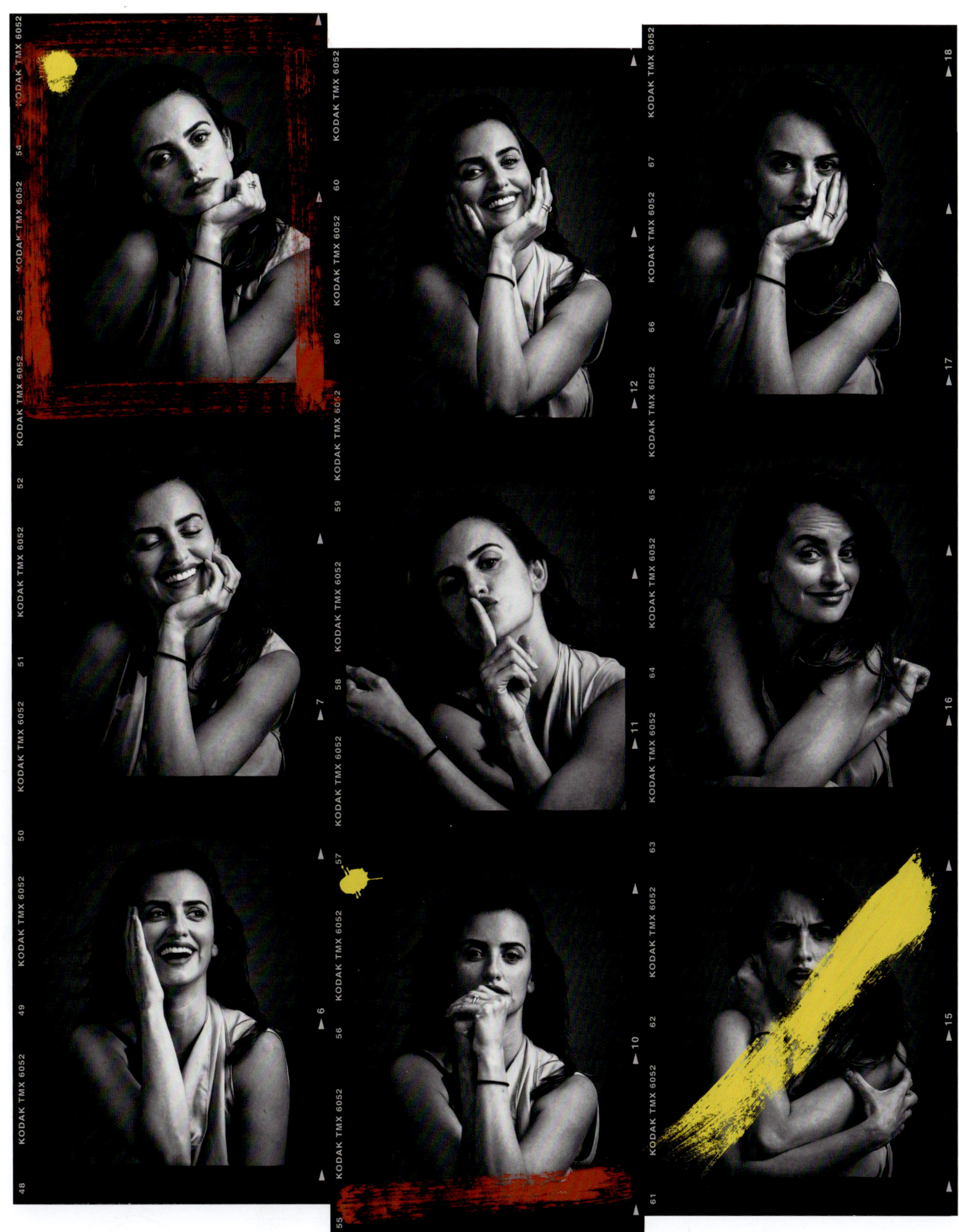

Peter Capaldi

Most famous people are pretty good at faking it, and especially good at faking being at ease – it's all part of the job description. But in Andy's pictures what you are seeing are some of the most famous, most photographed people in the world having fun and feeling completely relaxed; securing that trust is just one of his gifts.

I suspect that those whose success is absolutely wedded to their appearance put their faith in Andy because they know he is a brilliant photographer. In other hands, the 'ideal' image is likely to be one that leans into popular ideas of beauty or cool; one that displays the subject at their most seductive. But a key element that distinguishes Andy's pictures from others is that they remain unedited after the event: never touched-up, edited or tampered with in any way. They are unflinching, stark, raw in their depiction of the vagaries of skin and bone, and age. The image that Andy captures at that particular moment, on that specific day, is the one that you get to see, and the only manipulation is in the choice of published shot. His monochromatic style sees almost photo-journalistic lighting merge in a painterly way with shadow, light and perfect composition.

Like all great photographers, he's capturing moments: framing them, arranging them, finding the best space in which to communicate them. And, ironically, this approach complements the subjects beyond measure, makes them gratifyingly relatable and, if anything, more attractive.

In this wonderful collection of contact sheets, you get to see all of the images taken during the sessions, not just the ones chosen for publication, and I hope you enjoy looking at them as much as the subjects enjoyed having them taken.

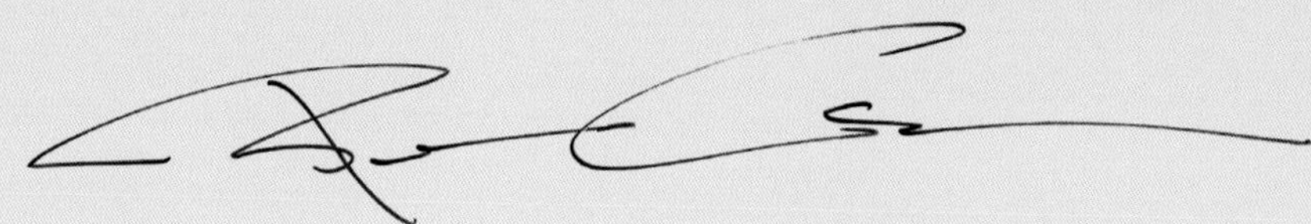

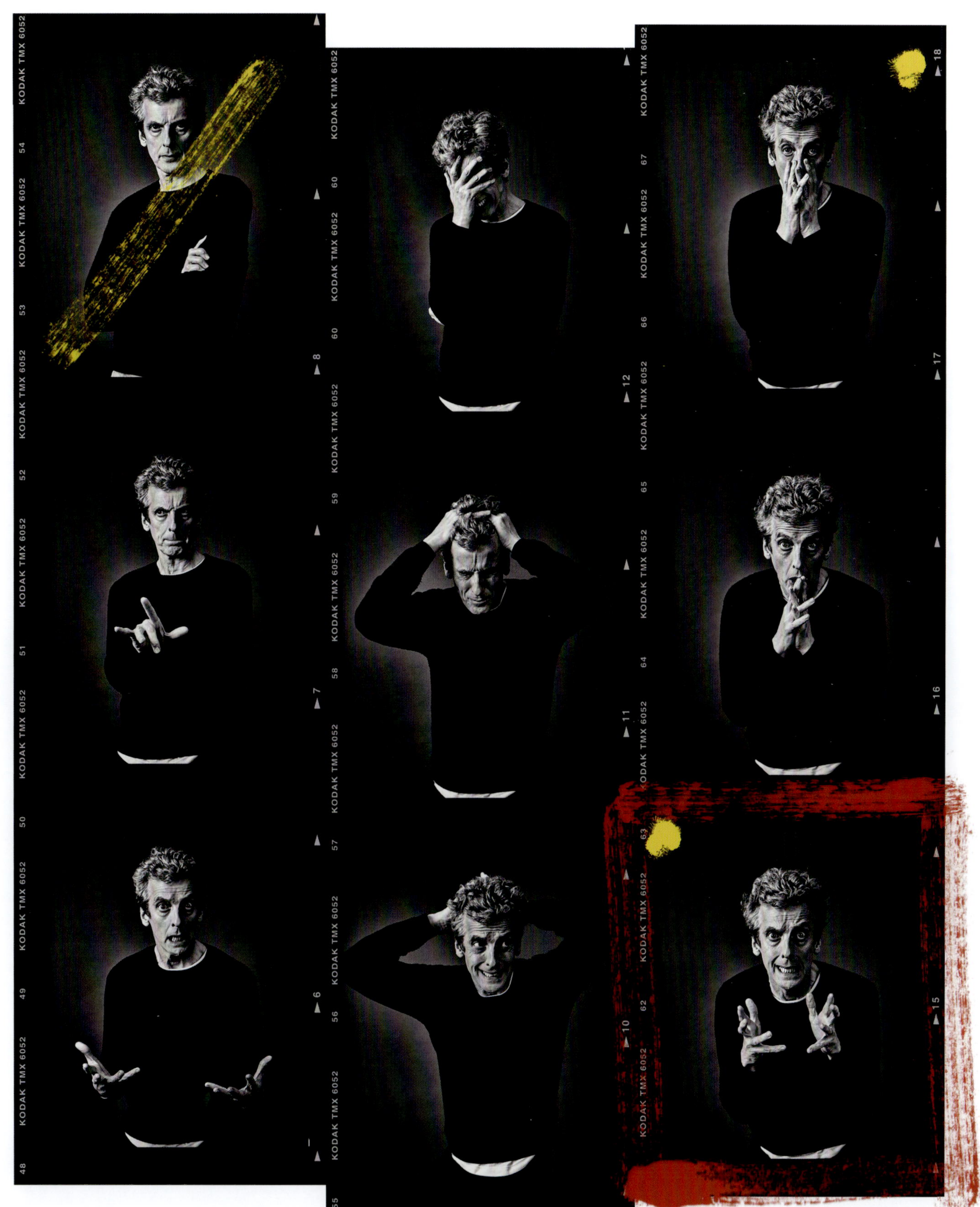
KODAK TMX 6052

Phil Collins

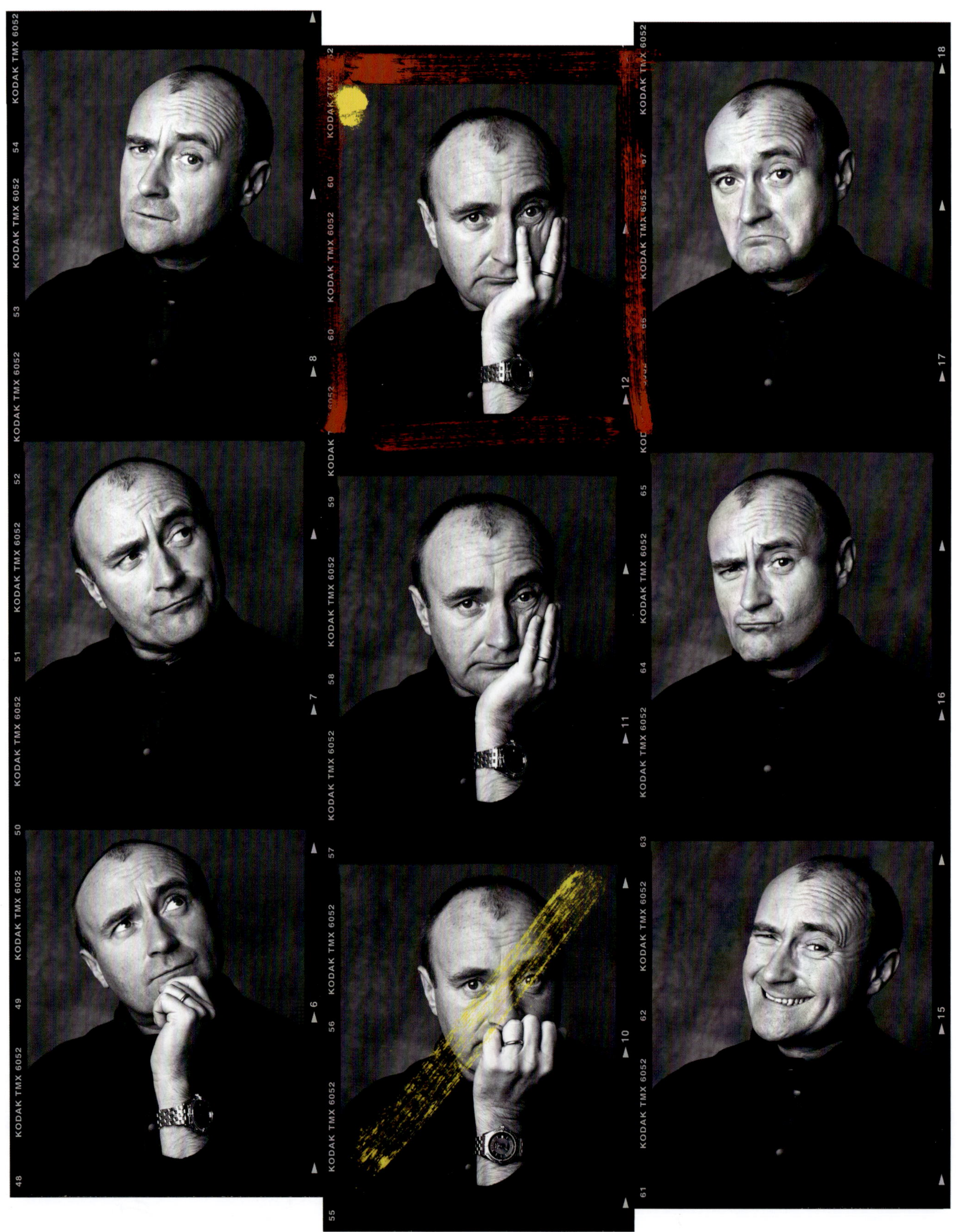

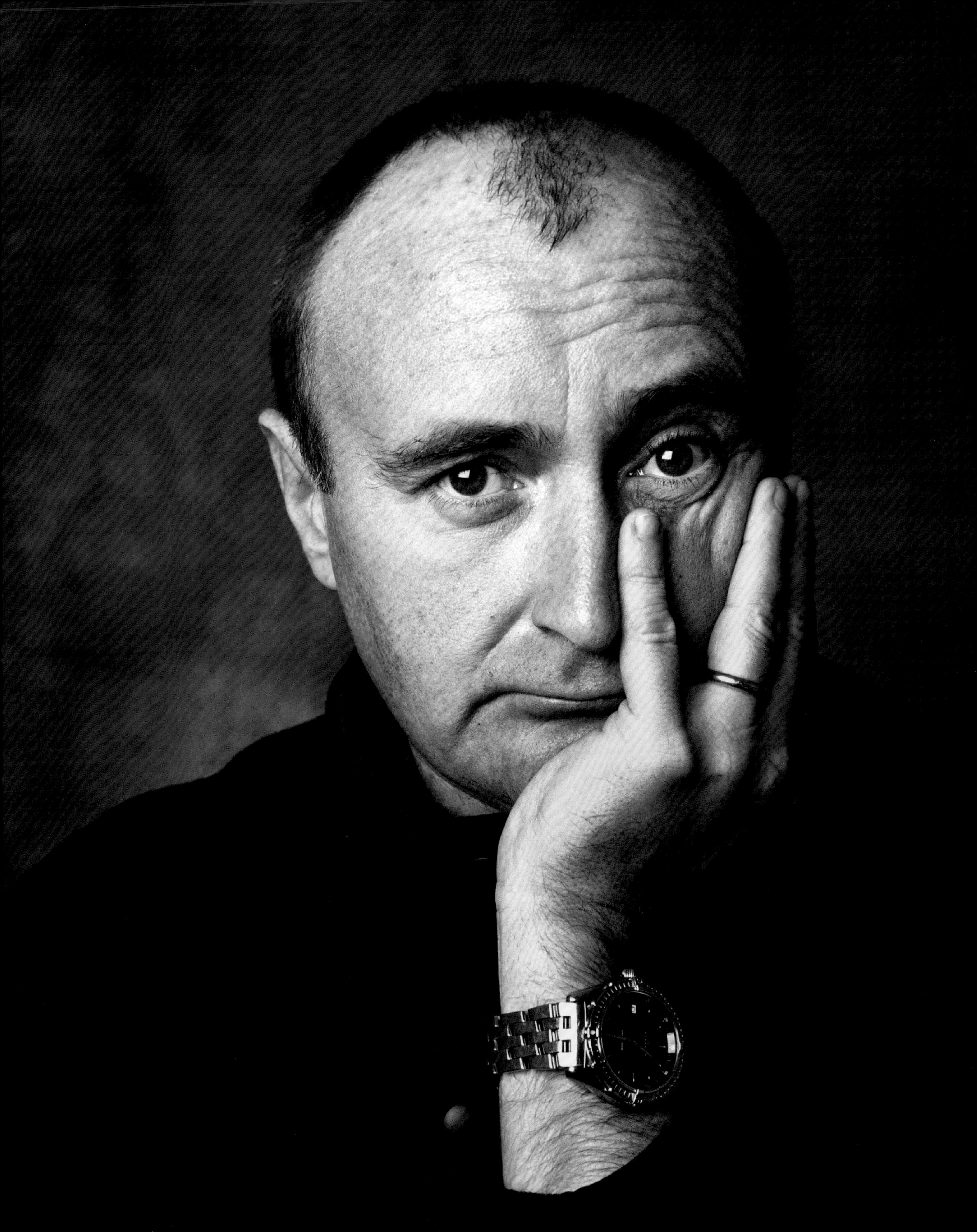

Pierce Brosnan

The original shoot was to be in his house in Malibu but there was a big fire days before we were meant to meet, so it took place in a rental property down the street. Pierce is a relaxed man and I met him on the street walking his dog. When he saw me he called down the road "Ah! Mr Gotts, I've been expecting you", which I found very amusing as I'm an avid 007 fan. He was casting a new movie to be filmed in Ireland and he was picking my brain on actresses that I may have photographed that he did not know. Since *Remington Steele*, Pierce has been cast as a good-looking, charismatic man. In photos he either does his classic smouldering face or wide mouth. So my mission was to get him to do silly faces, and Pierce termed this request as 'interesting'. Ultimately, Pierce still sees himself as James Bond from the mid to late '90s. I think he finds it hard to accept he is greying and time is no-one's friend.

Normally when he sees pictures after photo shoots, they have been retouched, therefore keeping alive his James Bond perception of himself. Like most people, he would probably like the world to see a polished version of himself, but I believe my shots show handsome Pierce in a new playful light, which is a nice change.

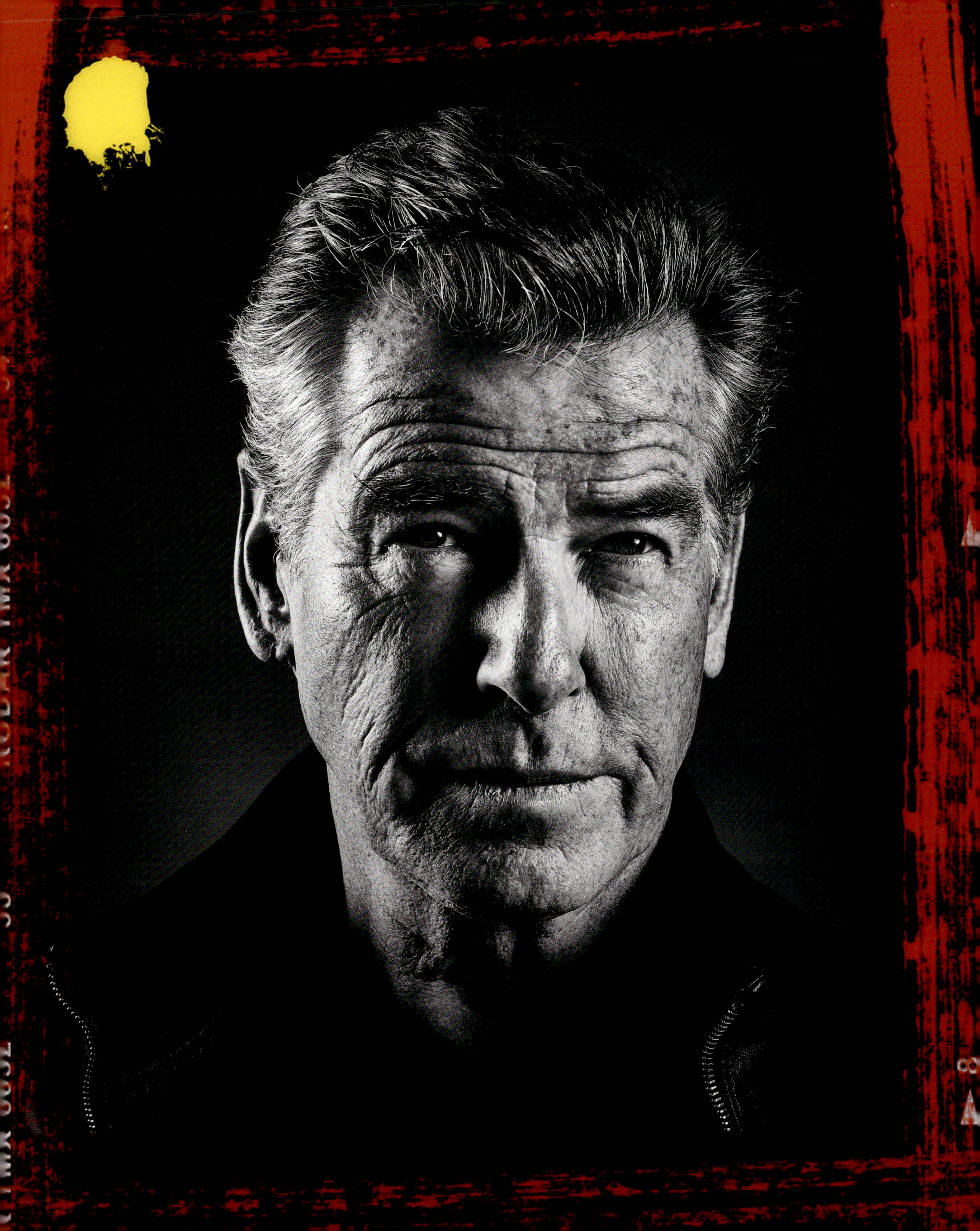

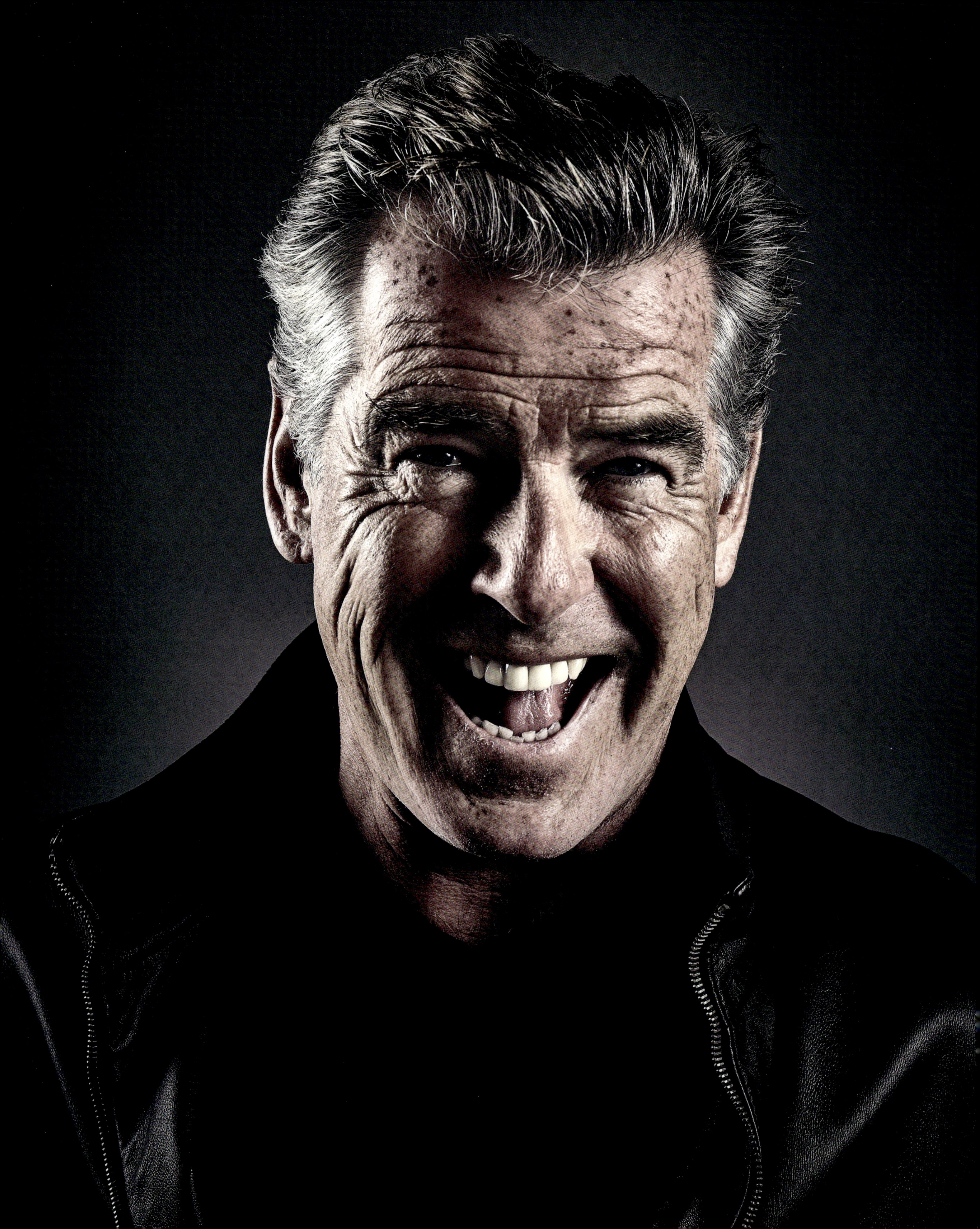

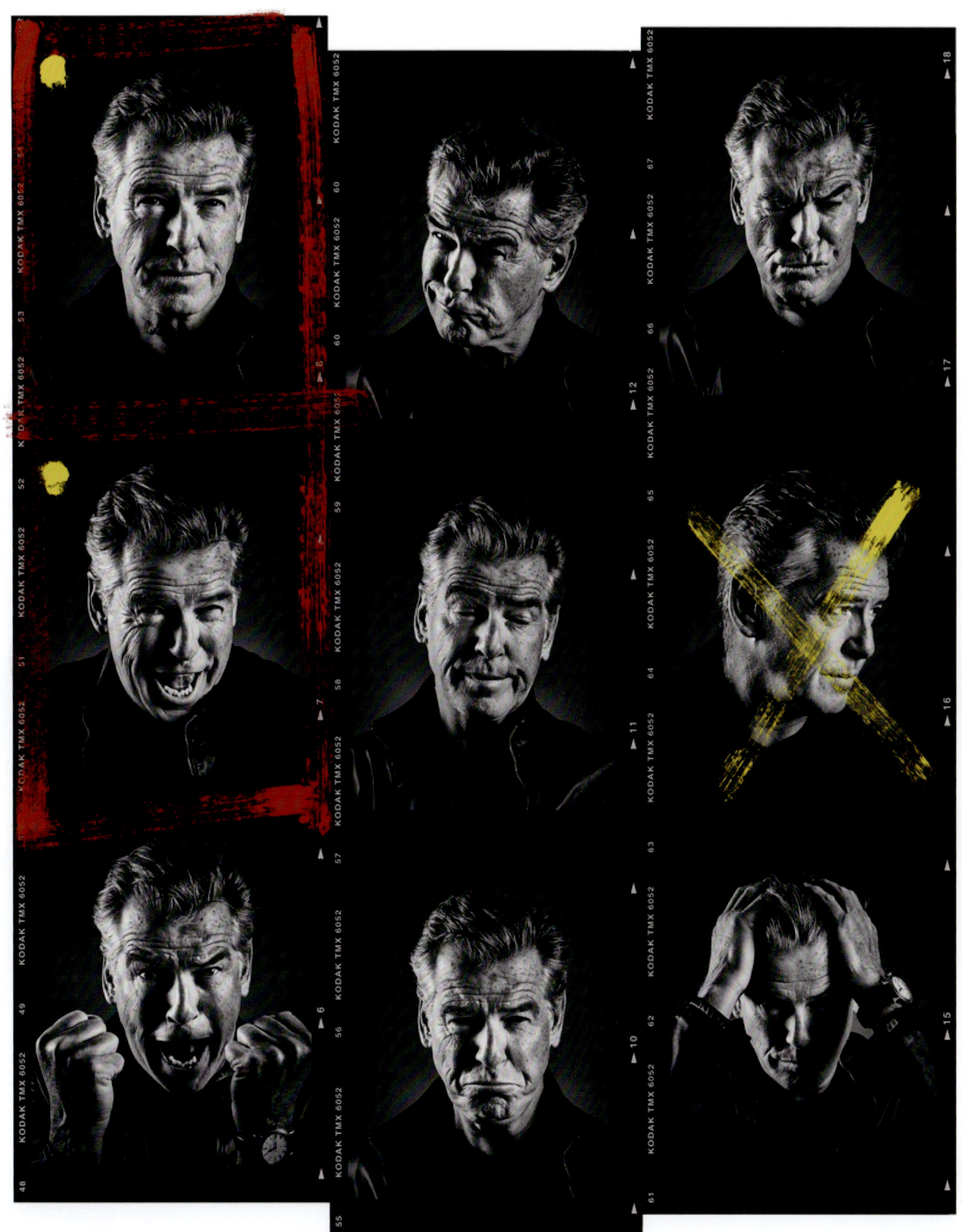

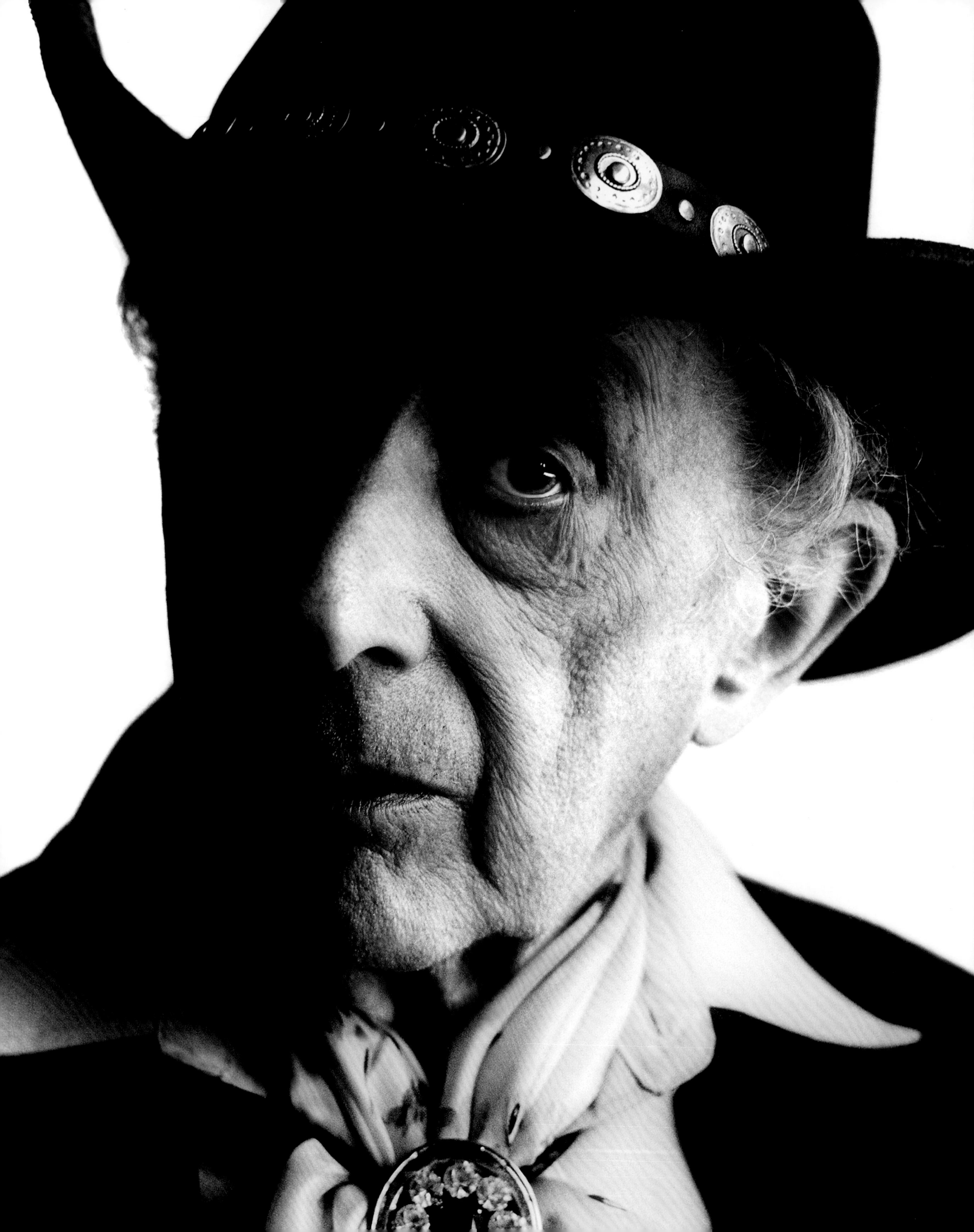

Quentin Crisp

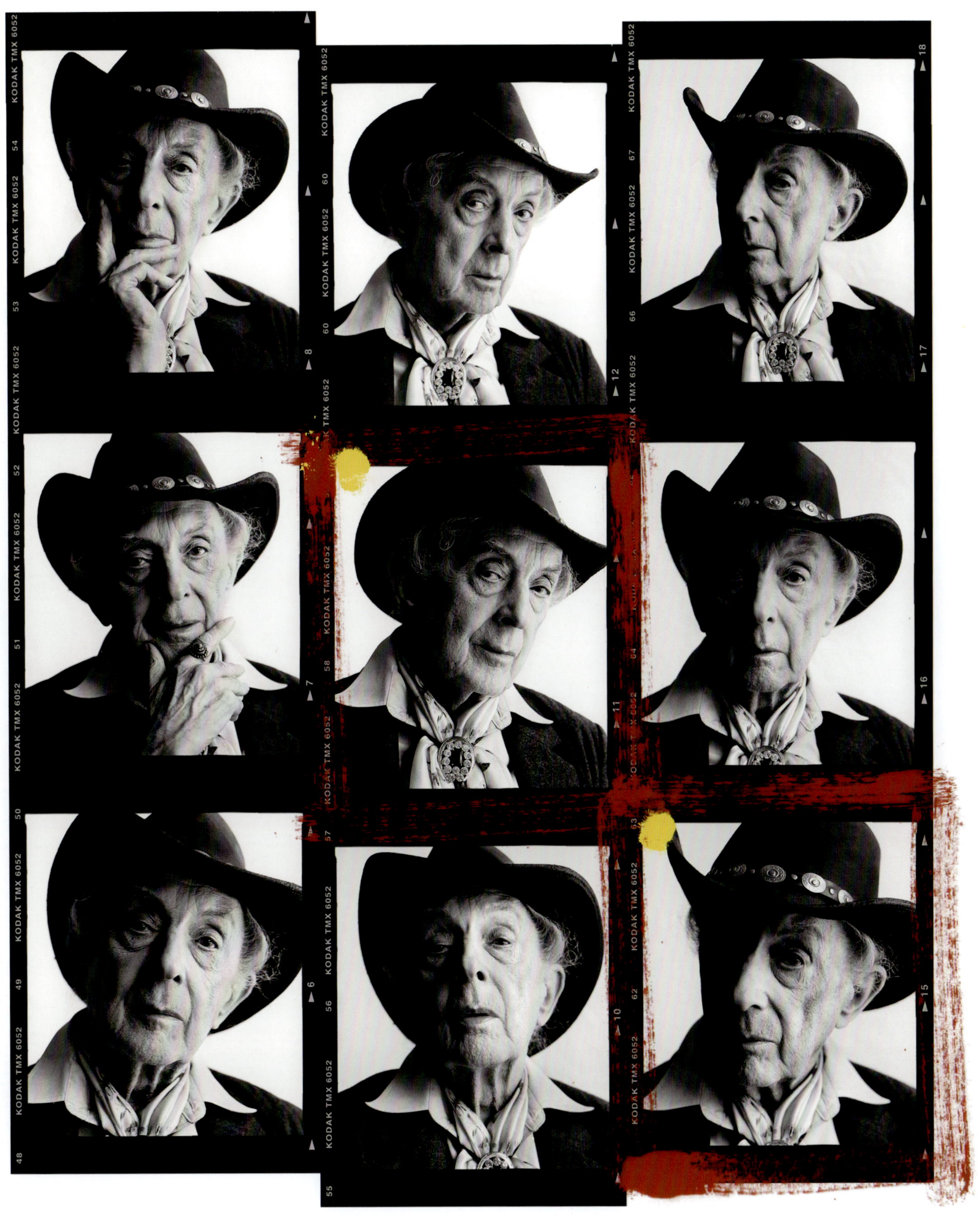

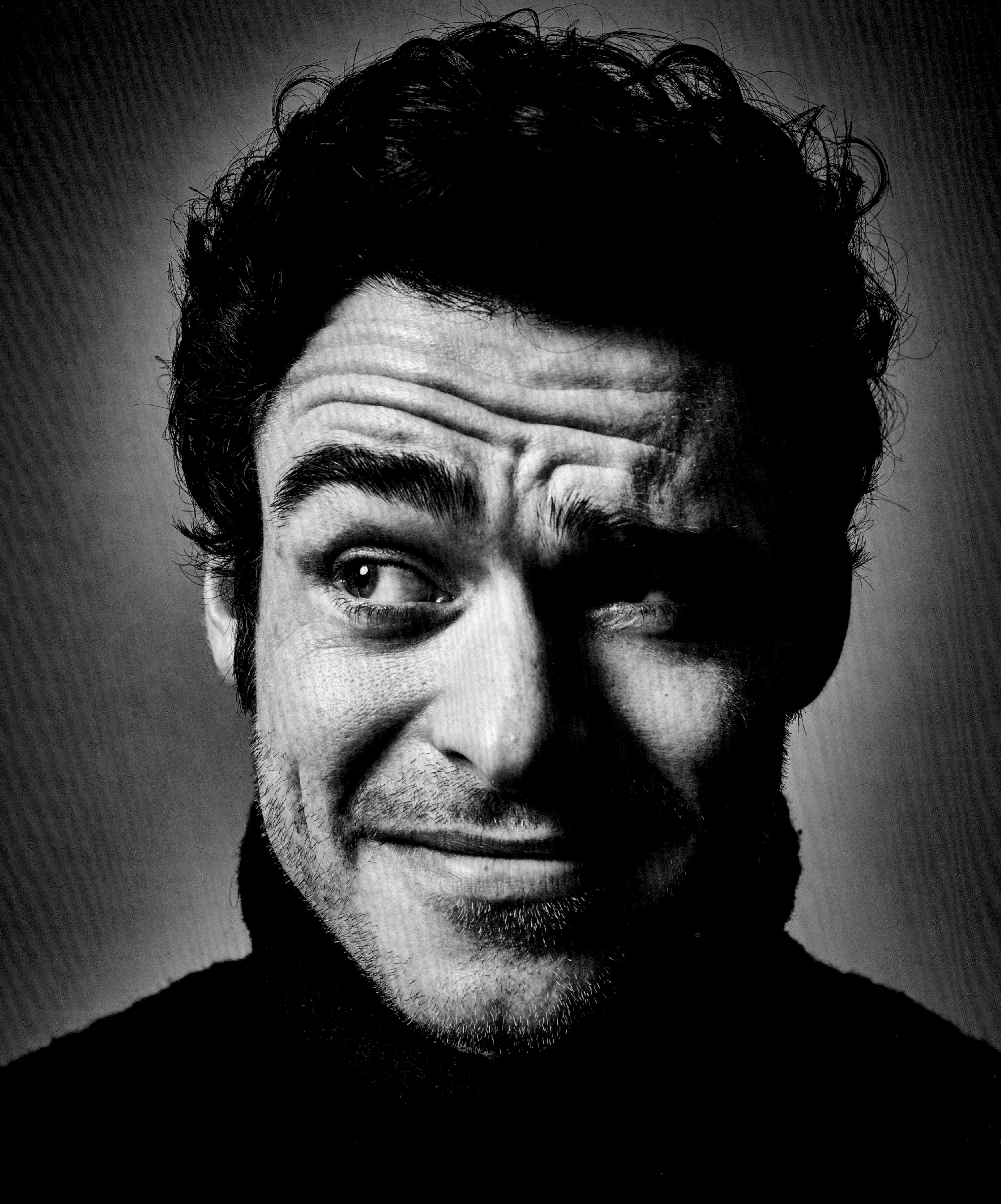

Richard Madden

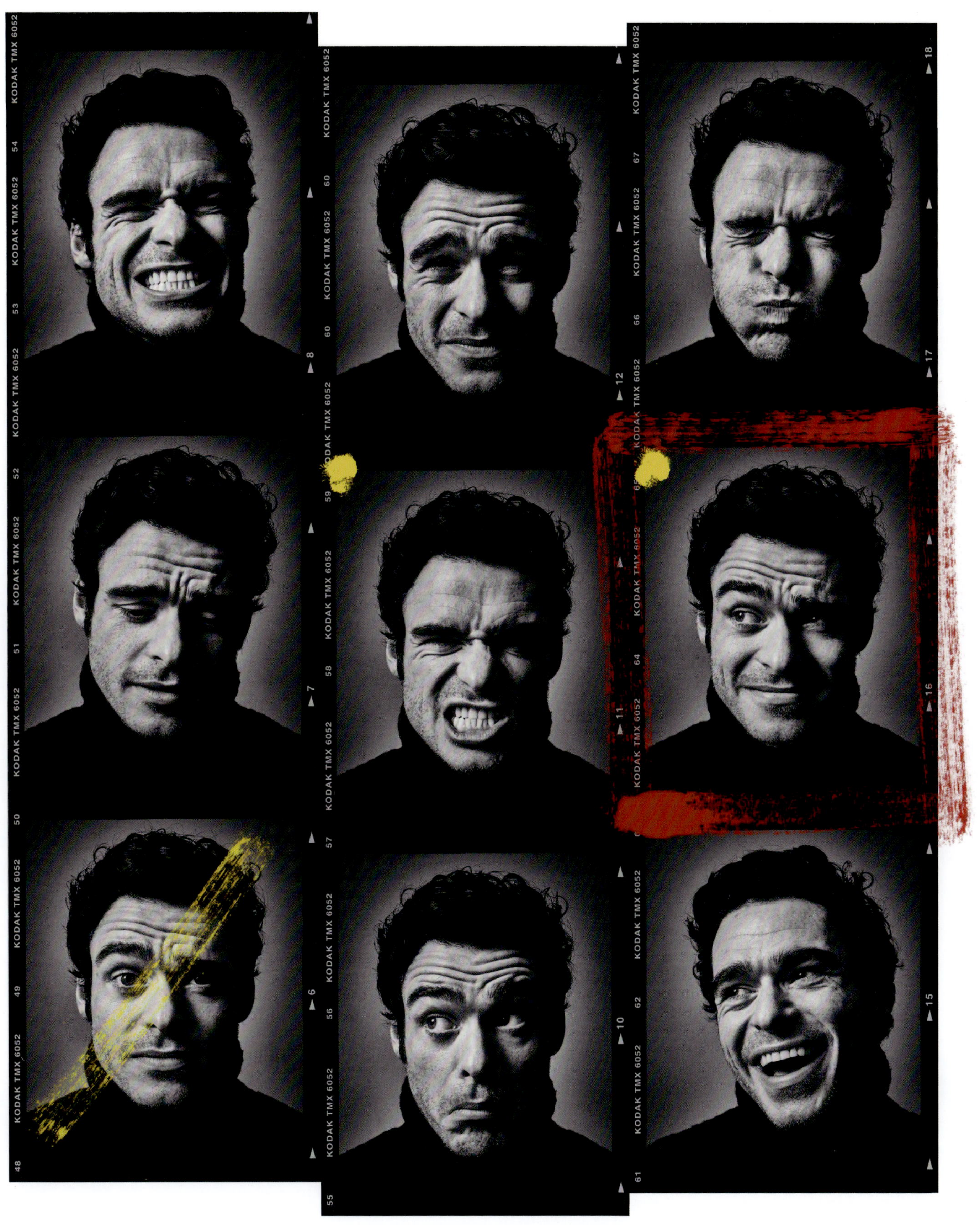

Ringo Starr

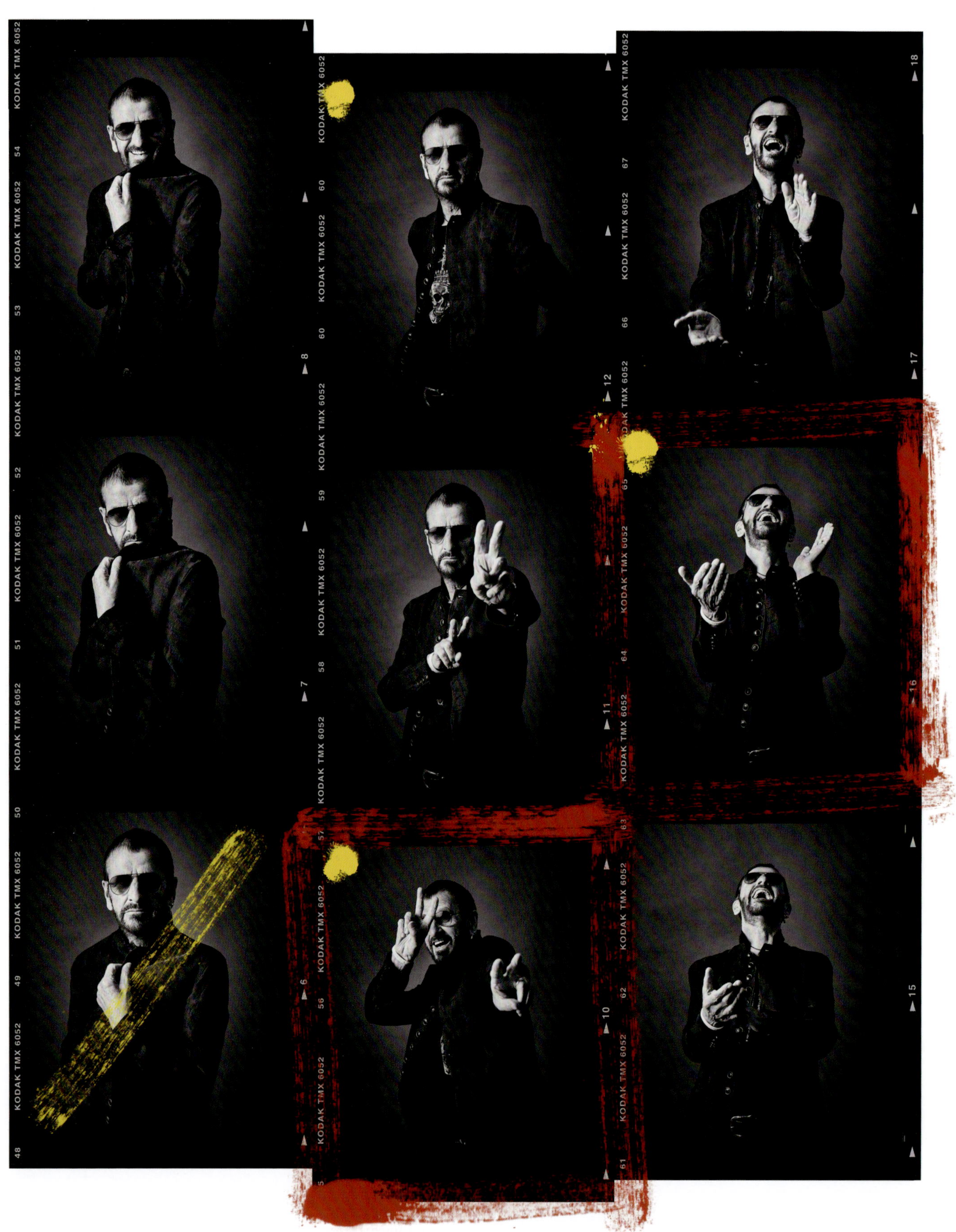

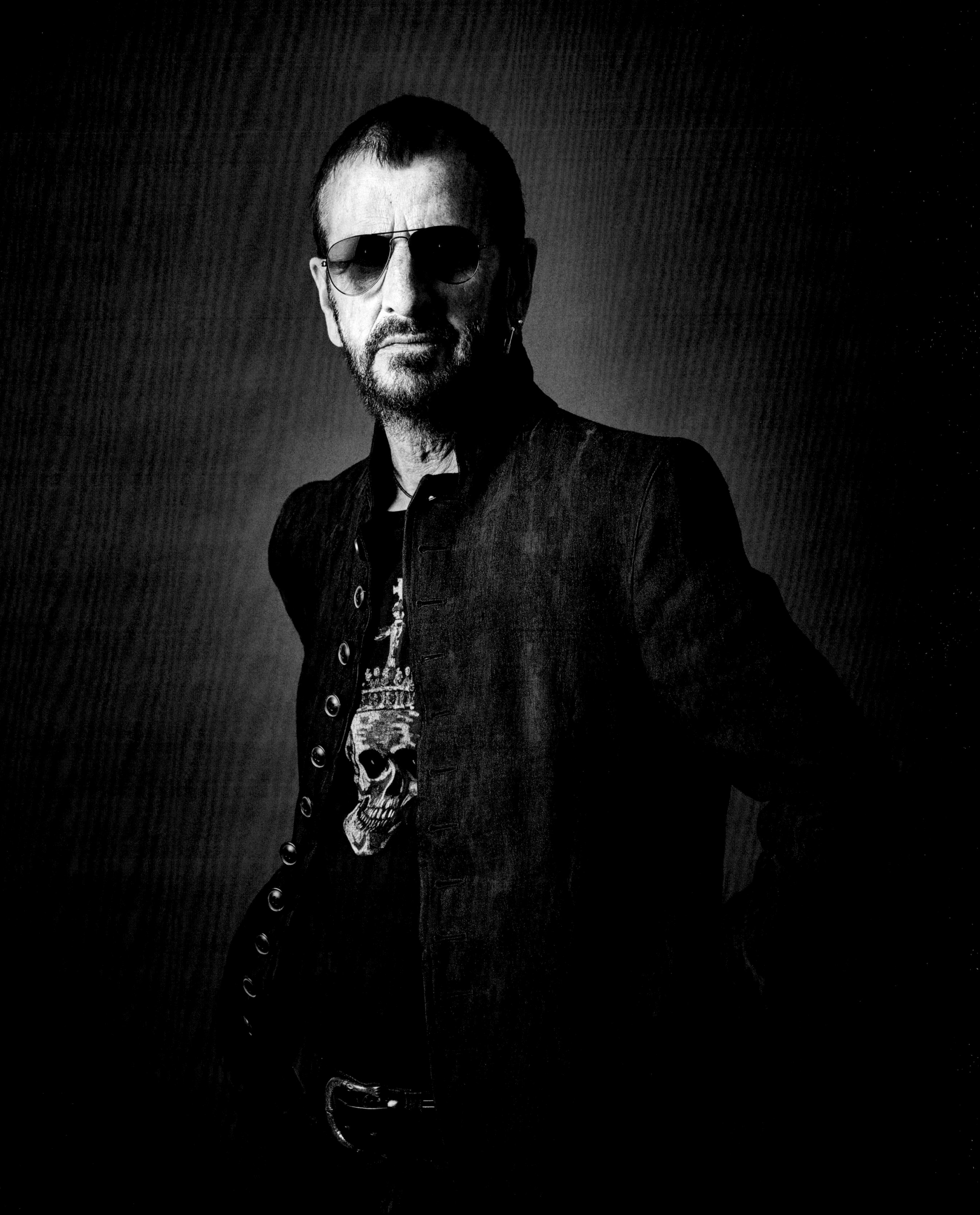

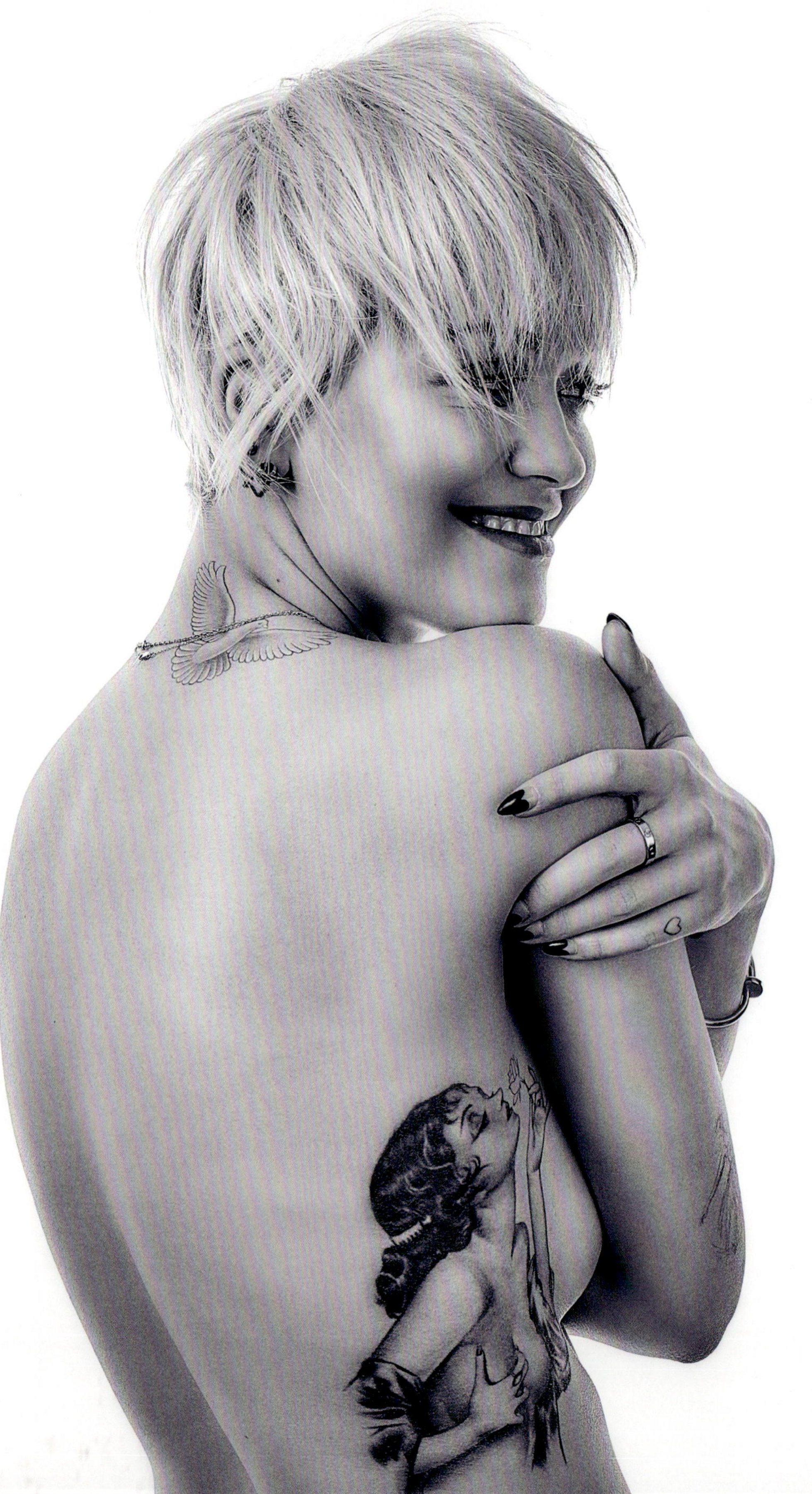
KODAK TMX 6052
58
KODAK TMX 6052
59

Rita Ora

I shot Rita in Flemings Mayfair. My concept for the shoot was a close-crop shot of her face, as she has very striking features. She turned up to the shoot in a wool jumper with quite a high collar, which was no good. I asked if she could take it off, and I assumed she would have a t-shirt or vest underneath. To my surprise, when she pulled the jumper off, she was totally naked! I had no idea she had SO many tattoos over her body and she was very happy to show them off for the shoot.

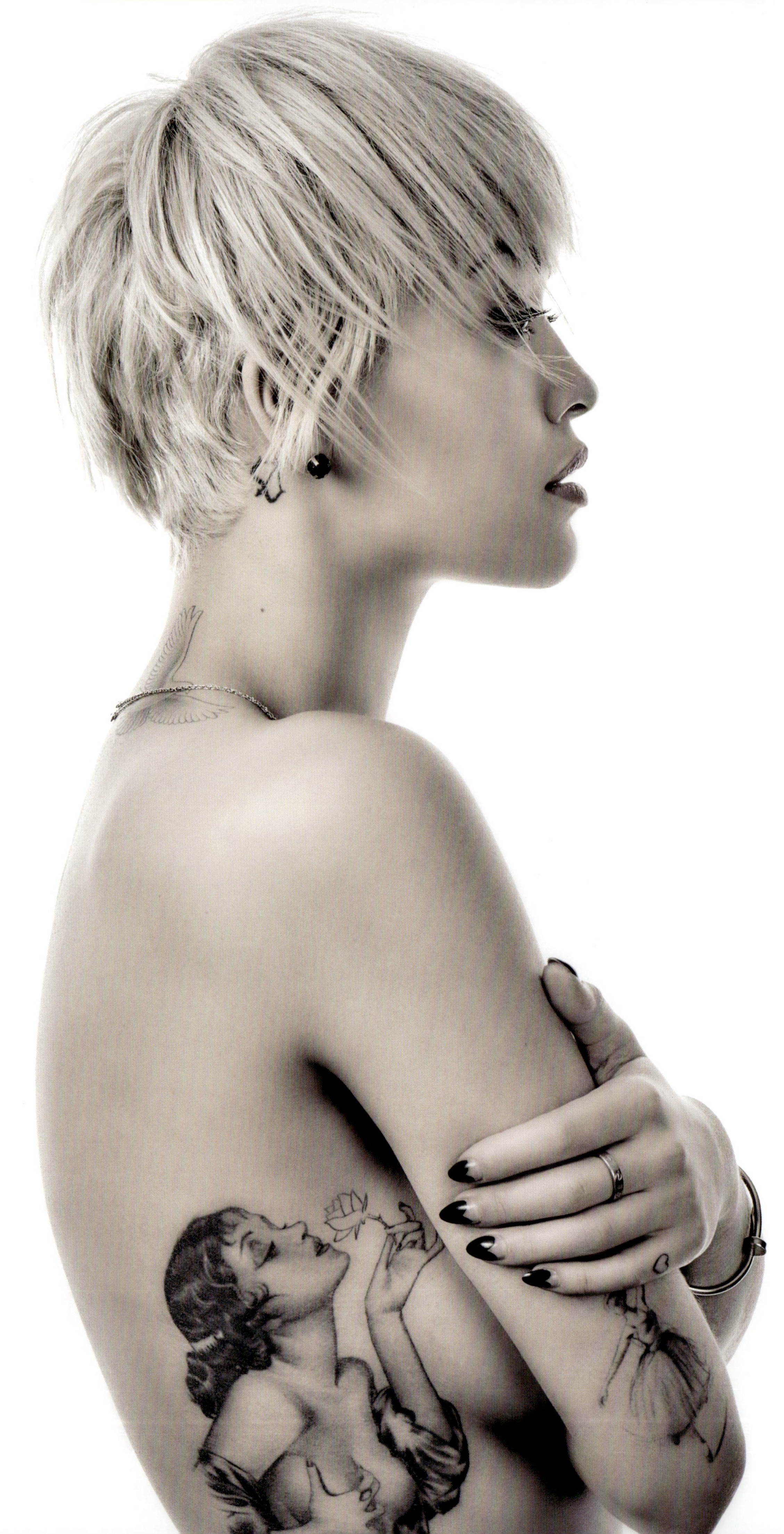

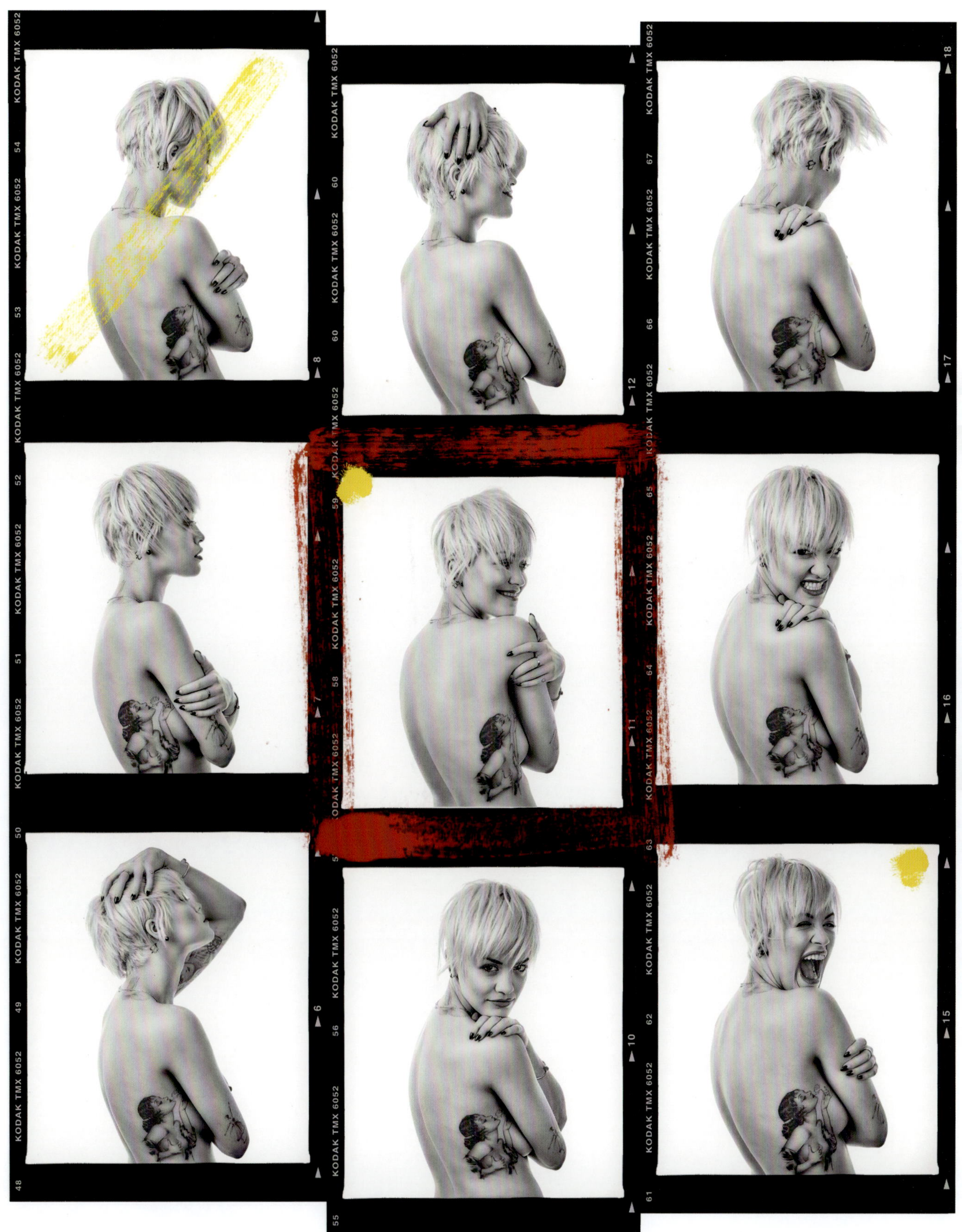

Robert De Niro

When I first asked Robert De Niro to be shot for my Icons project he said "No" in the same week that Al Pacino had also refused. Strangely, he then said "Yes" in the same week that Al Pacino agreed.

The shoot was done at the Dorchester Hotel in London. He was an hour late coming from Manchester and was further delayed making his way through the Dorchester whilst being besieged by adoring fans. He arrived in an old blazer and captain's hat. He sat as close as possible to me, put his arm around me asking if he could call me Andy, and saying for me to call him Bob. I could not shoot Robert De Niro without doing some iconic shots, which he breezed through in the matter of moments. I knew what I wanted and he knew what he wanted to give.

The conversation turned to voices and impressions. I asked him if he ever gets bored of people mimicking the iconic line his character Travis Bickle says in *Taxi Driver* – the infamous "You lookin' at me?" He said this didn't bother him, but asked if I had seen Al Pacino do the impression? In the blink of an eye he over-exaggerated his own expression and barked out several times "You lookin at me?" Luckily I still had my camera in hand to capture this photography gold. De Niro doing an impersonation of Pacino, doing an impersonation of De Niro!

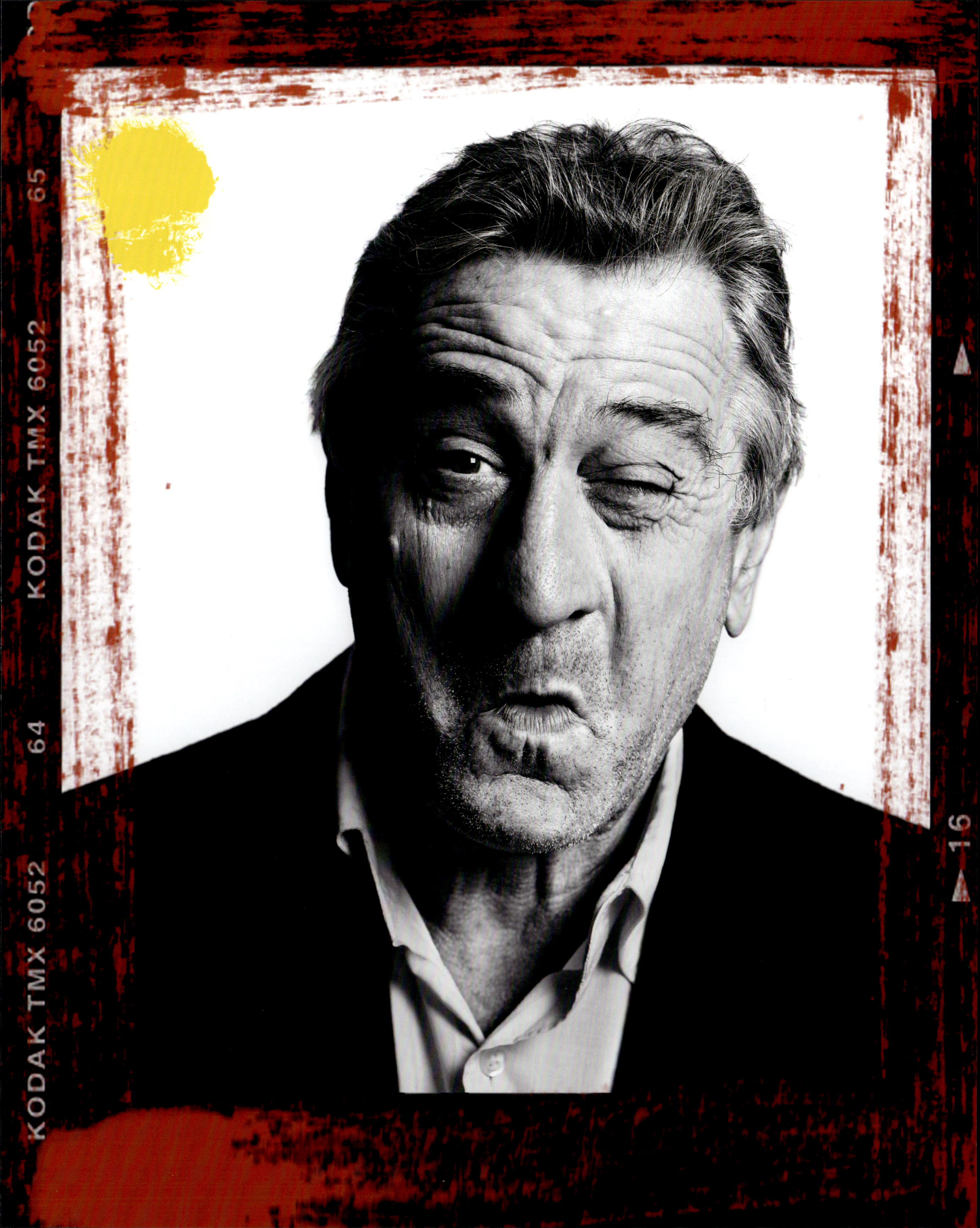

KODAK TMX 6052 65

KODAK TMX 6052 64

16

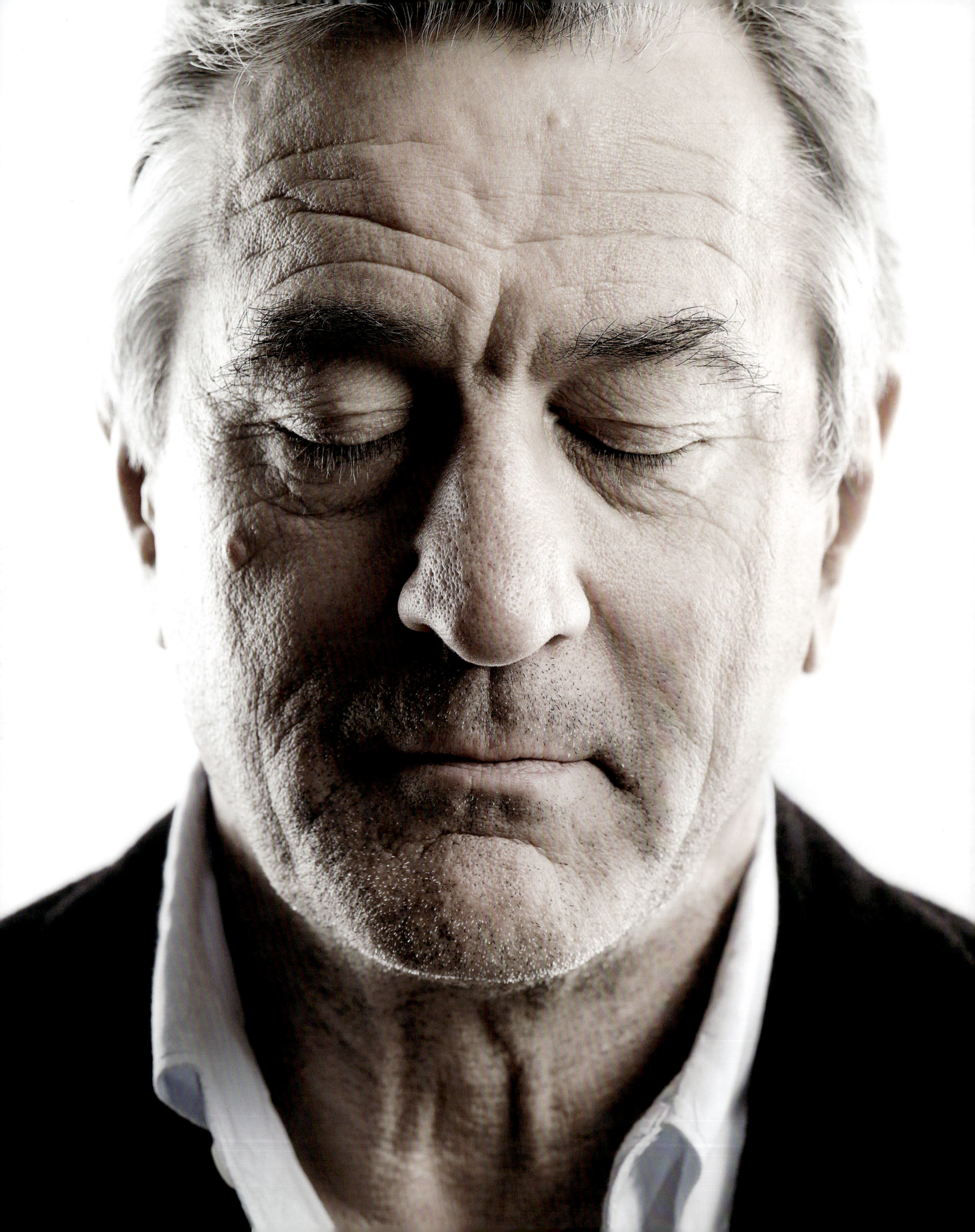

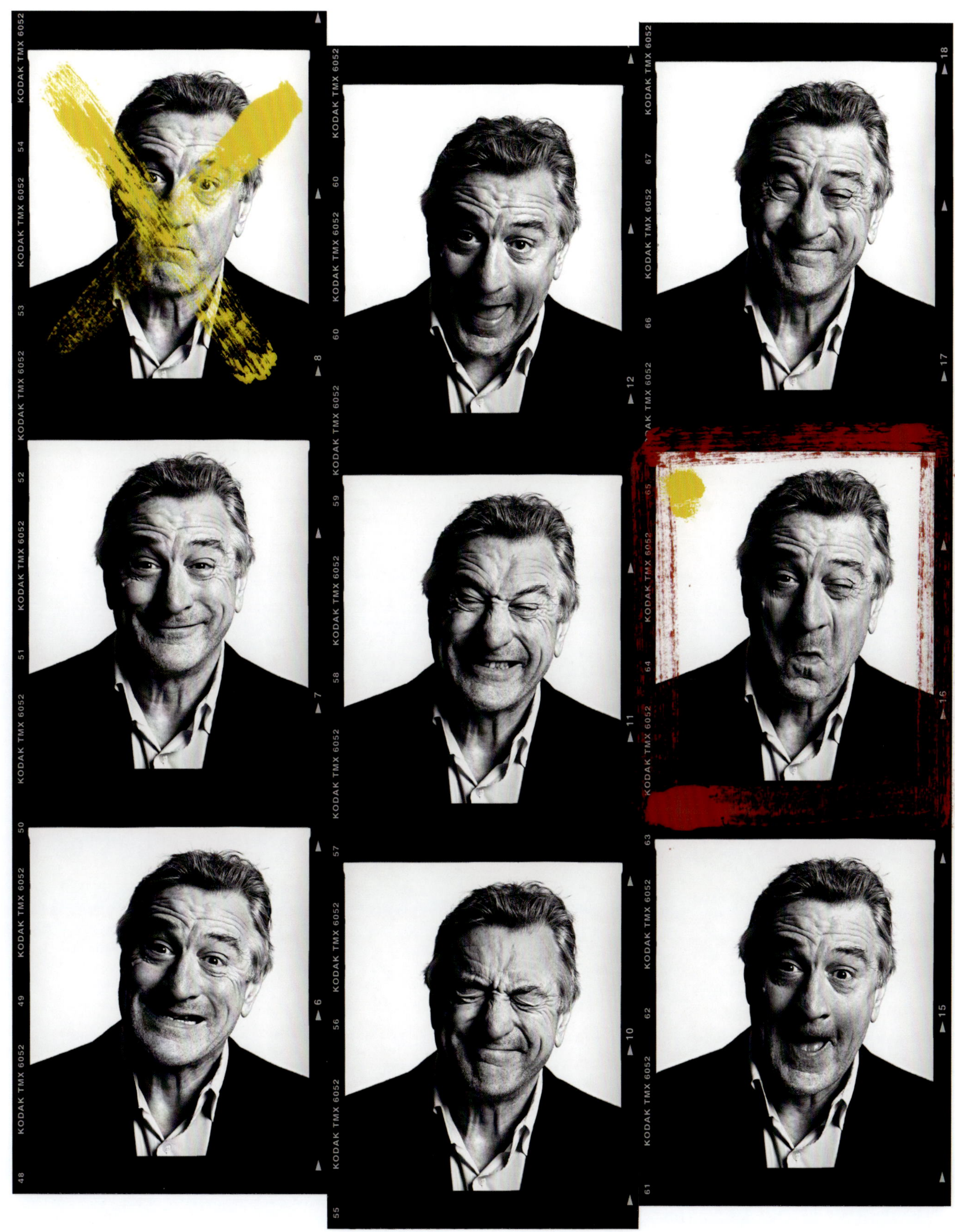
KODAK TMX 6052

Robin Williams

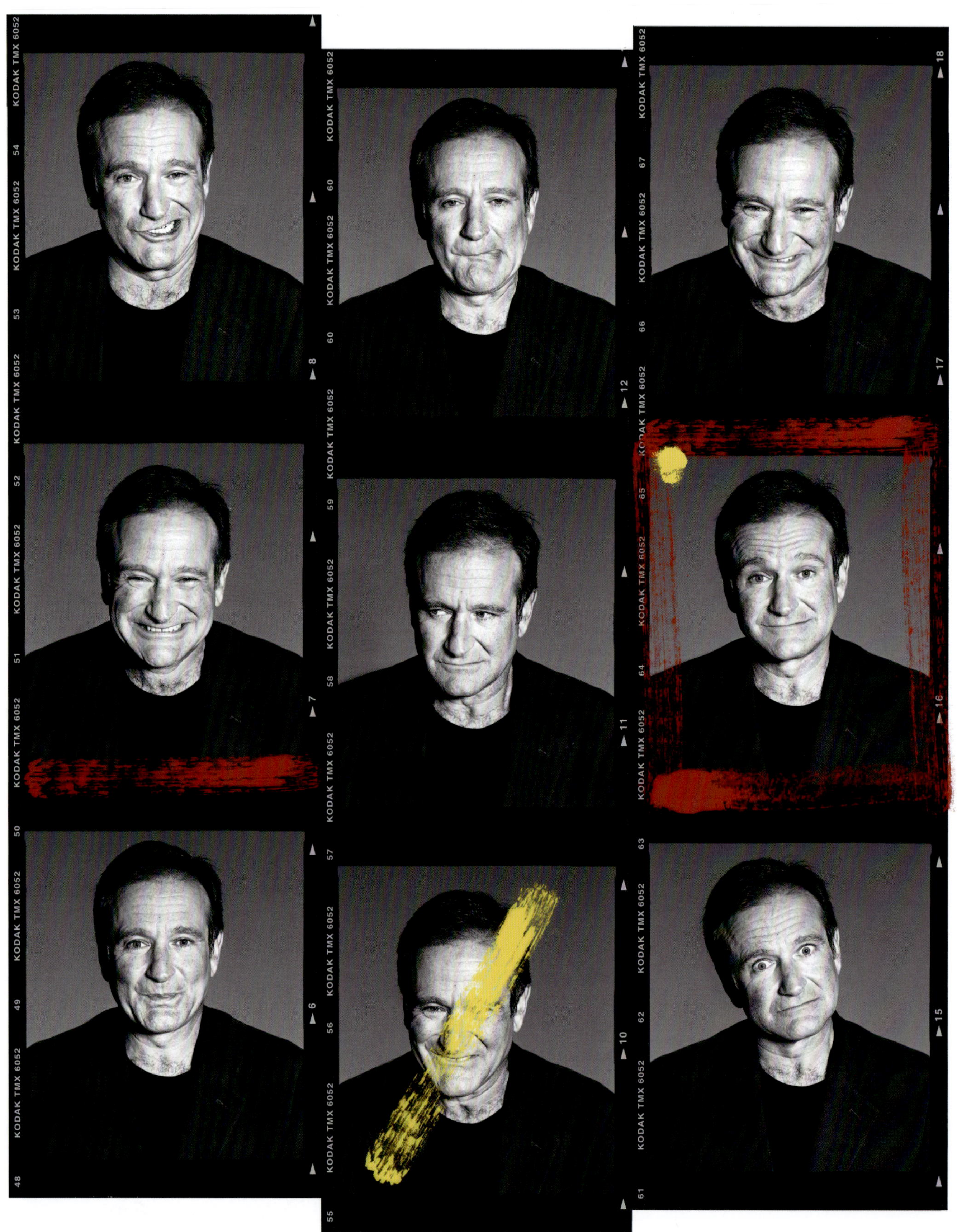

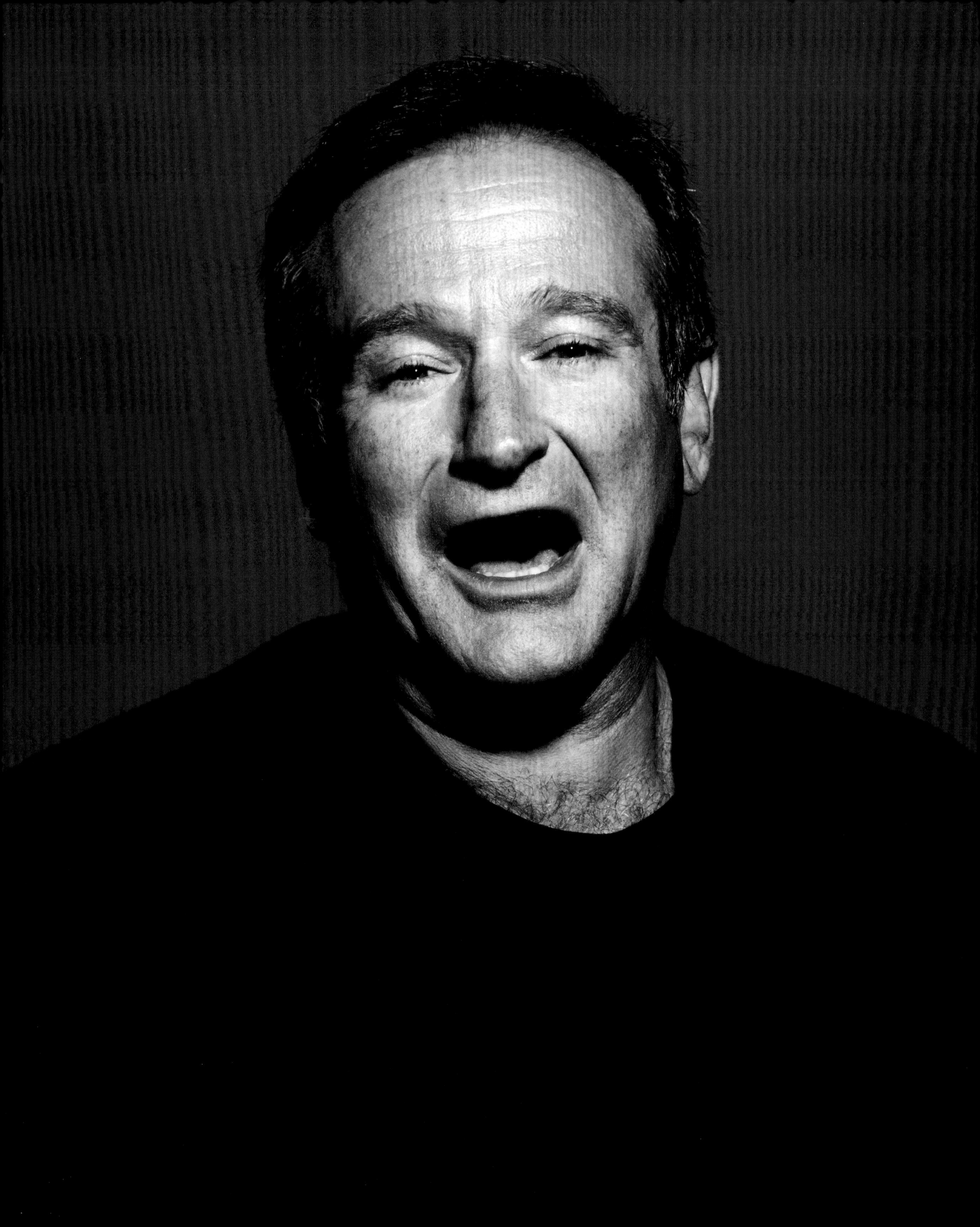

Samuel L. Jackson

The location for this shoot was his publicist's office on Rodeo Drive. To this day I have never understood why they flew me to LA from London to shoot Samuel, who was doing the shoot on his way to the airport to fly to London. The change was instantaneous the minute Samuel entered the building. The atmosphere lifted as he addressed every member of staff on his way through. Also, you could not miss him with his bright orange cap, t-shirt and green shorts. I got the measure of Samuel very quickly when he insisted on making a phone call before the shoot, only to inform me that he needed a new suit and so was sending flowers to his tailor's wife for his troubles. After a quick wardrobe change, we began shooting. Samuel, being a busy man, was was on his phone. Yet this did not stop him giving me what I wanted while he chatted on loudspeaker between shots. And by the time his call had ended, the shoot was a wrap and it all had been done on an office swivel chair. Samuel oozes charm and coolness. He has a wonderful ability to make you feel good about yourself, it's a real privilege to be in his company.

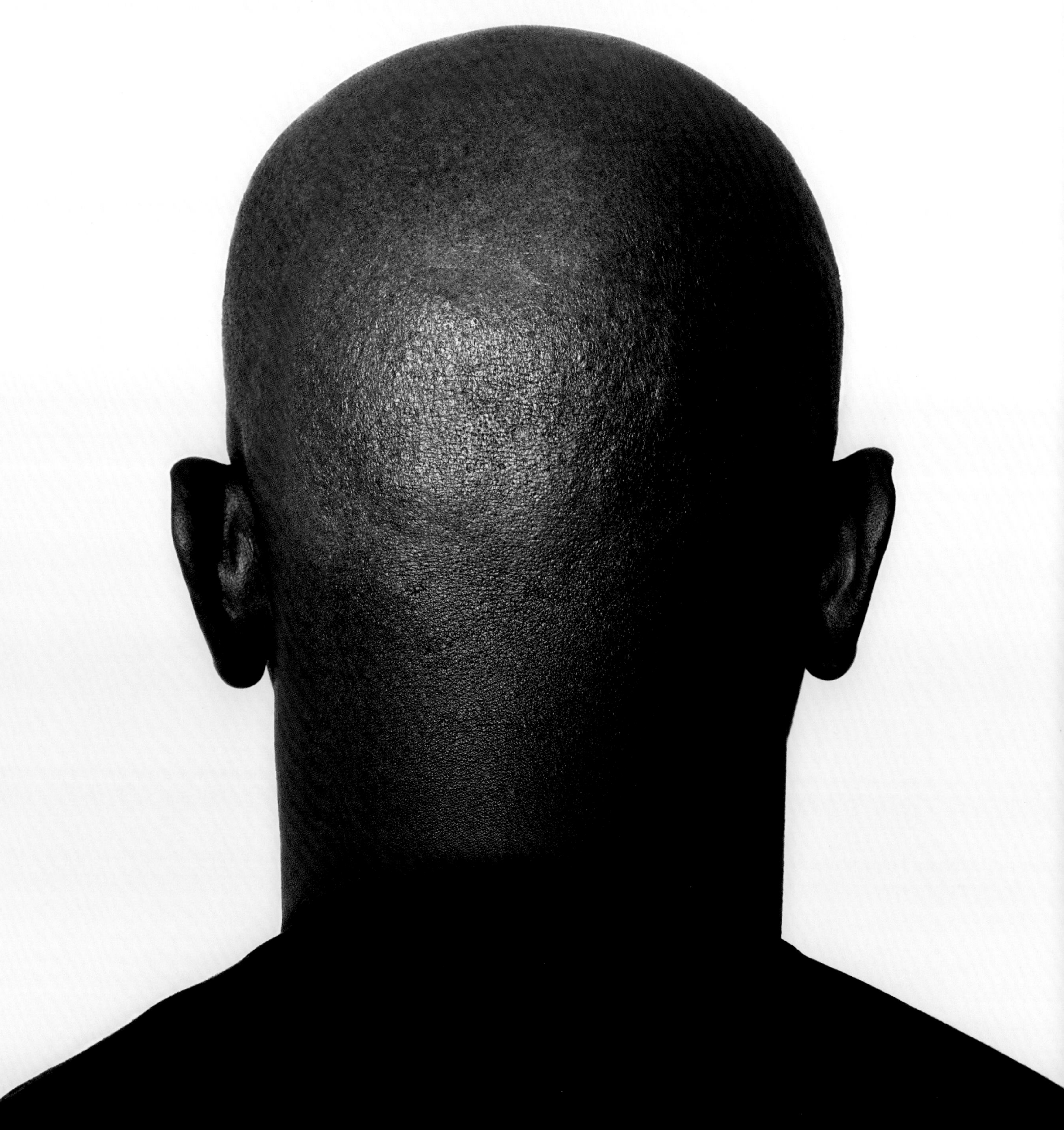

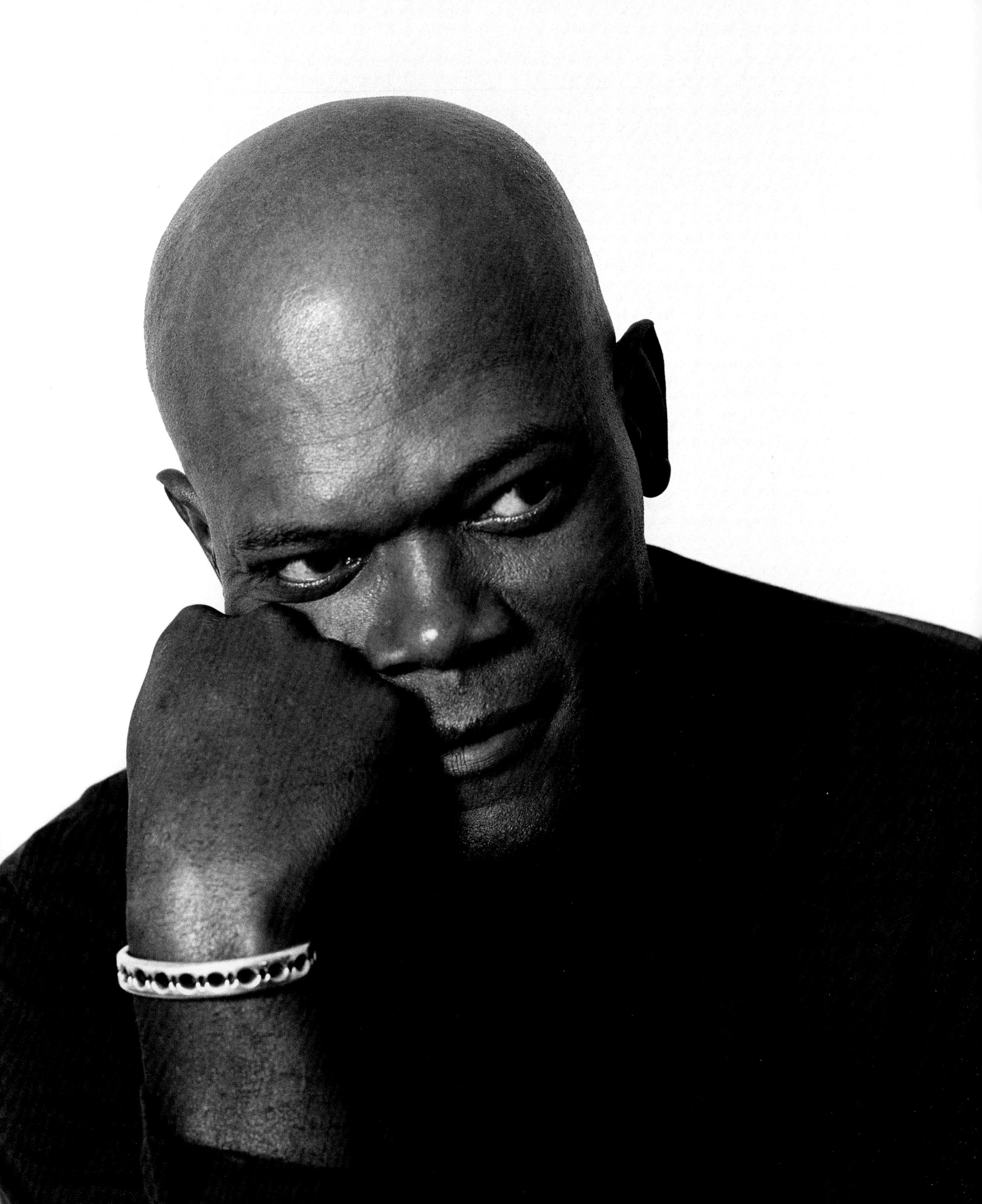

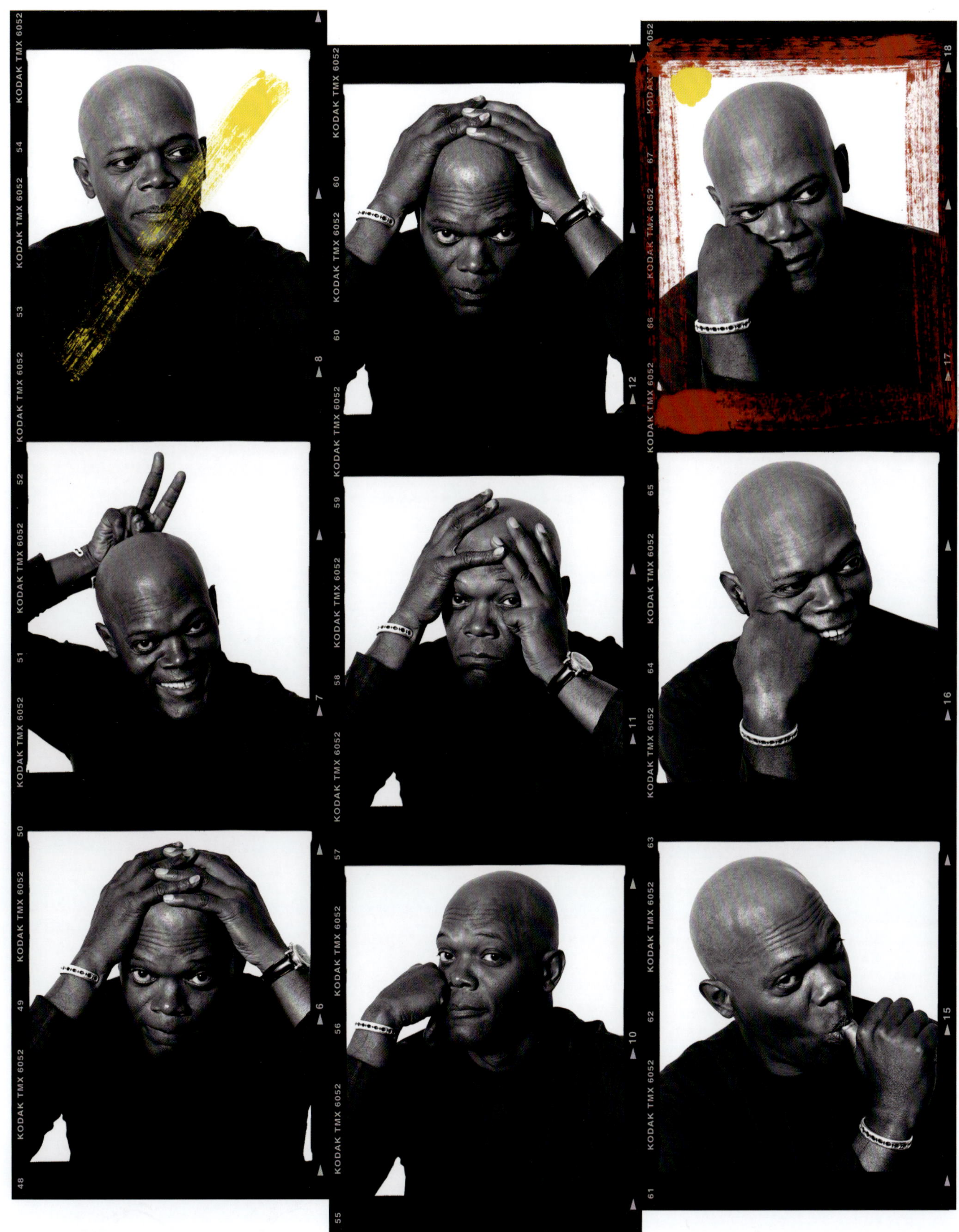

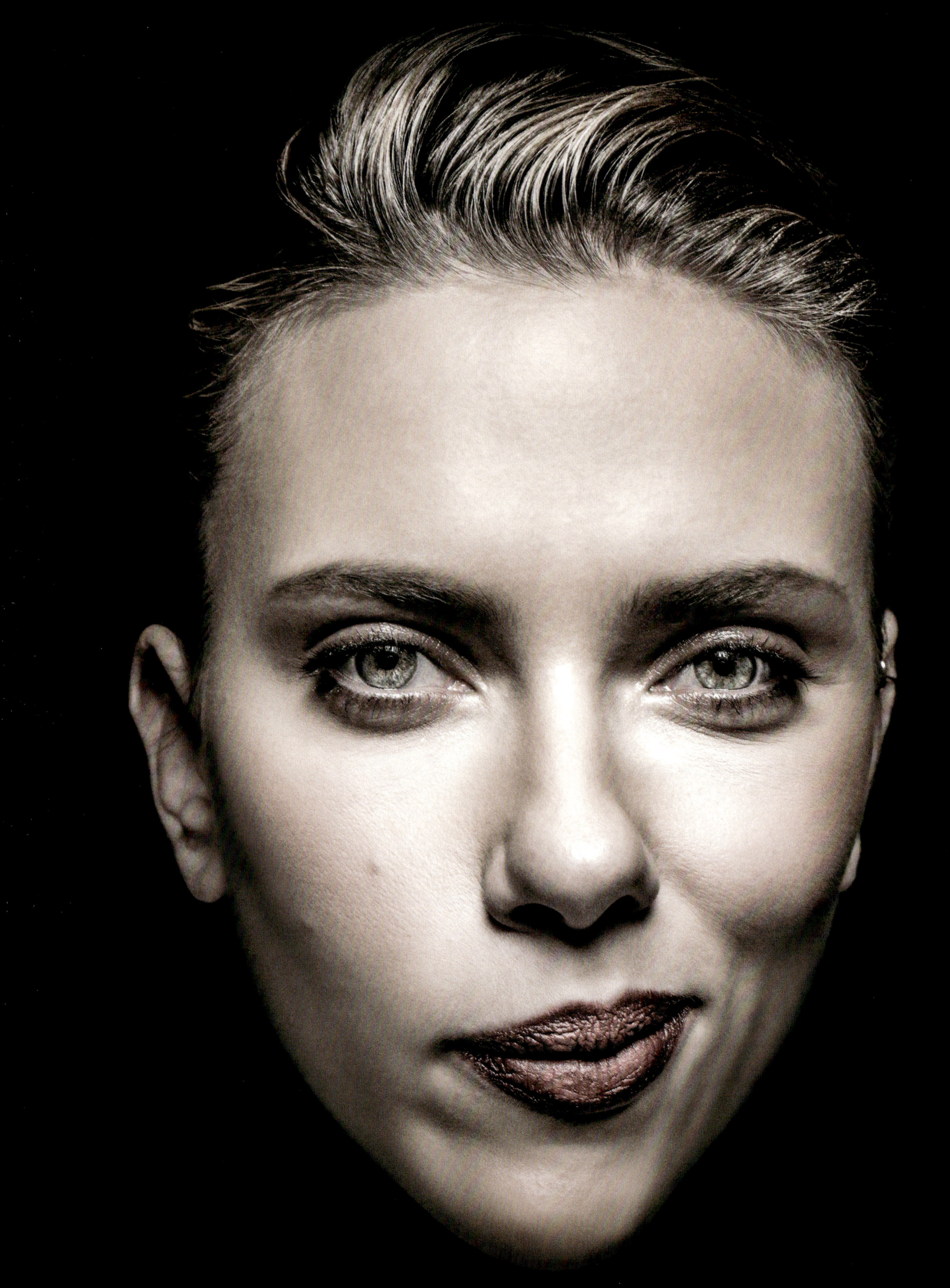

Scarlett Johansson

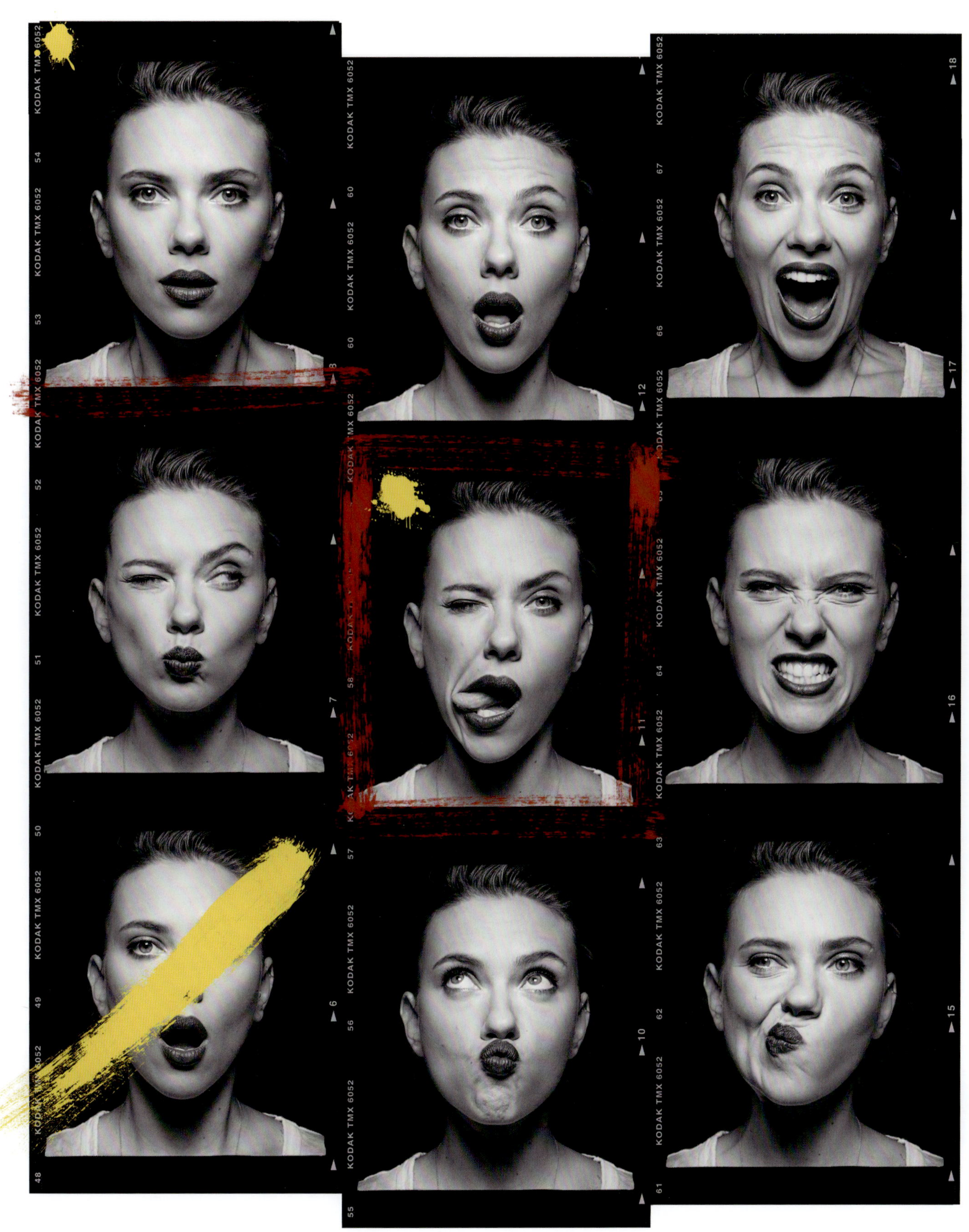

Sharon Stone

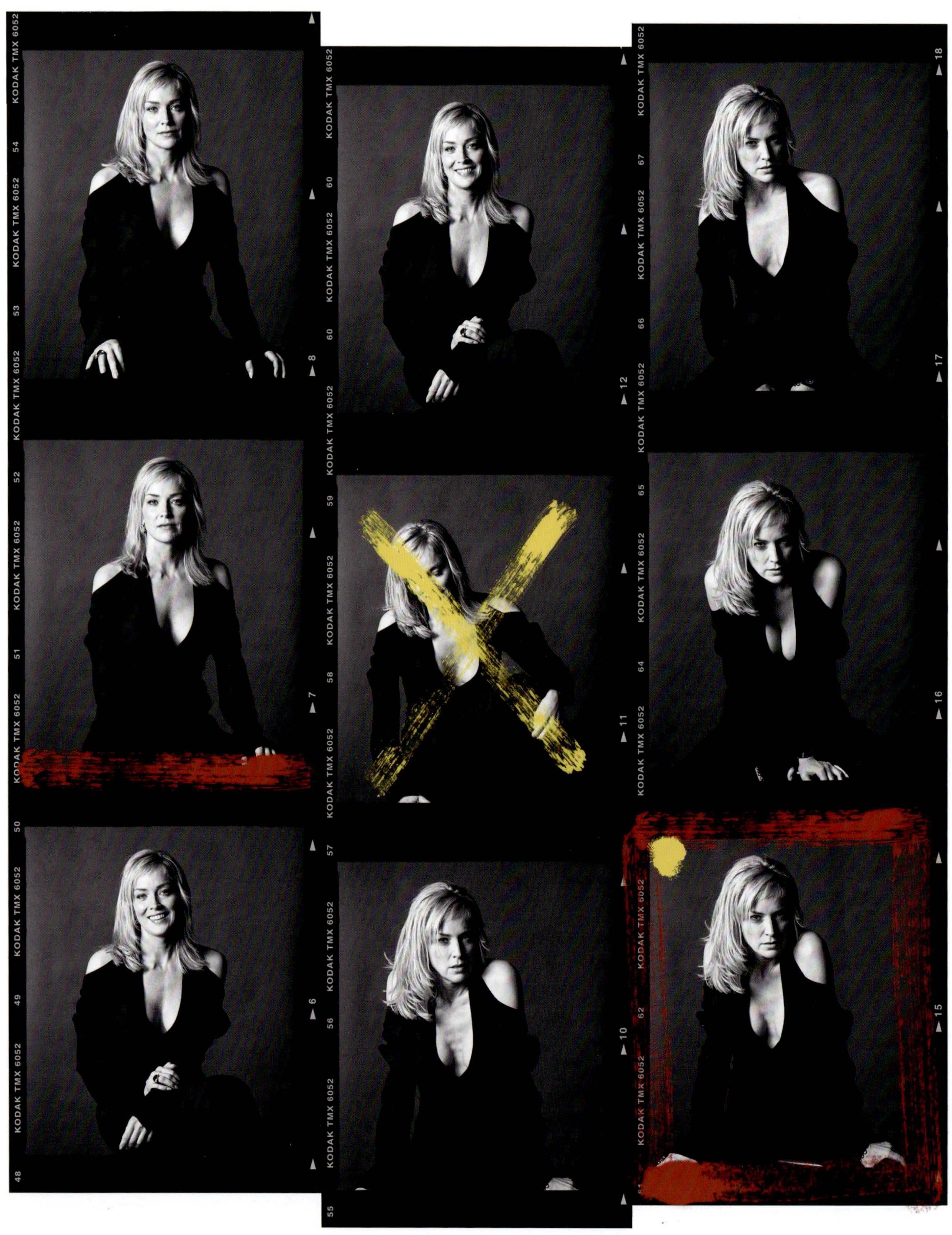

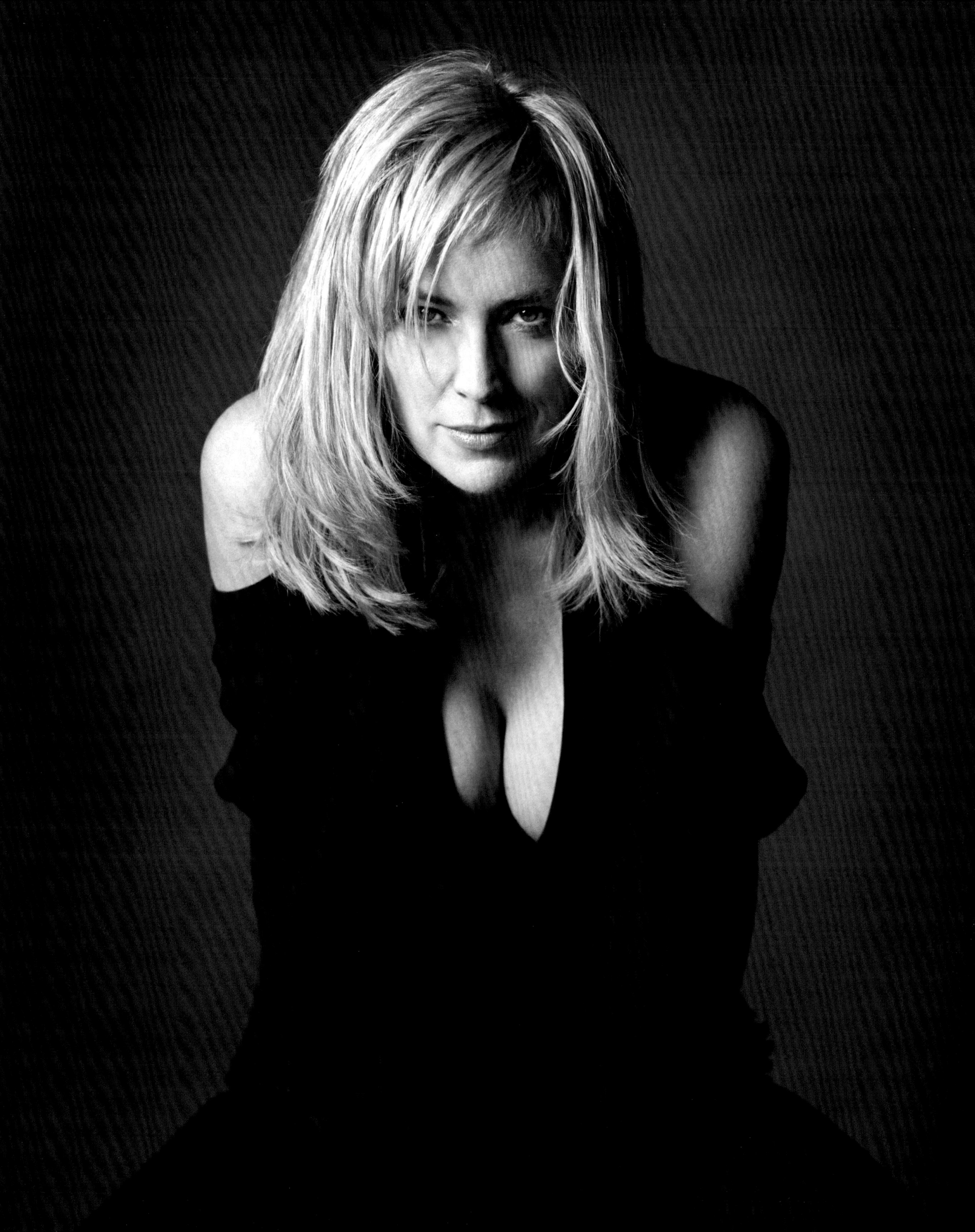

Simon Pegg

The digital age is replete with forgotten interfaces, physical exchanges made obsolete by a new era of intangible convenience. These lost moments of connection span numerous aspects of our daily life, perhaps no more so than the realm of photography. As an art form, photography has evolved steadily from the first meticulously created daguerreotypes to the thousands of barely regarded images we now carry in our pockets. For the photographer, the means of expression has become increasingly convenient, aided by digital shortcuts that arguably bypass some of the artistry.

The tension of that brief moment when the shutter allows light into the camera has been alleviated by the promise of post-production fixes and visual edits; automatic surrogates that compensate for a lesser understanding of the moment. Almost gone is the silent alchemy of the darkroom and the nose-stinging whiff of developer. Almost gone is the physical image, its weight and presence a tangible culmination of artistic endeavour. And almost gone is the contact sheet, that forgotten record of the moments that, for one reason or another, may not have been selected to represent the session.

Perhaps it's wrong to bemoan evolution. To suggest that things were better when art was harder to achieve is somewhat reactionary. Surely, art is democratic and should be available to every human being. Any improvements to the process by which art can be created must be welcomed and embraced. It's just a shame that the contact sheet got lost along the way.

The contact sheet catalogues the combined experience of the photographer and the subject over the course of the shoot. When the subject is a living thing, this experience is an exchange of ideas, a microcosmic relationship recorded in still images. For every usable shot, there are glimpses behind the process – mistakes, accidents, moments of vulnerability, truth and honesty perhaps not required in the final image. This is not because the photographer deals solely in artificiality, every good photographer captures truth. It is, however, a single truth selected from many and it is fundamental to the contact that the photographer has with his/her subject. It is the art.

One of Andy Gotts' many talents as a photographer is his ability to interface with his subjects. I know this because I've had the pleasure of sitting for him on more than one occasion. Having your picture taken can be an awkward affair when it's not candid. The very definition of the word 'candid' is truthful and straightforward, or frank. These are the things a photographer looks for, even in the most posed moments. One might

KODAK 59 KODAK TMX 6052 KODAK 58 TMX 6052 KODAK

11

assume that obtaining candidness from a posed moment is counter-intuitive, but for a good photographer it is an essential skill. A good photographer puts their subject at ease and then captures them between the spasms of forced naturalism.

Nowhere is this process more evident than the contact sheet. Andy's decision to collate his contact sheets (which he still produces physically) is very telling. Each contact sheet presented here, tells the story of Andy and his subject(s). Sometimes their reticence or self-consciousness or the gradual loosening of inhibition, as Andy charms and assures them into a more relaxed state, and eventually their willingness to give Andy some truly fun moments of raw personality. Funny faces, laughter, genuine enjoyment – Andy has a knack of eliciting these moments from even the most uptight of subjects.

Here, then, is a collection of lost interfaces. The fragments of truth, one might assume, fell between the clicks. Shots that some photographers might disregard as mistakes or unusable takes, Andy sees as valuable and important steps on the journey towards achieving the most appropriate, not the most valuable image. Art is a process, not a product and if the image used in a magazine, book, newspaper or even exhibition is the product of a photo shoot, then these glimpses of the images that didn't fit the remit must surely represent the process. In that respect they are far more representative of the true art of photography. Art, truth, silly faces, all tangible and remembered here in one convenient place.

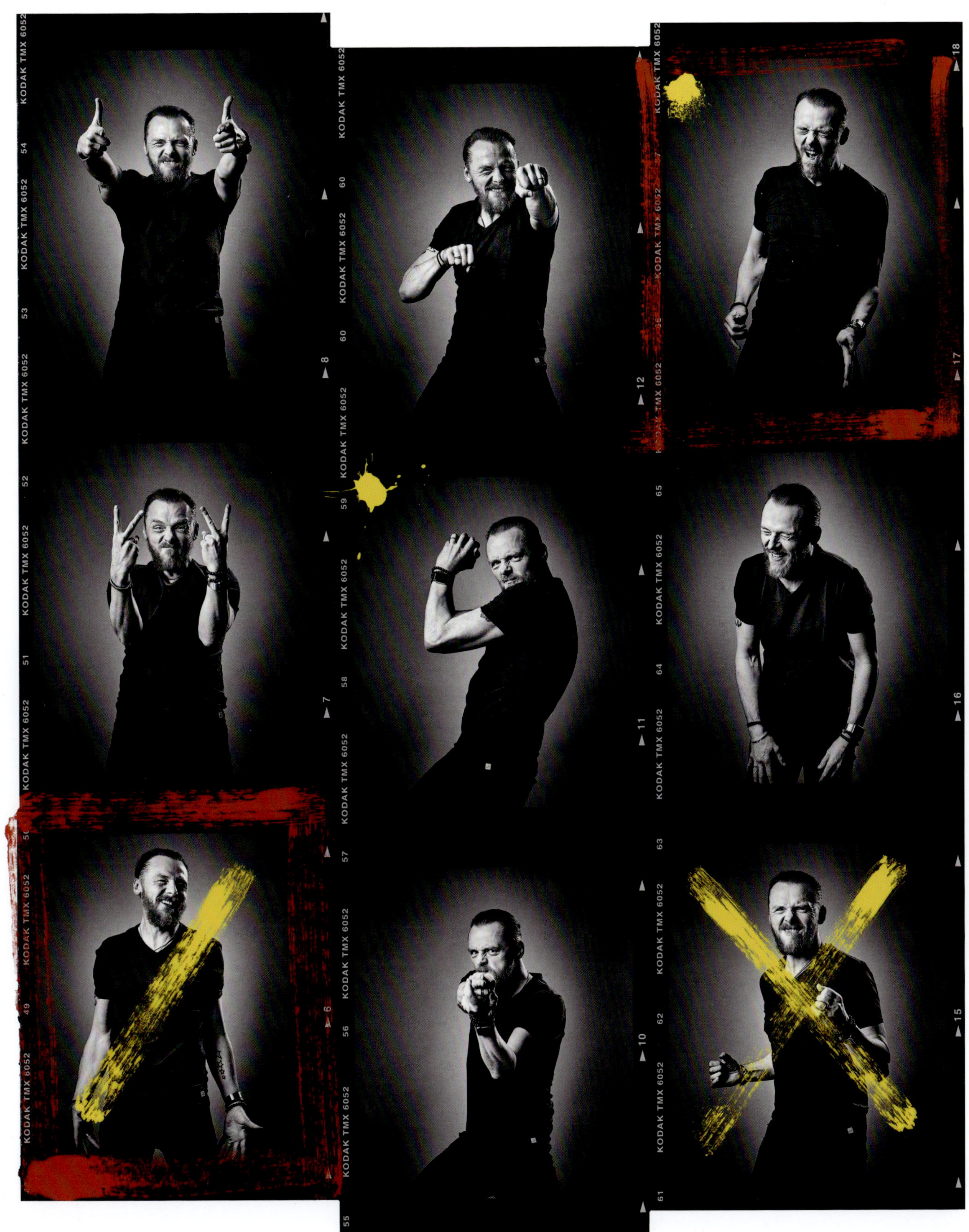
KODAK TMX 6052

Steven Tyler

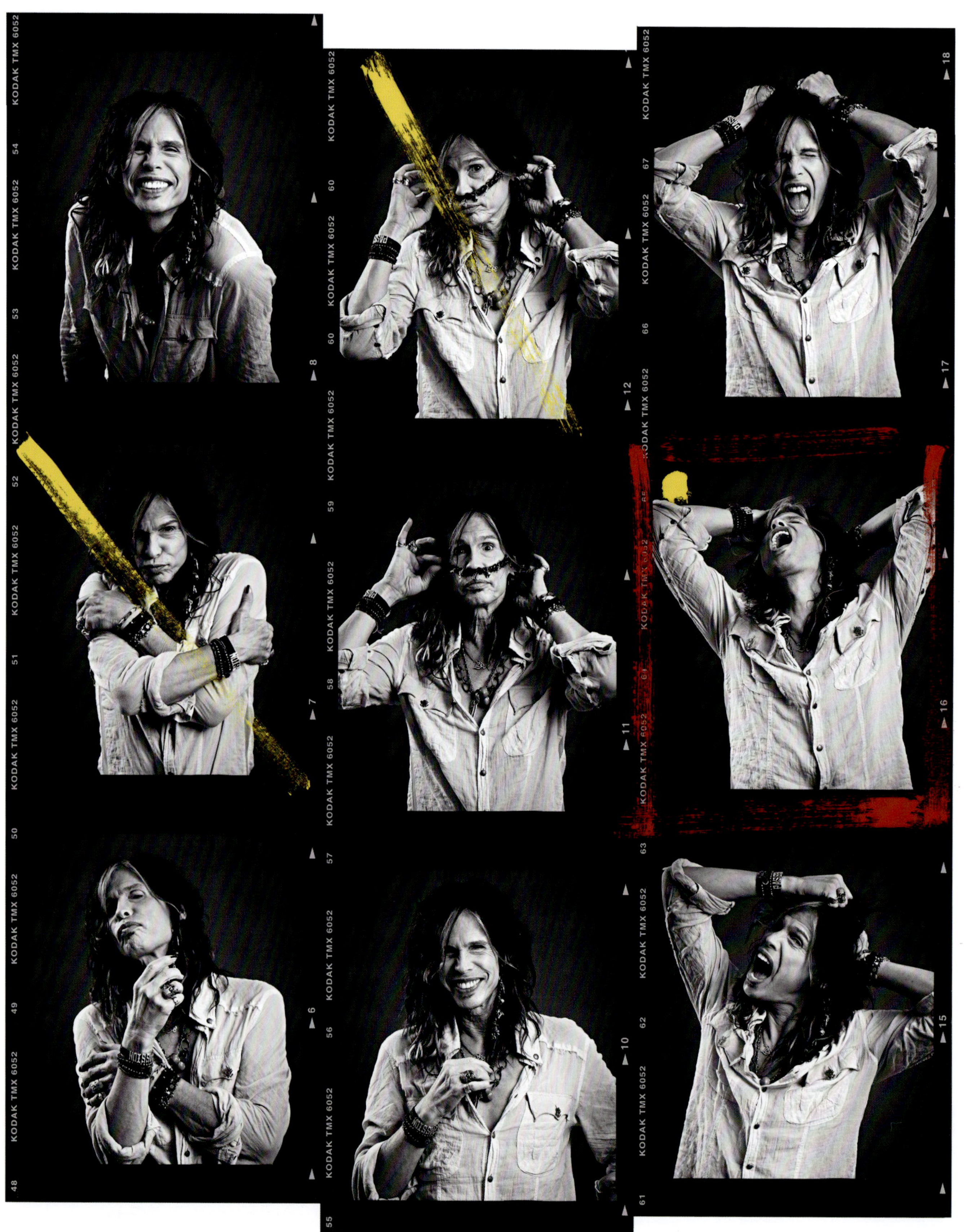

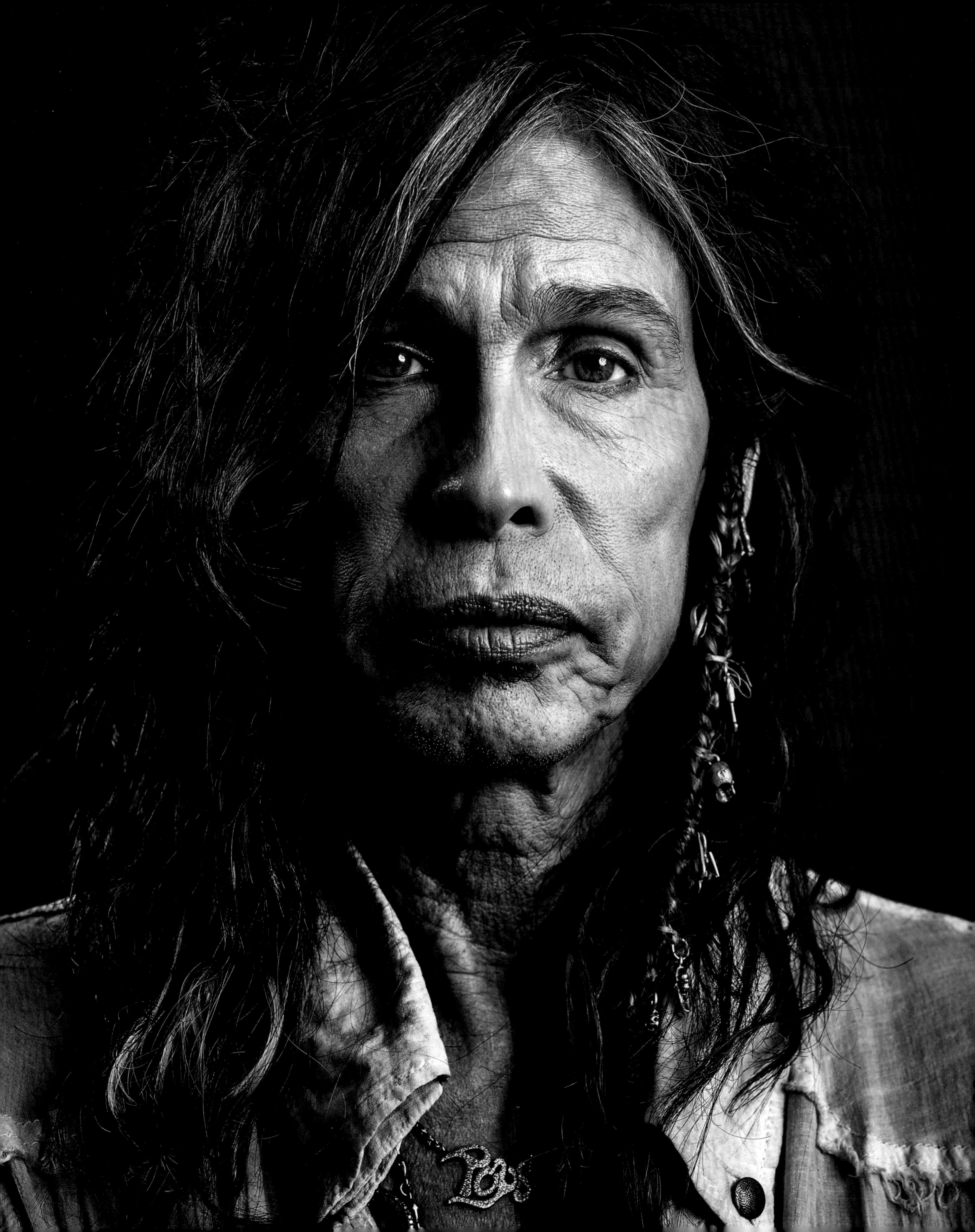

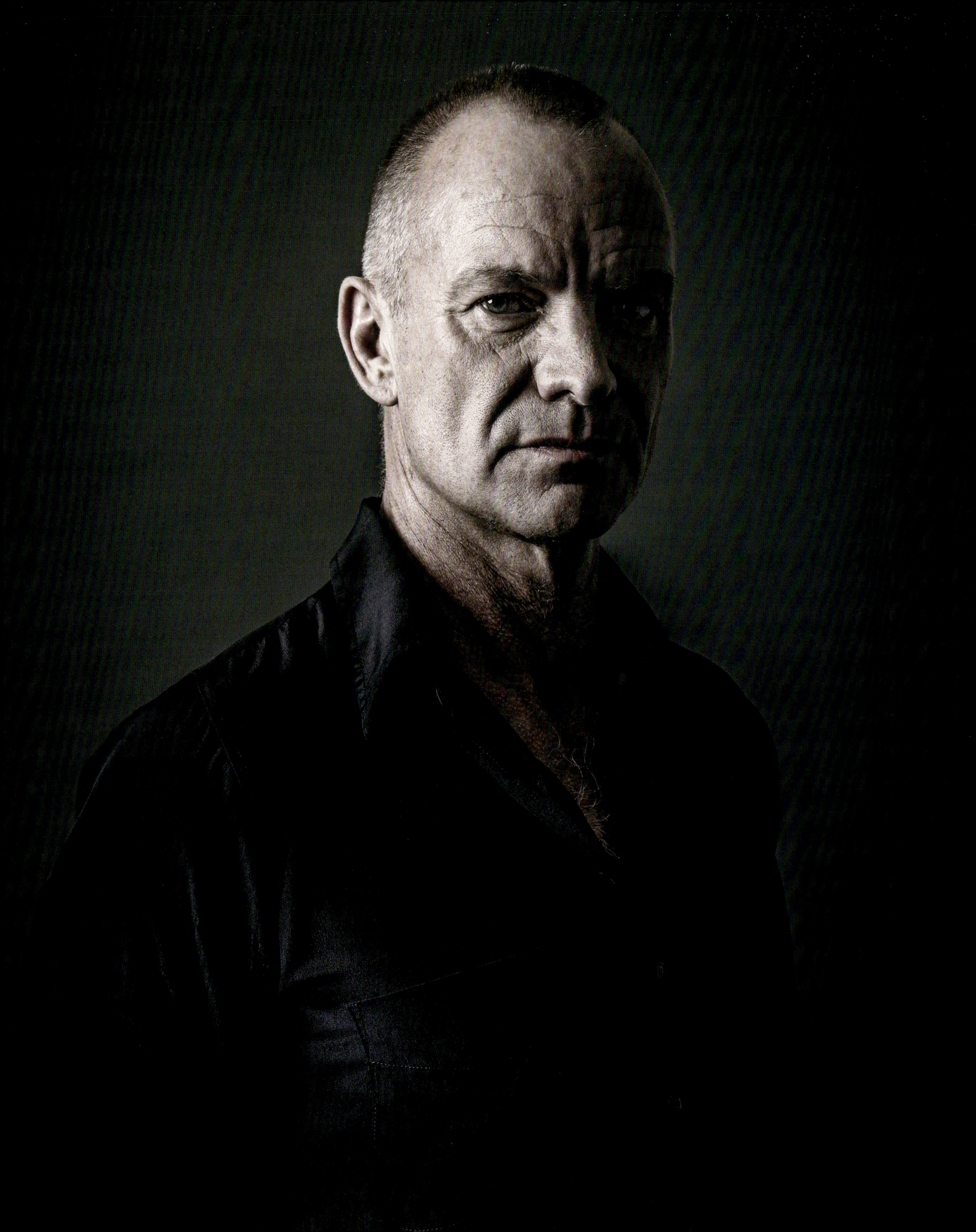

Sting

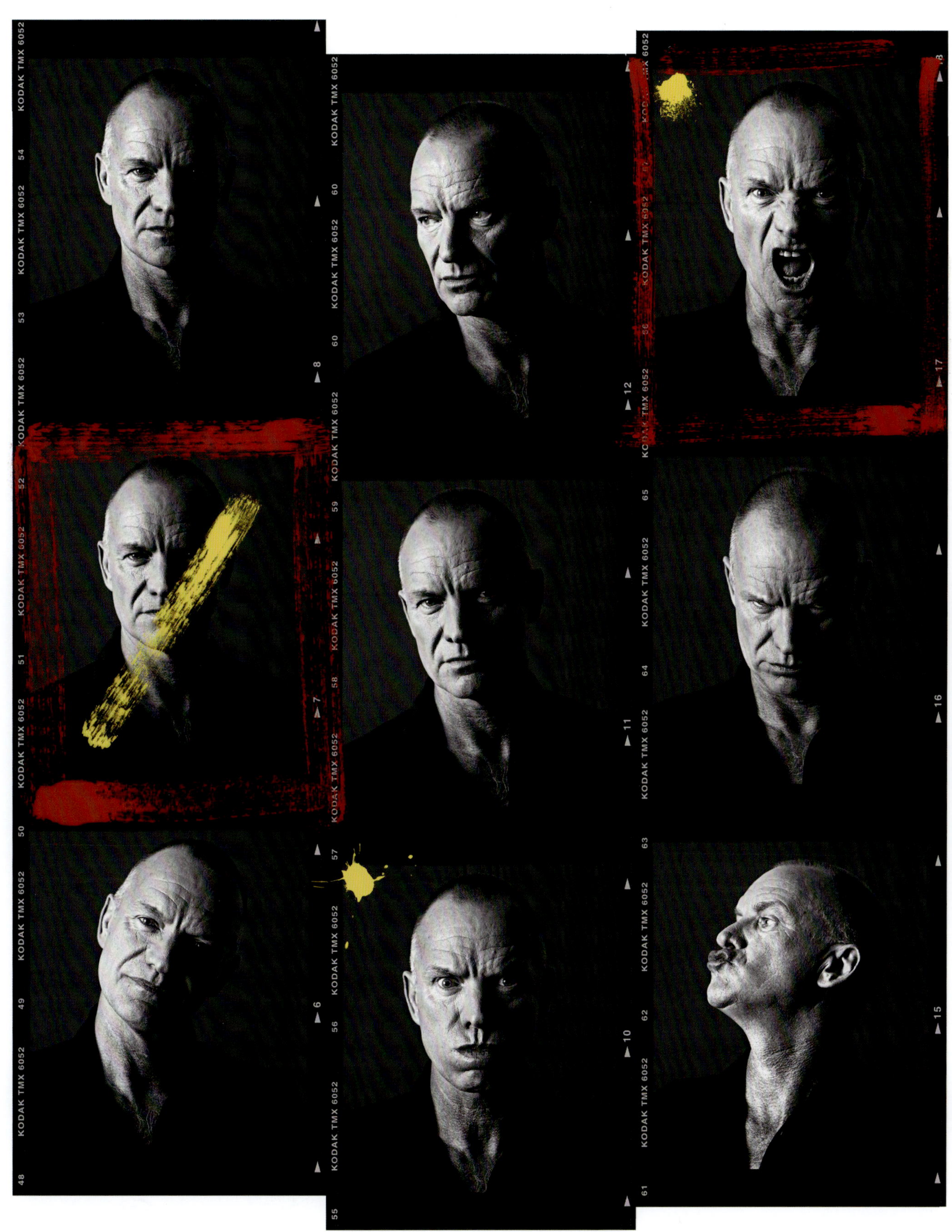

Susan Sarandon

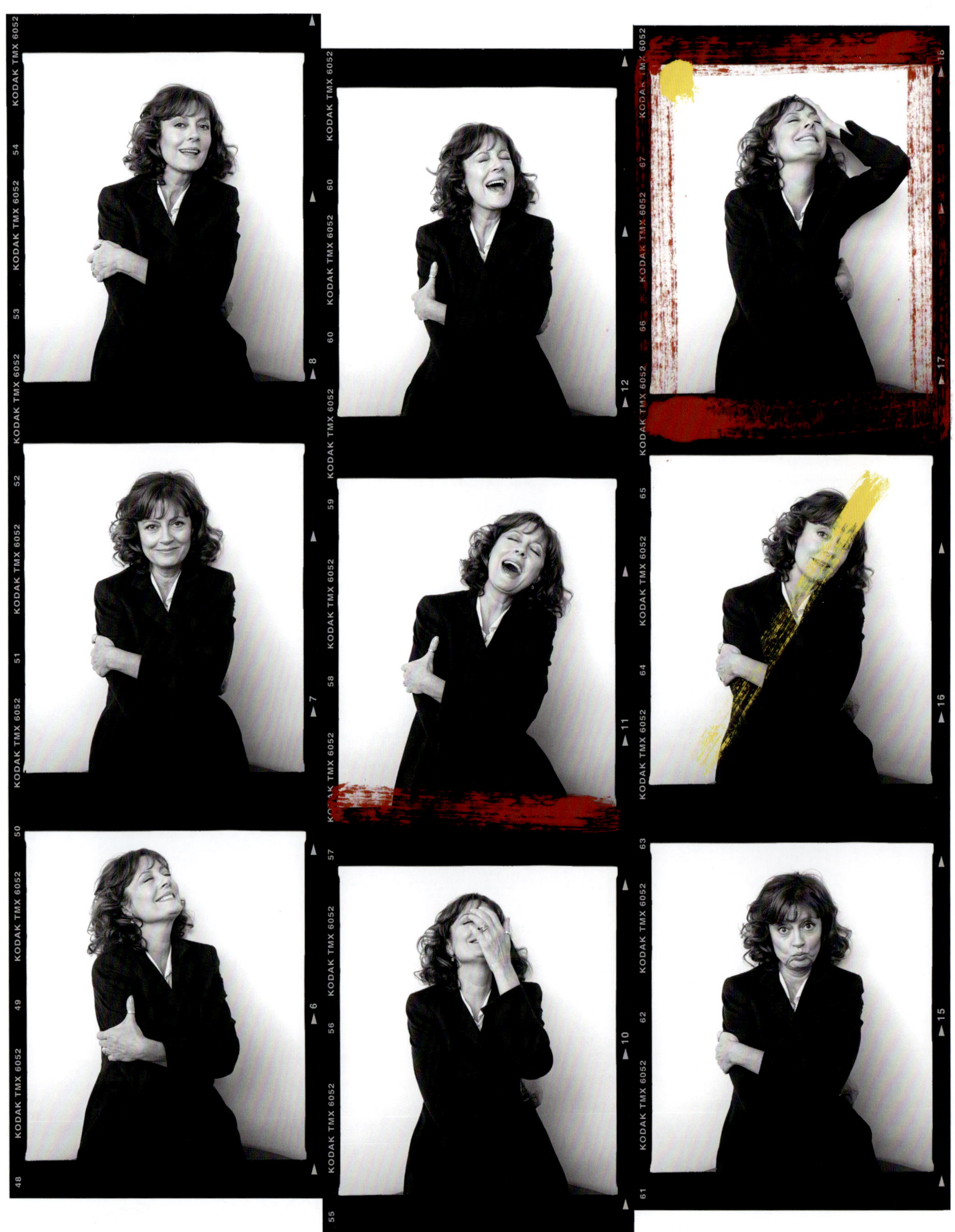

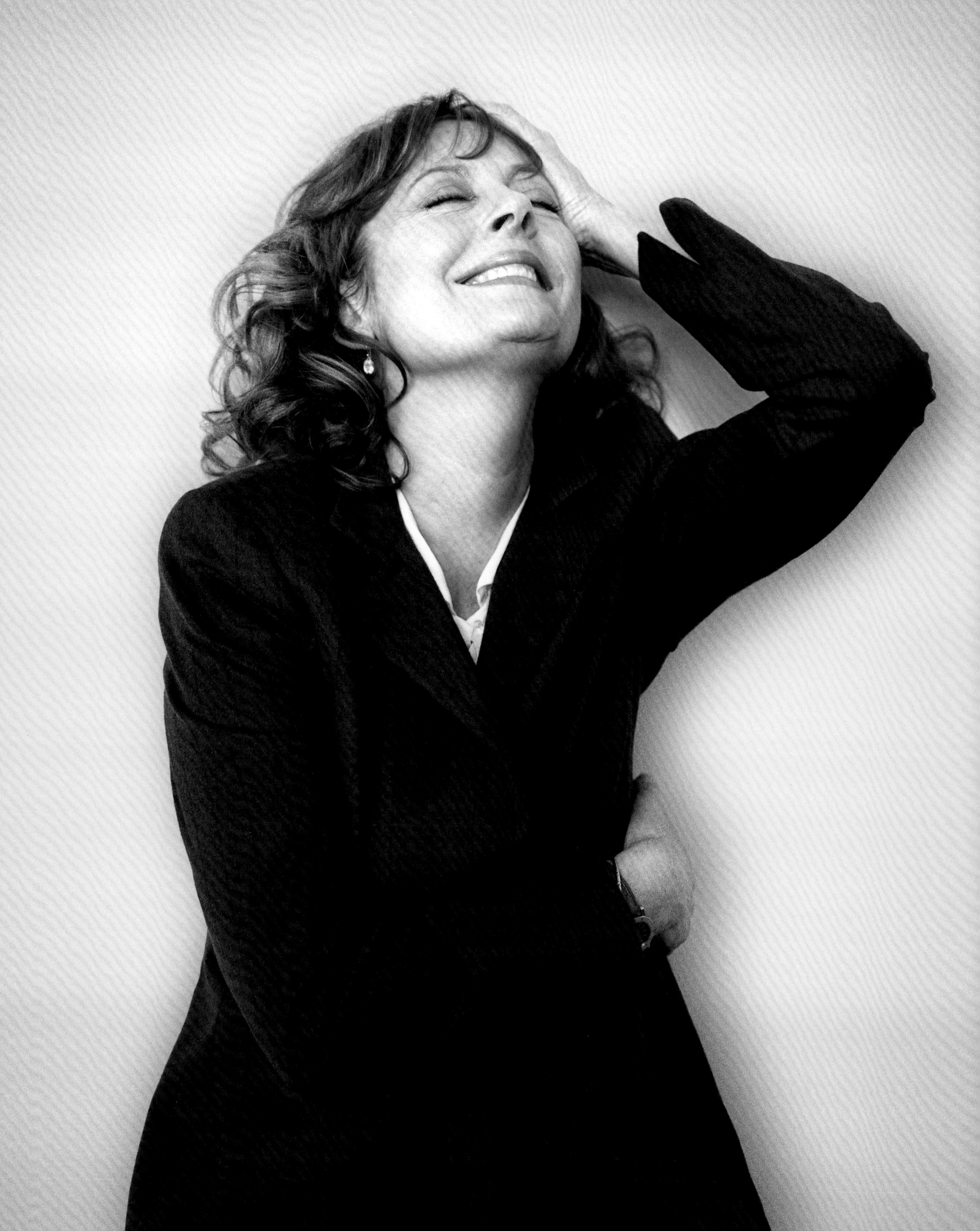

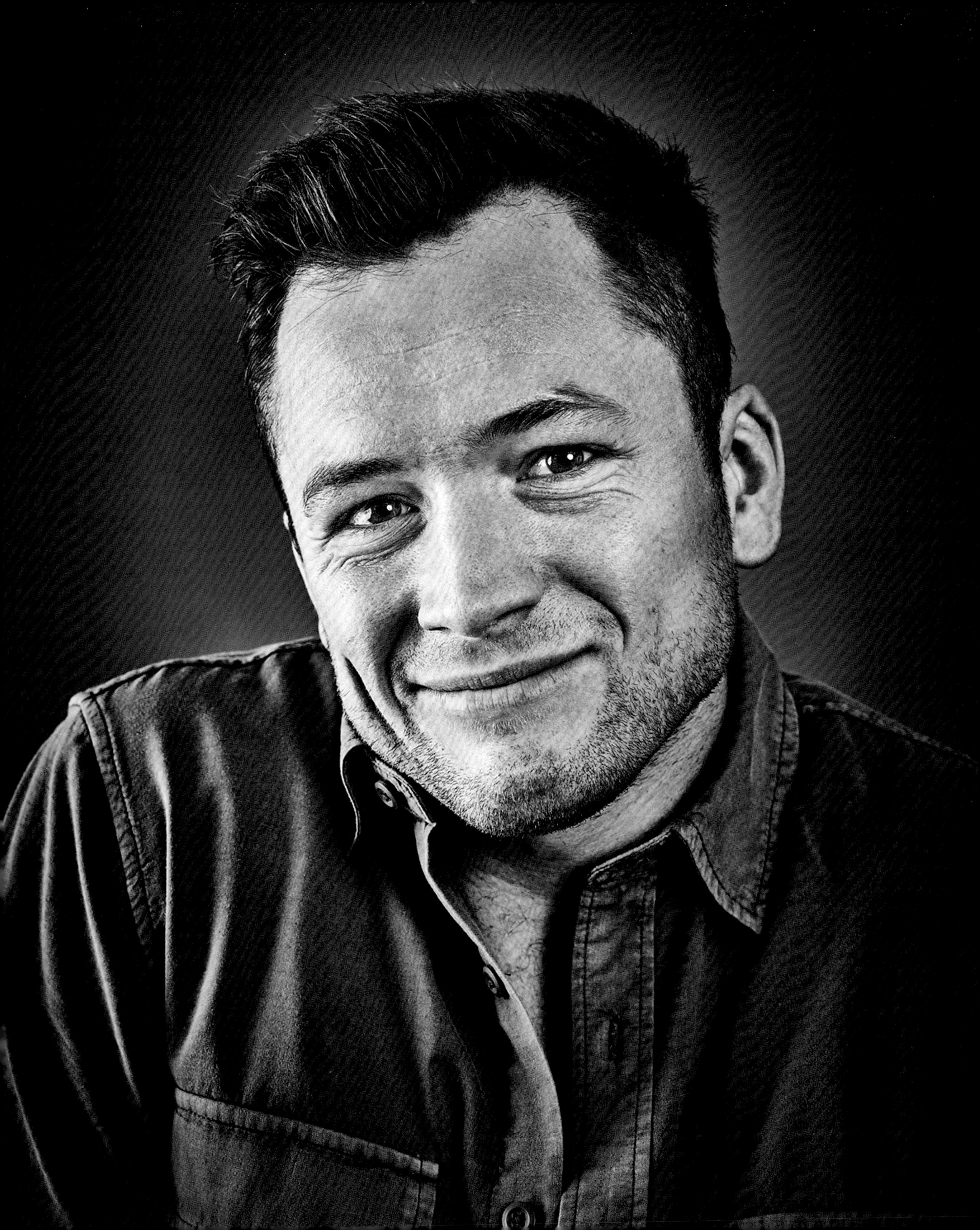

Taron Egerton

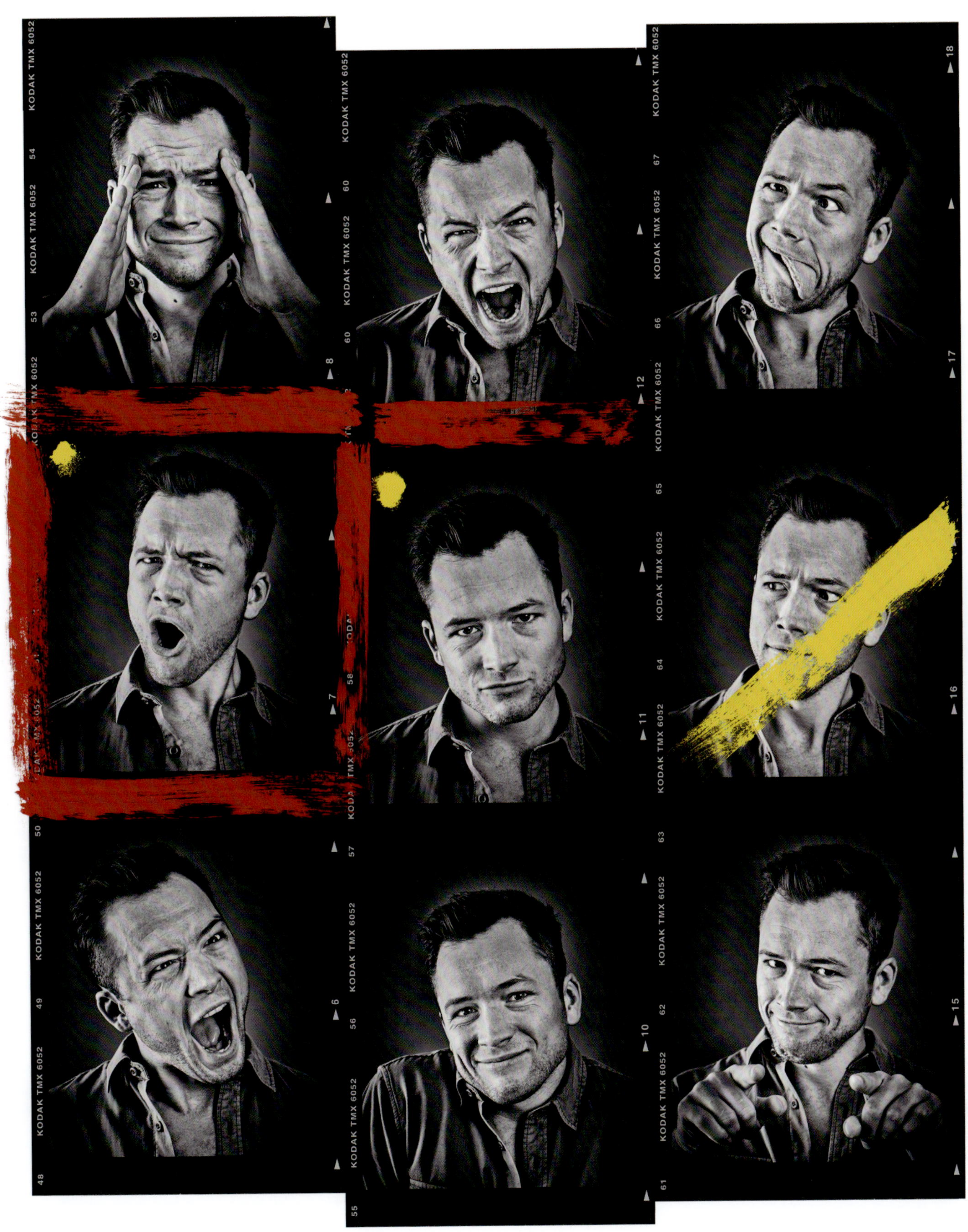

Thandiwe Newton

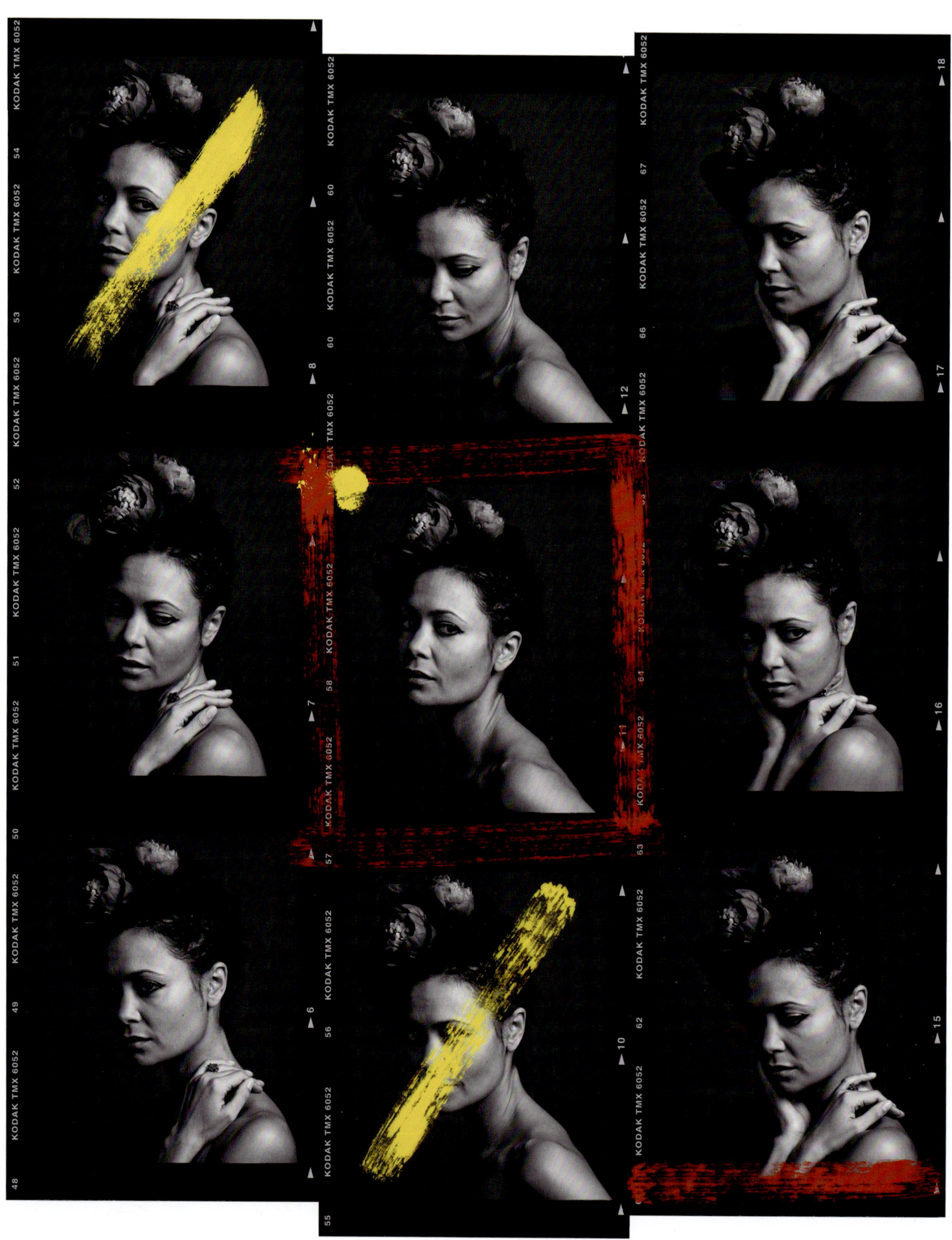

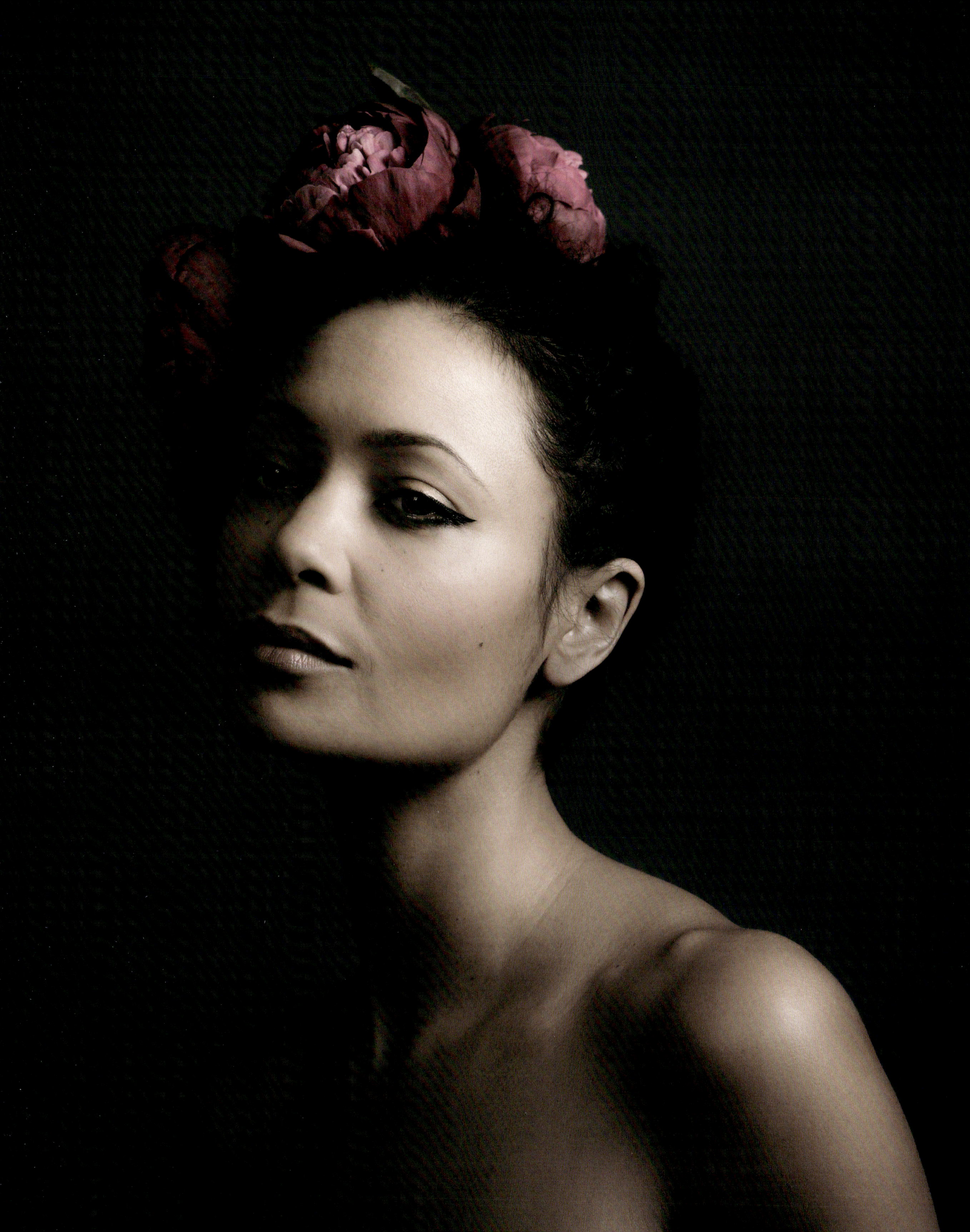

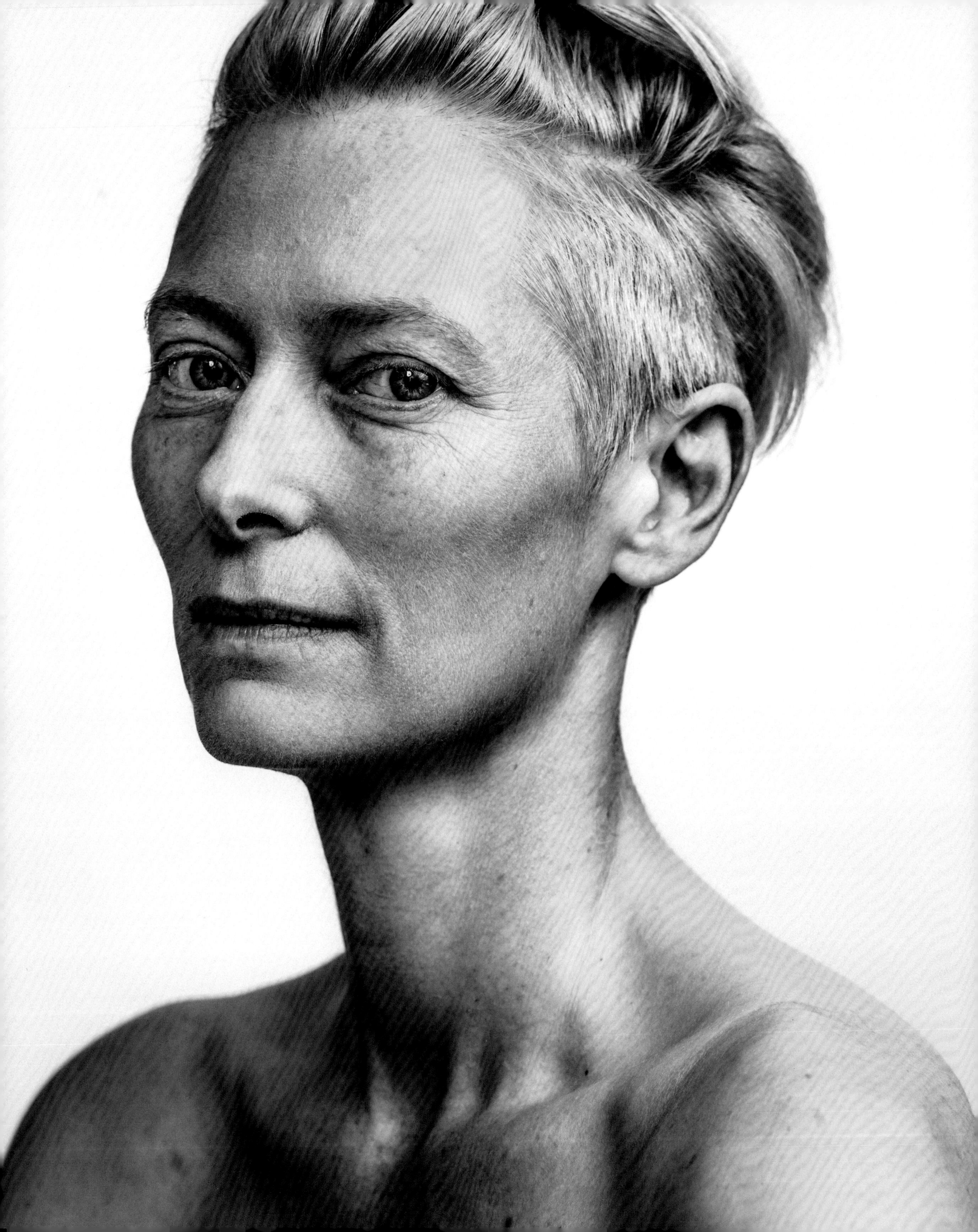

Tilda Swinton

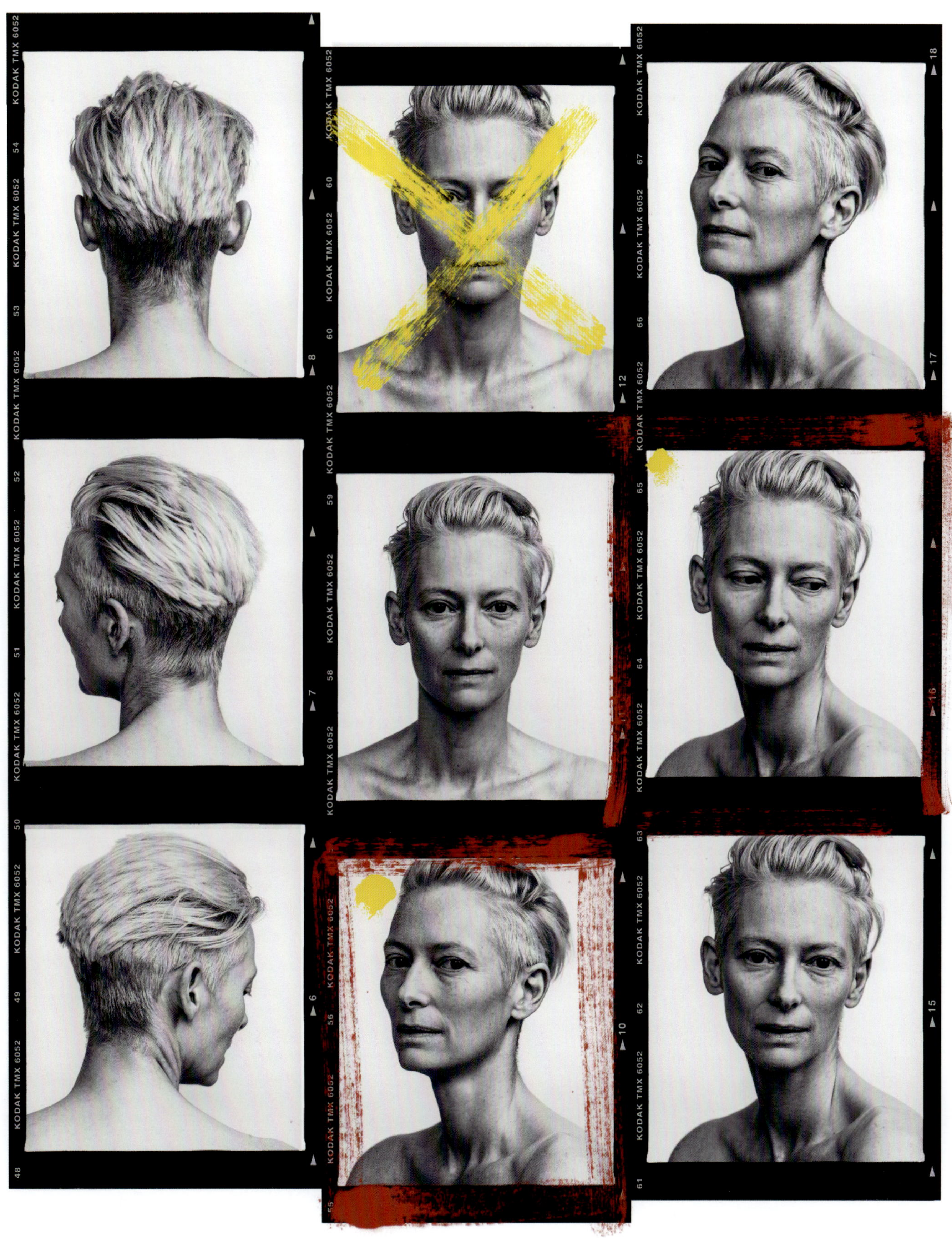

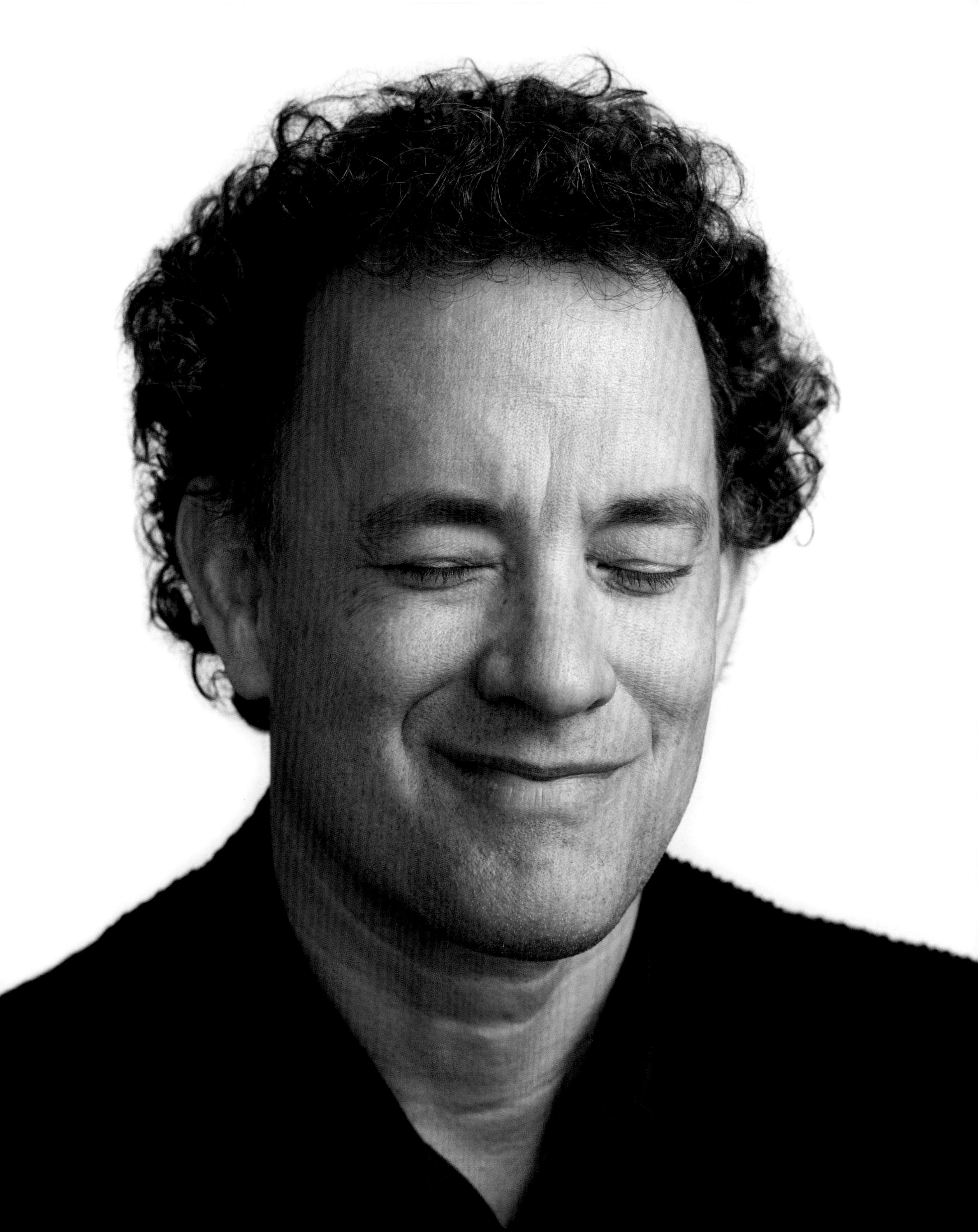

Tom Hanks

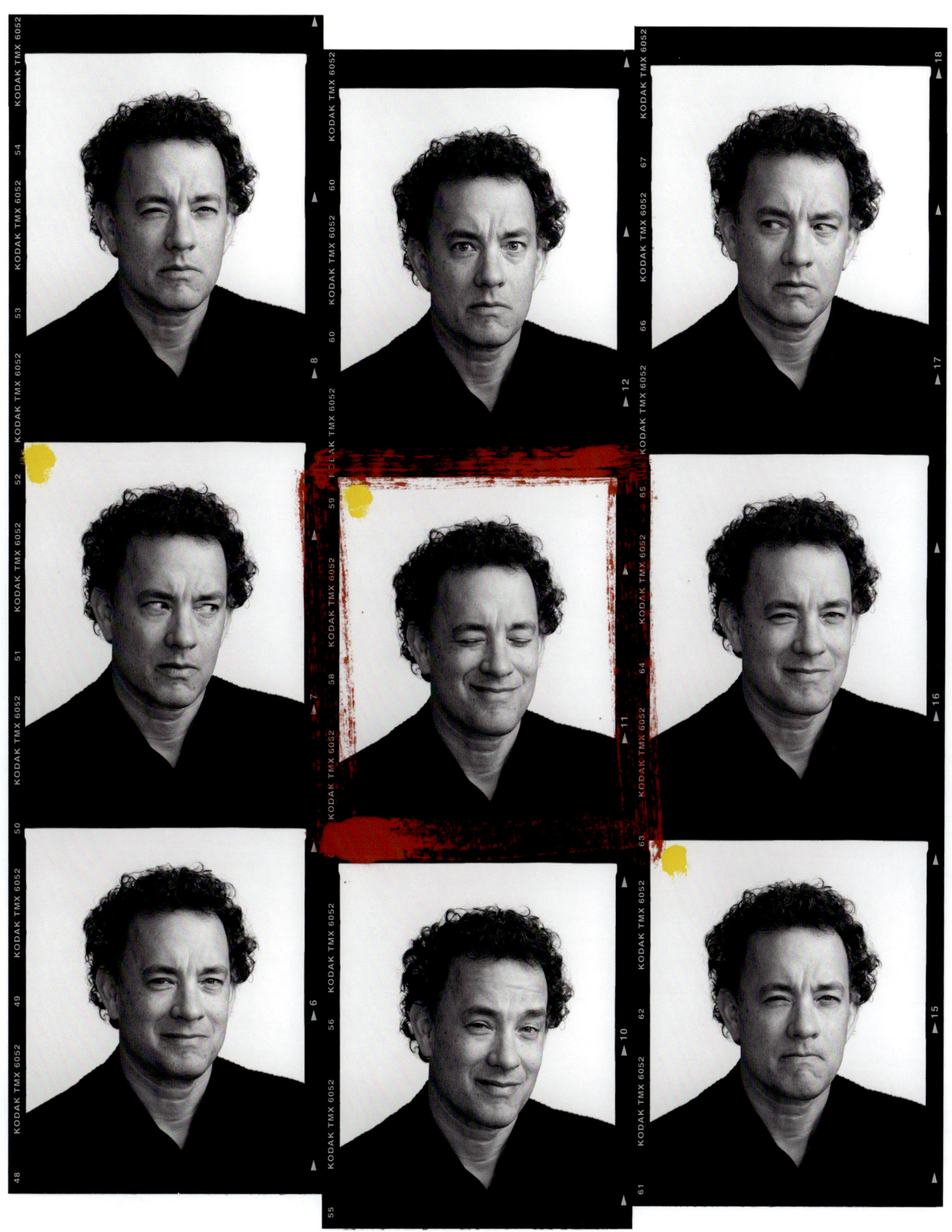

Tom Hiddleston

I shot Tom near Belfast whist he was shooting the bizarre film *High-Rise*. He had just finished a big scene, which was the last shot of the day, and he knew there was a line of adoring fans awaiting autographs and selfies outside the studio. I knew from the outset what I wanted and we got my shot in literally two minutes. We then talked for a while about his filming project based on Hank Williams, *I saw the light*. I asked if he had practised the singing, to which Tom said "Nah, I'm going to wing it." Then he gave me a wink and chuckled in a playful way. He asked if I wanted to take any more shots when the crowds of fans had subsided. Not wanting to miss the chance, I quickly unpacked the camera and took a handful more. He was a very giving and kind guy.

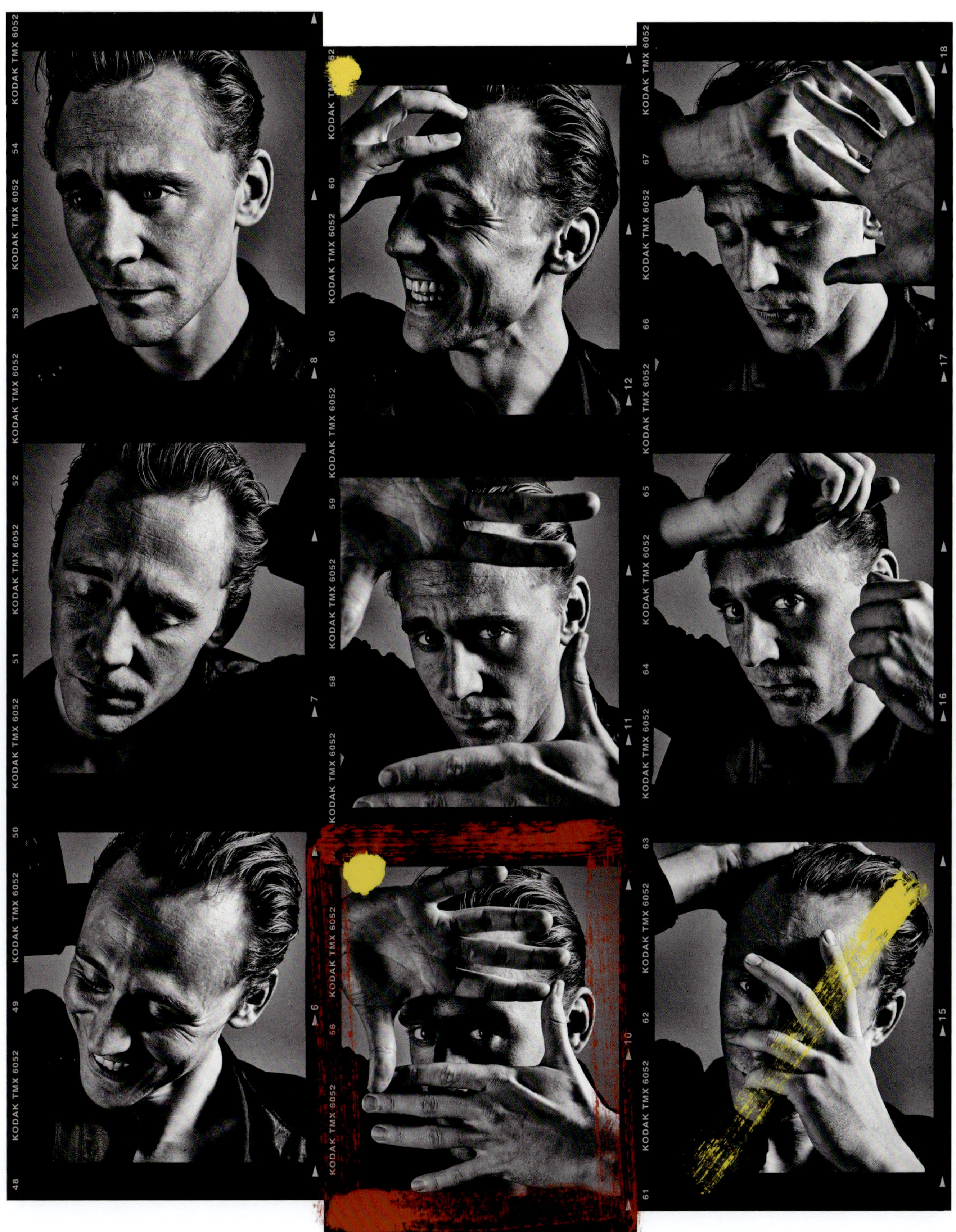

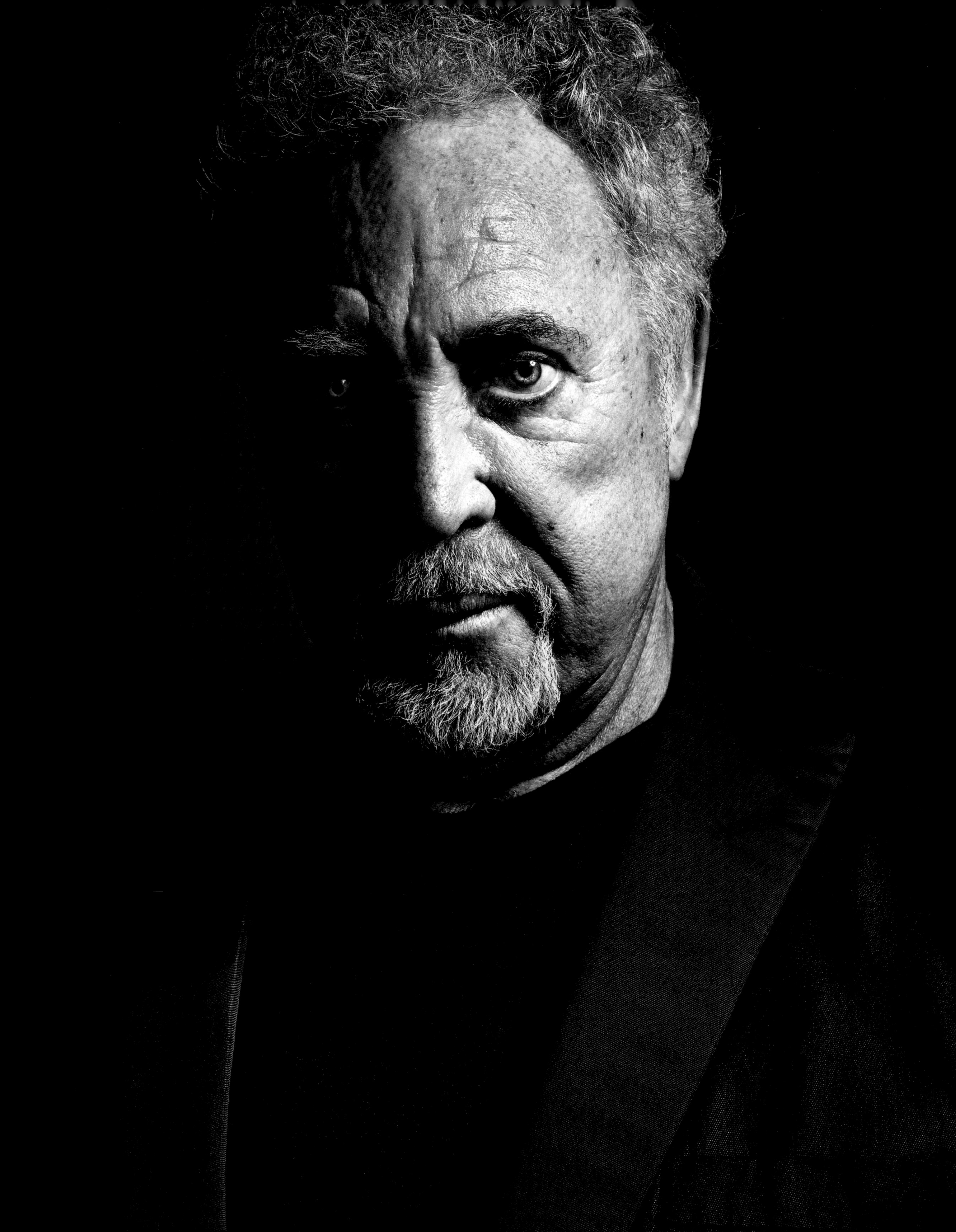

Tom Jones

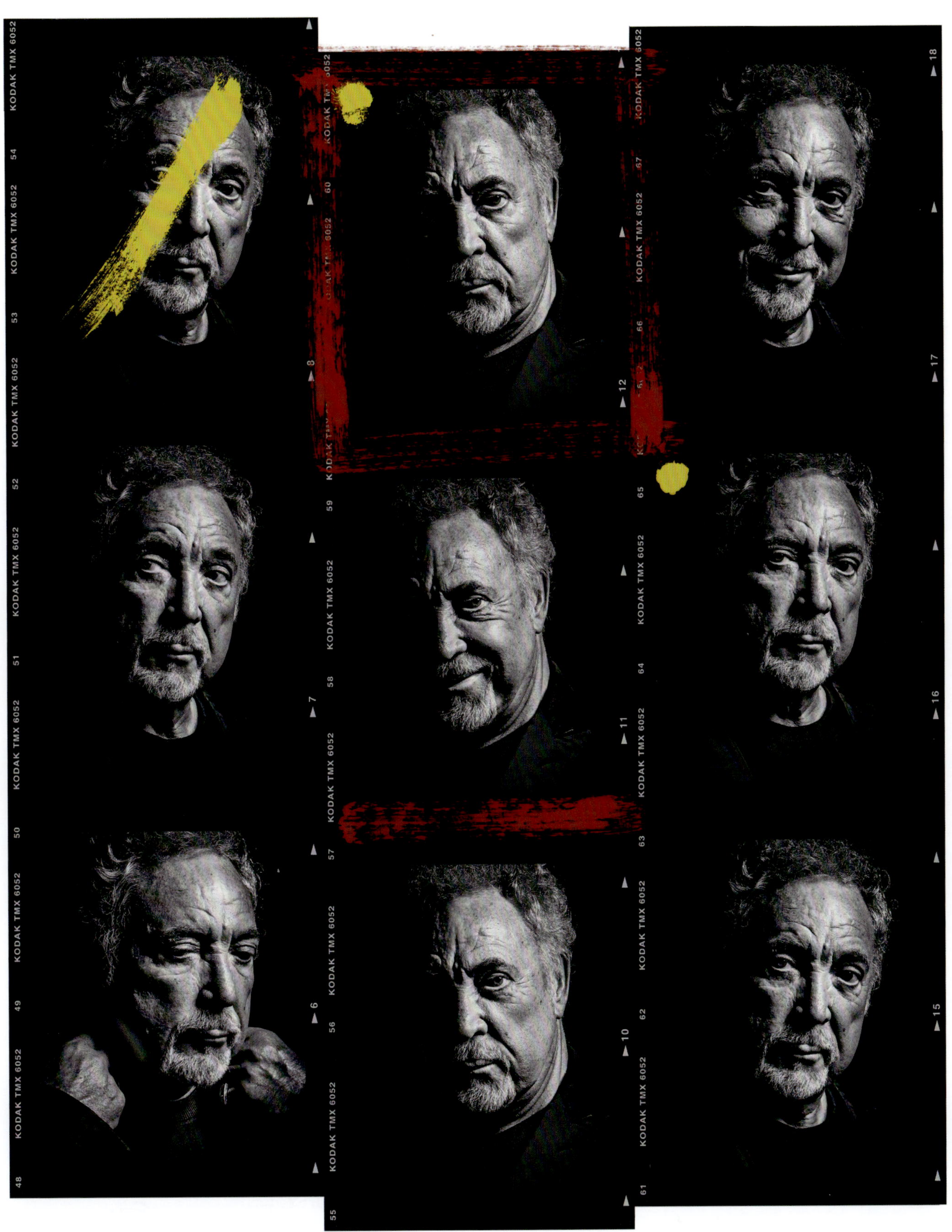

Twiggy

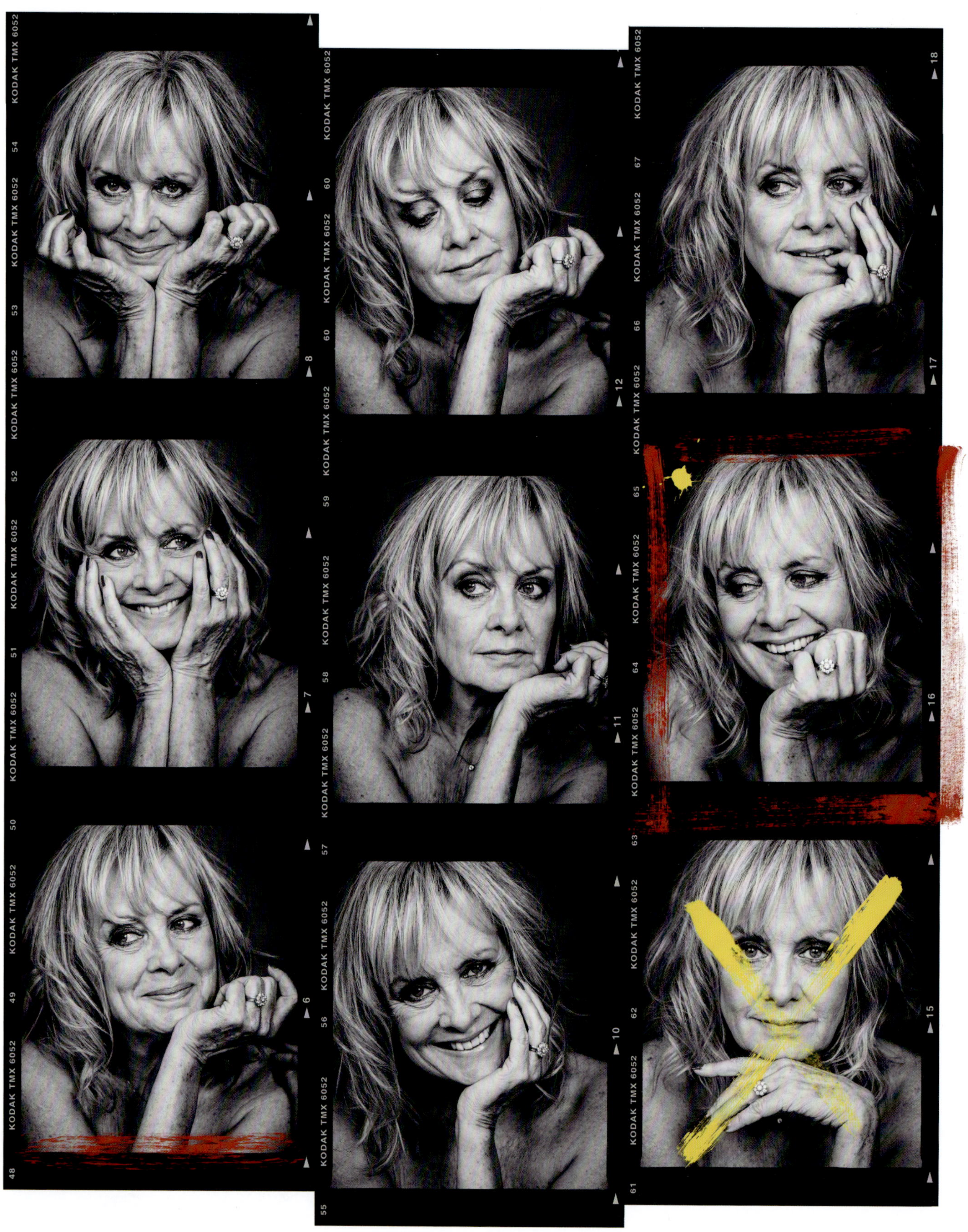

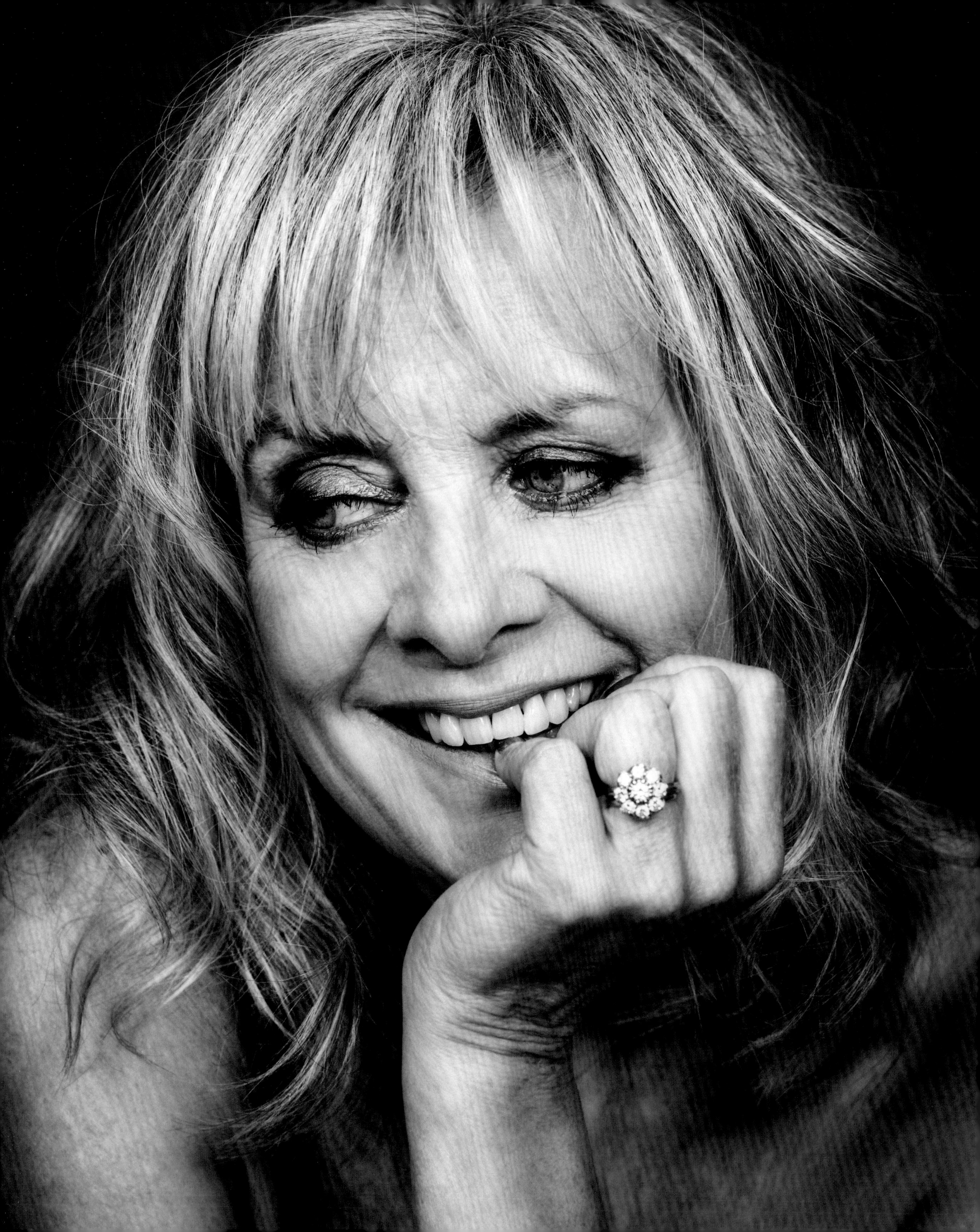

Vivienne Westwood

I shot Vivienne in Flemings Mayfair. I have shot her many many times over the years. I worked on a project for her and Greenpeace entitled SAVE THE ARCTIC and ever since we have supported each other's projects. Dame Viv commented that a few shoots she had modelled for recently (by other photographers) made her look old. So, I suggested she came over to see me and we could do some fun shots. We started shooting and she was on good form and wanted to move and lark around. I cranked up the tunes and we had a little boogie around the room... Now and again I would grab a shot of the dancing dame; this coupled with afternoon tea made it a very pleasurable shoot.

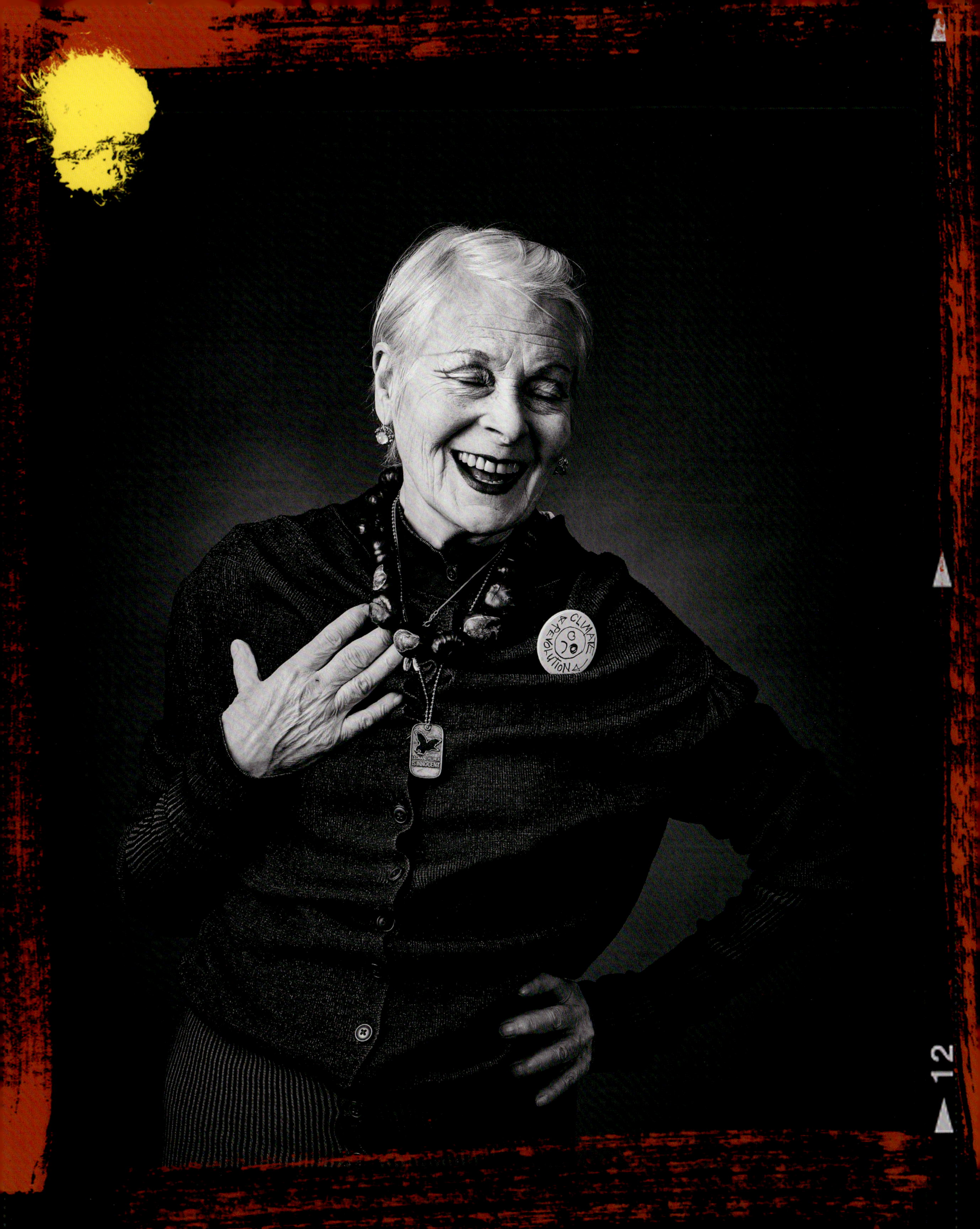
CLIMATE REVOLUTION
LEONARD PELTIER IS INNOCENT
12

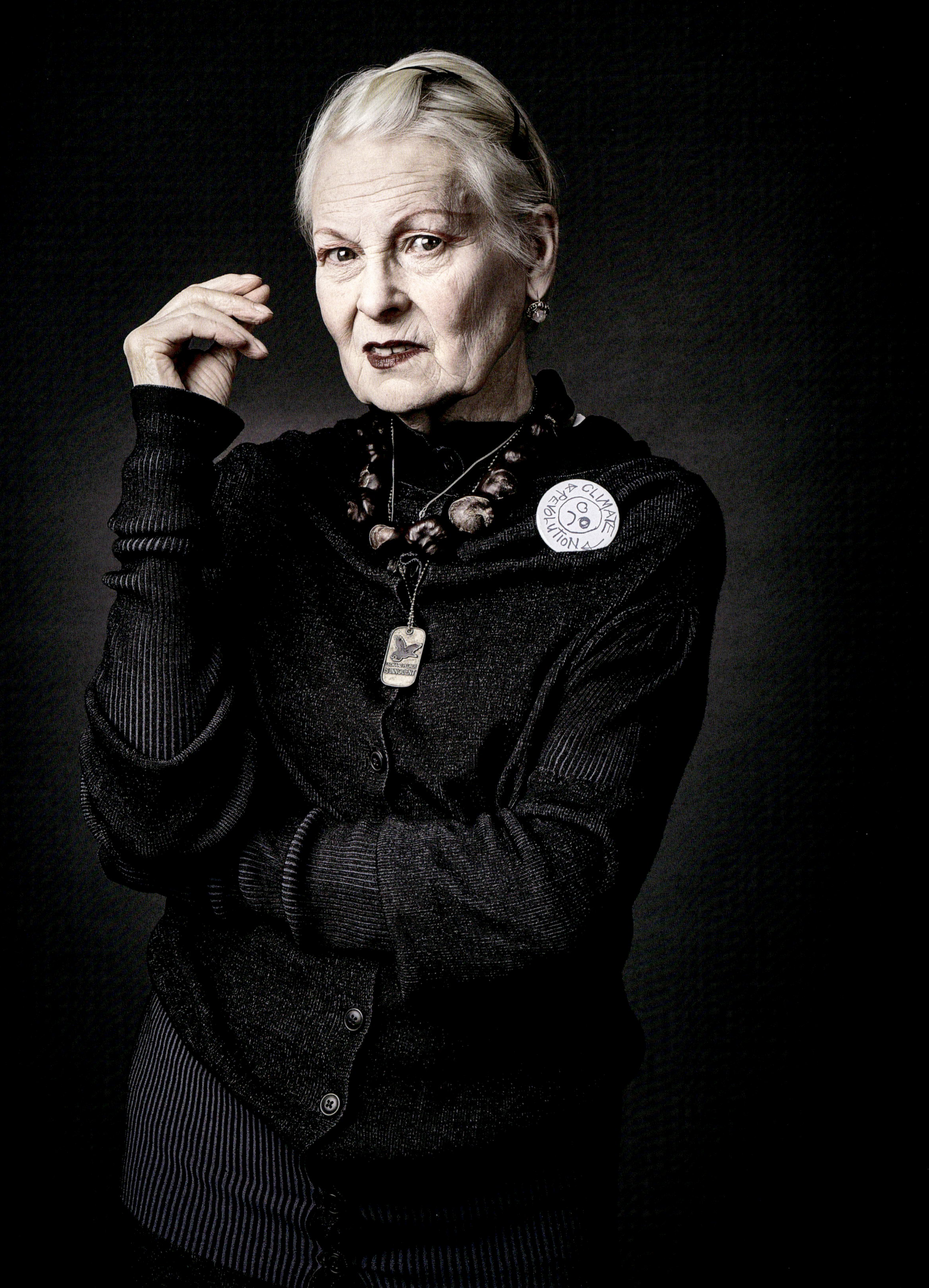
A CLIMATE REVOLUTION
IS INNOCENT

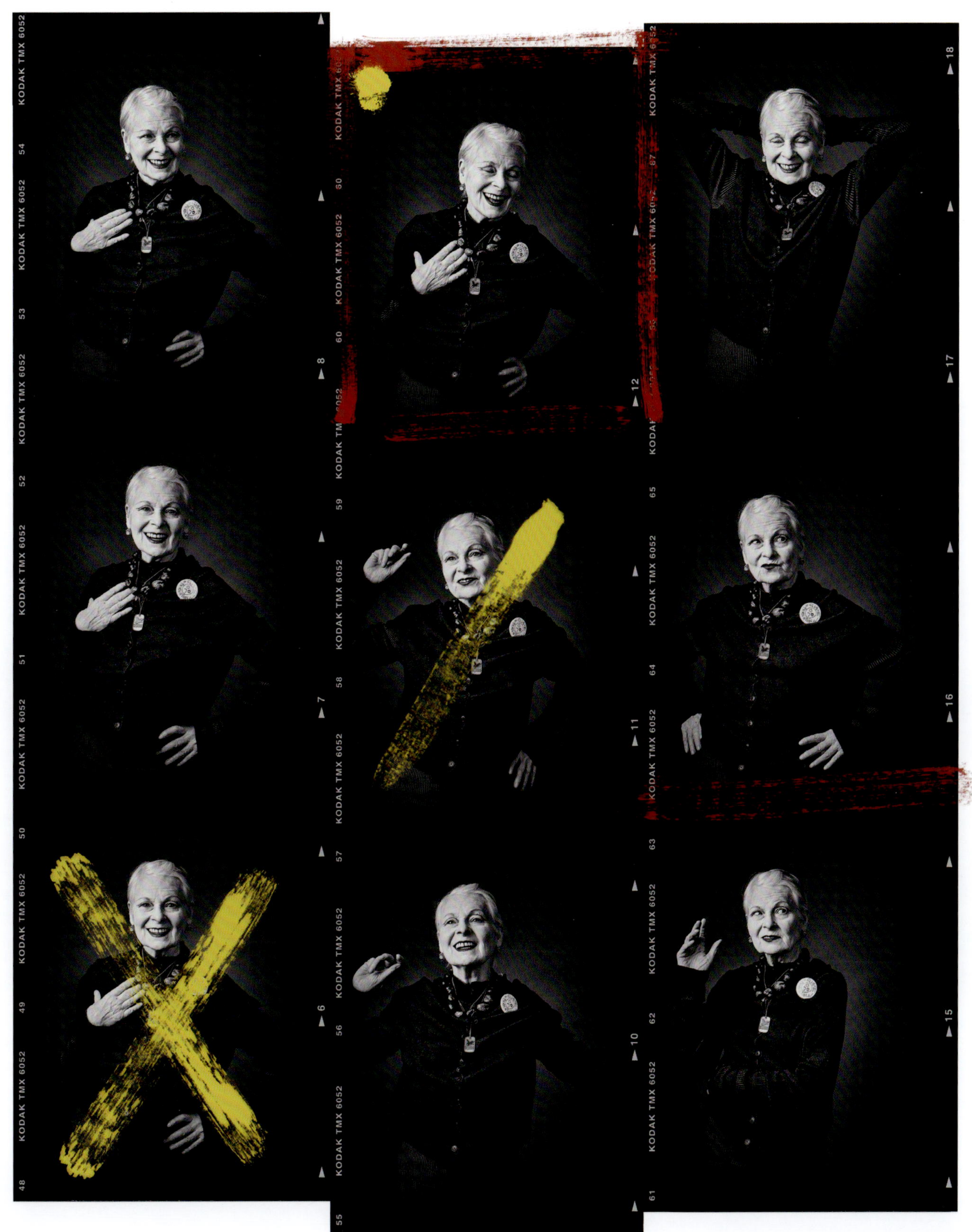

Acknowledgments

In May 1990 I was coming to the end of my first year studying photography at college. The course was a two year BTEC in Design Photography. I remember sitting in the common room debating what I should devote my entire second year to ... as I had to spend this final year specialising in a specific topic. Nothing sprang to mind. Nothing leapt up and grabbed my attention. I did love all aspects of photography – landscapes, still life... but could I devote a whole year to either? Then I heard the televisual superstar Stephen Fry was going to attend the college to hand out the end-of-year diplomas and give a talk. It was this nugget of information that stirred something in me and a hint of a plan manifested.

The day Mr Fry came to the college I found out, by stealth mode, the room in which he would be giving his talk. In the adjoining room I set up a makeshift studio with a couple of lights and a backdrop, then I went to the Q and A and awaited like a lion stalking his prey. After a very entertaining talk and batting a few questions back and forth (mostly about *Blackadder*) to us goggle-eyed students he uttered the magical line I was waiting for: "Are there any other questions?". In a flash, I put my hand up and bleated out, "Please can I take your portrait next door Mr Fry, Sir, please?". After rolling his eyes and checking his watch, he agreed.

This massive frame sat before me and gave me ninety seconds. I took ten shots. And there it was – my eureka moment. All at once I knew this was the photography I wanted to be doing as a career – celebrity faces. Was there a set career path? No. Did I know anyone in the entertainment industry? No. But over the next thirty years I slowly, very slowly, climbed the ladder, and it was all due to the kindness of Mr Fry and those beloved ninety seconds.

Looking back, I would firstly like to give my heartfelt thanks to all who gave their time to be photographed over the past three decades. Photography is quite an intimate experience when there are only two people in the room, and to get the shots I do there has to be a little dance between us to make the magic happen.

Huge cheers to all who have contributed texts and words of wisdom: Kylie Minogue, Jeff Bridges, Simon Pegg, Gene Simmons, Alan Cumming, Ian McKellen, Peter Capaldi and the guv'nor Michael Caine.

I would like to kick in the shins all the agents, managers and publicists that have dragged their feet in organising shoots and are the reason for thirty years of headaches and bitter emails!

A massive high-five to each and every champagne vineyard that has kept me going during those times.

Deep thanks to family and friends that have coped with my vast mood swings: Enid, Ivor, Steven, Deborah and Isabelle.

HUGE thanks to all the lovely, shiny people without whose help this project would have been not as much fun: Henrik and the staff of Flemings Mayfair. Margo and Cassie for their MUA talents. Mamiya, Elinchrom and Phase One for the magnificent equipment. Additional gratitude goes to Duncan and the Unseen team who have championed my photography.

Most importantly, a plethora of thanks to all the people who have believed in me and have given a bumbling photographer from North Norfolk a chance over the last three decades. It has not been an easy ride, but I have done it my way. Don't dream it ... be it.

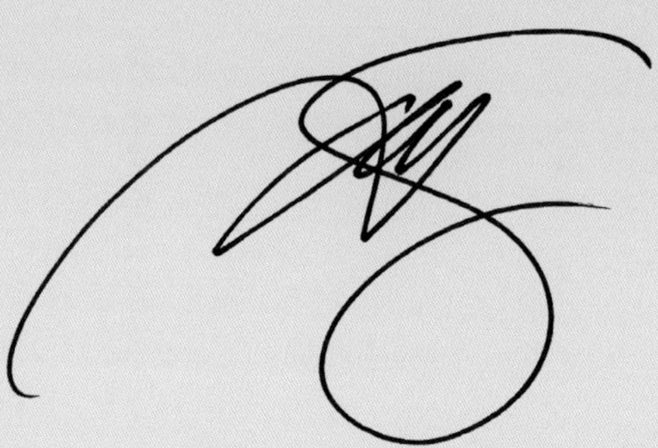

ISBN: 978 1 78884 280 8

First published by ACC Art Books in 2021 in large format
This edition published by ACC Art Books in 2025

A CIP record for this book is available from the British Library

Design: Mariona Vilarós

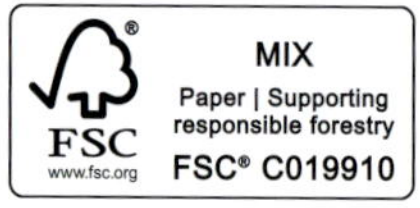

Printed in China
for ACC Art Books Ltd, Woodbridge, Suffolk, UK

www.accartbooks.com

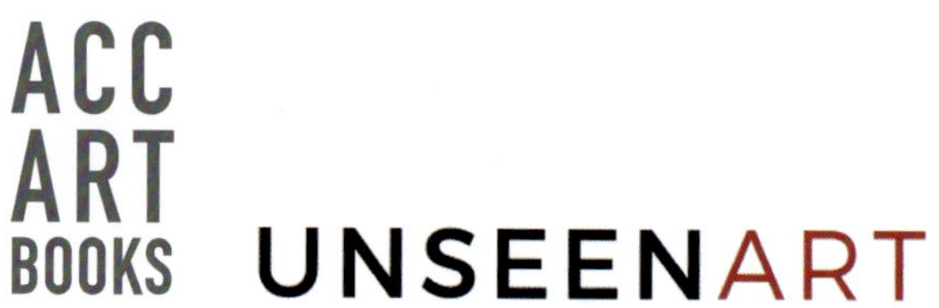